LANGUAGE IN SOCIETY 6

The Sociolinguistics of Language
Introduction to Sociolinguistics Volume II

Language in Society

GENERAL EDITOR
Peter Trudgill, Professor in the Department of Language and Linguistics,
University of Essex

ADVISORY EDITORS
Ralph Fasold, Professor of Linguistics, Georgetown University
William Labov, Professor of Linguistics, University of Pennsylvania

Titles in Print

The Sociolinguistics of Language

RALPH FASOLD

BLACKWELL
Oxford UK & Cambridge USA

Copyright © Ralph W. Fasold 1990

First published 1990

Reprinted 1991, 1992

Blackwell Publishers
108 Cowley Road, Oxford, OX4 1JF, UK

3 Cambridge Center
Cambridge, Massachusetts 02142, USA

British Library Cataloguing in Publication Data
A CIP catalogue record for this book is available from the British Library

Library of Congress Cataloging in Publication Data
Fasold, Ralph W.
  The sociolinguistics of language / Ralph Fasold.
    p.   cm. — (Introduction to sociolinguistics ; v. 2)
(Language in society ; 6)
  Bibliography: p.
  Includes index.
  ISBN 0–631–13386–0
  ISBN 0–631–13825–0 (pbk.)
  1. Sociolinguistics.   I. Title.   II. Series.   III. Series:
  Language in society (Oxford, England); 6
  P40.I58   vol. 2

Typeset in 10 on 12 pt Times
by Photo·graphics, Honiton, Devon
Printed in Great Britain by TJ Press Ltd., Padstow

Contents

Editor's Preface

This book is the companion volume to Ralph Fasold's *The Sociolinguistics of Society*. Between them, these two books cover the entire spectrum of scholarly activity within the very broad discipline of sociolinguistics, and they thus provide an excellent introduction to the subject as a whole. They are therefore ideal for beginning students in the area, but they are also highly original in their approach and interpretation to the extent that scholars carrying out research in sociolinguistics will themselves wish to ensure that they are familiar with the contents.

Sociolinguistics, as is well known, is a science that combines linguistic and societal concerns in varying degrees. Fasold's earlier volume concentrated on those areas of the subject that lie towards the societal end of the language and society continuum. *The Sociolinguistics of Language* complements this work and completes the picture by concentrating on those aspects of sociolinguistics which are of more central concern to linguists, dealing as it does with the influence of social factors on language and with topics of concern to linguistic theory, albeit in a way that makes the book accessible to non-linguists such as social scientists with an interest in language and society. As I pointed out in my preface to the previous volume, Ralph Fasold is very much a practitioner of sociolinguistics, having himself carried out research in a number of areas of the discipline, both theoretical and applied. He is also one of those people working within sociolingusitics who is clearly very much a linguist: it is apparent from this book that one of his major concerns is to improve our understanding of how language works, and to gain insights into the nature of the human language faculty. This book stresses, however, that such insights depend not only on the study of language as an autonomous system, but also on the study of its relationship with society.

Peter Trudgill

Introduction

In one sense, writing a book is an arrogant act, since writers implicitly assume that a substantial number of people are going to want to read their views. Writing a textbook may be even more arrogant because authors really make the additional assumption that their vision of the field is good enough to serve as the perspective through which perhaps hundreds of students will be introduced to that field. If I had seen it in this light at the outset, I might never have attempted this book. As it is, I think I should use the introduction to reveal something of my vision of sociolinguistics, so that users will at least know something about the field-glasses they are about to peer through.

My view of language and linguistics in general, and of sociolinguistics in particular, is that it must be segmented to be thoroughly understood: reductionism, if you will. This motivated my decision to place the topics in this book and the ones in its companion, *The Sociolinguistics of Society*, in separate volumes. I am not able to see very much in common between the issues about the forms and use of language on a small scale that are treated in this book and the large-scale sociopolitical issues that are addressed in the other.

I also see a sharp distinction between language and use or, more accurately, grammar and language. I am developing a conviction that the phenomenon of language is the product of the interaction of two very different sets of principles. Some of what we find in language is clearly due to the need people have to communicate to other people not only their thoughts, but also their self-concepts and their perception of the relationship between them, their audience and the situation.

Other aspects of language seem to be just as clearly due to principles of grammar that have nothing to do with communication. These principles keep language from being used to say things it would be very useful to say, while making it possible to say other things that are really not likely to be needed. The study of the former principles I have begun to think of as *linguistics proper* and the latter as *grammatics*. This perspective has particularly shaped chapters 5 and 6 on pragmatics, where I try to establish a clear distinction between semantics and pragmatics (assuming a distinction between both and syntax). My dualist viewpoint also influences chapter 8, on variation analysis, particularly in the attention I give to 'developmental linguistics'. Developmental theory maintains a similar fundamental distinction between the 'sociocommunicative' and the 'neurobiological', which parallels my notion of linguistics proper and grammatics (although I am not fully convinced that the 'neurobiological' principles of developmental linguistics are necessarily neurobiological).

Although it might make some sense to equate 'linguistics proper' with 'sociolinguistics', no unified theory of sociolinguistics will be found here. Instead, I present sociolinguistics as a series of topics with some connections between them, as was done in the companion book. The reason for this is that I am not able to detect an overall theory, even of the portion of sociolinguistics that is addressed here. If there are any candidates for an overall theory, perhaps developmental linguistics (C.-J. Bailey, forthcoming) and systemic grammar (Halliday 1985, 1987) would be two of them.

The principal reason for my pessimism about sociolinguistic theory is that I take it that the requirements for what might be called a theory are rather strict. A successful theory is one which does not have to stipulate very many basic principles, but can account for a large range of facts from very few principles and their interactions. Perceptive description of people's intuitions about how something works – even if everyone has the same intuitions – is not enough. In fact, I take it to be a hallmark of a really successful theory that it will propose convincing arguments in favor of *counter*intuitive principles, as has happened in particle physics in this century. In other words, a really successful theory will eventually lead to surprises, and I am not sure we have yet been really surprised.

Although what you find in this book has been shaped by my outlook, I realize that many other sociolinguists take a very different view. I feel most strongly that the author of an introductory textbook bears the full responsibility for presenting currently accepted thinking in the field, even if he or she disagrees with it, and summarizing the research of the leading scholars in the field in the way they themselves would summarize it, at least as far as this is possible. I have made a considerable effort to do just that. I hope I have succeeded in representing the work of the scholars I cite in a sympathetic manner, even in those instances where my leanings are in a different direction. I have also tried to make it clear when I am introducing my own ideas which are not part of generally accepted thinking in sociolinguistics. I consider this a duty.

Each of the chapters focuses on a topic concerning the effect of relatively small-scale social influences on language. The subject of the first chapter, address forms, might appear to be too limited a phenomenon to deserve an entire chapter. Still, address forms are a good way to start because the linguistic forms involved are simple, limited in number and their distribution is almost totally directed by social factors. Address forms make the fundamental point in sociolinguistics clearly: social context is an important influence on language and language use. Address form phenomena differ considerably from one cultural setting to another so this topic leads naturally to the ethnography of communication, the subject of chapter 2. On the border between sociolinguistics and anthropology, the ethnography of communication nicely illustrates anthropological methods and approaches to sociolinguistic themes.

Chapter 3, on discourse analysis, was possibly the most difficult to write. Discourse analysis has a wide scope and a large and growing scholarly literature; so much so that there was no hope of providing an overview of it. I see discourse analysis as having two subdivisions: one about conversation, and one about the structure of texts, whether oral or written. I tried to give the flavor of what is done in each of these areas by discussing an important topic in each. For conversation, research on turn-taking provides the theme. For text analysis, it was the relationship between grammar and discourse. The topic of chapter 4, language and sex, has been an important one for quite some time now. Very recent work has indicated that it may soon be considered a central factor in sociolinguistic variation, and the interaction between language and sex is clearly seen in everyday life.

The chapters on linguistic pragmatics, chapters 5 and 6, may not seem to be matters of sociolinguistics at all. Yet many of the main ideas in pragmatics – conversational implicature, speech acts, presupposition, indexicals and politeness – have shed considerable light on just that aspect of sociolinguistics that this book is about and this, I think, justifies their inclusion. In fact, as I point out at the end of chapter 6, the whole book might be seen as a book about pragmatics in the broad-scope tradition that Levinson (1983) calls the 'continental' approach.

In chapter 7, pidgins and creoles are the subject. Research on pidgins and creoles has inspired many of the insights in sociolinguistic variation studies. Chapter 7 includes a rather long section on US Vernacular Black English (VBE), since it has been widely assumed that it has creole origins. The creole origin hypothesis has been called into some question with the development of the 'divergence' controversy. The divergence issue involves evidence that the vernacular variety of US Black English is becoming progresively *less* like other varieties of American English, rather than becoming slowly more similar by the process of decreolization. This controversy is discussed in some detail. Chapter 8 is an overview of what has been the centerpiece of the sociolinguistics of language over the past 30 years or so, variation analysis. The work of William Labov, which has been the major force in variation studies, is the subject of much of the discussion. I have also included the substantially different view of sociolinguistic variation found in the developmental linguistics approach pioneered by Charles-James Bailey.

The final chapter is about the applications of the research discussed in the earlier chapters to social problems and issues. In preparing this chapter, I was surprised to discover how much applied research there has been since the 1960s, when applications of variation research to language arts education made up the great bulk of what existed. Since then there has been more work on first language teaching, but a lot has been done in areas like medicine, law, bilingual education, advertising, and second language teaching. In fact, the chapter is titled '*Some* applications of the sociolinguistics of language' precisely because I found myself unable to give all the applied areas the attention they really deserve.

A number of friends and colleagues have taken the time to read and comment on portions of the manuscript, and I am very grateful to all of them: Charles-James Bailey, Derek Bickerton, Gae Fasold, Esther Figueroa, Patricia Giegerich, Robin Lakoff, Pan Yuling, Deborah Schiffrin, Roger Shuy, Deborah Tannen, Wang Chih-kang, and Walt Wolfram. Their efforts have made the book better than it would have been otherwise, but I am sure all of them will find much that I have said that they cannot fully endorse.

1

Address Forms

INTRODUCTION

When people use language, they do more than just try to get another person to understand the speaker's thoughts and feelings. At the same time, both people are using language in subtle ways to define their relationship to each other, to identify themselves as part of a social group, and to establish the kind of speech event they are in. To take a simple example, I can communicate more or less the same idea in either of the following two ways:

Bring it over here, wouldja?

Could I ask you to bring that paintbrush over here?

However, the two ways of making the request make very different assumptions about my idea of the relationship between me and the person I am talking to, and what kind of social situation I think it is. I might use the first utterance either because I am on close personal terms with the person I am talking to, or because I am in a clear position of authority over that person. By putting my request this way, I show that I am confident the other person is willing to carry out my request and will not be offended that I asked. Using the second request, I am not sure I am close enough to, or have enough authority over, the other person such that he or she will willingly do what I have asked. In either case, it is clear enough that the content of my message is that I want the other person to bring an item, but the setting and social relationship assumptions cause me to convey that message in two strikingly different ways.

In no area of sociolinguistics is this second function of language more clearly highlighted than in address forms. Address forms are the words speakers use to designate the person they are talking to while they are talking to them. In most languages, there are two main kinds of address forms: names and second-person pronouns. Just a brief moment's reflection will show you that you can, in principle at least, address anyone in either of two ways: by their first name or by their title and last name. I say 'in principle' because it's clear in a lot of cases that I could scarcely use one or the other form. It makes me flush with embarrassment even to think of addressing the president of my university as 'Tim' and it makes me want to chuckle to think of calling my brother 'Mr Fasold'. But there are times when it is an agonizing problem to decide just how I am supposed to address someone; for example, a next-door neighbor who is a generation older than I am. For most Americans, it is expected that you will address neighbors by their first name (and they will address you the same way) as soon as the introductions are over. On the other hand, there is considerable reluctance to address people who are old enough to be friends of your parents by their first name. The result is a real conflict.

English speakers have it easy compared to speakers of most languages in the world.[1] We need only decide what name to use and can probably even avoid using any name at all for quite a long while. Speakers of French, German, and Italian, like speakers of almost all European languages, have to make a choice in the word for 'you' as well. These languages have two forms for 'you'; one is for people who deserve deference either because their social station is above the speaker's, or because the speaker does not have a sufficiently close personal relationship with them. The other one is used for people who are either close to the speaker, or of lesser social standing. In some languages, like French, the deferential pronoun is grammatically and historically a plural form (*vous*) but is used when speaking to one individual who deserves deference, rather than the grammatically singular *tu*. In others, the deferential pronoun comes from somewhere else in the language. The German deferential *Sie* is the same as the *third*-person plural pronoun, except it is capitalized. Some speakers of Italian use the second-person plural *voi* but the more modern deferential pronoun is *Lei*, historically a contraction of *La Vostra Signoria*, 'your Lordship' (Bates and Benigni 1975). It is much more difficult to avoid saying 'you' than it is to avoid saying someone's name.[2]

The address systems of even these European languages are simple to use compared with the choices in many Asian languages. In Hindi, for example, there are *three* second-person pronouns to select from. In Thai, speakers not only have to select from a long list of second-person forms, but have several socially determined words for 'I' to choose from, in addition to sentence-ending particles that convey social information. In Japanese and in the Indonesian language Javanese, speakers must master not only pronouns but entire systems of honorific particles. In Javanese, there are even alternate forms of nouns and verbs (like the word for 'eat') and grammatical endings that are determined by level of formality (Geertz 1960/1972).[3] We will see how the Javanese system works in a little more detail later in the chapter.

Before we examine how address systems work, we should understand the limitations of the topic. Address forms are really part of complete semantic systems having to do with social relationships. As Bean (1978) points out, it is not really sufficient to look only at addressing by name and second-person pronouns. As I have just mentioned, there are languages like Javanese in which many other devices are used for the expression of social relationships. Furthermore, there is the whole question of *kin terms* (words for kinship relationships like 'mother', 'brother', 'cousin'). We will mention kin terms only where they are used to address people, as in 'Uncle Harry'.[4] Another related phenomenon is how a person is *referred to* as well as how he or she is addressed. A man can be expected to address his wife by her first name, but may refer to her as 'Mom', 'my wife', 'Mary', 'Mrs Harris', or 'Tommy's mother', depending on who it is he is talking to (cf. Geiger 1979). We must carefully distinguish address forms from *summonses*.[5] Address forms are used when a speaker already has the listener's attention; summonses are used to *get* their attention. This can be an important distinction. It is common for American English speakers to get the attention of virtually *any* adult male by calling him 'sir', but it would most likely sound overly stiff to use 'sir' once you have his attention. For example, if a driver in a car wanted to get directions from a pedestrian, this might well be achieved by saying something like: 'Sir, how do I get to the airport?' It would be odd for the same person to say, in the middle of the conversation, something like: 'Did you say three stoplights before I turn, sir?' Our discussion will be limited to address forms only. We will not go into kin terms in any depth and terms of reference and summonses will be left out.

BROWN AND GILMAN

The classic and most influential study of address forms and the social relationships they reveal was published by Brown and Gilman in 1960 (Brown and Gilman 1960/1972).[6] Using a variety of methods, such as informal interviews, the analysis of works of literature (particularly drama), and the results of a survey questionnaire, they investigated second-person pronoun usage in French, German, Italian, and Spanish.[7] They proposed that pronoun usage was governed by two *semantics*, which they called *power* and *solidarity*.

The power pronoun semantic, like the power relationship, is nonrecipro-cal. A person has power over another person to the degree that he or she can control the other person's behavior. This relationship is nonreciprocal because two people cannot have power over each other in the same area. In the same way, the power semantic governs the nonreciprocal use of the two pronouns. The less powerful person says V (the term Brown and Gilman use to designate the deferential pronoun in any of the languages, taking the first letter from Latin *vos*) to the more powerful one and receives T (the familiar pronoun, from Latin *tu*). The bases of power are several. Older people are assumed to have power over younger people, parents over children, employers over employees, nobles over peasants, military officers over enlisted men. The power semantic appears to Brown and Gilman to have been the original one. They theorize that the Latin plural pronoun was used first to the emperor during the fourth century. The reason may have been that at the time there were two emperors, one in Rome and one in Constantinople, and addressing either was considered the same as addressing both. Or the emperor might have been considered 'plural' in the sense that he represented all the people he governed. Royal persons often use 'we' in self-reference and the plural of 'you' might have been the extension of that. In any case, the use of the plural form seems to have become generalized and came to be used to address all 'powerful' people.

The power semantic would be sufficient only if a society were so finely stratified that each individual had an asymmetrical relationship with every other individual; in other words, there were no power equals. Since this was never the case, at least in Europe, a residual rule for power equals was necessary. This rule called for the reciprocal use of the same pronoun between power equals. This is, you use the same pronoun to a power equal that they use to you. Since the V form entered European society from the top, the V form was associated with the noble classes, and nobles originally addressed each other with mutual V. Among the common people power equals used T with each other.

Since not all differences between people are connected with power, a second semantic, the *solidarity* semantic, developed. Two people can be equally powerful in the social order, but be from different families, come from different parts of the country, and be in different, if equally respected, professions. In other words, the need developed to distinguish a degree of common ground between people which went beyond simply having equal power. This is where solidarity came in. Solidarity implied a sharing between people, a degree of closeness and intimacy. This relationship was inherently reciprocal; if you were close to someone else, in the most natural state of affairs, that person was close to you. Wherever the solidarity semantic applies, then, the same pronoun is used by both people.

Originally, according to Brown and Gilman, the solidarity semantic came into play only where it did not interfere with the power semantic. This would be, of course, between power equals. If two people were equally powerful, but not 'solidary' – they did not share anything significant, like family background or origins in the same village – they would exchange V, as the noble classes did before the solidarity semantic developed. The difference was that now mutual V would be used between nonsolidary equals, among common people as well as among nobles. If power equals *were* solidary, they would exchange mutual T, even if they were members of the higher classes. Brown and Gilman illustrate this as in figure 1.1

Figure 1.1 should be taken as a sort of instruction diagram for a speaker trying to decide what pronoun to use with the person he or she is talking to, although only in the metaphorical sense. I do not mean to imply that people actually go through this process when they are talking. The speaker determines power relationships first. If the person is more powerful, then the speaker gives T and expects to receive V. If the other person is less powerful, then the speaker will give V and get T. If there is no power difference, then the speaker decides if he or she and the other person are solidary. If so, then both will use T; otherwise both will use V.

Logically, however, power and solidarity can conflict. A restaurant patron has power over a waiter such that the power semantic entitles the customer to address the waiter with T, but they may be total strangers with no basis for solidarity; the solidarity semantic dictates V. Parents and children could scarcely be more solidary, so mutual T is called for by the solidarity semantic, but the power semantic would lead a child to address his or her parents with V. As the solidarity semantic gained in importance, conflicts of this type arose. This tension in the system is illustrated by Brown and Gilman as in figure 1.2. The middle sections of figure 1.2 are identical with those of figure 1.1; there is no problem there in selecting pronouns. In the top right quadrant, both power and solidarity indicate that a superior and not solidary addressee should receive V. Similarly power and solidarity both call for T to the inferior and solidary

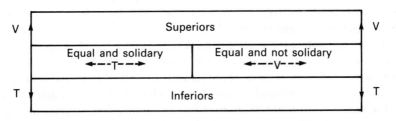

Figure 1.1 The two-dimensional semantic in equilibrium
Source: Brown and Gilman (1972:259, figure 1a)

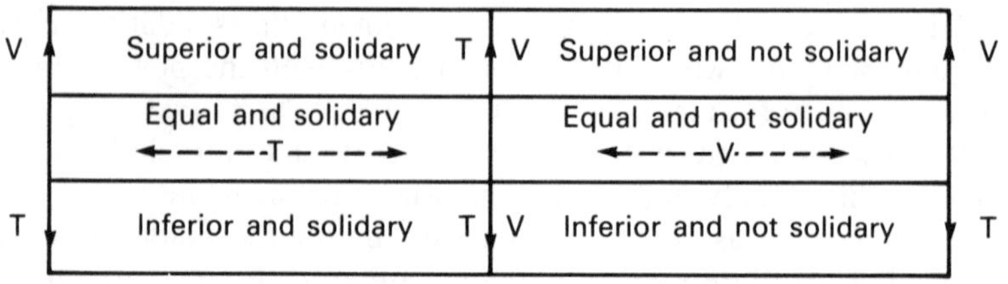

V	Superior and solidary T	V Superior and not solidary	V
	Equal and solidary ←———·T————→	Equal and not solidary ←———–V·————→	
T	Inferior and solidary T	V Inferior and not solidary	T

Figure 1.2 The two-dimensional semantic under tension
Source: Brown and Gilman (1972:259, figure 1b)

addressee in the lower left quadrant. There is no conflict between the two in either case. But in the remaining two quadrants, the two semantics call for the opposite choice. The addressee defined by the upper left quadrant is superior (and so should receive V by the power semantic) but is also solidary (and so should receive T by the solidarity semantic). The opposite conflict surfaces in the lower right quadrant.

Brown and Gilman's data indicate that, by the mid-twentieth century, solidarity had almost completely won out over power as the dominant governing semantic. The patron addresses the nonsolidary waiter with V despite the power difference and children and parents exchange mutual T. The net result is that there is a substantial increase in the number of reported reciprocal uses of pronouns, either mutal V or mutal T. In Brown and Gilman's survey results, speakers of French, Italian, and German indicated that the nonreciprocal pattern would be used in only a minority of social situations. Furthermore, the use of mutual T, as opposed to mutual V, seems to be increasing as well. This would indicate that not only is the power semantic receding as a choice-governing factor, but the grounds for solidarity are becoming broader too. But the power semantic remains in force in one subtle way. If solidarity increases between two people as they get to know each other better, it might sooner or later become appropriate to shift from mutual V to mutual T. It is the individual with more power, in the traditional sense, who is the one privileged to suggest the switch.[8]

Apart from their major analysis of the development and changes in the power and solidarity semantics, Brown and Gilman made other discoveries worth mentioning. First, although solidarity had succeeded power as the dominant semantic in French, German, and Italian, and the basis for solidarity seems to be broadening for speakers of all three languages, speakers of these three languages seemed to pick out different factors as the favoured bases for solidarity. For example, family relationships were more likely to lead to mutual T for German speakers, while 'shared fate' (such as being fellow-students or fellow-countrymen abroad) appeared to be more important for French speakers. Italian speakers said they would use mutual T within the family to almost the same extent as German speakers would, and they surpassed even the French in their willingness to use T on the basis of camaraderie.

Second, there was a striking correlation between reported individual usage of mutual T and political radicalism. The French students studying in the USA who had answered the pronoun survey questionnaire were also asked to take a test designed to measure radicalism. Radicalism was measured by asking people to report their agreement or disagreement with statements on issues like the nationalization of industry, capital punishment, and trial marriage. The test was constructed in such a way that a high score meant the person was more radical. The pronoun survey had asked for the students to report their usage of T or V with various other people, such as mother, elderly female servant, grandfather, male fellow-student, female fellow-student, older brother's wife, and top boss. A respondent who would use T with all seven of these addressees would get a score of 7, with lower scores going to those who would use T with fewer addressees. The scores for the 50 French speakers for pronoun usage ranged from 1 to 7. The correlation between pronoun scores tabulated this way and the results of the radicalism test was almost perfect. If Brown and Gilman's results were typical of French students as a whole, it would mean that if you heard a male French student address a woman fellow-student with *tu*, you could almost bet money that he believed in free love and the weakening of religious loyalties.[9]

Since Brown and Gilman reported their research, a number of other scholars have conducted research on the same and other languages, among them Lambert and Tucker (1976) and Bates and Benigni (1975). Lambert and Tucker analyzed a mass of survey data from French-speaking communities in France and Canada and Spanish communities in Puerto Rico and Colombia. Bates and Benigni conducted their research on Italian in Rome. Both studies confirm the broad outlines of Brown and Gilman's earlier work. Bates and Benigni (1975:273) find Brown and Gilman's work 'remarkably farsighted'. Lambert and Tucker (1976:144) seem to think that the two-semantic model is a little too simple, but they do state that role and status merge into solidarity, although you might expect them to be associated with the power semantic. This would be in line with Brown and Gilman's notion of a shift away from power towards solidarity as the major influence. These two studies are both in total agreement, with each other and with other studies, that there is considerable variation in pronoun choice based on the background of the speaker. Not only is this true across languages, as Brown and Gilman stated, but even within the same language and community, depending on the speaker's social class, age, sex, and other social factors. We will try to work out later in the chapter what implications the variation in pronoun use has for Brown and Gilman's account.

AMERICAN ENGLISH ADDRESS

Related to the use of T and V pronoun forms is the choice of the name which one person will use to address someone else. This choice is available for manipulation by speakers of English as well as in languages that have T and V. The address system of American English, in particular, has been analyzed by Brown and Ford (1961/1964) and by Ervin-Tripp (1972).[10] Each of these studies has become something of a classic. In addition, Slobin et al. (1968) have done a small follow-up study of the Brown and Ford research.

Although there are other options which we will mention later, the principal choices in American English are between first name (FN) and title with last name (TLN), with FN roughly analogous to T and TLN to V.[11] Brown and Ford used a variety of data in their investigation of which forces influence this choice. Like Brown and Gilman, they used literary sources (a set of modern American plays). They also had records of more than 200 interactions involving about 80 people in a Boston drafting firm. This information came from an employee of the firm who made brief notes of his colleagues' address behavior (the anthropologist's 'participant-observer' technique). In addition, they had records of observations involving some 56 children in the American Midwest for a psychology research project on another topic, in which address forms were frequent. Besides this they used questionnaire data on the reported usage by 34 business executives.

The three patterns that are possible with the two forms are the mutual exchange of FN (including such common nicknames as 'Bob' and 'Jim'), the mutual exchange of TLN (with Mr, Mrs, Dr, and so on as the 'titles'), and the nonreciprocal pattern in which one person gives FN and gets TLN. According to Brown and Ford, the two reciprocal patterns are governed by a single dimension, ranging from acquaintance to intimacy. Americans call someone they are merely acquainted with by TLN and expect the same in return. People who are friends call each other by FN. But Brown and Ford point out that the difference between the two relationships for Americans is very small. Five minutes' conversation is often enough to move from a TLN relationship to a FN one. In my own experience, even five minutes will not be allowed to elapse if some relatively permanent basis for solidarity is beginning. For example, when new employees first meet their co-workers or when a person who has just moved into a neighborhood meets the new neighbors, mutual FN is commonly exchanged as soon as the introductions are over. This is characteristic of Americans and would not be true of speakers of other languages, or even other English speakers. In fact, the meaning of such notions as 'solidarity', 'power' and 'intimacy' from one country to another, and even from one social group to another in the same country, is a major source of variation in address form usage.

The nonreciprocal pattern is governed by two dimensions: age and occupational status. The member of a dyad who is older (a difference of 15 years or more seems to be significant) will be called by TLN and call the younger person by FN.[12] The person with the higher occupational status also has the privilege of being addressed with TLN while addressing the other person with FN. It is not always the case that older people have higher occupational status than younger ones. When there is a conflict, for instance between a young executive and an old janitor, it will be occupational status that takes precedence; the janitor will be called by FN and address the executive by TLN (Brown and Ford 1964:237).

The discovery that all the address form usages in their varied data sources were consistent with these principles is no doubt the major point in Brown and Ford's research. Although they refer to the earlier work of Brown and Gilman, the terms 'power' and 'solidarity' are not used. Yet it is easy to see that the Brown and Ford results are remarkably similar to the earlier work on T and V. The mutual exchange of FN, like mutual T, marks a socially acceptable level of solidarity. In the absence of sufficient solidarity, but with no difference in power, mutual TLN will be used in the same way that mutual V is. If we interpret age and occupational status as manifestations of power, and it is clear that this is what Brown and Gilman intended, then the nonreciprocal pattern seems to be very much like the receding use of nonreciprocal T/V in the European languages.

Apart from the main pattern, Brown and Ford made a number of other interesting observations. They noticed that there was a natural progression from mutual TLN to nonreciprocal TLN/FN (provided the necessary social differences were present) to mutual FN: that is, two people might start out calling each other by TLN, then the older or higher-status person might begin calling the other by FN and later they might use mutual FN.[13] The upper right-hand portion of figure 1.3 illustrates the most frequent path of progress through the system, using the three patterns I have mentioned so far. By including three additional forms, with their associated reciprocal and nonreciprocal usages, Brown and Ford get the nine-step display illustrated in the left-hand portion of figure 1.3. These three forms are: (1) T (title alone, the most formal address term), (2) LN alone (last name alone, less formal than TLN but not so intimate as FN), and (3) the 'multiple names' we are going to discuss next. This is the full progression that accounts for all the various sources of data that Brown and Ford used.

The progression might move more or less rapidly – one of the middle steps (or even the first step) might be skipped – but one thing that will

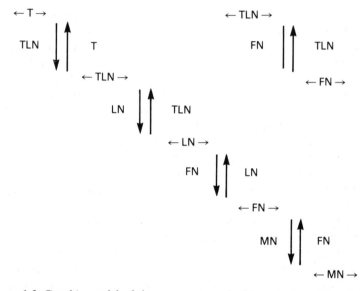

Figure 1.3 Graphic model of the progression of address in time (from left to right)
The upper portion of the figure represents the major progression; the lower
portion represents the full progression
Source: Brown and Ford (1964:241, figure 1)

not happen is for either progression to move backwards. Once a speaker
has begun using FN, for example, he will never use TLN again with the
same addressee, with two exceptions.

One of these exceptional circumstances has to do with using the address
form system to express anger or reproof. If people are angry enough with
someone they usually address with FN, they might withdraw to TLN to
symbolize the disruption in the relationship. When the issue that caused
the trouble is resolved, they return to FN. Brown and Ford mention a
special case of this in connection with a premature shift from TLN to
FN. As is the case with T and V, the switch from a nonreciprocal TLN/
FN to mutual FN is appropriately initiated, at least tacitly, only by the
person with the higher status or greater age. Suppose the person in the
less favorable social position assumes wrongly that tacit permission has
been given, and begins using FN. The other person, who has always
addressed him with FN, might use TLN in order to show that the other's
FN is not acceptable ('Hi, Jack!' may be answered by 'Good morning,
Mr Jones').

The other exceptional situation is the use of 'multiple names'. Brown
and Ford discovered that when people become very good friends, the
exclusive use of mutual FN no longer seems enough to symbolize the

friendship. In this case, they will address each other with multiple names: 'sometimes saying TLN, sometimes FN or LN or a nickname, sometimes creating phonetic variants of either FN or the nickname' (Brown and Ford 1964:238). These multiple names (MN) are not used to express anger; they are used in more or less free variation. The use of the more formal options, like TLN or LN, are not taken seriously. The use of MN need not be reciprocal. In fact, Leeds-Hurwitz (1980) reports how a woman who had been promoted to a somewhat ambiguous position in a business concern used nonreciprocal MN to help her carve out her place in the institutional hierarchy. We will take a closer look at her creative use of the address form system a little later.[14]

Slobin et al. (1968) were able to confirm the major pattern presented by Brown and Ford in a study of a San Francisco insurance firm. Eighty-seven employees (57 men and 30 women) were interviewed at four levels of management: (1) upper management, (2) middle management, (3) lower management, and (4) nonmanagement. They were asked the names they used to address subordinates, a subordinate's subordinate, their boss, their boss's boss and their fellow-workers. Typical of the American readiness to use first names, all the respondents reported that they addressed everyone at the same or lower level by FN, as table 1.1 shows. A large majority even reports addressing immediate superiors by their first name. Everyone without exception reported receiving FN from fellow-workers and only four individuals reported receiving TLN from superiors. Some of the managers reported that subordinates or subordinates' subordinates addressed them with TLN, mostly those in middle and upper management. Of all the responses, leaving aside a few interviewees who said that the address form they would use depended on the situation, only four (the four who reported receiving TLN from their superiors) reported mutual TLN. All the other uses of TLN were nonreciprocal and in every case the higher-status individual used FN and was addressed with TLN.

Just as Brown and Ford discovered, age is less important than occupational status for determining address form. There were 26 cases in the insurance company data in which a younger person had higher status than an older person. It never happened that the younger higher-status person used TLN to the older lower-status person and received FN in return. Reciprocal TLN was exchanged in only two of these cases. In five other cases, the subordinates said they were called by FN and what they called the superior would depend on the situation. The rest were on a mutual FN basis. But these same results also indicate that age cannot be totally ignored. There were no clear instances of a superior addressing an older subordinate by FN and getting TLN back. Except for the five situation-dependent reports, all of these 'reverse' age-difference dyads used one of the reciprocal patterns, almost always mutual FN. As Slobin et al. (1968:293) put it: 'The data suggest that pairs of individuals. . . feel

Table 1.1 Frequency and percentage of reported address forms given, by organizational level of speaker and status of addressee

| | Organizational level of speaker | | | | | |
| | Nonmanagement | | Lower management | | Middle and upper management | |
Addressee	FN	TLN	FN	TLN	FN	TLN
Boss's boss	14	31	3	13	10	7
	31.1	68.9	18.8	81.3	58.8	41.2
Boss	43	5	13	2	12	5
	89.6	10.4	86.7	13.3	70.6	29.4
Equal or	76	0	49	0	49	0
subordinate	100	0	100	0	100	0

Source: data from Slobin et al. (1968:290, table 1)

uncomfortable with nonreciprocal naming when the elder is of lower status.'

Ervin-Tripp (1972) took a quite different approach to the study of American English address form use. She presents the address form system as a series of choices, using the computer flow chart format developed by Geoghegan (1971). Figure 1.4 is a reproduction of the address system she finds valid for 'a competent adult member of a western American academic community' (Ervin-Tripp 1972:226–7). The diamond-shaped junctures are to be taken as decision points. The 'E' beside the juncture labelled 'adult' marks the entry point, the point where you begin the process. There are two exits from each decision point depending on whether the indicated condition is met (+) or not (−). To work out the correct address form to use, you simply follow the appropriate path through the chart. For example, a faculty member (F) who wants to address the dean (D) would recognize him or her as an adult, then check to see if it was a 'status marked setting' (like a formal faculty meeting with parliamentary procedures in effect). If not, whether or not F knows D's name would be checked (almost certainly F would), then whether or not D is a relative (presumably not). Next, F decides if D is a friend or colleague (D is a colleague, at least), then if D is of higher rank (D is), then if F has a 'dispensation' to address D by his first name.[15] 'Dispensation' simply means that D has made it clear, explicitly or tacitly, that it is acceptable for F to call him or her by D's first name. If F has a dispensation, then F addresses D by D's first name; if not, F then has to decide if there is an 'identity set' of occupational or courtesy titles like 'Senator' or 'Doctor' that applies. In this case, presumably there *is* an applicable title of this kind, namely 'Dean'. As a result, F addresses him

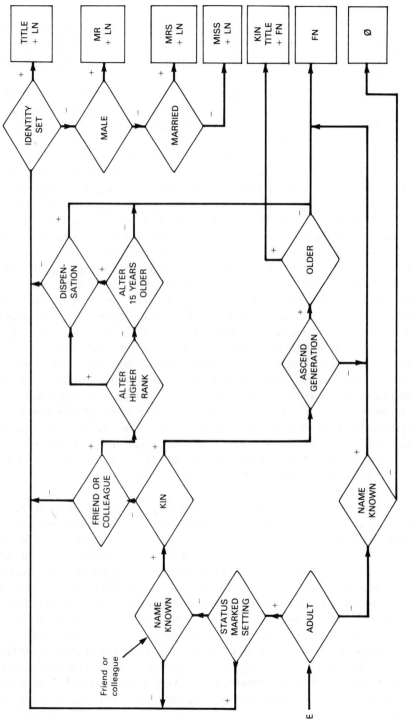

Figure 1.4 Flow chart representation of one American address form system
Source: Ervin-Tripp (1972:219, figure 1)

as 'Dean' + LN in the absence of a dispensation. Ervin-Tripp's model leads to a decision under other sets of circumstances in a similar manner. It is important that neither Ervin-Tripp nor any of the other scholars who use the model suggests that it actually represents the thought processes a speaker goes through in deciding address forms. It is simply a logical model designed to include all the critical information organized in a way that gives the right results. As Ervin-Tripp (1972:226) says, it is like a formal grammar.

It is instructive to see if Ervin-Tripp's notion of what is crucial in addressing is substantively different from what Brown and Ford and Slobin and his colleagues found. Notice first that Ervin-Tripp calls for a decision about whether or not the other person is an adult. Her model calls for addressing any child by his or her first name if you know it and not using any name if you do not. (An adult, according to Ervin-Tripp, is a person who has reached the age appropriate for completing secondary school; about 18 in the USA.) You would not expect that the business firm data that these two projects investigated would have had any instances of address forms directed to children. Brown and Ford did have data on address to children but they have almost nothing to say about it, so the earlier research neither supports nor contradicts Ervin-Tripp. The next two junctures in Ervin-Tripp's chart involve 'status marked settings' and whether or not the other person's name is known. Neither of these is mentioned in the earlier research, but setting is surely important and probably accounts for the 'depends on the situation' responses that Slobin et al. received from some of their interviewees. Brown and Ford (1964:236) mention in passing that 'generic first names', like the 'Mack' or 'Buddy' of taxi drivers, sometimes occur when the addressee's name is not known, but taxi drivers would not be members of a 'western American academic community'! Similarly, address to kin is not mentioned in either of the earlier reports.

As for the middle of the top part of Ervin-Tripp's display, there is striking agreement with the other two. If the speaker is not on intimate terms with the addressee (that is, not a 'friend or colleague') then some form of TLN will be used. This agrees with what we know about the use of FN to people the speaker is on reasonably close terms with. Notice that rank precedes age; if the other person is of higher rank, the age juncture will not enter into the decision. Again, we have agreement with what we have already seen: rank dominates age as a criterion. It is possible for a younger or lower-status person to address an older or higher-status person by FN, but only if there is a 'dispensation'. In other words, the older or more highly-ranked person is privileged to decide how he or she will be addressed, as we have already seen. Where there is overlap between Ervin-Tripp's work and the other studies, there is agreement.

There is one more detail in Ervin-Tripp's chart that needs to be mentioned. It would appear that no one who follows this address system would ever avoid some kind of name unless the addressee were a child, but this is clearly not true. There are two situations under which a speaker might simply avoid using any name at all. One case might be when a condition at one or other juncture is ambiguous. You may not know if the other person considers your friendship to be close enough for you to use a first name. Perhaps you think you may have a tacit 'dispensation' to use a higher-status individual's first name, but you are not sure. Maybe the other person is older than you are, but not a great deal older. Will that person be insulted if you use a first name, or hurt if you do not? In cases like this, the decision-making system 'breaks down' and the speaker cannot make a reliable decision. The English language gives its speakers the option of avoiding the use of a name temporarily until the nature of the relationship becomes clearer. In my opinion, it is appropriate for this problem *not* to be included in the flow chart because it represents the failure of the system to provide an answer. (I mean a failure of the real *system*, not Ervin-Tripp's representation of it; it is clear, I think, that in real life, the American English address system will sometimes leave its users confused, no matter how accurately it is described).

The other case is when the speaker simply does not know the other person's name. It is possible, of course, to step out of a discourse and ask for an introduction ('I'm sorry, I didn't get your name'), but this ploy is awkward and embarrassing. Failing this, Ervin-Tripp's chart leads us to 'title', 'Mr', 'Mrs', or 'Miss' plus an empty last name.[16] But while it is perfectly acceptable to address a priest, for example, as 'Father', or a physician as 'Doctor', it is odd to address someone as just 'Mrs'. Ervin-Tripp (1972:228–9) proposes that this problem be solved by changing metaphors, so to speak, and adds rules of the following form to her model:

Father + Ø ---> Father

Mr + Ø ---> Ø

In other words, 'Father' plus an empty last name adds up to 'Father', but 'Mr' plus an empty last name adds up to nothing and the speaker uses no name at all.

VARIATION

So far, we have emphasized the uniformity among the European languages that Brown and Gilman analyzed and the agreement among the three studies of American English address. But the truth is that there is considerable variation in address form usage, across languages, across national boundaries, across social groups within the same country, from one individual to the next, and even in the behavior of the same person from one instance to another. It would be foolhardy to try to predict exactly what address form will be used at any given time, even if you know exactly what the relationship is between the speaker and the person he or she is talking to. If there is a small number of principles that govern address forms, as there seems to be, how can there also be so much variation? Is the research that seems to lead to uniformity misleading? Are the scholars misled? Or is there some way to understand both the uniformity and the diversity in a consistent manner? I am not aware that this issue has been addressed before in a general way, but it certainly seems worth exploring.

I am able to identify at least two sources of variation in the use of address forms. First, there are group differences. Second, even within the same social groupings, there is considerable freedom to select one or other of the acceptable general patterns on an individual basis. Sometimes individuals vary from their own usual usage to convey temporary moods and feelings.

Group differences

Without exception, all scholars who have done research on address forms beyond well-defined, relatively homogeneous groups report variation according to social groups within the society. Bates and Benigni (1975) used a modified version of the Brown and Gilman questionnaire administered as an interview, rather than a written instrument. They found striking social class differences in the use of T and V in Italian, with the direction of difference not exactly the expected one. The younger upper-class respondents were by far the least formal. Lower-class young people were significantly *more* formal in their use of T and V, with older speakers falling between. The correlation Brown and Gilman found between political radicalism and the tendency to report use of T was replicated by Bates and Benigni, but with a much lower correlation coefficient (0.48 for all social classes as opposed to Brown and Gilman's 0.96, although 0.48 is still significant). But the correlation is much weaker when the upper-class young people are removed (a Spearman's *rho* of only 0.26; no longer significant at $p<0.01$). These results cast the earlier work of Brown and Gilman in entirely new light. Their respondents were Italian college students studying in the USA and so naturally would be young and upper class.[17] If there are such clear class differences among Italian speakers, the same is no doubt true for the French and German speakers as well. Still, if we stay with equivalent social groups, we find that Brown and Gilman's results are fairly well replicated.

Many of the lower-class subjects have a third pronoun in their system that almost no one else reports using. The older deferential form *voi* is used along with the usual V form *Lei* and T form *tu*. *Voi* is still commonly used in rural and southern parts of Italy, and many of Bates and Benigni's lower-class subjects have their origins there. The result is frequently 'a tripartite system, in which *Lei* is reserved as the respect form for nonfamilial superiors and/or distant acquaintances in the city, while *voi* is used in the family, and may also be extended to superiors and distant acquaintances "back home"' (Bates and Benigni 1975:279).

This use of *voi* shows up again in the analysis of nonreciprocal use. Recall that Brown and Gilman's contention was that solidarity was gaining at the expense of power as the dominant semantic. Since the power semantic requires the use of the nonreciprocal pattern, their hypothesis would lead to a prediction that reciprocal usage would be virtually the only pattern found. One rough means of testing the hypothesis statistically would be to test the mean scores for the pronouns people say they receive against the mean scores for pronouns they say they give, to see if they are significantly different. If most people are really reporting reciprocal usage most of the time, then there should be no significant difference between the pronouns they say they give and the ones they say they receive. Bates and Benigni tested this difference with the t test and, contrary to expectations, got a t of 3.27, which is significant at $p<0.01$ (Bates and Benigni 1975:283). The same test on only the data from upper-class subjects, though, resulted in a nonsignificant value for t. This means, of course, that upper-class subjects *are* reporting predominatly reciprocal usage. This might simply be further evidence that Brown and Gilman's students studying in the USA were not typical, but the use of *voi* in the lower class was also part of the reason for the significant t value. Many lower-class speakers use nonreciprocal *voi/tu* within their families, whereas upper-class speakers use mutual *tu* in their families. This was no doubt another cause of the unexpected result. But with the questionnaire items that ask about usage of T and V with family members left out (thereby eliminating most reported usage of *voi*) there is still a significant difference between pronouns given and pronouns received, but at a lower level ($p<0.05$). Again, there is no significant difference for the upper-class speakers, with the family items left out.

To find out where this difference was, Bates and Benigni examined each of the 22 items in the questionnaire individually. They found that nonreciprocal use was reported at statistically significant levels for only six items. Three of these involved ascending generation family members and are the result of the use of *voi* by some the subjects. Of the remaining three items, two of them indicate that it is *age*, not acquired social status, which is triggering the nonreciprocal use. A number of subjects responded that they would address an elderly maid who had been with the family for years with *Lei* and receive *tu*. This means that the age of the older woman would outrank both the solidarity that goes with long acquaintance and the power of higher social rank as a considertion in pronoun choice. The fifth item that was significantly nonreciprocal was address to the 7-year-old son of the President of the Republic. Here, speakers said they would address the boy with *tu* and receive *Lei*. This example might be taken as the same as the case of the elderly maid, but working in the opposite direction. This time, the higher-status person is younger, and (presumably) not solidary, but neither social status nor the lack of solidarity counts, only his age.[18] This case is not quite so clear, though, since address to children might cancel out everything else, as it does in Ervin-Tripp's model.[19] The sixth item appears to be a counterexample. Here, many subjects said that in an office setting, they would address a 'boss whom you rarely see' with *Lei* and expect to receive *tu*. Although this item gives statistically significant results (at $p<0.05$ by a χ^2 test), it involves only a few subjects (most would use reciprocal *Lei*) and most of those were young. Bates and Benigni (1975:283) suggest that the nonreciprocal usage might be triggered as much by the probable age difference as by the difference in acquired social status. In the main, then, if you allow for the use of *voi* within the family by some people, and the effect of age rather than other kinds of social status, it seems that Brown and Gilman's contention about the victory of solidarity over power is substantiated by Bates and Benigni's results.

Another study involving languages mentioned by Brown and Gilman was conducted by Lambert and Tucker (1976). Using a questionnaire asking for pronouns given and received in 34 'interacts', they collected massive amounts of data from two age groups of school children in two areas of the province of Quebec. The 'interacts' involved both family (paternal grandfather, female second cousin) and nonfamily (bus driver, young female stranger) interlocutors. Children aged from 9 to about 16 years of age completed the questionnaire, and their responses were divided into two age groups, elementary school age subjects (9–13 years old) and secondary school age subjects (13 to a little over 16 years old). In addition to the original study, they report the results of replications in French-speaking communities in France and on St Pierre-et-Miquelon, an island territory governed by France, but located in Canadian waters off the coast of Newfoundland. Additional replications in Spanish-speaking communities were conducted in Puerto Rico and in Colombia. There were substantial and statistically significant differences between the two language groups and within the different commmunities speaking each language. Furthermore, patterns of difference in the use of address forms were discovered based on demographic characteristics, such as urban versus rural location, social class, age, and sex of the youngsters who supplied the data.

Lambert and Tucker's research results are far too detailed to summarize effectively, but it will be helpful to take an example or two of the sorts of difference by social group that they found in the Quebec study. In addressing parents, there are two general patterns, reciprocal *tu* and the nonreciprocal pattern in which the parents are addressed by *vous* and address their children with *tu*. Rural versus urban location has an influence on these patterns, in a way that is similar in some respects to Bates and Benigni's results in Italy. There is a tendency for rural children to report the nonreciprocal pattern and urban children to report reciprocal usage. This reminds us of the use of deferential *voi* within the family by Italian speakers with rural roots. *Statistically* significant results by location were found only for girls in the younger age group and for boys in the older age group, however (Lambert and Tucker 1976:13).

An interesting difference shows up among the urban respondents in the intertwining influence of sex and age. There were four 'interacts' that clearly contrasted the exchange of address forms between the young respondents and adults of each sex. These interacts were the ones with older male and female adult acquaintances and older male and female adult strangers. The general tendency was for younger children to address adults of either sex and either degree of acquaintance with the V form *vous* and be addressed by *tu*. If there were any differences between the younger children and the teenagers, it was a tendency for the adults to use *vous* to the teenagers.

However, there were striking differences depending on the sex of both the youngster and the adult. Male acquaintances were significantly more likely to use mutual *vous* with teenage girls than with young girls, where they used the nonreciprocal pattern. There was no parallel difference where boys were being addressed; the nonreciprocal pattern tended to be used to the same degree with both age groups.[20] Besides this, there was no difference between younger boys and younger girls in the use of T or V with men they were acquainted with. But teenage girls reported significantly more use of mutual *vous* than teenage boys did. Where women acquaintances were concerned, there were no significant differences either by the age or sex of the youngster.

With adult male *strangers*, there was a significant trend towards using mutual *vous* to adolescents of both sexes compared to behavior towards younger children. But the trend was stronger where girls were concerned, so that significantly more teenage girls than boys said they would be called *vous* by an unfamiliar man. (There were no differences by sex for the younger children.) With unfamiliar adult women, only the data on the urban girls also showed a significant shift toward mutual *vous* to the older girls. The shift to mutual *vous* by female strangers to older youngsters was not significant in any other subgroup, not even urban teenage boys. There were no significant differences between how boys and girls would be addressed by women strangers at either age.

Notice that a shift from nonreciprocal T and V to mutual V as a young person gets older does not require them to make any changes in their own usage. The young person keeps on using V to adults; it is the adult who shifts from T to V. What these data show is that adult males in Quebec took sharp notice of the difference between an elementary school age girl and a secondary school age young woman. As she grows towards womanhood, a girl can expect more and more grown men to use *vous* to her than was the case when she was a child. Men are significantly less likely to treat boys the same way as they grow up. Grown women are significantly less likely to let the difference between a pre-adolescent and an adolescent influence their pronoun usage with young people of either sex; the difficult-to-explain address form shift by adult female strangers to teenage urban girls is the only exception.

Paulston (1975), in her study of address forms in Swedish, also noticed distinct differences in usage by social class. Paulston depended much less on questionnaire data than is usually the case in studies of this sort. She supplemented and verified her interview and questionnaire results by taking 'copious field notes' during social events in which she was a participant, employing the participant-observer technique used in anthropology (Paulston 1975:2). She reports that there are conflicting semantics, separately governing the Swedish T form *du* and the V form *ni*. These semantic differences are class related, generally not consciously recognized by Swedish people.

Paulston detected a difference between 'solidarity' *du* and 'intimacy-familiarity' *du*. Solidarity *du* is intended as the form of address between equals known and unknown. Users of solidarity *du* may also call the other person by their first name, but more often they will avoid using the other person's name at all, even if they know it. Solidarity *du* expresses shared group membership, but not the intimacy associated with using a person's first name. Some speakers deal with the inconvenience of having to avoid names altogether by making up a sort of nickname to go with solidarity *du*, often by simply stripping off the '-son' that commonly ends Swedish names, and calling the person by the rest of his last name. Intimacy *du* overlaps with solidarity *du* and may merge with it but Paulston was able to distinguish the two. Speakers who use the intimacy *du* semantic always also address the same person by their first name or by a kin term. Furthermore, before speakers begin using intimacy *du*, they have to talk about it explicitly. As we by now expect, it is the higher-status person who is privileged to initiate it.

Intimacy *du*, used only between people who have a close relationship, is characteristic of the highest social class. Paulston's (1975:9) questionnaire survey data showed that all but one of the 26 highest class respondents wanted to preserve the use of *ni* (the Swedish V form) and/or the use of titles. This, of course, allows *du* to be reserved for intimate friends and relatives. Fifty-one of the 55 respondents from the lowest class said they wanted to see *du* used generally with everyone, a sure sign of solidarity *du*. Responses from the middle social group were mixed.

The form *ni* also has varying semantic controls over it. Like the rural Italian use of *voi* within the family and the tendency in rural Quebec for children to be involved in a nonreciprocal *tu-vous* pronoun pattern with their parents, Paulston (1975:12) reports a 'peasant *ni*' in which the form *ni* is used for parents and other older relatives and for 'worthy elders in the community'. She reports that the use of peasant *ni* is 'totally rural' and disappearing.

In urban areas the use of *ni*, for reasons that are not entirely clear, is considered impolite by speakers in the two lower classes, especially if the addressee is also called by TLN. Members of the highest class use *ni* – and TLN – freely within their social group to people they do not address with *du*, but tend to avoid it with people from other social classes. These differences in the unconscious rules for the use of the two pronouns by social class frequently cause misunderstandings when people from one class talk to someone from another class.

Individual differences

Researchers who use the flow chart model that Ervin-Tripp uses uniformly make it clear that the same chart cannot be expected to fit all uses. As I pointed out, Ervin-Tripp herself limited the system in figure 1.4 to members of an American academic community located in the West. 'A shared language,' she says, 'does not necessarily mean a shared set of sociolinguistic rules' (Ervin-Tripp 1972:230). Although she attributes to the academic community a rule that prohibits using the title 'Professor' without LN, non-academic university personnel do use 'Professor' or 'Doctor' alone to members of the faculty (Ervin-Tripp 1972:229). Mitchell (1979) presents a different flow chart for each of four Swedish speakers, in another study of the Swedish address system. The four charts are not variations on the same basic system, but differ from each other in substantial ways. Jonz (1975) analyzed the address terms used within the US Marine Corps, and came up with three flow charts, based on the marine's military rank. There can be no doubt that different population subgroups use somewhat different rules of address.

There can be variation from one person to the next, even when their social characteristics are identical. To some extent, this reflects inherent problems in sociological research. Sometimes the criteria assigning a person to one social class or another cause a person to be classified in a way that may be consistent with objective criteria, but which does not match the person's self-identity. For example, Paulston (1975:9) reports that four lower-class respondents to a questionnaire gave answers that resembled the answers from upper-class respondents. Three of these four could be shown to be upwardly socially mobile. Questionnaires can also simply be erroneously marked by the person who is filling it out. In Lambert and Tucker's data, for example, two out of 318 urban secondary school age boys indicated that they addressed their grandfathers with T and were called V in return. It is hard to avoid the conclusion that they either mistakenly marked their questionnaire forms or they were not taking the task seriously.

In the third place, a survey questionnaire might not specify all the criteria a person would need to make the decision called for. In a case like this, the respondent will consciously or unconciously fill in the missing information and may not do it the same way as someone else. The typescripts of interviews conducted by Blocker (1976) nicely illustrate the potential for this kind of problem. She interviewed a number of Indiana University faculty members in their offices and asked them about their address form practices. A typical interview went, in part, like this:

Interviewer: And how do you address the chairman of your department?

Professor: By his first name, Dale.

Interviewer: What if he were here in front of us, would you still call him Dale?

Professor: No, I'd call him Dr W.

If this individual were marking a questionnaire that simply asked how he would address the chairman, he would probably mark FN, thinking of an informal situation. Another respondent, with exactly the same rules for address, might mark TLN thinking of a situation in which students were present.

Cases in which people change pronoun use to express social relationships are more interesting. Brown and Gilman (1972:276–80) give a number of examples of 'violations' of address form usage in English and French literature that were used to help define a dramatic character or express temporary shifts in relationships. Shakespeare was a master of this use of address forms, sometimes making the point quite explicit. Brown and Gilman (1972:278) quote, as an example, this line of Sir Toby Belch in *Twelfth Night*: 'Taunt him with the license of ink; if thou thou'st him some thrice, it shall not be amiss.' Footnote 19 shows how a reversal of the rules for pronoun usage was used to accent the degradation in Nazi concentration camps in the film version of *Sophie's Choice*. Ervin-Tripp cites a real-life example of the same thing, taken from a magazine article written by the black American psychologist, Alvin Poussaint. In an autobiographical anecdote, Dr Poussaint told of being asked his name by a white policeman, who addressed him as 'boy'. Poussaint gave his name as 'Dr Poussaint', adding 'I'm a physician.' The policeman then demanded his first name and went on to address Poussaint by his first name only. Simply by his manipulation of the address form system, the officer was able to show that, as far as he was concerned, no black person could possibly be treated any more deferentially than a small child, even if he were an adult member of a respected profession.

Paulston (1975) reported a less depressing example of the use of a shift in address to express speakers' attitudes towards others. In her discussion of the unique insulting connotation of the Swedish V form *ni*, Paulston reports that the notes from her observations of salespeople's address to customers over five months' time showed only two instances in which *ni* had been used: When she returned to the same department store the first day it opened after Christmas, she found the sales personnel enduring the frustration of large numbers of exchanges and returned gifts. According to Paulston's notes from that day, 'The clerks gave an impression of kranky [sic] sullenness. . . and I heard so many *ni*'s that I lost count' (Paulston 1975:14). It appeared that the clerks were expressing their mood by using an address form they normally avoided.

An extraordinarily creative use of the address form system by a woman administrator in a business organization is reported by Leeds-Hurwitz (1980). The managerial organization of the concern involved a director in the highest position and ten associate directors. The director had a staff of four individuals (two of whom themselves had secretaries). The associate directors each had at least one secretary; some had an additional staff member or two. There was also a support staff called the 'Committee Control' office. The manager of this office reported directly to the director, as did each of the associate directors and, of course, the members of the director's own staff. The work of the Committee Control office was important, but somewhat peripheral to the function of the organization. A woman identified as 'Sue' by Leeds-Hurwitz was promoted to manager of the Committee Control office from a position as a member of the staff of one of the associate directors.

Sue's position in the organization was ambiguous in two ways. First, her new job made her the equivalent to an associate director in some respects, but not quite of the same status in others. Second, the address form patterns between her and other people in the organization had been established when she held a position on the associate director's staff. She was now in a position of authority over five people in the Committee Control office with whom she was already on a reciprocal FN basis. This use was now not quite so appropriate as it once was. Yet, as Brown and Ford discovered, it is not possible to move up and to the left in either section of figure 1.2. The option of addressing her five subordinates with

FN and demanding TLN from them would have caused far too much resentment.

Sue solved this problem by using one of the minor options in the larger portion of figure 1.3, namely the nonreciprocal FN <---> MN option. To facilitate this, Sue had to construct nicknames for several of the Committee staff, names which are apparently not used to these people by anyone else. For example, Sue called a woman named Betty by the name 'Betty B' (the 'B' from the first letter of her last name) and another woman named Wendy (actually Leeds-Hurwitz herself) by either 'Wendy-Loo' or 'Lendy-Woo'. These people continued to call her 'Sue'.[21] By this device Sue was able to symbolize her new authority with a nonreciprocal pattern without demanding any change in the address forms used by her subordinates.

Sue's new status with respect to the associate directors presented a different problem. On the basis of her earlier status, she addressed them by TLN and received FN. In her new position, she was in some ways their equal. If she wished to emphasize the equality, she could begin addressing them by FN. But this would not be appropriate, since an invitation to use FN is supposed to come from the person with the clearly higher status. Apparently few if any of the associate directors invited Sue to use their first names. She could conceivably have initiated the minor pattern in the lower part of figure 1.3 and begun addressing them by LN only. But there would have been several things wrong with that solution. First, it represents an increasingly intimate step in the address progression, and so, playing by the rules, it should be initiated by the associate directors. Second, the use of LN alone is in general rare in American English, and is common only in certain occupation groups, and normally among people of the same sex. Mutual LN is exchanged, under some circumstances, in the armed services (predominantly men), and also, if I am correctly informed, among nurses (predominantly women). Outside these domains, addressing someone by LN can be mildly insulting (something like Swedish *ni*, I suppose). Finally, LN alone as an address form is especially unexpected coming from a woman addressing a man. A third option Sue could have resorted to would have been to avoid using the associate directors' names at all. But this could not have lasted; sooner or later she would have found herself in a position in which the use of one name or another could not have been avoided.

The solution Sue hit upon was ingenious. She initiated an address form that does not appear anywhere in figure 1.3. She began addressing the associate directors by FN + LN (for example, 'Charles Johnson'). Except as used by angry parents in giving orders to children ('Johnny Jones, you come here!'), FN + LN is seldom or never used as an address form. Sue's use of the term to her colleagues would not have been confused with the 'angry parent' usage, and since the form was so novel, it would not have been intuitively obvious to the associate directors that their prerogative to increase the intimacy of the address pattern had been broached. But knowing what we now know, it seems clear that if FN + LN had to be inserted into the system, it would surely go above FN and below TLN. It seems to be roughly the equivalent of LN without its problems. Sue's solution in both directions seemed to fit her situation perfectly. The FN <---> MN pattern to her new subordinates 'lowered, them without making them change their established address term to Sue, and her FN + LN <---> FN pattern with her 'almost equals' seemed to capture that relationship very nicely without giving the associate directors any real grounds for complaint. Sue's address form usage was individual, even novel. But for the most part it conformed well to the overall rules of address in American English. Sue's 'modifications', in effect, of figure 1.3 are illustrated in figure 1.5.

A brief questionnaire experiment I carried out with a class of graduate students in 1972 produced another set of results with individual variations. I asked 22 students to report whether or not they would address various other people with FN, TLN, or avoid addressing them by name entirely. I systematically manipulated three characteristics of the addressees:

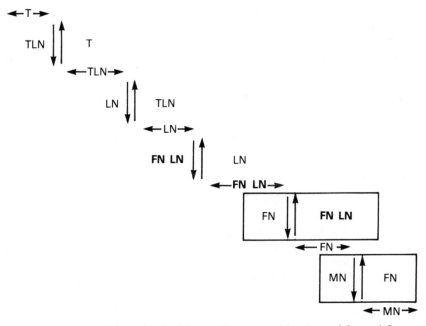

Figure 1.5 Graphic model of Sue's effective modifications of figure 1.3
Boxed areas represent Sue's exploitation of the address system to symbolize her new status. Area in bold face represents a level that she effectively inserted into the system.

membership in a religious order, sex, and degree of acquaintance. The latter two are well-known factors contributing to address form usage. I included the first because the students were all studying at Georgetown University, a Roman Catholic institution. Although about half the students were not themselves of Roman Catholic background, all had had the opportunity to become acquainted with members of Catholic religious orders. I combined the different values of the three variables in the following format:

Addressee is:

(1)   A member of a religious order (priest or nun), of the same sex you are, and is not a casual friend.[22]
(2)   Not a member of a religious order (priest or nun), or of the same sex you are, and is a casual friend.

All possible combinations of the three characteristics were presented in the same way. As tedious as the completion of the questionnaire no doubt was, the results show that the respondents, for the most part, completed it carefully. The results were not totally uniform in the sense that each of the addressees I defined received exactly the same address form from everyone. But the results conformed well to the Guttman scale technique (Guttman 1944). Guttman scaling was used also to some extent by Brown and Gilman and depends on implicational relationships. They illustrate Guttman scaling in the following way (Brown and Gilman 1972:273–4):

A perfect Guttman scale can be made of the statements: (a) I am at least 5' tall; (b) I am at least 5' 4" tall; (c) I am at least 5' 7" tall; (d) I am at least 6' 1" tall; (e) I am at least 6' 2" tall. Endorsement of a more extreme statement will always be associated with endorsement of all less extreme statements. A person can be assigned a single score – a, b, c, d, or e – which represents the most extreme statement he has endorsed, and from this single score all his individual answers can be reproduced.

If a person has said that he is at least 5' 7" tall, but he has said he is not at least 6' 1" tall, you may expect that he has said he is at least 5' 4" tall and that he is at least 5' tall, but that he is not at least 6' 2" tall. This scale would be 'perfect' for all rational respondents because there would be nobody who would endorse a greater height without also endorsing all lesser heights. In most sociological research, Guttman scales only approximate perfection; if less than 10 per cent of the responses are out of order, the approximation is generally considered acceptable. In my experiment I was fairly sure, for example, that anyone who claimed to address a lay person of the opposite sex who was not a casual friend with FN would address a lay person of the same sex who *was* a casual friend the same way. Similarly if the casual friend of the same sex were not addressed with FN, then I expected the less intimate acquaintance of the opposite sex would not be either. In other words, I expected the responses to be representable by a Guttman scale.

The resulting scale is presented in table 1.2. Asterisks mark responses that deviated from scalability. The scale in table 1.2 is 93.8 per cent scalable. It is clear that the interlocutor whom most respondents report they would address with FN is a same-sex 'casual friend' who was not a priest or nun. The interlocutor with the fewest FN address reports is the one with the opposite characteristics: a member of a religious order of the opposite sex who is not a 'casual friend'. Within these characteristics, it appears that membership in the religious order is the most important consideration of the three, degree of intimacy next and sex the third.

But an examination of four of the 'deviations' shows that perhaps the ordering of the interlocutor characteristics is not quite so fixed as table 1.2 might indicate. Pattern numbers 9 and 10 represent two individuals who either would or might address a priest or nun who was a casual friend by FN, but definitely would not address a lay person they knew less well by their first name. But this does not necessarily imply an error in filling out the form, or that the two have a totally different system from everyone else. It simply indicates that the acquaintance factor is more important to them than whether or not the other person is a religious. Patterns 4 and 11 also have asterisks in them, but they do not seem to be similar to each other at first glance. The pattern 4 respondent

Table 1.2 *Implicational scale for address form choice by 22 Georgetown University students, by three characteristics of interlocutor*

	Interlocutor								
	Priest or nun	N	N	N	N	Y	Y	Y	Y
Pattern	'Casual friend'	Y	Y	N	N	Y	Y	N	N
number	Same sex	Y	N	Y	N	Y	N	Y	N
1		+	+	+	+	+	+	+	+
2		+	+	+	+/−	+/−	+/−	+/−	+/−
3		+	+	+	+	+	+	−	−
4		+	+	+	+	+	−	+*	−
5		+	+	+	+	−	−	−	−
6		+	+	+/−*	+	−	−	−	−
7		+	+	+	−	−	−	−	−
8		+	+	−	−	−	−	−	−
9		+	+	−	−	+*	+*	−	−
10		+	+	−	−	+/−*	+/−*	−	−
11		+	−	+*	−	−	−	−	−
12		+	−	−	+*	−	−	−	−
13		+/−	−	−	−	−	−	−	−
14		−	−	+*	+*	−	−	−	−

Plus sign indicates FN use reported. A +/− means speaker is unsure or needs more information to decide. Asterisk marks a deviation from perfect scaling.

would address a priest or nun by FN, even if he or she were not a 'casual friend', as long as that person were of the same sex as the speaker. Pattern 4 speakers would not address a priest or nun by his or her first name, even a 'casual friend', unless that priest or nun were of the same sex. The pattern 11 speaker reports the same decision order, this time where the addressee is a lay person. Both treat the solidarity of shared gender as more important than the solidarity of acquaintance, as I defined it.

Whatever the ordering, two things are entirely clear: (1) The evidence in table 1.2 indicates that a lay person is more likely to be addressed by FN than a religious, a 'casual friend' than a less intimate acquaintance, and a person of the same sex than one of the opposite sex; and (2) the combination of these characteristics an interlocutor must have before he or she will be addressed by FN varies considerably from speaker to speaker. In other words, there seems to be considerable agreement on what characteristics lead to FN usage, but there is considerable individual variation about what combination of these characteristics represent enough solidarity to justify using FN. The speakers represented by the top line of the table (who would address everyone by FN) and the last no-asterisk speaker in the table (who would not use FN with anyone except possibly the person with the most favoring characteristics) would no doubt irritate each other if they met, but the behavior of both would be consistent with the same address form rule system. A person who, for example, called slight acquaintances by FN and 'casual friends' by TLN would be completely outside that system.

A striking demonstration of the fact that variations within the same general address term system are tolerated and even expected within a community is provided by Lambert and Tucker (1976:49–52) with their 'bicycle experiment'. In this social psychological experiment, 13-year-old girls attending a Montreal high school were asked to listen to a family discussion. They were told that the real conversation had occurred earlier and what they were hearing was a reconstruction of it by the same family. Actually, the recording was made by actors, who rehearsed the conversation so that it sounded completely natural. The conversation centered around a teenage boy who asks his parents for a bicycle. Different subgroups of the girls heard different variations on the conversation. In some of the conversations, the boy was told he would get the bicycle, in others that he would not. In some conversations, the boy and his parents used reciprocal *tu*; in others, the boy used *vous* to his parents and received *tu*. As you might expect, both address patterns were used with both outcomes of the conversation.[23] After a group of subjects had heard one of these conversations, they were asked to rate the families as a whole and each individual member on several scales.

Of the two conversations which ended with the boy getting the bicycle, the subjects rated the reciprocal *tu* family more positively in several ways.

For example, the family was rated as significantly more modern, the mother was rated more lively and active and the father more affectionate and tolerant than their counterparts in the nonreciprocal pronoun family. Of the two conversations in which the boy did *not* get the bicycle, the nonreciprocal pronoun family tended to receive the more positive ratings. They were seen as having a better family spirit and to be more religious, the mother was more strong and active, and the father more tolerant and courageous. These results are the more striking if we remember that the conversations were identical in every way, except for the pronoun use (and, of course, the associated verb agreement) and the few lines at the end where the decision is reached. A similar experiment was conducted on St Pierre-et-Miquelon with entirely consistent results.

These findings indicate that both pronoun patterns are expected and normal in these French-speaking societies. A family using either one can be seen in positive terms but, whichever pronoun pattern is used, the family's overall behavior should be consistent with it. It is as though the girls who listened to the tapes expected that the sort of family who would be on mutual *tu* terms with their son should respond favorably to his arguments for getting the bicycle. In the family in which the boy addressed his parents deferentially, the parents are apparently expectd to exercise their authority and hand down decisions to their son. Either address form pattern and either family structure could be looked on positively so long as the two factors were consistent.

UNIVERSALS OF WESTERN SOCIETY

In order to understand both uniformity and variation in rules for address, it seems we need a concept of an overall general pattern with room for individual and subgroup differences within that pattern. Brown and Gilman, I would say, were on the right track with their notion of 'power' and 'solidarity'. Reciprocal T pronoun and reciprocal FN address is surely a nearly universal result of relatively high 'solidarity' or intimacy. But from one society to another, and even from one individual to another within a society, the definition of solidarity, and the level of solidarity required for reciprocal address, varies substantially.

As I see it, there is also striking agreement in the Western societies we have looked at in the factors that induce people to use the nonreciprocal patterns. But I am less sure that these factors ought to be taken together and called 'power'. Something you could call 'power' certainly is involved when people with higher occupational status are addressed with the more remote form but return the more intimate one. However, it is less obvious that two other commonly recurring influences, age and sex, are special cases of 'power'. To some extent, greater age is likely to go with greater achieved power; the longer you work for a company, for example, the more opportunity you have for advancement. On the other hand, retired people often see their achieved social status slip away, but are still involved in nonreciprocal address patterns with younger people.[24] Brown and Gilman (1972:256) see this issue in Freudian terms. The power our parents had over us as children deters us from addressing people our parents' age or older in a familiar way. In their view, it might even be the root of the nonreciprocal use to people with social and political power: they are 'parent figures'.

If you find this argument convincing, then the age influence can be salvaged as a case of power. In the case of sex influences, on the other hand, it is more difficult. Traditionally, at least, if there is to be a nonreciprocal pattern on the basis of sex, it is the woman who receives the more deferential address form.[25] We have already seen how this works out in Quebec in the differential use of *tu* and *vous* to adolescent girls and boys by male adults. I suppose that few would argue that women have, or traditionally have had, more social power than men, yet the following passage from Brown and Gilman (1972:261) suggests that they see the influence of sex as an example of the power semantic.

There is an interesting residual of the power relation in the contemporary notion that the right to initiate the reciprocal T belongs to the member of the dyad having the better power-based claim to say T without reciprocation. The suggestion that solidarity be recognized comes more gracefully from the elder than from the younger, from the richer than from the poorer, from the employer than from the employee, from the noble than from the commoner, *from the female than from the male*. (emphasis added)

Perhaps a line of argument could be developed in which sex as an influence on address would be another special case of the power semantic. For the moment, though, I prefer to think of both age and sex as influences on nonreciprocal address form usage that are separate from, and parallel to, social power.

ADDRESS IN ASIAN LANGUAGES

Most of what I have had to say is about address usage in European languages. As we have seen, a considerable amount of work has been done on these languages. Indigenous languages of the Western hemisphere and African languages have received much less attention.[26] More has been written about Asian languages. The differences between Asian address systems tend to be substantially more complex than European ones.

Chinese

In Chinese, for example, the use of address terms has changed as the social and political situation has altered.[27] Chinese has forms for 'you' that roughly parallel the T and V forms in European languages with *ní* as the T form and *nín* as V. According to Fang and Heng (1983), this distinction largely fell out of use after the revolution of 1949. At present, *nín* has been largely replaced by *ní* in spoken usage in some parts of the country, including the south. Even in the south, *nín* might be used by educated speakers to show respect for the person they are addressing. In Beijing and other parts of northern China, *nín* is still commonly used when someone is talking to an older person. In writing, *nín* is sometimes still used, especially in the opening greeting formula *nín hao*, functionally something like 'Dear sir'.

The use of general honorific titles, particularly *xiānsheng*, 'Mr', *tàitai*, 'Mrs', and *xiaojiě*, 'Miss' (the English translations are somewhat rough), fell out of favor after 1949, as well as titles based on statuses that had no meaning in the new society, such as *lǎobǎn*, 'proprietor' (it was no longer possible to be a proprietor). This removed more titles than it would in English, since titles based on employment were and are more common than in English, where 'Doctor', 'Professor', and military ranks are the only common ones used like this. The form *tóngzhì*, 'Comrade', was the replacement, since it reflected the egalitarian ideals of the new order. Some titles were retained, like *lǎoshì*, 'teacher', *zhǔrèn*, 'director', and *shīfu*, 'master', in the sense of master craftsperson, used to skilled workers like machinists and carpenters (Scotten and Zhu 1983). *Tóngzhì* can be used alone to address someone, or with a name or another title. Some examples of usage are given by Scotton and Zhu (1983:484–5):

Tóngzhì (title alone) 'Comrade'
Wáng Tóngzhì (surname and title) 'Comrade Wang'
Wáng Wéiguó Tóngzhì (full name and title) 'Comrade Weiguo Wang'
Zhǔrèn Tóngzhì (two titles) 'Comrade Director'

It is also possible to use *tóngzhì* with a first name, especially between newly-acquainted people of equal standing in formal letters, and from superiors to inferiors.

During the Cultural Revolution of 1966–76, some supervisory positions were eliminated and their function taken over by revolutionary committees, making the titles associated with those positions obsolete. At the same time, workers were moved to professional positions while professional people were sent to work in factories. This led to some spread of *tóngzhì* where other titles were used before, and considerable increase in the use of *shīfu*, 'master craftsperson', because the virtue of working people was being emphasized and because working people were in positions of responsibility.[28] After the leaders of the Cultural Revolution were politically defeated and workers returned to factories, the use of *shīfu* declined, although it is still more widely used in some regions and segments of society than it was previously.

In spite of official support for the use of *tóngzhì* as a universal address title, it has not become the only form in actual use. On the basis of a substantial number of observations of actual use in China, Scotton and Zhu (1983:483) developed an analysis using the basic concepts of Brown and Gilman. However, like Paulston, they distinguish both *solidarity* and *familiarity* from *power* and from each other. Solidarity is a common characteristic 'that cannot be denied, such as kinship, nationality or party membership'. Familiarity refers to a history of *voluntary* encounters between individuals; basically, they choose to be friends. These three conditions do not exclude each other (in fact familiarity usually means that solidarity is also present), but one or another can become most salient.

When solidarity and familiarity are sufficiently strong, there are a number of forms that will be used. Kin terms can be used, or first names alone. Another possibility is to use *Lǎo*, 'old' (for people of the same age or older), or *Xiǎo*, 'little' (to younger people) before the surname. To address someone as *Lǎo Wáng*, 'old Wang' is very friendly in Chinese and does not have the slightly insulting flavor it might have in English.[29] When there is a power differential, and the person with the greater power has an occupational title, they can be addressed by that title along with their surname. This practice is not uncommon, although Fang and Heng (1983) find it contemptibly contrary to the ideals of Chinese society. In cases where people do not know each other well, so that power and solidarity remain unknown, *tóngzhì* (with or without a name) is to be expected. *Tóngzhì* is also used to an addressee whose occupation is known, but does not have a title, and solidarity and familiarity are not sufficient to allow a title to be left out.

According to Scotton and Zhu's analysis, the use of *tóngzhì* can have special effects when power and solidarity are both part of the social interaction precisely because other address forms are possible and a speaker deliberately chooses *tóngzhì*. When solidarity is part of a relationship, for example, even when one person has more authority, a form like *Lǎo Liang*, 'Old Liang', might be expected. If the speaker with more authority has to reprimand the other, *Liang Tóngzhì* might be used instead, as when a university vice-president tells a faculty member who wants to leave his job to take another position: 'Comrade Liang, we will help you if you are in trouble, but we won't let you go' (Scotton and Zhu 1983:487). As Scotton and Zhu explain it, this use of *tóngzhì* emphasizes not the solidarity between the speaker and the hearer, but the solidarity relationship between the addressee and the Chinese people as a whole. In other words, the vice-president is saying, in effect, 'I can't let our personal relationship influence me here, I have to treat you just like anybody else.' *Tóngzhì* ironically becomes a way of temporarily establishing a certain social distance between speaker and addressee.

Used to an addressee with greater authority who is well-known, *tóngzhì* has the opposite ultimate effect, but in a way by the same route. By emphasizing the solidarity that all Chinese people have, the power difference in the immediate relationship is reduced. So, for example, one of Scotton and Zhu's examples has a section head bringing a report to his superior. He first addresses the superior as 'Bureau Head Wang', and then delivers the report. But his goal is to get Wang to agree to some changes, so after finishing the report, he says, 'Comrade Bureau Head, I know our comrades have some opinions. Do you think you can make some changes in the project?' This tactic could be hazardous if you are approaching an official you do not know personally, according to Fang and Heng (1983:499). There is a chance that the official might be one who insists on the prerogatives of the office and would be offended at being addressed with *tóngzhì* instead of the occupational title and might not grant your request.

More recently, the use of *tóngzhì* is sharply declining, because it is associated with the era of the Cultural Revolution; an era that is now not looked at favorably. While *tóngzhì* might be used in writing and to address strangers, especially in the north, to use *tóngzhì* to address someone you know now seems unnecessarily formal to many Chinese people, and is often used to make jokes. The most common address forms are *lǎo*, 'old', and *xiǎo*, 'little'. *Shīfu* is still used to address an unknown man, and *dàjiě*, 'big sister', would be preferred for addressing an unknown woman if she is middle-aged or older. To some extent, the use of *xiānsheng*, 'Mr' and *xiáojiě*, 'Miss', are increasing, particularly in the coastal provinces, Guangdong and Fujian, where there is more contact with outsiders.[30]

The use of address forms in Chinese is fascinating for two reasons. The use of *tóngzhì*, *shīfu*, and other forms has ebbed and flowed with social and political change and reflects those changes. At the same time, the alternative forms available allow speakers to manipulate the tone of some encounters in quite subtle ways.

Javanese

A good example of how intricately social meaning can influence the choice not only of pronouns, but other parts of speech as well, is Geertz's study of Javanese, a major language of Indonesia (Geertz 1972).

In Javanese, there are three recognized levels of speech which manifest themselves by selections among near-synonyms for common words. These three levels are not just an anthropologist's construct, they are named in Javanese: *krama*, 'high', *madya*, 'middle', and *ngoko*, 'low'. For example, the word translated as 'now' in English would be *samenika* at the *krama* level, *saniki* at the *madya* level, and *saiki* in *ngoko* level speech. If one of these basic level-marking words is chosen in a sentence, and if the speaker needs the meaning of another level-marking word in the same sentence, he or she has to pick one that matches the level of the first. In addition, there is another set of words referring to people, their parts, possessions, and actions which also has sets of near synonyms. The difference here is that these words can be used in combination with the basic levels to raise the level of speech a sort of half-degree. For example, a middle-status, urbanized person might use the following sentence to say 'Are you going to eat rice and cassava now?' (Geertz 1972:169)

Menapa sampéjan badé neda sekul kalijan kaspé samenika
are   you   going to eat rice   and   cassava now

This sentence is a high-level (*krama*) sentence. Having chosen *menapa*, the speaker has to use *badé* and *samenika*. But if he wants to raise the level just slightly, he can use other words for 'you' and 'eat'. In this case, the sentence would be:

Menapa pandjenengan badé dahar sekul kalijan kaspé   samenika
are   you   going to eat rice   and   cassava now

In the same sentence at the low (*ngoko*) level, only the word for 'cassava' is the same:

Apa kowé arep mangan sega lan kaspé   saiki
Are you   going to eat   rice and cassava now

The social forces that govern the use of this system are analogous to those that apply in the European languages; what Geertz (1972:167) calls 'status and familiarity'. The factors that confer 'status' are similar to those that confer 'power' in Brown and Gilman's analysis: wealth, descent, education, occupation, age, and so on. 'Familiarity' is essentially the same as 'solidarity'. Variations in the use of the Javanese system operate in a way similar to the use variations we have just been looking at. There are three distinct but overlapping polite language subsystems depending on general social status. Within groups, the systems are used according to the personalities of individuals: 'Some people, . . . who tend to think the whole business rather uncomfortable and somewhat silly, speak *ngoko* to almost everyone except the very high in status. Others will shift levels on any pretext' (Geertz 1972:177). The Javanese way of showing deference and intimacy by means of language is much more elaborate than any examples in European languages. On the other hand, the forces that influence the use of the system, and the variations in its use, are rather similar to the equivalent language behavior in Western societies.

SUMMARY

Perhaps the most obvious point where social factors influence language is in the selection of address forms. In many languages, and in English at an earlier time in its history, there are two (or more) words for 'you'. One of these is used for people you are close to, or who have a lower social position than you do. The other is used for people you are less well acquainted with or who are socially superior. The use of these forms in several European languages was analyzed in a classic article by Roger Brown and Albert Gilman (1960/1972). They found that the use of the familiar pronoun T and the deferential pronoun V were governed by two forces, which they called 'power' and 'solidarity'. 'Power' derives from higher or lower social status, and 'solidarity' comes from intimacy and 'shared fate'. According to Brown and Gilman, European dual second-person pronoun systems originally expressed power primarily and solidarity only secondarily. Now, solidarity dominates power as the semantic that is most important in selecting T or V.

In English, as well as other languages, the choice between first name (FN) and title and last name (TLN) is in many ways parallel to the T/V dichotomy. Roger Brown and Marguerite Ford (1964) conducted a study on how these forms are socially distributed in American English. Their results indicate that, for the most part, only three patterns are used: reciprocal FN, reciprocal TLN, and nonreciprocal FN/TLN. The two reciprocal patterns are governed by intimacy (similar to solidarity) and the nonreciprocal pattern is governed by age and occupation status (related to power). Susan Ervin-Tripp (1972) conducted another classic study of American English address, using a computer flow chart model which has been much imitated since then.

Slobin et al. (1968) conducted a replication of the Brown and Ford research, which verified the main points they had made. Numerous scholars have followed up the Brown and Gilman research. While the broad outlines of Brown and Gilman's analysis seem to be valid, some refinements seem to be necessary. Several studies - for example, Lambert and Tucker (1976), Bates and Benigni (1975), and Paulston (1975) - make it clear that the application of the power and solidarity semantics can vary substantially not only from language to language, but from one community where the lanaguage is spoken to another, and from one social grouping to another in the same community. Furthermore, it is clear that there are even differences from one individual speaker to another.

Both uniformity and considerable group and individual variation are characteristic of address form systems. At least in Western societies, forces that can loosely be called 'power' and 'solidarity' govern address forms, but the relative strength of each, how they are defined, and how to apply them to everyday choices varies a good deal. A brief look at the use of *tóngzhì* and other address forms in Chinese (Fang and Heng 1983; Scotton and Zhu 1983) and at the Javanese system of 'linguistic etiquette' (Geertz 1972) shows that they are more intricate than is typical in European languages, but the influences on its use - and the variation in applying those influences - are quite reminiscent of what we find in Western societies.

NOTES

1 Earlier, of course, English had two second person pronoun forms, 'thou/thy/thee' in the singular and familiar, and 'ye/your/you' for the plural and deferential. Over time, 'you' replaced 'ye' in its own paradigm and the whole 'thou' paradigm.

2 See Paulston (1974, 1975) for an account of the lengths to which some speakers of Swedish go to avoid using the deferential *ni*.

3 References to Geertz's article will be to its rather more accessible reprinting in Pride and Holmes (1972), instead of the original.

4 As is its pronoun system, the English kinship system is an extremely simple one compared to those of other languages. It is not uncommon for a language to have six or more terms for 'aunt' and 'uncle' depending on whether the relationship is through the father or the mother, is a blood relationship or by marriage, and even whether the 'aunt' or 'uncle' is older or younger than one's parent.

5 For criteria for separating address forms and summonses, see Schegloff (1972).

6 Citations to Brown and Gilman's article will be to its reprinting in Giglioli (1972).

7 They also say quite a bit about the use of 'you' versus 'thou' in English, using literature from the period during which the contrast existed. Their data on other languages was not sufficient to support serious analysis.

8 This finding of Brown and Gilman's is consistent with a remark made by my father, an immigrant from Germany who lived most of his life in the USA. After a trip to Europe in the late 1960s, he remarked that Germany had changed since his youth. As evidence, he told about a group of high-school students on a guided tour of a certain tourist attraction. The tour guide, an adult male, referred to one of the girls as 'one of the ladies' and consistently addressed them all with *Sie*, the deferential German pronoun. This behavior struck my father as inappropriate and a little foolish.

9 If you have some acquaintance with statistics, you might be interested to know that the correlation test used was Spearman's rank-order correlation test, that the correlation coefficient was 0.96, and that, even with only 50 scores, 0.96 is 'very significant' (Brown and Gilman 1972:275).

10 Citations to Brown and Ford will be to its reprint in Hymes (1964). Ervin-Trip (1972) is an excerpt from Ervin-Tripp (1969).

11 The two choices do not necessarily go together in languages that have both T/V and FN/TLN distinctions. Addressing a person with T does not necessarily mean you can use their first name. Paulston (1975) offers some discussion of how this works in Swedish.

12 Dyads involving family relationships are an exception. Older family members are called by kin terms (Mother, Dad, Grandpa) or kin term plus first name (Uncle Harry, Cousin Mary) and younger members are called by FN.

13 Brown and Ford do not mention this, but notice that the implication is that even the nonreciprocal pattern is more intimate than mutual TLN. This strikes me as accurate.

I can imagine an employer addressing an applicant by TLN, but shifting to FN after the new employee has had the job a short time. The employee would continue to address the boss by TLN for a longer time, perhaps always.

14 I have noticed what I believe is another use of the address system to express greater intimacy than reciprocal FN. I know of several cases of women who are married to men who have names that are associated with very common nicknames, like David, Joseph, or Richard. These men's friends call them 'Dave', 'Joe', or 'Dick'; their wives call them 'David', 'Joseph', and 'Richard'.

15 The word 'alter' in the labels in this juncture and the one to the right is Latin for 'other'.

16 The original Ervin-Tripp article was written before 'Ms' was widely used as a title for women, allowing their marital status to remain ambiguous, as 'Mr' does for men.

17 A fact Brown and Gilman are well aware of. Not only are young upper-class individuals self-selected to a large degree when students studying abroad are the basis for the sample, but Brown and Gilman deliberately eliminated the occasional student from a working-class family in order to control for social class (Brown and Gilman 1972:263).

18 Interestingly enough, I included a similar item on a questionnaire I used with a class of sociolinguistics students at Georgetown University some years ago. I asked how they expected to address and be addressed by Caroline Kennedy, the daughter of the former US president, who was then 12 years old. Almost all said they would address her by her first name, though a few said they would avoid any address term. One respondent said she would call the girl 'honey'. No one said they would call her 'Miss Kennedy'. It seems it is as impossible for a child to acquire enough status to be called by TLN in American English as it is for a child to recieve V in Italian.

19 There is a scene in the award-winning film 'Sophie's Choice' in which Sophie, imprisoned in a Nazi concentration camp during World War II, is caught by the young daughter of the commandant as she is about to steal a portable radio for a group of prisoners trying to communicate with the outside. During this scene, the dialogue is conducted in German with English subtitles. The commandant's daughter, a child of about 10, addresses Sophie, an adult, with T (*du*) and receives V (*Sie*). This reverse nonreciprocal usage between an adult and a child powerfully underscores the degradation of prisoners in a concentration camp.

20 As is always the case with self-reported data, we cannot be sure the questionnaire results necessarily reflect what actually happens. Conceivably, adult males address teenage girls the same as they do little girls but the older girls, as they fill out the questionnaire, are being careful not to give the impression that they are the sort of girl a grown man can get too familiar with. Personally, I doubt that this explanation is the right one. By the way, Bates and Benigni (1975) provide valuable discussion of the difference between self-reported and observed events in the context of their study in Italy.

21 The status of commonly shortened forms of names like 'Sue' for 'Susan' complicate the notion of 'multiple names' considerably. Normally, you would not use a person's nickname until after you were already on first-name terms but, with names like 'Susan' and 'William', the reverse might be true. The use of the full FN form might imply a closer relationship than the use of the short form (cf. footnote 14).

22 My example of 'casual friend' was, for instance, another student in the same class as the person answering the questionnaire, with whom they might have an occasional conversation, not related to the course they were taking.

23 Two other conversation types were also recorded, an 'ambiguous' outcome in which it is not clear whether or not the boy will get the bicycle, and a 'neutral' condition conversation, in which bicycles are discussed, but no decision is involved.

24 When old people are utterly helpless and being cared for in nursing homes, this may come to an end. I have observed that in US homes for old people, young attendants,

some of them not yet 20, routinely address the old people by their first names.

25   It is commonly known that there are men who feel free to address even women they have not met with terms of affection like 'dear' and 'honey' (cf. Wolfson and Manes 1979). This is contrary to the traditional address pattern.

26   But see Evans-Pritchard (1964) for address in Nuer, in a Sudanese lanaguage, and Moles (1978) for an analysis of address in Quechua, an indigenous South American language.

27   Besides the sources cited, I have benefited from discussions of Chinese address with Professor Wang Chih-kang, of Nanjing University.

28   According to Professor Wang, the use of *tóngzhì* could provoke a challenge during the factional times of the Cultural Revolution. Since *tóngzhì* literally means 'having the same ideals', someone addressed with *tóngzhì* could challenge the speaker with 'and who is your comrade?' (With whom do you share ideals?) The use of *shīfu* would remove the risk of a response like that.

29   As is typical of address in many societies in Asia, there are combinations that allow intermediate degrees of solidarity or familiarity, like *Lǎo Wáng Tóngzhì*, 'Old Comrade Wang', or *Lǎo Tóngzhì*, 'Old Comrade'.

30   I am indebted to Pan Yuling for information on recent developments in the use of Chinese address forms.

2

The Ethnography of Communication

INTRODUCTION

The study of address form usage tells us quite a bit about how the speakers of a particular language, in a particular community, organize their social relationships. The approach to the sociolinguistics of language in which the use of language in general is related to social and cultural values is called the ethnography of speaking or, more generally, the *ethnography of communication*.[1] The acknowledged 'father' of this way of studying linguistics is Dell Hymes (1962/1968, 1972a, 1972b, 1974), so it is appropriate to pay close attention to what Hymes says the ethnography of communication is about.

In an early article, Hymes (1962/1968) defined the ethnography of speaking in a way that fits the work that was later done under that label very well: 'The ethnography of speaking is concerned with the situations and uses, the patterns and functions, of speaking as an activity in its own right' (Hymes 1962/1968:101). Hymes was concerned that both linguists and anthropologists were missing a large and important area of human communication. Anthropologists had long conducted ethnographic studies of different aspects of cultures – usually exotic ones – such as kinship systems, or indigenous views of medicine and curing. But language was treated as subsidiary; as a way of getting at these other topics. He noted (Hymes 1972b:50) that 'there are no books on comparative speaking to put beside those on comparative religion, comparative politics, and the like.' Linguists, in his view, were paying too much attention to language as an abstract system. They became interested in how to describe and explain the structures of sentences that speakers of a certain language would accept as grammatical. How anybody *used* one of those sentences – whether to show deference, to get someone to do something, to display verbal skill, or to give someone else information – was considered simply outside the concerns of linguistic theory. It seemed to Hymes that, 'linguists have abstracted from the content of speech, social scientists from its form, and both from the pattern of its use' (Hymes 1974:126).

The ethnography of communication would fill the gap by adding another subject (speaking or communication) to the anthropologist's list of possible topics for ethnographic description, and expand linguistics so that the study of the abstract structure of syntax, phonology, and semantics would be only one component of linguistics. A more complete linguistics would be concerned with how speakers go about using these structures as well.

ESSENTIAL CONCEPTS

Speech community

To understand what the enthnography of communication is all about, it is necessary to understand some fundamental concepts. It is one of Hymes's emphases that ways of speaking can vary substantially from one culture to another, even in the most fundamental ways. For example, it has been pointed out (for instance, Schegloff 1972) that most middle-class white Americans (and possibly members of other Western societies as well), have a 'no gap, no overlap' rule for conversational turn-taking.[2] If two or more people are engaged in conversation and if two speakers start to talk at the same time, one will very quickly yield to the other, so that the speech of two people does not 'overlap'. On the other hand, if there is a lull in the conversation of more than a few seconds' duration, the participants become extremely uncomfortable. Someone will start talking about something unimportant just to fill the 'gap' or the group will break up.

So profoundly ingrained is this rule for speakers who have it that they can hardly imagine a conversation being carried on in any other way. But Reisman (1974) found that it was quite the usual practice for Antiguans to carry on discussions with more than one speaker speaking simultaneously. On the other hand, Saville-Troike (1982) reports that there are American Indian groups where it is common for a person to wait several minutes in silence before answering a question or taking a speaking turn. Reisman (1974:112) tells the following story about his experiences in a Lapp community in northern Sweden, where conversational gaps are part of the ordinary way people talk:

We spent some days in a borrowed sod house in the village of Rensjoen . . . Our neighbors would drop in on us every morning just to check that things were all right. We would offer coffee. After several minutes of silence the offer would be accepted. We would tentatively ask a question. More silence, than a 'yes' or a 'no.' Then a long wait. After five or ten minutes we would ask another. Same pause, same 'yes' or 'no.' Another ten minutes, etc. Each visit lasted approximately an hour – all of us sitting formally. During that time there would be six or seven exchanges. Then our guests would leave to repeat the performance the next day.

Obviously, an ethnography of communication for middle-class white Americans would include the 'no gap, no overlap' conversational rule. The corresponding description of Antiguan speech rules would not include the 'no overlap' rule. And a description of the American Indian groups Saville-Troike refers to, or the Lapps that Reisman lived near, would not include the 'no gap' rule.

If the rules for speaking can be different from one social group to the next, how do we decide what a social group is for purposes of ethnographic description? It is clear that it cannot be all citizens of the same country; American middle-class whites and some American Indians have different rules for conducting conversations. It cannot be decided on the basis of speaking the same language, either. In England, for example, conversations in public places like restaurants are subdued such that people who are not in the conversing group cannot hear what is being said. American public conversations can easily be overheard by anyone else in the same average-sized room unless what the group has to say is particularly personal or secret. Yet the two nations share the English language. It is necessary, then, for ethnographers of communication to develop the concept of *speech community*: the group to which a particular ethnographic description applies.

Defining 'speech community' has proved to be far from easy. Numerous definitions have been proposed, most of them at least slightly different from the next. Hymes (1972b:53–5), for example, insists that all members of a speech community share not only the same rules for speaking, but at least one linguistic variety as well. Suppose people in a Czech village and people in an Austrian village just across the border were to have the same rules for how to greet other people, how many people can and must be speaking at a time and so forth; but suppose the Austrians spoke only German and the Czechs spoke only Czech. They would *not*, according to Hymes, be members of the same speech community. Saville-Troike (1982:20) speaks of a level of analysis at which a speech community need not share a language. By all definitions, though, a speech community must at least share rules for speaking.

Of the definitions of speech community I know about, only Saville-Troike's includes a component that I consider essential. Her discussion mentions *overlapping* speech communities. A college student, for example, might be a resident of a particular dormitory, a student at a particular college, a black person, an American, and a member of a Western, European-derived society, all at the same time. Each of these 'speech communities' might have at least some distinguishing communication rules. Some of these speech communities would be different from others by the addition of special rules of speaking. There might be particular slang terms or a specific greeting behavior that only students at the college know and use; otherwise their speech behavior would be just like that of other American college students. In other cases, rules of one community might conflict with those of one of the others. A black student probably uses speech in ways when talking to other black people that white students would not be able to understand or appreciate. Saville-Troike's insight is that it is not necessary for each speaker to belong to only one speech community or even to two or more completely separate communities. People can be, and normally are, members of several speech communities at the same time, just like you can be in the kitchen, on the ground floor, and in the house all at the same time. People alter their norms for speech behavior to conform to the appropriate speech community, by adding, substracting, and substituting rules of communicative behavior.

Situation, event and act

In order to study the communicative behavior within a speech community, it is necessary to work with units of interaction. Hymes (1972b:58–9) suggested that a nested hierarchy of units called the speech situation, speech event, and speech act would be useful, and his suggestion has been widely accepted. The three units are a nested hierarchy in the sense that speech acts are part of speech events which are, in turn, part of speech situations. Hymes described speech situations as 'situations associated with (or marked by the absence of) speech.' The examples he gives are ceremonies, fights, hunts, or lovemaking. As Hymes sees it, speech situations are not purely communicative; they may be composed of both communicative and other kinds of events. Speech situations are not themselves subject to rules of speaking, but can be referred to by rules of speaking as contexts.

Speech events, on the other hand, are both communicative and governed by rules for the use of speech. A speech event takes place within a speech situation and is composed of one or more speech acts. For example, a joke might be a speech act that is part of a conversation (a speech event) which takes place at a party (a speech situation). It is also possible for a speech act to be, in itself, the entire speech event which might be the only event in a speech situation. A single invocation which is all there is to a prayer when that prayer is the only event in a rite is the example Hymes gives.

The third level in the hierarchy is the speech act. 'Speech act' is the simplest and the most troublesome level at the same time. It is the simplest because it is the 'minimal term of the set' (Hymes 1972a:56). It is troublesome because it has a slightly different meaning in the study of the ethnography of communication from the meaning given to the term in linguistic pragmatics and in philosophy (for example, Austin 1962, chapter 4), and because it seems it is not quite 'minimal' after all. According to Hymes, a speech act is to be distinguished from the sentence and is not to be identified with any unit at any level of grammar. A speech act could have forms ranging from, 'By the authority vested in me by the laws of this state, I hereby command you to leave this building immediately', to, 'Would you mind leaving now?, to, 'I sure would like some peace and quiet', to, 'Out!' (all interpretable as commands, if the context is right). For Hymes, a speech act gets its status from the social context as well as grammatical form and intonation. As he puts it, 'the level of speech acts mediates immediately between the usual levels of grammar and the rest of a speech event or situation in that it implicates both linguistic form and social norms' (Hymes 1972a:57). We will later see (in chapter 6) that other approaches to speech acts link them more closely to the syntactic level of grammatical theory and handle the variation in speech act form according to context in another way.

Although speech acts were proposed as the minimal component of speech events, it has become clear that they are not actually quite 'minimal' (Coulthard 1977:40). Hymes mentions jokes as an example of a speech act, but some jokes, like knock-knock jokes or riddles, require speech moves by more than one speaker. For example:

Knock knock.

Who's there?

Joe and Angie.

Joe and Angie who?

Joe momma angie daddy! (Your momma and your daddy)

or:

What do you get when you cross a watermelon with a persimmon?

I don't know, what?

A fruit that's impossible to spit the seeds out.

Other apparent speech acts, like greetings and summonses, are made up of pairs of conversational moves – each made by a different speaker – that go together. In a greeting, for example, if one person greets another, you would expect a return greeting. If the other person does not return the greeting, it is not as though nothing had happened; the absence of the returned greeting is itself significant. It might mean that the greeted person is angry with the original greeter, or that he or she did not hear the greeting. If the greeting is a speech act, then what do we call each of the utterances by the two people greeting each other? If each move is individually taken to be the speech act, then we have no term for the whole two-move greeting as a unit. Regardless of how this problem is ultimately solved, Hyme's insight about the units of communication being hierarchically organized in this way has proved useful.

Speaking

In addition to looking at communication as composed of speech situations, speech events, and speech acts, Hymes suggests that there are certain *components* of speech that the ethnographer should look for. Although there are more than eight such components, Hymes (1972a:59–65) puts them into eight groups, each labeled with one of the letters of the word 'speaking'. (This technique, of course, has no theoretical significance; it is merely a mnemonic device.) The 'situation' (S) is composed of the setting and the scene. The setting is about the physical circumstances of a communicative event, including the time and place. The scene is the 'psychological setting'; what kind of speech event is taking place according to cultural definitions. The 'participants' (P) include not only the speaker and addressee, but also the addressor and the audience. The distinction between the speaker and the addressor (source) is illustrated by formal scenes among the Wishram Chinook in which the words of a chief (addressor) are repeated by a spokesman (speaker). An example in which the addressor is not even present would be the case in which the addressor is a head of state or other dignitary whose message is read to reporters by a press agent. In some scenes, the audience is not being addressed directly, but is essential for the kind of speech event in progress. The ritual insults called 'sounds' among black American adolescents described by Labov (1972b) require other youngsters to be around who evaluate the insults with remarks like 'Ooo, what a bust! or 'That's stale.' These members of the audience are not spoken to directly, but it would be unthinkable for one person to 'sound on' someone else if there were no one else around to hear it.

The 'ends' of a speech event (E) can be divided into outcomes (the purpose of the event from a cultural point of view) and goals (the purposes of the individual participants). In all sorts of bargaining events, for example, the overall outcome is to be the orderly exchange of something of value from one person to the other. The goal of the seller, of course, is to maximize the price; the buyer wants to minimize it.

Message form (how something is said) and content (what is said) together are called the 'act sequence' (A). Both message form and message content involve communicative skills that vary from one culture to another. Speakers have to know how to formulate speech events and speech acts in ways that their culture values and also how to recognize what is being talked about, when a topic changes, and how to manage changes in topic. One way to get a feel for the difference between message form and message content is to consider the difference between direct and indirect quotations. If someone were to say: 'He advised me, "Listen! If you buy a used car from that guy, you'll really regret it"', that person has reported both the form and content of the message; both what the advice was and how it was given. If the same speech were reported as, 'He advised me not to buy a used car from that guy', only the content is reported.

'Key' (K) refers to the manner or spirit in which a speech act is carried out: for example, whether it is mock or serious, perfunctory or painstaking. Often, certain keys are closely associated with other aspects of communication, like setting or participant (you expect the key to be solemn in a church but a clown to communicate in a jovial key). A possible result of conflict between the content of an act and the expected key is sarcasm. 'Instrumentalities' (I) include both channels and forms of speech. By channel, Hymes simply means the way a message travels from one person to another. Probably the most commonly used channels are oral or written transmission of a message, but messages can also be transmitted by such means as telegraph, semaphore, smoke signals, or drumming. By forms of speech, Hymes means languages and their subdivisions, dialects, codes, varieties, and registers.[3]

Communication also involves 'norms' (N), both of interaction and interpretation. We have already seen that Americans typically follow the 'no gap, no overlap' norm of conversational turn-taking, and that this norm is not followed in every other culture. To be competent in communicating in a certain culture, you have to follow norms of interpretation as well. Interpretation, in the sense in which Hymes uses it in this context, is more or less what we mean by the expression 'reading between the lines'.[4] It involves trying to understand what is being conveyed beyond what is in the actual words used. Although it is possible to make mistakes in interpreting communicative acts by other members of your own culture, it is far more common across cultures. Gumperz (1977) cites an incident aboard a bus in London that is an example of this. The bus was being operated by a West Indian man. As is customary, he would periodically announce 'Exact change, please', with roughly the following intonation:

Exact cha$_n$nge ple^{ase}

If a passenger did not have the money ready or tried to give him a large note, the driver would repeat 'Exact change, please', only this time his 'please' was louder, had higher pitch, and there was something of a pause between 'change' and 'please', something like:

Exact change $PLE_{A_{SE}}$

One passenger who had received the repeated request went on down the aisle looking angry and muttering 'Why do these people have to be so rude and threatening about it?' Why did it sound rude and threatening? To speakers of British or American dialects, to separate the word 'please' from the rest of the sentence by a brief pause, and to say it with higher pitch and greater loudness than usual would mean that the word 'please' was being given special emphasis: that the hearer was supposed to pay special attention to the word. Furthermore, the falling intonation would indicate finality to British or American English speakers: that is, the speaker considers the speech act concluded. This conclusiveness, in turn, seems excessively direct. The passenger would note the special emphasis on 'please' and take it to mean that the driver was emphasizing the fact that he was making a request. When something is emphasized, the hearer has to work out why; in this context it would seem to mean something like 'This is a REQUEST which I have to repeat because you ignored the first one.' Furthermore, the finality implied by the falling intonation might seem to be saying, 'You are in the wrong so there is nothing further to be said or done except for you to make it right by paying the fare with the exact change.' The whole utterance would sound rude and impolite because it seems to place the hearer entirely in the wrong. The problem, according to Gumperz, is that the norms of interaction for West Indian English call for such a slight pause, higher pitch and increased loudness for routine emphasis, with no expressive overtones. That is to say, the word 'please', spoken the way the driver spoke it, is not a clue to look for a hidden 'between the lines' meaning, but simply as a way of emphasizing the word 'please'. If anything, then, the driver was trying to be polite, by emphasizing the politeness word 'please'.

'Genres' (G) refer to categories like poems, myths, proverbs, lectures, and commercial messages. It is often the case that different genres have defining formal characteristics. In Hymes's view, casual speech is not the absence of any genre, but a genre of its own. Genres often coincide with speech events, but have to be distinguished from speech events since a speech genre can occur in more than one kind of speech event. Hymes gives the example of a sermon as a genre occurring outside the context of a church service for serious or humorous effect.

METHODOLOGY

The information that you can expect to get from the study of some phenomenon depends to some extent on how you go about getting it. As a result, there is a close relationship between the analyses that emerge from an academic discipline and the methodology that is used in that discipline. The ethnography of speaking, as an approach to the study of language in social context, is in practice a branch of anthropology. The analyses that come out of ethnographies of speaking, then, are ones that come naturally from the methods used in anthropology.

Unlike much of the work in sociology and psychology, anthropological studies typically do not involve research projects predesigned to control variables and yield statistical results. The goal of work in the ethnography of speaking, and other anthropological studies, is to gain a global understanding of the viewpoints and values of a community as a way of explaining the attitudes and behavior of its members. Information of this kind is not likely to come out of laboratory-style research designs. Rather, what is required is an intimate understanding of the community by the investigator. Saville-Troike (1982:118–34) presents seven procedures for collecting data for an ethnographic analysis of communication, but two of them are the most important. 'Participant-observation' is the staple method that has served anthropology for a long time. The other method, 'introspection' is used when a scholar studies his or her own speech community. Some of the others that Saville-Troike suggests, such as (more-or-less detached) observation, interviewing, and philology (the use of written material, like etiquette books or newspaper advice columns, as well as descriptions of communities that no longer exist), are really auxiliary to the two major methods. Others, like ethnosemantics (for example, the study of how a particular community views medicine and healing, quite apart from the 'scientific' Western approach) and ethnomethodology (a particular kind of detailed analysis of conversational interactions), are for specific kinds of ethnographic work.

Participant-observation is absolutely required for the ethnographic analysis of cultures that the ethnographer does not belong to. To find out what beliefs and values motivate a community of people, the investigator must go as far as he or she can towards becoming a part of the community, filling a role that makes sense in that setting. Usually, he or she has to be content with the role of a relative outsider; perhaps even the role of a guest or stranger. Essentially, the investigator tries to learn to see the world just as the members of the community see it, no matter how foreign that may be to his or her experience so far. Above all, the investigator has to avoid passing judgement on the community's customs. In conducting research in a community where sick people were treated by incantations, for example, no competent ethnographer would ever report that aspect of the culture as a 'silly superstition'. On the contrary, he or she would attempt to understand the community point of view that it is a valid and efficacious way to heal someone. Participant-observation demands considerable commitment to the research. The researcher spends months – more often years – in the community before he or she feels confident of understanding their outlook. In developing parts of the world, this will mean accepting a reduced material standard of living for that length of time.

Introspection means the investigator tries to analyze his or her own values and behaviors and those of people in his or her community. This is by no means as simple as it sounds. For one thing, the way people operate in their own culture is automatic and largely below the level of conscious awareness. As a result, important facts that a participant-observer in a foreign culture would notice almost immediately might be overlooked entirely. Furthermore, it can be extremely uncomfortable to have to function in the community after the certain formerly implicit rules have been made explicit. For instance, in my own classes, to illustrate how the ethnography of communication is conducted, I conduct a group discussion of the American rules for greetings, using collective introspective. It turns out that people are usually not consciously aware of most of the rules for greetings until we make them explicit. In a way I dread these classes. If a student has to talk to me soon afterwards, it becomes painfully embarrassing for both of us simply to say 'hi' or 'hello' (or decide not to). Each of us is wondering if we are following the rules we have just discussed!

Besides the discomfort that results when a formerly unconscious behavior pattern is suddenly brought to explicit awareness, in the objective analysis of someone's own culture the analysis might easily bring out some of the less flattering practices of the community. To take a mild example from our analysis of greetings, we always discover that one of the rules of greetings is that there must be eye-contact between potential greeters. This leads us to admit that we often deliberately *avoid* eye-contact with another person under some circumstances, as a way to avoid greeting them. For example, we might not be sure if the other person will think it is appropriate for us to greet them, or we do not want to be rude, but we simply do not have the time to risk beginning a long conversation with an acquaintance. It is far easier to be objective and detached about such facts in someone else's culture than in your own.

In a sense, introspection is a late stage of the participant-observation method. When someone studies a speech community which he or she is not a natural member of, that person must become a part of the community to whatever degree possible. From this position, he or she will try to get a deep, almost intuitive understanding of the culture. The final analysis is, in a sense, an 'introspection' of this newfound understanding. Ethnographers must be very careful that the understanding they *think* they have is really accurate since learning second cultures, like learning second languages, is almost always imperfect: you 'behave with an accent' in the new culture. Ethnographers do this by making sure all the observed behavior and the information that they might get from interviewing members of the community is consistent with the understanding they think they have.

By the way, information obtained by direct questioning of subjects might reflect more the way they think things ought to be, rather than the way they are. The speech community member, after all, is being asked to do on-the-spot introspection without the benefit of education in the methods of anthropological research. We use the term introspection as distinct from participant-observation since, when someone is working in his or her own community, it is assumed that that person is a participant. Ethnographers using introspection in their own community should be just as careful that their explicit understanding of the practices and beliefs of their own culture is as consistent with independent evidence as participant-observers in a foreign community would be.

The dangers from using participant-observation/introspection in a nonnative community and in a native one are real in both cases, but of different kinds. In making observations in a foreign community, an ethnographer is likely to notice most of the relevant facts, since so much will be new and unexpected. The danger comes in trying to reach an accurate interpretation of these facts in terms of the culture. The investigator is hampered by the temptation to interpret what is going on around him or her from the perspective of his or her own culture, or even to see the folkways of the new community as technically and morally inferior to the ways of his or her own community. Hymes (1972b) suggests using an 'etic grid' to overcome these hazards. The term 'etic' is derived from the linguistic term 'phonetic' as opposed to 'phonemic'. In phonetic analysis, linguists try to write down the sounds of a new language as accurately as they can, without assuming that they are phonologically related to each other in the way they are in the linguists' own language. Phonemic analysis involves discovering the sound system of the new language, using the phonetic data. Similarly, the ethnographer has to make 'etic' observations of behaviors, at first assiduously refusing to interpret what they might mean. Only after weeks or months of observations have been collected will the ethnographer begin to place confidence in their 'emic' meaning: the significance they have within the cultural system of the community under observation. The 'grid' Hymes referred to in this early article seems to be a forerunner of the categories of the SPEAKING mnemonic. By focusing on each of these components and making 'etic'-style observations, the ethnographer improves his or her chances of avoiding the characteristic pitfalls of participant-observation in another community.

Work done in the ethnographer's native community will not suffer from interference from some other cultural system; rather, the danger is that some things people do which have significance will be overlooked simply because they seem so mundane and their meaning so obvious. As we have seen, becoming too aware of the communicative rules in your own culture can make it painful when you find you have to conform to them in daily life. It is tempting to avoid this kind of discomfort simply by not analyzing some of these rules. Perhaps the greatest hazard is the natural tendency to avoid conclusions that might seem to place your own culture in a bad light, even when the facts point in that direction. Native community ethnographers, unlike investigators of a foreign community, then have to live with the fact that they are part of a community that has those possibly unattractive characteristics. This result, of course, could be avoided if investigators, consciously or unconsciously, come to the wrong conclusion, or simply leave that aspect out of the analysis altogether. Interestingly enough, a Hymesian 'etic grid' is also a useful tool for avoiding the dangers of native-community research.

THE WHORF HYPOTHESIS

In the discussion of methodology, I have emphasized the difficulty that ethnographers face in trying to avoid interpreting other community mores in terms of their own cultural values. The special role of language, though, has not been mentioned. The rules of behavior within a community are often unconscious, but still quite binding on members of the community. Similarly, linguistic rules are for the most part not apparent to the speakers of a language, but they none the less conform to those rules in speaking. These observations led two scholars – the second a student of the first – to the hypothesis that the structure of the vocabulary and grammar of an individual's language actually *shape* that person's view of the world. The two scholars were Edward Sapir and his student, Benjamin Lee Whorf. The hypothesis is accordingly known as the Sapir–Whorf hypothesis, or simply the Whorf hypothesis, since Whorf was the one who gathered evidence in support of it.

Sapir (1929: see also Mandelbaum 1958:162) expressed the hypothesis in these words:

Language is a guide to 'social reality.'. . . Human beings do not live in the objective world alone, nor alone in the world of social activity as ordinarily understood, but very much at the mercy of the particular language which has become the medium of expression for their society. It is quite an illusion to imagine that one adjusts to reality essentially without the use of language and that language is merely an incidental means of solving problems of communication or reflection. The fact of the matter is that the 'real world' is to a large extent unconsciously built up on the language habits of the group. No two languages are ever sufficiently similar to be considered as representing the same social reality. The worlds in which different societies live are distinct worlds, not merely the same world with different labels attached. . . We see and hear and otherwise experience very largely as we do because the language habits of our community predispose certain choices of interpretation.

These words of Edward Sapir are quite striking. He speaks of societies being 'at the mercy' of their languages and speakers of any two different languages as living in 'distinct worlds'. Whorf (1940, and Carroll 1957) gave a number of examples of how this could be so. One way has to do with different words for similar concepts. Whorf's most famous example is of the different words in Eskimo for falling snow, wind-driven snow, slushy snow, snow on the ground, and hard-packed snow. Eskimos would be tempted to think of an English speaker as cognitively deprived if they discovered there was only the English word 'snow' for all these substances. In the same vein English speakers are inclined to wonder how the Hopi, a native American group in the western US, get along with only one word – *masa'ytaka* – that means airplane, insect, and aviator.

Even more profound differences between languages are possible when grammar is taken into account. Whorf goes on to describe some of the startling differences between English and Hopi grammar. In English, as in most European languages, a fundamental division of words is into nouns and verbs. But Whorf argues that this division is an artefact of certain particular languages; nature is not polarized in this way. For example, if verbs are defined as denoting events of relatively short duration, such as 'hit' or 'fall', then 'fist' might well qualify as a verb, although of course it is a noun in English. Similarly, nouns like 'lightning', 'noise', or 'spasm' are events that might well be verbs if verbs are supposed to denote events. On the other hand, verbs like 'dwell' or 'adhere' are situations that are as stable and enduring as 'apple', for instance, or 'newspaper', and those concepts could be denoted by nouns, if stability is the criterion. Is it really so inconceivable that in some language, people might say the equivalent of 'Her dwell is in that house over there', or 'Those kids out there are noising too much'? As it turns out, in Hopi, notions like 'lightning', 'flame', and 'wave' are not nouns at all, but verbs. In Hopi, duration is the criterion for nominal or verbal status and these events are all far too brief to be denoted by nouns. According to Whorf, in Nootka (a language spoken in western Canada) *all* words seem to a native speaker of a European language to be verbs. The Nootka use the equivalent of 'it used to cabin', for example, to express 'there used to be a cabin'.

A possible consequence of this would be that speakers of different languages could stand side by side and experience precisely the same event and yet understand it in profoundly different ways. Furthermore, each would find it difficult or impossible to understand the event from the other's perspective. Whorf provides a speculative scenario in which a physicist from a society in which verbs are not inflected for time becomes involved in a conversation with a Western physicist. The first physicist would have no formulas that involved 'time' or 'velocity'. 'Time' might be replaced by 'intensity', perhaps, and 'velocity' by 'variation'. For a while, each would think the other simply had different words for the same concepts. But eventually the first physicist would become puzzled by the Western physicist's use of the notion 'rate' to describe an object falling to the ground and the progress of a chemical reaction in a beaker. The first physicist would not understand how his or her colleague could speak of an event that takes place in the same spot (like the beaker) in the same terms as a falling object in which there was movement in an obvious plane. The Western physicist would wonder why this other person, who seemed otherwise so knowledgeable and intelligent, could not understand a reasonably elementary concept like the rate of progress of a chemical reaction. It is possible that neither of them might ever come to understand the source of the difficulty.

Needless to say, such a striking hypothesis very quickly became controversial. Critics were quick to point out that, while there certainly were substantial differences between European languages (Whorf was fond of referring to SAE, or Standard Average European) and the indigenous North American languages that Whorf cited, it did not necessarily follow that these differences induced profound differences in the way speakers of each language perceived the world. The Whorf hypothesis has been examined experimentally numerous times since the early 1940s when Whorf published his work on the subject. Most of the experimental research had to do with lexical differences and the different divisions in semantic field that go along with them. Perhaps the best-known example of this research was the work on color terms by Berlin and Kay (1969). One experiment that is based on grammatical categories was conducted by Carroll and Casagrande and published in 1958.

What has been concluded after all these decades of research on the Whorf hypothesis? For a number of reasons, it was difficult to come to firm conclusions. In the first place, as Joshua Fishman (1982) points out, it is not totally clear exactly how far Whorf was willing to carry his hypothesis. Whorf was still developing and clarifying his ideas when he died in 1941 at the age of 44. Much of the controversy, then, is about what Whorf 'really' meant. Another reason, again pointed out by Fishman, is that in general there is a profound difference between Whorf and his supporters on the one hand and his critics on the other about what methods should be used in this kind of research and what kind of evidence is taken seriously. The critics tend to use carefully-designed experiments with attempts to control variables, along with the use of statisical procedures to evaluate the results. Whorf himself and those who are impressed with his work are more inclined to rely on methods in the spirit of participant-observation and the data that it produces. Nevertheless, it is at least clear that there are several possible degrees of 'Whorfianism'. It is common for scholars to write about 'strong' and 'weak' versions of the Whorf hypothesis (for example, Miller and McNeill 1969). According to the strong version, people's cognitive categories are determined by the languages they speak. According to the weak form, people's behavior will tend to be guided by the linguistic categories of their languages under certain circumstances. As you would expect, it is easier to get someone to agree with the weak form than with the strong form. To a large degree, the argument has become one of how strong a version of the Whorf hypothesis is credible, rather than whether Whorf was right or wrong. As McCormack (1977:4) puts it, 'Nowadays the Sapir–Whorf hypothesis is neither wholly accepted nor wholly rejected.'

AN EXAMPLE

Background

An example of an approach to the study of sociolinguistics is often a much better way of understanding how the approach works than any amount of discussion of it. In this section I will describe one of the finest examples of the ethnography of communication I know of, the work of Elinor Ochs on a rural Malagasy village in Madagascar (Ochs 1973, Ochs Keenan 1974, 1975, 1977; Keenan and Ochs 1979). Her work was based on extended participant-observation in a small hamlet in the Vakinankaratra region of south-central Madagascar. The rules for behavior and value system of that community were substantially different from what a Westerner would ordinarily expect and this has a great effect on the rules for communication. As Keenan and Ochs (1979:138) put it:

The European learner of Malagasy who had perfected his knowledge of the sound system of the language and the various ways of forming words, phrases, and sentences would . . . still find himself unable to perform successfully most social acts requiring the use of speech in the type of peasant community in which we lived.
  He would frequently draw many incorrect inferences from what people said and equally frequently be misunderstood and find that his attempts at communication prompted reactions quite different from those he intended.

The reason for the difficulty that even a fluent speaker of the language would have is based on several critical facts about the folkways of the Malagasy villagers. Villages are based on a near-subsistence peasant economy, and have very small populations. This means that, in day-to-day life, people will see and work with the same people and be involved in similar activities. Except at harvest time, people seldom see other people from outside the village or leave the village themselves. This means there is never very much new information. Villagers all know each other and what happens in the village is pretty much public knowledge. Information from outside the village is seldom available. Most villagers are not literate, and could not afford newspapers, magazines or books if they could read them. Radios are too expensive to be common. Any new information, then, is passed from one individual to another. Since news is scarce, a person who has information that not everybody else knows is very much sought after. In order to prolong this status, someone who has new information is inclined to keep it for as long as possible.

At the same time, the society is very egalitarian, in particular with respect to actions that might involve guilt or blame. If something goes wrong, or if something desirable does not occur when it is expected, the fault should ideally be shared by everyone. Except for government posts imposed from outside, there is no individual leadership. Families are an important unit of social organization. Rice plots are cultivated by family units and all members – men, women, and children – are involved. The success of the crop becomes the responsibility of the whole family. Actions that go beyond the concerns of any one family are taken by the village elders, called *ray-aman-dreny* (which literally means 'father and mother'). People become elders if they have children and grandchildren, guaranteeing that they will be ancestors (who are very important to the Malagasy villagers). These actions are taken collectively by the elders as a group; no individual takes full responsibility. For example, Keenan and Ochs (1979:143) report that on one occasion six men, jointly and by turns, participated in sawing one single board during the construction of a coffin. If it later turned out that the coffin was poorly constructed, then the blame would not belong to just one builder.

These facts of Malagasy village life have two important consequences for personal interaction. First, if a person has even the simplest scrap of information that is not common knowledge, he or she has, in effect, a valued commodity. Therefore, the privileged person will not want to part with it too soon or all at once. Second, the strong egalitarian principle causes each individual to avoid doing anything that would set him or her apart from the rest of the group. In particular, confrontations with other villagers are carefully avoided.

Information exchange

Keenan and Ochs illustrate the contrast between Western European or North American norms for information exchange and Malagasy village norms. They do this by showing that a Malagasy villager would conceal the same information that a Westerner would reveal without a moment's thought. Imagine a Western man walking down the street and being asked by a neighbor, 'Where are you off to?' He would think nothing of saying, 'Just down to the hardware store to get some nails. Eddie and I are going to build a treehouse today.' A Malagasy would never dream of revealing that he was going precisely to the hardware store, what he was going to buy there, and why he was buying it in two short sentences and in response to such a general question. A Malagasy man who met a friend on the road might, after a greeting, be asked where he was headed. But he would simply say something like, 'Just a little to the north there.' The response does not provide any information at all. It would have been obvious before he said anything what direction the man was taking, but even that statement would be likely to include reduplicated forms for 'North' (*avaraparatra*, unreduplicated *avaratra*). Reduplication has the effect of minimization, as if the walker is not going quite as directly northwards as it is possible to go. An incident of this type would illustrate Keenan and Ochs' point about even a fluent Malagasy-speaking European making wrong inferences. To the European, the Malagasy's apparent evasiveness would mean that he has some special reason for not wanting to say where he is going, maybe because it is exceptionally personal or perhaps even involves some activity that is not quite honest. That inference would be completely wrong; the Malagasy is probably not going anywhere more special than the local equivalent of a hardware store. As strange as it seems to outsiders, the information in a Malagasy utterance is more likely to be something the hearer knows or could work out than something he would not know unless someone told him.

Another kind of information-concealing is involved in referring to individuals in conversation. On one occasion, a teenage boy mentioned to Keenan and Ochs that 'Bosy's mother is a little sick', as a way of indirectly asking for some medicine. A European would normally assume that Bosy's mother is not the boy's mother, even if there was every reason to believe that Bosy is his sister. The European would assume that the boy would refer to his own mother as 'my mother'. But 'Bosy's mother' was in fact the boy's mother, too. To refer to her as 'my mother' would have called too much attention to him by Malagasy standards; it was much more appropriate to deflect that attention by identifying his mother through a third party, his sister. Another way to avoid calling too much attention either to yourself or to the person you are talking about is to use the generic expression *olona*, 'person'. Someone from a Western culture who heard a woman ask, 'Is the person still sleeping?' would have no doubt that she did not know the person and might be mildly puzzled about why she was not a little more precise in indicating which 'person' it was. The 'person' was actually the woman's husband (Ochs Keenan 1977:261).

Malagasy grammar has a particular grammatical device that makes it easy for a speaker to avoid referring to individuals, the circumstantial voice. Like European languages, Malagasy has an active and a passive voice, for example:

manasa ny lamba amin'ity savony ity Rasoa
wash   the clothes with this soap   this Rasoa

'Rasoa is washing clothes with this soap'

The verb occurs first, the subject last and the object in between, as is typical in Malagasy. In the passive voice, the sentence would be:

sasan-dRasoa   amin'ity savony ity ny lamba
washed-by-Rasoa with this soap   this the clothes

'The clothes are washed by Rasoa with this soap'

or, with the subject deleted:

Sasana amin'ity savony ity ny lamba
washed with this soap   this the clothes

'The clothes are washed with this soap'

In these sentences *ny lamba*, 'the clothes', occupies the subject position, in a manner similar to English sentences. In the second example, there is no mention of who did the washing, but at the cost of making 'the clothes' prominent in the sentence. The circumstantial voice allows some other noun phrase to be made prominent: one which refers to neither the agent or the patient of the action, but to some circumstance connected with the action. Using the circumstantial voice, it is possible to say:

anasan-dRasoa   ny lamba ity savony ity
wash-with-by-Rasoa the clothes this soap   this

'This soap is wash-the-clothes-with by Rasoa'

or, more loosely and more naturally, 'This soap is used to wash the clothes by Rasoa.' As in the passive, the agent can be left out in the circumstantial voice, giving:

anasana   ny lamba ity   savony ity
wash-with the clothes this soap   this

'This soap is wash-the-clothes-with' or,
'This soap is (used to) wash the clothes'

The Malagasy speaker has a way of avoiding the agent of an action in an utterance without necessarily making the patient prominent.

Another feature of the Malagasy language – a usage rule rather than a particular syntactic structure – involves the existential construction with the verb *misy*, 'exist' (Keenan and Ochs 1979:128–9). The verb *misy* is morphologically and syntactically an ordinary verb taking the usual inflections and is used in such ordinary existence statements as:

misy liona any   Afrika
exist lion there Africa

'There are lions in Africa'

misy Andriamanitra
exist God

'God exists'

But the verb *misy* is regularly used with another verb to indicate an activity without revealing who it is that performed the action, as in:

misy mitomany
exist cry

'There is crying' or 'Someone is crying'

misy mitady
exist look-for

'(Someone) is looking for (something)'

Notice that it is impossible even to translate this construction into understandable English without using an overt subject, at least an indefinite one. In Malagasy, there is no mention at all of either the agent or patient of the action. The second sentence, as Keenan and Ochs (1979:153) point out, could be used by a friend who knows your brother well to tell you your brother has been looking for you. In English, of course, if someone says 'Someone is looking for you', you would most naturally assume that the speaker either never saw who it is who is looking for you or did not recognize the person. This inference would be completely invalid in a Malagasy village.

Giving orders and making requests

When we come back to the topic of speech acts in chapter 6, we will see that orders and requests are socially somewhat hazardous communicative activities. If you give someone an order or make a request, you expect that he or she would be willing to do something that is for your benefit. Typically, it means either that you think that you are in a sufficiently superior social position for the other person to be obliged to carry out the order or request, or that the solidarity between you is sufficient for that person to be willing to act for your benefit. If your assessment is wrong – he or she does not accept your social superiority or acknowledge the right amount of solidarity between you – the other person might openly refuse to carry out the order or fulfil the request, making you look foolish. Even if that person does do what you want, it may be with reluctance and damage will be done to your friendship. From the point of view of the person who is receiving the order or request, there are two choices, neither of them particularly attractive when you think about it. If you are given an order or a request, you can accept it and put yourself momentarily at the service of someone else; or you can risk an open confrontation with the other person by refusing to do what is wanted or by doing it with poor grace. Since the Malagasy value equality and the avoidance of confrontation, you would expect them to manage these speech acts so that the risks are minimized, and they do.

The passive and circumstantial voices can be used in the imperative mood for giving orders and very often are. A passive order in Malagasy would look like:

Sasao   ny lamba
Be-washed   the clothes

'(Let) the clothes be washed'

It would also be possible, but less likely, to say:

Sasao-nao   ny lamba
Be-washed by-you the clothes

'Let the clothes be washed by you'

The circumstantial imperative would be:

Anasao   ny lamba ity savony ity
Be-washed the clothes this soap   this

'This soap is to be used to wash the clothes'

or less often:

Anasao-nao   ny lamba ity savony ity
Be-washed by-you the clothes this soap   this

'This soap is to be used by you to wash the clothes'

These constructions, especially with the form meaning 'by you' omitted, have the effect of emphasizing the item that is going to receive the effect of the action, or some other aspect of the act – like the clothes or the soap – at the expense of emphasis on the recipient of the order, and even on the action itself. It is grammatically possible to give orders in the active voice, by saying:

Manasa lamba
Wash   clothes

'Wash the clothes'

This form of request is considered very rude and brusque and would only be used by someone who was provoked. Because of its similarity to imperatives in European languages, European speakers over-use the active imperative and seem haughty and rude to the Malagasy as a result.

Requests are de-emphasized in several ways. To begin with, the speech action is likely to take the form of a hint rather than an overt request. Second, even the hint will not be mentioned right away; it will be brought up after considerable conversation has taken place. In the third place, the hint that reveals the desired act will often not be dropped by the person who will benefit, but by someone else on his or her behalf. In fact, requests are often group acts, rather than individual ones.

Keenan and Ochs (1979:154) give the following example of how all this works out in practice. On one occasion, a group of boys arrived at their house for an unannounced visit. After about 20 minutes of talk, someone mentioned a cut foot. Somewhat later, one of the boys in the back of the group showed Keenan and Ochs a badly cut foot, which required first aid.

Clearly, there is considerable potential for misunderstanding between Europeans and Malagasys where requests are concerned. The much more direct requesting style of a European strikes the Malagasy as confrontational and arrogant. And the ordinary Malagasy request seems exasperatingly devious and time-wasting to the European.

It would be mistaken to leave the impression that there are never confrontations or direct substantive revelations of information among the Malagasy. There are times when Malagasy interactions are relatively more direct. For example, if a request is made for something unimportant, such as for a piece of tobacco, it will be reasonably direct. More serious requests, such as for a bride, will certainly be indirect. More straightforward speech events are also more likely between relatives and close acquaintances than if one or more participants are outsiders. Furthermore, there are marked differences between men and women in their communicative activity. Women are permitted, and expected, to be much more straightforward than men are. In fact, the difference in communicative expectations for men and women is exploited within the culture. For example, women do most of the buying and selling in markets, especially in town markets where some of the clientele will be European. Buying and selling in a setting where bargaining is customary means there will be a series of minor confrontations where an initial price is going to be refused and a counteroffer madè, with the item for sale perhaps alternatively praised and denigrated. This kind of event is considered easier for women.

EVALUATION

The ethnography of communication has been controversial since its beginning. One controversy is about its relationship to the field of linguistics as a whole. Most scholars who study the ethnography of communication are convinced that the limitations that linguists have placed on the study of language during the last 30 years have been too strict. Linguists have deliberately ignored the uses of language by its speakers, as an automotive engineer might be interested in the mechanics of automobiles to the exclusion of whether they are used to bring home the groceries, provide a getaway after a bank robbery, or anything else. Ethnographers of communication take the position that language is intimately human (in a way that automobiles are not) and that it is a mistake not to take into account the cultural values and beliefs connected with its use. Most of them would agree with Saville-Troike (1982:3–4) when she says:

The ethnography of communication takes language first and foremost as a socially situated cultural form, while recognizing the necessity to analyze the code itself and the cognitive processes of its speakers and hearers. To accept a lesser scope for linguistic description is to risk reducing it to triviality, and to deny any possibility of understanding how language lives in the minds and on the tongues of its users.

The more technically-oriented linguists readily admit that their study of linguistic structure abstracted from its use eliminates the possibility of 'understanding how language lives. . . on the tongues of its users', but believe their work leads to profound insights about how language exists 'in the minds' of users and would vehemently deny that their work is trivial; so the controversy continues.

A second controversy centers on the status of the ethnography of communication as an intellectual discipline. One concern is that work done in the field has produced only a series of descriptions of communicative interaction in a variety of exotic cultures, like the work on the Malagasy village I have just summarized, rather than a cohesive theory of human communication. Joel Sherzer (1977a:47), who has himself produced some of the best ethnographic research, had this to say:

> The ethnography of speaking has thus amassed a growing collection of ethnographic tidbits from around the world, relating to various theories of language and language use, either as confirmation or as refutation or corrective. At the same time, in spite of the theoretical and methodological impetus provided by Gumperz, Hymes, and others, recent research has offered relatively little new theoretical or methodological perspective of its own which draws on this valuable ethnographic data.

According to Hymes (1974:108), ethnography can learn a lesson on explicitness and falsifiability from linguistics:

> Linguists write rules, or formalize relationships in data in other ways, and study the conditions in which one or another formalization is to be preferred, not to ape mathematics, but in order to do a decent job of work. Rule-writing commits one in explicit terms, as to what is being claimed and comprised.

Ben Blount (1981), another student of the ethnography of communication, calls for improvements in the practice of ethnography precisely so that the descriptions it produces will be adequate for theory-development. It seems, then, that the ethnography of communication is open to the criticism, even by its own advocates, that it has not been rigorous enough in developing precise theoretical formulations about its subject matter.

Related to the problem of precision and theory-building is the issue of the methods used in the ethnography of communication. In the search for precision, other social sciences have relied heavily on carefully designed experiments where extraneous factors are controlled. In psychology, for example, it is common to bring people into a laboratory and ask them to do certain tasks without telling them the reason for the experiment. Investigators doing research in this way consider the participant-observer method an open invitation to hopelessly contaminated results due to the lack of controls. To the ethnographer of communication, the controlled experiment method seems so flagrantly intrusive into the natural life of human societies as to dash all hope of seeing life as the community under study sees it. In any case, whatever the validity of experimental methods in an investigator's own society, their use in other cultures is likely to be grossly inappropriate (Saville-Troike 1982:9–10). The controlled experiment methodology produces results whose interpretation is clear and replicable, but limited in scope and potentially invalidated by the intrusion of the controls. Using participant-observation as a method does not disturb the phenomena being observed nearly so much and is potentially capable of deeper insights, but the interpretation is much more dependent on who it is that is doing the observing and results are not nearly so easily replicated.

My own observation is that ethnographic work on speaking and communication routinely exceeds the work of other social sciences on language-related topics where comprehensive understanding and depth of insight are concerned. But this is true only when the research is done by the most skilled ethnographers. On the other hand, in my judgement the ethnography of communication, even after some 20 years of development, has not developed theoretical models of the cultural aspects of human communication that are both precise enough to be tested for accuracy and general enough to be applied to any human society in the world. One reason might simply be that ethnographers of communication prefer to make clear the human values displayed in the cultures they describe, and do not think the methods used in the physical sciences are appropriate. Another reason is that they may be right. Quite possibly human culture is too complex and too varied to be captured by understanding a small number of principles and a handful of units, as is true in the physical sciences and even in the study of the syntax of languages. If so, it would be beside the point to complain that the ethnography of communication has not developed theories that look like the ones that a physicist would produce.

SUMMARY

The ethnography of speaking – or, more generally, the ethnography of communication – is the study of the organization of speaking as an activity in human society. The study of the ethnography of communication was initiated by Dell Hymes in the early 1960s and numerous studies of the communication patterns in various societies around the world have been conducted since. A central concept is the speech community. 'Speech community' is difficult to define, but most ethnographers would agree that it refers to a group of people who share the same rules and patterns for what to say, and when and how to say it. A valuable addition to understanding speech community was made by Saville-Troike (1982), when she proposed that speech communities should be understood as overlapping. That is, each individual speaker can, and probably does, belong simultaneously to several speech communities; some of the smaller ones included in larger ones, and some separate from the others.

The units of interaction that Hymes proposed as the focus of ethnographic study include the situation, event, and act. Situations are general settings, such as a party, in which communicative events, like conversations, can occur. Within events, speech acts occur, such as asking a question. Speech acts are somewhat of a troublesome concept because the same term is used by philosophers of language and linguistic pragmaticists who take a different approach to them from the one taken by ethnographers of communication, and because some speech acts can be divided into components and would not be the minimal units that Hymes originally thought they were.

As an aid to organizing the information that is collected in an ethnographic research project, Hymes suggested that observers look for eight groups of components, grouped under labels whose first letters spell out the word SPEAKING to make them easier to remember. The components are the situation, participants, ends,. act sequence, key, instrumentalities, norms, and genres. The data that ethnographers of communication use are collected largely by two methods: participant-observation and introspection. Participant-observation is the traditional method used in anthropology and means that the investigator will move into a community (typically a little-studied group in a remote part of the world), attempt to find some role to play as at least a marginal member of the community, and try to gain an intimate feel for group values and communicative patterns. The researcher is normally a participant-observer for a period of months or years. Introspection is used in the study of the investigator's own culture. Using introspection, the researcher tries to make explicit the rules and values unconsciously absorbed while growing up in a particular community. Each method has its own particular hazards and advantages.

Even before the development of the ethnography of communication as a field of inquiry, the study of the relationship between language and human thought by Edward Sapir and Benjamin Lee Whorf led to a startling hypothesis now known as the Sapir–Whorf hypothesis. According to the hypothesis, a language influences or even determines the way its speakers understand the world around them because of the way the words in the language divide up the field of meaning, and because of the patterns found in the grammar of the language. Whorf speculated that even some of the basic concepts in physics would be understood very differently if they had been developed by speakers of certain non-European languages. The Sapir–Whorf hypothesis has been investigated over a period of some 40 years, but the results are unclear because of conflicts among scholars over what methods should be used and because it is not fully clear just how strong a version of the hypothesis either Sapir or Whorf really intended. At the present time, the Sapir–Whorf hypothesis is accepted as having some validity, but few scholars would agree with the strong version that says a speaker of a particular language is locked into a particular world-view by that language.

The ethnography of speaking conducted in a Malagasy village in Madagascar by Elinor Ochs shows us a community whose speech activity is substantially different from what is typical in European and North American cultures. An emphasis on equality, the subordination of individuals to the group, and the scarcity of new information lead the Malagasy villagers to organize their speech behavior in interesting ways. From the Western perspective, Malagasy speakers are uninformative in the content of their conversations, evasive in the way they make reference to other people, and extraordinarily indirect in giving orders and making requests. This is the normal way of speaking in the village and it is completely consistent with the society's values.

Research in the ethnography of speaking is sometimes criticized for the repetitive collection of data from numerous societies at the expense of an attempt to build a general theory of human communication that would have some generality over all societies. The participant- observation and introspective methods are faulted by researchers in other social sciences as being insufficiently rigorous and too dependent on the particular intuitive skills of the ethnographer. Ethnographers of communication, on the other hand, find the controlled, laboratory-style research favored by the other social sciences to be so intrusive and unnatural that using them would destroy exactly what the ethnographer is most interested in. The criticism, it seems, will not end until it becomes clear how much of the rigorous methodology and theory-construction that is used in the sciences is appropriate, or even possible, in the ethnography of communication.

NOTES

1 Earlier Hymes used the term 'ethnography of *speaking*', but I think the wider scope suggested by the term 'ethnography of communication' is more appropriate, and I am sure Hymes would agree.
2 We will look at turn-taking in conversation in detail in the next chapter.
3 All these will collectively be called 'lects' in later chapters.
4 Formal theories about how it is possible to understand more than what is said have been developed in a subject area called linguistic pragmatics, the subject of chapters 5 and 6. The range of cases covered in linguistic pragmatics has a tendency to be narrower than what is studied in this area in the ethnography of communication.

3

Discourse

THE SCOPE OF DISCOURSE RESEARCH

Discourse analysis is possibly the field within sociolinguistics that has undergone more research activity in recent years than any other. The language issues treated within discourse analysis are myriad: in a sense the study of discourse is the study of *any* aspect of language use. Sociolinguists have not been the only ones to do research on discourse. Discourse has been studied by general linguists, anthropologists, sociologists, communication scientists, psychologists, scholars in artificial intelligence, and rhetoricians. Although there are no doubt many ways to subdivide the study of discourse, one way is to consider the study of *texts* as distinguished from the study of *interactive events*. By the study of texts, I do not mean only research about written texts, but work on sound recordings or transcriptions of spoken language as well. Discourse studies on interactive events concern the problems and successes people have using language in their interactions.

The study of texts, often called, appropriately enough, *text linguistics* (van Dijk 1980; de Beaugrande and Dressler 1981; de Beaugrande 1983; Longacre 1983), is a prominent area of linguistics in Europe. An important feature of the study of texts, written or oral, are the notions of *coherence* and *cohesion*; those features that contribute to the sense of unity in a text. An influential book developing the notion of coherence in language was written by Halliday and Hasan (1976). The structure of oral narratives has been studied about as much as the structure of written texts (cf. Linde and Labov 1975; Sherzer 1977b; Linde 1977, 1984; Chafe 1980; Schiffrin 1981, 1984a; Polanyi 1982; Polythress 1982; Wolfson 1982; Mittwock 1983; and the contributions to Tannen 1982a, 1982c, and 1983b).

The analysis of discourse behavior shows two tendencies. One trend is to analyze how people manage their discourse behavior with respect to their cultural backgrounds and their interactive goals at the time of talk (for example, Labov and Fanshel 1977; Merritt 1977, 1982; Grimshaw 1982; Gumperz 1982, 1983b; Schiffrin 1984b; Tannen 1984b).[1] The other tendency is to try to discover explicit rules for the management of conversational problems, such as turn-taking, closings, and error correction. This kind of research often treats the people involved in the conversation as secondary to the fact that a structured event is in progress. Often these studies are designed to contribute to a larger sociological theory (Allen and Guy 1978; Schenkein 1978). In other research the goal is to construct abstract models of conversation which show conversations as systematic exchanges of turns to talk that are independent of who is talking and what they are saying (Jaffe and Feldstein 1970; Cappella 1979, 1980; Brady 1980; Cappella and Planalp 1981; Reardon 1982). Naturally, many studies contain elements of both these trends.

Rather than attempting to summarize the immense amount of information available on discourse analysis, I will concentrate on one theme from each of the two areas of discourse analysis.[2] As an example of research in discourse behavior, we will take up turn-taking. Turn-taking is a central issue in the study of the management of discourse events and has received a great deal of attention from a wide variety of perspectives. Turn-taking research leads in a natural way to another important interactional theme, interruption. It is reasonably typical of what interactional discourse analysis is about. Our examples of text analysis will come from studies of the relationship between discourse and grammar. Although the discourse–grammar branch of text linguistics is not quite as representative of text linguistics as turn-taking is of interactional discourse analysis, discourse and grammar research brings us in touch with the most central traditional concerns in general linguistics.

TURN-TAKING

The 'Simplest Systematics'

Perhaps the most influential proposal about turn-taking was made by Sacks, Schegloff, and Jefferson (1974). The three authors, leading scholars in the approach to sociology called *ethnomethodology*, noticed that conversational turn-allocation proceeded in an orderly manner, and were eager to discover what the sytem behind this was.[3] Their study was based on audio recordings of actual conversations. Certain readily apparent facts emerged from the examination of the data, and these facts would have to be accounted for by any serious model of turn-taking. The most crucial of these observable facts were the following (Sacks, Schegloff, and Jefferson 1974:700–1): first, speaker-change occurs. A single person does not continue speaking indefinitely; instead one person stops talking and another begins. Second, 'overwhelmingly', one party talks at a time. Third, in spite of this overwhelming tendency, occurrences of more than one speaker at a time are common, but brief. Fourth, exchanges of turn (transitions from one to the next) with no gap and no overlap are common. If the no gap and no overlap cases are combined with instances with only slight gap or overlap, a great majority of exchanges are accounted for. Fifth, there are turn-allocation techniques; the person currently speaking can select the next person (for example, by directing a question to a particular individual), or the next speaker may be self-selected. In addition, there is typically no pre-planning: neither the order nor the length of individual speakers' turns is specified in advance; and the length of the conversation, what will be talked about, how many people will participate, or the relative distribution of turns is not predetermined.

Sacks, Schegloff, and Jefferson divide the rules needed to account for these facts into two components, the turn-constructional component and the turn-allocation component. Turns are constructed of *units* which, for English at least, turn out to be syntactic units: words, phrases, clauses, and sentences. The authors' data consists of examples of turns which are constructed of only one of each of these units. Each such unit has a *projectable* completion point; roughly, participants can be expected to know what it would take for an instance of that unit type to be completed. The completion of such a unit constitutes a *transition-relevance place* and turn exchanges occur at these places. It follows that a current speaker is initially entitled to at least one such unit.

The turn-allocation component is the more interesting of the two. It turns out that the facts that Sacks, Schegloff, and Jefferson set out to account for follow from three rules. The rules come into play in order at each transition-relevance place. These are the rules (Sacks, Schegloff, and Jefferson 1974:704).

1 If the turn is constructed so as to involve the 'current speaker selects next' technique, then the person so selected has both the right and obligation to speak and no one else has such a right or obligation.

2 If the turn is *not* so constructed, then another speaker may self-select at the next transition-relevance place, but no one has to self-select. If self-selection is instituted, the first person to do so gets the turn and turn exchange occurs there.

3 If the 'current speaker selects next' technique is not being used, and no one else has self-selected, then the current speaker may continue, but need not.

If neither of the first two rules has applied, and the current speaker continues to speak as allowed by the third rule, the rules recycle and are in effect at the next transition-relevance place and continue to apply recursively until there is an exchange of turns.

The rules apply in order, which means the later rules only come into play if the earlier ones have not been invoked. On the other hand, the presence of the later rules in the system imposes constraints on the earlier ones. Since the second rule allows self-selection, if the current speaker wants to select the next person to speak he or she must make it clear that that is what is happening before the next transition-relevance place. If it is not clear by the time the next transition-relevance place is reached that the 'current speaker selects next' rule is to be used, another participant might self-select under the second rule before the current speaker gets the chance to designate the next. Since the third rule exists, it is important for a participant who does not hold the current turn to exercise the second rule before the current speaker decides that rule 2 is not going to be invoked and continues by rule 3. An example given by Sacks, Schegloff, and Jefferson illustrates all of this.[4]

Claire: So then we were worse o- 'n she an' she went down four.
          (0.7)
Claire: But uhm
          (1.5)
Claire: ⌈Uh
Chloe: ⌊Well then it was *her* fault ⌈Claire
Claire: ⌊Yeah she said one no
          trump, and I said two, an' then she went back t'two

In her first turn, Claire reaches a transition-relevance place at the end of her sentence. After seven-tenths of a second (rather a long time in a conversation), it is apparent to her that no one else is going to self-select by rule 2, so she tries to continue by rule 3 saying 'But uhm'. She really does not have anything more to say and so stops again.[5] This time the silence is twice as long. Now, Claire half-heatedly starts again, applying rule 3 at the same time as Chloe self-selects under rule 2. Chloe gets the next turn, at the end of which she intends to select Claire as the next speaker, by addressing her by name. But a transition-relevance place can be *projected* after the word 'fault'; Chloe's utterance would be a complete unit, namely a sentence, at that point. Claire actually self-selects at the projected transition-relevance place by rule 2, instead of being selected by Chloe under rule 1, resulting in the overlap between the beginning of her new turn and Chloe's utterance of 'Claire'. Of course, it all worked out well in this case, since the participant who would have been selected by the current speaker was the one who self-selected and actually took the next turn. To be sure of selecting Claire, Chloe could have said something like: 'Well then, Claire, it was *her* fault.' Possibly she thought it was safe enough to designate Claire at the end of her sentence, since Claire seemed to have run out of things to say under her own initiative.

The rule set accounts for the facts listed earlier in the following ways. The possibility for speaker-change occurrence and recurrence is built into the system by the existence of turn-allocation rules that can bring about speaker change in an orderly manner.[6] Overwhelmingly, one party talks at a time as a consequence of two features of the turn-allocation rules. First, the rules assign only one turn at a time. A current speaker will not say anything like, 'What do you think, Joe and Paul?' assigning simultaneous turns to both Joe and Paul. Second, no one has the right to a new turn except at a transition-relevance place. Within units, the current speaker has exclusive rights to the turn to talk.

Almost paradoxically, though, the rule system also has to account for the fact that there *are* times when more than one person is speaking, and that they are common, if brief. First of all, the rules guarantee that any such instances will be localized to transition-relevance places. Rule 2 makes overlap likely since the next turn is awarded to the first self-selector. If more than one speaker wants the next turn, it is quite likely that each will begin talking at the next transition-relevance place, thereby overlapping each other. An example of these simultaneous self-selections is as follows (Sacks, Schegloff, and Jefferson 1974:707):

Mike: I know who d'guy is.
Vic: ⌈He's ba::d.
James: ⌊You know the gu:y?

Another source of overlaps, this time between the current speaker and a self-selector, has to do with a slight misprojection of a transition-relevance place. We have already seen an example of this in the example conversation between Claire and Chloe. Chloe's third line was projectably complete after 'fault', and Claire in fact self-selected there, resulting in an overlap with Chloe's continuation, her utterance of 'Claire'. Another source of misprojections is variation in the current speaker's articulation. In the example below, speaker A took longer than projected to say the word 'ask', although a unit completion was actually iminent, thereby producing an overlap between the completion of 'ask' and the initiation of a self-selection by B.

A: Well if you know my argument why did you bother to
   a: ⌈ sk?
B: ⌊ Because I'd like to defend *my* argument.

The common occurrence of exchanges of turn (transitions from one to the next) with no gap and no overlap is another feature of turn-taking to be accounted for; especially since these cases, along with instances with only slight gap or overlap, constitute a great majority of exchanges. It is fairly clear how the proposed system produces exchanges with no overlaps or only slight ones. If the current speaker selects next, there is no provision for any overlap at all. If the current speaker continues in the absence of a self-selection by some other speaker, there will be no overlap, since only one speaker is involved. Even in cases of self-selection, if there is only one self-selector, and he or she projects the transition-relevance place accurately (or waits until it actually occurs), no overlap results. Only when there is more than one self-selector, or an inaccurate projection of the transition-relevance place, will there be an overlap. Where there is misprojection, the overlap is really brief, since the self-selection is usually only slightly misplaced and the original speaker reaches the actual end of the unit very quickly. Even when more than one speaker self-selects, one of them ordinarily stops almost immediately.[7]

It is not quite so obvious why there are no gaps. The rules *provide for* continuous talk with no gaps or overlaps, but the rules are not stated in such a way that someone has the *obligation* to speak if no one else does. The crucial third rule states that the current speaker may continue if no next speaker has been selected or no one self-selects, but does not say that he or she must. If the speaker does not, the rules recycle (rule 1 applies vacuously, since there is now no current speaker). If again there is no invocation of rule 2 by some other speaker, and the last speaker still does not continue by rule 3, the rules go through another cycle. Consequently, there is always the possibility this could continue so long that a *gap* becomes a *lapse*. While gaps do not result in discontinuous talk, lapses do.

In spite of the fact that there is no explicit provision in the rules to guarantee gapless – or even lapseless – talk, Claire's behavior in the conversation between Claire and Chloe is quite typical. After her first turn, she chose not to select Chloe and Chloe did not self-select within a half-second gap. Claire then continued her turn, but without any content that advanced the conversation ('But uhm'). After another gap, this time 1.5 seconds, Claire began again (with 'uh'), but was overlapped by Chloe who finally decided to self-select. In spite of rule 3, Claire behaved as if she were responsible for the brief silence, and moved to fill the silence with 'talk' even though she had nothing to say. Sacks, Schegloff, and Jefferson have little to say about behavior like Claire's, but they do point out (Sacks, Schegloff, and Jefferson 1974:714–15) that a current speaker can convert a gap into a *pause* by exercising the option in rule 3 and continuing to talk. Since gaps (and lapses) only occur between turns, once the same speaker resumes the silence suddenly is seen to have occurred *within* a turn instead of between turns, so that it developed into a pause. Although Sacks, Schegloff, and Jefferson do not say so, the implication is that pauses are not as bad as gaps and lapses. When turn change has not occurred the last speaker who was talking still has the turn by default. As a result he or she 'owns' the gap. Gaps are socially undesirable and like people who own other things that are socially undesirable – a dog who barks all the time, for example – the 'owner' of the gap is expected to do something about it.[8] Incidentally, a gap apparently begins to seem 'too long' in Sacks, Schegloff, and Jefferson's materials before one second has passed; two seconds is a virtual eternity! Although it is true that no gap, no overlap, and brief gap or overlap transitions are usually what happen, there are cases in which gaps become lapses of some 15 seconds or more. In a brief footnote Sacks, Schegloff, and Jefferson (1974:714) comment that transition-relevance places at which lapses occur have to do with the organization of sequences, rather than with the turn-taking system itself. What they seem to mean is that lapses mark the end of one event and the beginning of another one. Their examples imply that the sequences they are referring to are sequences of *topics*. It is as though potential self-selecting speakers will only select themselves immediately if they have something to contribute on the current topic. Otherwise, there appears to be a felt obligation to be reasonably sure no other member of the group has anything more to say on the same topic. If the turn-taking rules have recycled enough times for the silence to become a substantial multiple of a 'decent' gap (14 seconds would be seven times a 2-second gap), a member of the group may assume that indeed no one else has anything else to say about what the group was talking about, so a new topic can safely be introduced. If something like this is correct, there is a connection between turn-taking and topic-change. The remaining features of turn-taking behavior that Sacks, Schegloff, and Jefferson observed are also accounted for in a reasonably direct way.

High-involvement style

Sacks, Schegloff, and Jefferson's basic analysis might leave the impression that simultaneous speech would result only from a misjudgement by participants in the conversation about when to begin their talk as self-selecting next speakers. By extension, it might appear that a conversational participant might sometimes talk simultaneously with the current speaker in *violation* of the 'simplest systematics' and that this might be a useful way to define interruptions. As a matter of fact, it is sometimes the case that speakers deliberately begin their talk at other positions besides transition-relevance places with the intention of dislodging the current speaker from his or her turn before a natural ending point. Not only is this so, but there are both intonational (French and Local 1983) and lexical (Schiffrin 1986, 1987) devices that speakers use for this purpose. However, there are other simultaneous talk events which do not involve any attempt to get the turn to talk from the current turn-holder. Such phenomena were noticed in early work by Duncan (1974), who labelled them 'auditor back-channels'. Back-channels are largely brief, quietly uttered expressions of support for the current speaker, such as 'yeah', 'mhm', or brief restatings of the current speaker's most recent thought. Back-channel behavior could be incorporated as a modification of the Sacks, Schegloff, and Jefferson analysis without too much disruption. It would be less easy to do this for some of the conversational phenomena discovered by Tannen (1983b, 1984b) in her work on conversational style.

Tannen has given a thorough analysis of a conversational style which she finds common among natives of New York City, especially if they are of East European Jewish background, as well as numerous other groups of people around the world: the Antiguan interaction described by Reisman (1974) might well be another case. Conversational overlap is one of the salient characteristics of this *high-involvement* style.[9] For speakers in this style, simultaneous talk is valued, even required. Tannen (1983b) gives three kinds of overlap which are common in this style:[10]

(1)   Cooperative sentence-building: here, the overlap occurs as the speaker and auditor try to complete the utterance together. Tannen provides the following example:

Steve:	The Huntington Hartford is on the ⌈ Sóuth side.
Deborah:	⌊ on the óther?
	across.

(2)   Requesting and giving verification: one of the participants asks for verification during the ongoing talk of the current speaker. Without a change of turn taking place, the current speaker may skilfully work the verification into his or her ongoing turn. Tannen gives these examples:

Steve:	Right where Central Park West met Bróadway. That build ⌈ ing
→ Deborah:	⌊ By
Steve:	shaped like that
Deborah:	Columbus Cir ⌈ cuit? . . . that Columbus Circle?
→ Steve:	⌊ Right on Columbus Circle. Here's Columbus
	circle, . . . ⌈ hére's Central Park West,
→ Deborah:	⌊ Nòw it's ⌈ the Huntington Hartford Museum.
→ Peter:	⌊ That's the Huntington Hártford,
	right?

The contribution by Deborah at the first arrow is a request for verification of the location described as 'where Central Park West met Broadway' and overlaps the description of the shape of the building (done with the aid of hands in the shape of a pyramid). At the next arrow, Steve verifies the location 'Columbus Circle', even while overlapping the talk that contains it and without disrupting the stream of his talk. At the last two arrows, Deborah and Peter verify that they know what building Steve is referring to in the preceding line, overlapping not only Steve's talk, but each other as well. In spite of the complexity of the attempt to represent this segment of conversation on paper, there are no turn changes. Steve has the floor and the contributions by Deborah and Peter are supportive of it.

(3) Choral repetition: participants repeat (or rather anticipate) what the current speaker is saying, thus producing a simultaneous near-repetition of what the turn-holder is saying. The overlapped repetition by Deborah and Peter at the last two arrows in the preceding example are an example of choral repetition.

Tannen (1984b:30) lists these pacing aspects of high-involvement style, the features that are most directly related to turn-taking:

1 faster rate of speech;
2 faster turn-taking;
3 avoid interturn pauses (silence shows lack of rapport);
4 cooperative overlap;
5 participatory listenership.

High-involvement style seems to modify the 'simplest systematics' design for the avoidance of both gaps and overlaps by treating an overlap as rather a good thing if used properly, while displaying a virtual abhorrence of gaps.[11] Even where there is no overlap, gaps are avoided by fast, pauseless turn-taking if it is possible. One high-involvement style feature that depends on gapless turn change is the 'machine-gun question'. Machine-gun questions are asked by one participant of someone else. The questions are timed to begin at the instant the previous speaker's answer is complete, often beginning a little early, producing overlaps. Machine-gun questions among people who interact in high-involvement style are designed to produce a feeling of familiarity, casualness, and rapport (although when used with speakers unaccustomed to high-involvement style, they may produce distress, cf. Tannen 1984b:62–6). The following example is from Tannen (1984b:64–5; the machine-gun questions are marked with arrows):

Steve: That what góod it's dòne is . . . outwéighed by
                      dec
                the dámage.
→ Deborah: Did yóu two grow up with télevision?
Peter: Véry little. We hád a TV⌈ in the Quonset
→ Deborah: ⌊ Hów old were you when your

Steve: parents got it?   We hád a TV but we didn't watch it
                   all the time . . . We were véry young. I was fóur when
→ Deborah: my parents got a TV.   You were fóur?
Peter: I even remember thát.

In this example, Deborah's questions follow immediately the preceding
speaker's talk and the second one starts while Peter is still talking. Yet
Peter continues talking and, by his own report when he heard a tape-
recording of the conversation played back, did not feel that he had been
interrupted. It is particularly interesting to notice that Steve answers
Deborah's first question, 'Did you two grow up with television?', at the
instant she finishes the second one ('How old were you when your parents
got it?'). Then he goes on to answer the second even though it was
partially overlapped by Peter's answer to the first. At no time do any of
the participants feel that they were not given enough opportunity to say
what they wanted to say.

An interesting bit of convergence on the interpretation of brief between-
turn gaps signalling heightened involvement in conversations comes from
a very different research tradition. Tannen's work is based largely on
records of conversations in which she was a participant (sometimes her
students were participants), and on playbacks in which conversational
participants are asked to comment on the replay of recordings of
conversations they were in. In other words, the analysis comes from the
analyst-as-participant, and from the analysis of interpretations by other
participants about what is going on.

Cappella and Planalp (1981) follow a sharply contrasting research
approach. In this approach, strict objectivity is valued and abstract models
are sought that will predict turn-taking, quite apart from the linguistic
structure or meaning of what is said. In fact what is said is not taken
into consideration and even the notion of 'turn-taking' is derived from
the more basic phenomenon, 'talk-silence sequences', since 'turns' cannot
be observed directly. Data for this kind of study are collected in a
laboratory. In a typical procedure, Cappella (1980:131–2) asked subjects
to sit in chairs across from each other in a small room with a low table
between them. A microphone was placed on the table and vibration-
conduction throat microphones were fitted to each participant. The throat
microphones were necessary to make sure that each person's speech could
be distinguished from the other; something that cannot be guaranteed
with ordinary microphones. The signals from the throat microphones and
the table microphone were recorded on a recorder in another room.
Sequences of talk and silence were measured by means of a computer
program. The results Cappella and Planalp (1981:127) obtained with this
methodology led them to a conclusion strikingly similar to Tannen's.

If the between-turn times are brief, this may be interpeted as interest or *involvement* [emphasis added] by one partner and mimicked by the other in an effort to show similar interest or involvement. When the between-turn reaction times are slow, they may be interpreted as disinterest, distance, or pensiveness by the person, who may mimic this separation from, or thoughtfulness about, the conversation by the slow-reacting partner.

Beside the differences in research outlook and methodology, there is another important difference between Tannen's work and that by Cappella and Planalp. The subjects in Cappella and Planalp's research were students at the University of Wisconsin and presumably of a similar social background for the most part. Hence their conversational styles were probably largely the same and the timing adjustments mentioned by the authors are likely to have been individual adjustments within the same overall style. Tannen's research has shown that, when speakers of different styles find themselves in the same conversation, their assumptions about how the conversation should be going might be so different that they find it impossible to adjust automatically, and some degree of stress and conflict can be the result. What was intended as a 'cooperative overlap' may be taken as an interruption when a high-involvement speaker is interacting with an 'overlap-resistant' speaker.

DISCOURSE AND GRAMMAR

Most of the work on turn-taking is involved with the management of silence, overlap, and single-speaker talk during interactions. Elements of language are involved in the analysis, of course, but the kind of discourse analysis we have been discussing so far, called *interactional sociolinguistics* by Tannen (forthcoming), looks to the linguistic phenomena to provide a basis for understanding social interactions. Another approach, to which I am going to turn now, uses records of speech as a source of data for understanding the linguistic units found in the recordings.

The study of *discourse markers* by Deborah Schiffrin (1985, 1986, 1987), is fundamentally interactive in its focus, but features linguistic units as well. Items like 'and', 'but', 'so', and 'well' turn out to have definite and fairly intricate functions in managing conversation. For example, 'well', in general, seems to signal that the speaker anticipates that the hearer might have to work a little harder than usual to relate the speaker's current contribution to what has just been said (Schiffrin 1985). Part (but only part) of the evidence for this is the relation of 'well' to two of the basic kinds of questions. Content, or WH, questions such as 'Where did you find that beautiful chair?' have many potential answers; essentially any response that can be interpreted as a replacement for the WH word in the corresponding statement. Yes–no questions, on the other hand, while they are often answered by other responses than simply 'yes' or 'no', still most often receive responses that can be *interpreted* as affirmative or negative. Since this is so, you would expect that replies to content questions might be potentially more troublesome for whoever has to respond to the question than replies to yes–no questions with their more limited potential responses. If you are asked a content question, you have to give an answer out of a number of possible ones that are truthful, to the point, not likely to be offensive, and so on. Sometimes the difficulty in doing this induces a respondent to say something that is not 'exactly' an answer to the WH question. For instance, if someone asks you 'What is your favorite Chinese food?' when you do not really like Chinese food, it would be hard to give an answer that includes the 'what'. Here would be the ideal spot for a reply like 'Well, I am not too fond of any kind of Chinese food.' This answer is potentially a small problem for the person who asked the question, because he or she will not directly find an answer to 'what'. Since 'well' is a marker of potential difficulty in the 'well'-sayer's talk, 'well' would be expected more often at the beginning of a reply to a content question, especially one like this, than to a yes–no question. Schiffrin found that this distribution actually does occur to a statistically significant degree.

Another place where 'well' serves a useful function is in events that might be considered interruptions. For example, if someone starts to talk at a position other than a transition-relevance point, and what they say is not supportive as back-channels or high-involvement style overlaps are, it might seem disruptive to other people in the conversation. Schiffrin has shown that 'well' occurs with this kind of interruption substantially more frequently than do discourse markers that indicate continuation rather than trouble, such as 'and' and 'so'. On the other hand, within high-involvement conversations where overlaps are expected, we might expect the continuation markers 'and' and 'so' to appear with the overlaps rather than 'well', exactly because high-involvement conversationalists in general do not find overlap to be troublesome.

The proposed discourse basis for grammatical forms

The same general approach, a close analysis of the forms observed in records of natural conversations, has been applied to the discourse dynamics which influence the selection among syntactic forms available in a language. One such case is the so-called 'historic present', involving the use of present-tense forms in past contexts. For example, someone might say 'So I was driving down the road minding my own business and this idiot *cuts* in front of me and I *have* to hit the brakes.' This usage seems to have discourse implications (for example, Schiffrin 1981; Wolfson 1982; cf. Contini-Morava 1983).[12] Erteschik-Shir (1979) is one of a number of analysts who have discovered discourse constraints influencing alternatives of what seem to be the same basic construction. The analysis involves the alternatives: 'John gave the book to Mary' and 'John gave Mary the book'. Erteschik-Shir argues that *dominance* – the intention of the speaker to draw the attention of the hearer to a sentence constituent – accounts for the choice of one or the other of these. In particular, whichever noun phrase ('Mary' or 'the book') the speaker wants to be dominant will come first, and the speaker chooses the alternative accordingly. The proposal appears to solve certain problems in earlier (but since abandoned) transformational analyses of this structure.

The success of analysis of this sort suggested to many linguists that the formal syntactic analyses which became commonplace under the influence of Noam Chomsky could be replaced by discourse-based analysis. A group of linguists who had been students of William Diver questioned whether an independent study of syntax was necessary at all (Zubin 1979; Kirsner 1983; Klein-Andreu 1983; and especially García 1979). Talmy Givón (1979a, 1979b), although he has come to acknowledge the necessity for structural syntax, is one linguist who has taken the lead in searching for origins and explanations of syntactic form in the requirements of discourse.[13]

An example of how this might happen can be illustrated with the passive construction in Kimbundu, a Bantu language (Givón 1979a:85). A construction far simpler than passive sentences is a concatenation of object topic followed by comment, or 'left dislocation'. A Kimbundu example is:

Nzua, a-mu-mono
John they-him-saw

'John, they saw him'

There is a structurally similar passive construction in the same language:

Nzua a-mu-mono   *(kwa mene)*
John they-him-saw   (by me)

'John was seen (by me)'

Of course, the interlinear gloss for *a-mu-mono* ('they-him-saw') makes absolutely no sense in the passive interpretation. The original function of *a* as an agreement marker for third person plural subjects is no longer its exclusive use. In passive sentences it is becoming, or has become, a morpheme for marking a passive verb form. At the same time *mu*, the third-person singular object marker in the first example, is a morpheme marking agreement in the subject of a passive in the second example.

In many languages, there are verbs that have both a basic meaning like 'take', 'go', or 'give' and also function in the same way that case markers, as case suffixes, prepositions and postpositions do in other languages. For example, in Yatye, the way you say 'The boy shut the door with a stick' is (Givón 1979a:95):

oywi awa itsi   iki   utso
boy **took** stick **shut** door

'The boy shut the door with a stick'

The sentence no doubt once meant 'The boy took a stick and shut the door' (and, in some sense perhaps, still does). But *awa* has come to be a marker of instrumental case (like English 'with') instead of just the verb 'took'. In the same language, the word for 'went' has become a locative marker:

oywi awa onyahwo awa   otwi
boy **took** book   **went** house

'The boy brought the book home'

Here *awa* doubles as a locative marker, besides meaning 'went'. Givón suggests that in languages with case morphology or prepositions, these more abstract kinds of case morphology might have arisen from such serial verb constructions that seem to underlie case indicators in languages like Yatye. Serial verb constructions, contends Givón, are well suited for face-to-face discourse because they are relatively easy to process quickly. The more abstract means of marking case (like prepositions and case suffixes) found in more 'removed' forms of discourse are seen as originating from more loosely-coded constructions (like serial verb constructions).

The transitivity hypothesis

Some of the most detailed research of this type has been carried out by Paul Hopper and Sandra Annear Thompson (Hopper 1979, 1983; Hopper and Thompson 1980, 1984; Thompson 1983). They developed a new notion of *transitivity*, which is both a label for a number of grammatical phenomena that occur together in a large variety of languages, and a bridge between discourse and syntax. Normally, the notion 'transitive' is taken to mean that the verb in the construction has a direct object. For Hopper and Thompson, however, transitivity concerns a number of facets of the transfer of an action from one participant to another. Their concept allows transitivity to be characterized on a scale of *more or less* transitive. If more – and the more important – facets of transitivity appear in a particular clause, it is to be considered more transitive. They give us a large amount of evidence that many languages are sensitive to degrees of transitivity in their grammatical properties.

Hopper and Thompson give a list of characteristics of transitivity and their high and low values (Hopper and Thompson 1980:252) as shown in table 3.1. The term *kinesis* refers to the contrast between 'I hugged Sally', where Sally receives an action and 'I like Sally', where she does not. A *telic* action is viewed from the point of view of its endpoint; 'I ate it up' refers to a telic action, 'I am eating it' is atelic. A *punctual* act has no intermediate phase between its beginning and ending; 'kick' is punctual, 'carry' is not. *Volitionality* means the agent is acting with purpose as in 'I wrote your name' contrasted with 'I forgot your name'. *Affirmation* is the contrast between affirmative and negative clauses. A realis *mode* event happens in the real world; an irrealis event either does not happen at all or happens in a possible rather than real world. In 'George startled me', the *agent* is higher in potency than in 'the picture startled me'. The *affectedness of O* refers to how thoroughly the action affects the object: more so in 'I drank up the milk' than in 'I drank some of the milk'. *Individuation of O* refers to the distinguishability of an object from the agent (reflexives – as in 'Harold shaved himself' – are low on this parameter) and from its own background.

The interrelationship between the components of transitivity and their coding in various languages has led Hopper and Thompson (1980:255) to the *transitivity hypothesis*: 'If two clauses (a) and (b) in a language differ in that (a) is higher in Transitivity according to any of the [just cited] features, then, if a concomitant grammatical or semantic difference appears elsewhere in the clause, that difference will also show (a) to be higher in Transitivity.' Among the many examples cited by Hopper and Thompson as illustrative of the transitivity hypothesis, we will consider

Table 3.1 Parameters of transitivity

Characteristics	High	Low
Participants	2 or more participants Agent (A) and Object (O)	1 participant
Kinesis	action	non-action
Aspect	telic	atelic
Punctuality	punctual	non-punctual
Volitionality	volitional	non-volitional
Affirmation	affirmative	negative
Mode	realis	irrealis
Agency	A high in potency	A low in potency
Affectedness of O	O totally affected	O not affected
Individuation of O	O high individuated	O non-individuated

Source: reprinted with permission from Hopper and Thompson 1980:252.

two: one where differences in transitivity are due to individuation of the object, and one where aspect is the crucial characteristic.

There are several properties that contribute to *individuation*. If an O is animate, definite, human, and has a specific, extant referent, it is more individuated than otherwise. In Spanish, an individuated object – in the following example due to having a human referent – will be marked with *a*; a less individuated object will not be.

Busco mi sombrero
I seek my hat

'I'm looking for my hat'

Busco a mi amigo
I seek   my friend

'I'm looking for my friend'

In Chukchee, an ergative language in which subjects of transitive clauses are marked differently from subjects of intransitive clauses, there are no fewer than four morphosyntactic indicators of the higher transitivity in the second of the two examples compared with the first:

Tumg-e   *na-ntəwatən   kupre-n*
friends(ERG.) set(TRANS.) net(ABS.)

'The friends set the net'

Tumg-ət   *kopra-***ntəwat**-gʔat
friends(NOM.) net-set(INTR.)

'The friends set nets'

In the first example, the object meaning 'net' is more highly individuated than in the second because it is referential and the second is not (in the first case, but not in the second, there is a particular net). The higher transitivity that results is coded by the ergative ending on the agent in the first case versus the nominative case on the second, the transitive marker on the first verb versus the intransitive marker in the second case, the independent word status of *kupre-n*, 'net', in the first sentence, while the form *kopra-* is incorporated into the verb in the second, and the absolutive case ending on the object in the first case, which is not possible in the second since the object is not a separate word.

In Hindi, the subject receives the ergative suffix only in transitive clauses that are highly transitive due to the telic action of a *perfective* clause. In perfective clauses with objects, the agent gets the ergative marker and gender–number agreement is between the verb and the object. Clauses that are less highly transitive because they are imperfective, even though they have an object, differ in both these morphological features. Agents of imperfective clauses have no ergative endings even when there is an object, and gender–number agreement is with the agent, as the following two examples illustrate.

Gariib aadmii mandir-kee   saamnee phuul   beectaa
poor   man   temple-of(OBL.) front   flowers selling(MASC. SG.)

thaa
was (MASC. SG)

'The poor man used to sell flowers in front of the temple'

Kisaan-nee   bail-kii oor   chaRii   pheekii
farmer(ERG.) ox-of   direction stick(FEM.SG) threw(FEM.SG)

'The farmer threw a stick at the bullock'

Simple presence of an object is not enough to trigger the ergative suffix and object-verb agreement. The higher level of transitivity associated with perfective aspect is required. When there is no object, whether or not the clause is perfective, there is no ergative ending and agreement is with the subject.

There is a great number of other examples from a wide range of languages that similarly support the transitivity hypothesis. But what about the link to discourse? According to Hopper and Thompson, the connection is in grounding, foregrounding, and backgrounding. Foregrounded clauses are the ones that advance the sequence of action. They form the basic structure of a narrative, with the background clauses providing a durative context or backdrop against which the foregrounded events take place. It is characteristic of foregrounded clauses that a change in order among them would cause the audience for the text to interpret the difference as a difference in the ordering of the real-world events. Backgrounded clauses are not ordered among themselves. Linguists who have studied the properties of texts have analyzed certain morphological and syntactic devices that reflect grounding. Hopper and Thompson go on to argue that the same features of morphology, syntax, and semantics are those associated with high transitivity predominant in foregrounded portions of texts. One way they demonstrate this, using English written texts, is to tabulate the facets of transitivity which occur in foregrounded and backgrounded clauses. In every case, the high-transitivity values of the feature are more frequent in foregrounded clauses. With respect to aspect, for example, 88 per cent of the foregrounded·clauses in the three texts were telic, while only 27 per cent of the background clauses were. Volitional clauses made up 76 per cent of foregrounded clauses and 36 per cent of backgrounded ones.

The conclusion that Hopper and Thompson draw is that, while transitivity has a certain validity at the sentence level, to understand the cluster of phenomena thoroughly it is necessary to see how transitivity features are related to foregrounded and backgrounded discourse. A possible difficulty with this conclusion is lack of a rigorous means of characterizing foregrounding and backgrounding. Given that the features which contribute to transitivity are more common in foregrounded clauses, can it be possible that a clause is identified as foregrounded because it has these features? While this does not seem to me to be the case in the work of these two, without a fully independent, clear set of criteria for identifying the two kinds of grounding, there is always the nagging doubt that the argument may turn out to be circular.[14]

To some extent, Thompson's (1983) study of the detached participial clause in English provides independent evidence of the association of transitivity features with foregrounding. A detached participle is illustrated by the italicized part of the following example (Thompson 1983:43): 'The Spanish infantry desperately hurled themselves against the palisades, *hacking at the logs with axes.*' These constructions can be identified by the following criteria: being set off by pauses, exhibiting a clause-final falling intonation contour characteristic of independent clauses, or being preceded by a clause ending in a clause-final falling contour. In written texts, where the overwhelming majority of detached clauses occur, these intonation characteristics are almost always marked by commas. Thompson shows that detached participles are used in texts as a particular kind of background, local background, to the event depicted in the associated main clause.

I will assume that Thompson's analysis can be accepted without reviewing its details. Her analysis would lead us to expect that detached participles, since they are a kind of backgrounding device, would be very *low* in transitivity, since transitivity is associated with foregrounding. If detached participles, which can be identified by means of fairly clear criteria, actually are low in transitivity, it would add credence to the link between transitivity and discourse that Hopper and Thompson have presented. To test the hypotheses, Thompson examined three of the aspects of transitivity, existence and individuation of the object, punctuality, and aspect, in 418 detached participial clauses collected from written texts. She found that only 30 per cent of detached participles had highly individuated objects by virtue of being referential and extant. The remaining clauses had either poorly individuated objects or none at all; most did not have any object. Detached participles contained nonpunctual verbs in an overwhelming 91 per cent of the cases. With regard to aspect,

80 per cent of the participial clauses in the data were atelic, since there was no specified end-point to the action. The data strongly support the co-occurrence of at least these three low-transitivity features with detached participles. To the extent that detached participles themselves are demonstrable indicators of a kind of backgrounding, it can be said that another level of objective support has been found for the discourse explanation for transitivity.

The categoriality hypothesis

In a more recent article, Hopper and Thompson (1984) have developed a similar analysis of the major lexical categories, noun and verb. Instead of accepting absolute grammatical criteria for these categories, they note that there are *prototypical* instances of nouns and verbs, but also uses of lexical material which are less fully typical of the categories than the prototypical ones are. As in their study of transitivity, Hopper and Thompson relate the categories noun and verb to discourse functions. Prototypical nouns are used to introduce participants in a discourse which are eligible to be *manipulated* in a subsequent discourse. Prototypical verbs are used to report *discourse events*; possible answers to the question 'What happened?' To the extent that these central discourse functions are not being served by lexical items which might otherwise be thought of as nouns or verbs, they depart from prototypical categorial status. The categoriality hypothesis states that items which are used for these primary functions display the full range of morphological and syntactic oppositions that are available to that category and none of those that pertain to another category. When items are not used for such purposes in the discourse, the morphological and syntactic distinctions between nouns and verbs will be blurred.

To take one example, a major function for predicate nominals is to name the class of entities to which something belongs. The nominative that appears in the predicate position is not usually a participant to be manipulated later. If I were to say, 'Sam is a dolt', it is *Sam* that is most likely to apper later in the discourse, not a dolt. In some languages, the occupants of predicate nominal positions lose some of the grammatical characteristics that are possible for occupants of major discourse positions. In French, for example, predicate nominals do not take determiners as in the following example:

*Jeanne est (*une) étudiante*
Jeanne is (a-FEM.) student(FEM.)

'Jeanne is a student'

In some languages, predicate nominals may even be inflected like *verbs* as the following example from Bella Coola shows. The word for chief takes the intransitive verb suffix:

staltmx-aw   wa-ʔimlk
chief(3pl.)(INTR.)(PROX.)man

'The man is a chief'

A painfully literal translation might be, 'The man chiefs'.

The case of body parts is also interesting. If 'Sarah's face' is mentioned in the discourse, it is more usual for the subsequent discourse to be about Sarah than about her face. In German or French, inalienably possessed body parts do not take possessive modifiers:

Er hat sich   die Hand verletzt
he has himself the hand injured

'He injured his hand'

Il s'est   blessé   la   main
he himself-has wounded the hand

'He injured his hand'

The form *sa*, 'his', in French or *seine* in German would be distinctly odd in these sentences.

The facts are much the same for verbs. Since the discourse-primary verbs are to be found in sentences that answer the question 'What happened?', stative verbs like 'resemble' or 'want' are not readily eligible. At the same time, some of the morphological possibilities with action verbs are not as easily used with stative verbs in many languages. In English, for instance, 'I was eating a three-bean salad' is a perfectly acceptable utterance; 'I was resembling my Uncle Horace' is decidedly less so. Copula clauses are also not for reporting discourse events, so the categorial hypothesis leads us to expect copulae will be 'defective', in some ways, as verbs. In many languages, there is no lexical copula at all. The Chadic language Ngizim is one example:

ja maalam-cin
we teacher(PL.)

'We are teachers'

In Swahili there is no copula form in the first or second person. There is a copula for third-person subjects, but it is the invariant form *ni*:

Tu wa-pishi
we(SUBJ.)cook

'We are cooks'

Hamisi ni   m-pishi
Hamisi (COP.) (SUBJ.)cook

'Hamisi is a cook'

Hamisi na Ali ni wa-pishi
Hamisi and Ali are (SUBJ.)cook

'Hamisi and Ali are cooks'

Not only does *ni* lack number agreement, but it is not marked for subject or object agreement, it does not take tense/aspect markers, and it cannot be negated. Negative copula clauses take a special suppletive negative copula particle.

These examples are only a small sample of the evidence Hopper and Thompson give in supporting the categorial hypothesis. The major point is that the lexical categories noun and verb are based in discourse. In fact, their final conclusion is quite striking (Hopper and Thompson 1984:747):

We should like to conclude, however, by suggesting that linguistic forms are in principle to be considered as *lacking categoriality* [emphasis in the original] completely unless nounhood or verbhood is forced on them by their discourse functions.

What they mean is that there is really no such thing as a noun or a verb independent of discourse. Depending on their discourse function, just about any form can come out as either a noun or a verb. Some forms have a latent 'propensity' to be either nouns or verbs and it often takes special morphology to reverse this 'momentum' (such as derivational morphemes like the English '-tion' which makes nouns of items that have the propensity to become verbs). This propensity, though, will not emerge unless there is pressure from the discourse for it to happen.

Obviously, Hopper and Thompson's conclusions are not accepted by all linguists, or even by all discourse analysts. Nevertheless, their work is some of the most provocative and best-supported analysis in text linguistics.

SUMMARY

Discourse analysis is an active research arena that can be separated into two general subdivisions: analysis of interactive events and analysis of text. An important and widely-studied topic in conversational interaction research is turn-taking. Sacks, Schegloff, and Jefferson (1974) propose three ordered rules which account for the major features of conversational turn-taking in their recorded materials. These rules 'conspire' toward the production of no-gap, no-overlap conversations. In many data sets of recorded interactive events, turn-taking in the vast majority of instances takes place with no or very brief gaps and overlaps. One possible use that conversationalists seem to make of exceptionally long gaps is as a warrant for topic change. The occurrence of simultaneous talk at places in a conversation where turn-changes are not expected suggests itself as a possible definition for the concept interruption. In fact, people involved in an interaction sometimes do attempt to wrest the turn to talk away from whoever is speaking by beginning their talk in the middle of the current speaker's turn. On the other hand, Duncan (1974) noticed that 'auditor back-channels' were a common kind of mid-turn overlapping talk and, far from being interruptions, were elements of support for the current speaker. Tannen's (1984b) analysis of conversational style reveals that there are speakers with high-involvement conversational styles where extended periods of simultaneous speech, rapid tempo, and gapless – often even overlapping – turn changes are the norm.

Research on text linguistics is as varied as the work in interactive events. One current line of research has led to the proposal that lexical, morphological, and syntactic aspects of languages have their origins and purpose in narrative. Givón (1979b) has attempted to demonstrate how features like passive constructions and prepositions and case morphology could have arisen out of simpler structures with little syntactic complexity that are easier to produce and understand and so are more appropriate to face-to-face discourse. Hopper and Thompson (1980, 1984) have pursued this kind of investigation with considerable rigor. They argue that transitivity, long considered a purely syntactic concept, is better understood as a means of indicating foregrounding and backgrounding, which are fundamental aspects of narrative structure. Similarly, they propose that the major syntactic classes – noun and verb – are not so much an inherent property of the individual words of a language as forced on the words by two other basic aspects of narrative. Reference to participants in a narrative that are later to be manipulated leads to the most prototypical noun-like qualities. Reference to events that carry forward the narrative is associated with prototypical verbs. Distance from either of these two functions has the effect of blurring the category distinctions between nouns and verbs.

NOTES

1 One interesting theme in research of this type is the notion of convention or routine in conversations (Coulmas 1979, 1981; Greif and Gleason 1980).

2 Very fine overviews of discourse analysis are found in Brown and Yule (1983) and Stubbs (1983).

3 *Ethnomethodology* is a term to be taken as analogous to 'ethnomusic' or 'ethnomedicine'; as these studies investigate how music and medicine are viewed from the perspective of a particular culture, ethnomethodology is concerned with how given social groups deal with problems of methodology (in this case, the methodology of conversational turn-taking).

4 Most of the transcription conventions used by Sacks, Schegloff, and Jefferson are reasonably straightforward, but two in this example bear a little explication. The use of a large square bracket to enclose parts of two people's talk means that there was a brief period of time when they were both talking at once. The numbers in parentheses are seconds and tenths of seconds.

5 I am trying to give this example a little human interest by attributing motives to the speakers for their behavior. Ethnomethodologists themselves frown on this, since it is really guesswork; nobody but Claire really knows why she stopped talking at this point.

6 Actually, the rules do not account for the fact that speaker-change *does* occur, but only for the fact that it *can*. There is nothing in the turn-allocation rule set that would prevent conversations from happening where rules 1 and 2 were not invoked at *any* transition-relevance place. In such a situation, the current speaker could continue under the sanction of rule 3 until the social event ended. It seems to me that such conversations almost never occur. I can conceive of such an event if the speaker were someone with higher status than any of the other participants such that they felt it would be presumptuous for any of them to self-select. It would also be necessary for the high-status speaker to be willing to hold an exclusive turn so that he or she would never select a next speaker, or allow a long enough gap at any transition-relevance place so that it would be clear that he or she wanted someone else to self-select.

In fact, I have been told a story about a prominent American linguist of an earlier era who was given to just such conversational behavior. At parties attended by a few faculty members and many graduate students, with arm draped over the mantle, this gentleman is said to have held forth for long periods of time on his ideas about language. The man's wife, on at least one occasion, gently suggested that he let other people have the chance to talk. 'But my dear,' the scholar is supposed to have protested, 'They want to *know!*'

7 Rule 2, however, says nothing about how conflicts in which each self-selector believes he or she is first are resolved. One way that conflicts between simultaneous self-selectors are resolved is when the speaker who continues the longest, thereby getting his or her speech 'out from under' the overlap, gets the next turn. The cultural value that only one speaker should talk at a time generates enough pressure so that one of the speakers involved in an overlap will usually soon stop talking.

8 There are several studies which indicate that other members of conversations besides the last speaker are expected to do their part in minimizing the length of gaps; some of this literature is reviewed in McLaughlin and Cody (1982). One such study (Arkowitz et al. 1975) suggests that allowing long gaps can be hazardous to a young man's social life! They found that males with low dating frequency allowed significantly more 10-second lapses in a 10-minute conversation with a woman confederate than did males with high dating frequency.

9 One of the most important insights to have come out of Tannen's work on discourse is the idea that those features of discourse which have been considered part of spoken versus written discourse should rather be understood as contributing to various degrees of personal involvement. 'That is', she writes, 'the features we have come to expect . . . in spoken language . . . all grow out of and contribute to interpersonal involvement' (Tannen 1984b: 17–18). The complementary discourse features have been identified with written language, but are a means to 'ignore personal involvement, a way of honoring participants' needs to avoid the negative effects of involvement'.

10 I have modified the transcription by replacing the initials Tannen used in Tannen (1983b) with the names used in Tannen (1984b).
11 For extended discussions of the interpersonal difficulties that can arise due to style conflict – and suggestions on what to do about them – see Tannen (1984b) and especially Tannen (1986).
12 The use of unmarked forms in past contexts in the analysis of second language acquisition is the source of a bit of controversy about how much discourse factors are the explanation rather than structural factors. See Wolfram (1985) and the references cited there.
13 Sankoff and Brown (1976) had earlier proposed that certain grammatical forms in Tok Pisin, a creole language of Papua New Guinea, had arisen out of discourse structure.
14 In her review of Givón (1979a), Green (1982:675–6) makes exactly this point in her discussion of Hopper's contribution to Givón's book.

4

Language and Sex

INTRODUCTION

A major issue in the sociolinguistics of speech is the relationships between sex and language.[1] Since the mid-1970s research on language and sex has concentrated on the role language plays in the location and maintenance of women in a disadvantageous position in society. Before this, linguists had taken an interest in sex and language in two other respects. The earlier of these was the presence in a few languages of lexical, phonological, and morphological forms that are used only or predominantly by speakers of one sex or the other. More recently, in early research in sociolinguistic variation, sex was investigated as an independent variable related to linguistic variables, along with social status, style, age, and ethnicity.

MEN'S AND WOMEN'S LANGUAGE FORMS

An early study of forms in certain languages used by speakers of one sex and not the other is Mary Haas (1944/1964). She found that in Koasati, a native American language spoken in western Louisiana, there were several systematic differences between men's and women's versions of the indicative and imperative verbal paradigms. Haas presents these differences in the form of rules deriving the men's forms from the women's, but I will only give some examples of what the net effect is in certain words (see table 4.1).[2]   In addition to her description of Koasati in this connection, Haas went on to review what was known at the time about the phenomenon in other languages. Besides cases where the sex of the *speaker* determines the form, there are other cases where the sex of the *addressee* is a determining factor, although these languages are even less common than the Koasati type. Rarer still are languages where the sex of both the speaker *and* the hearer is important. For example, a

Table 4.1 Examples of women's and men's forms in Koasati

Women's form	Men's form	Gloss
o:tîl	o:tís	I am building a fire
ó:st	ósc	you are building a fire
ó:t	ó:c	he is building a fire
lakawwîl	lakawwís	I am lifting it
lakáwc	lakáwc	you are lifting it
lakáw	lakáws	he is lifting it
ka:hâl	ka:hás	I am saying
í:sk	í:sks	you are saying
ka:	ká:s	he is saying

Source: data from Haas 1944/1964.

woman might use a different form when she is talking to another woman compared with when she is talking to a man, while a man might use a third form, meaning the same thing as the first two, regardless of to whom he is talking.

An example of a language like this is presented by Francis Ekka (1972) from Kūṟux, a small-group Dravidian language spoken in India. In Kūṟux, there are several morphological forms used by women only when addressing another woman; they are not used by men or by women to address men. Some representative forms are given here (see table 4.2). They are taken from the first-person singular and the first-person plural exclusive verb paradigms, and the noun plural.

Verb morphology in the second-person singular is even more sensitive to sex. There is one form used by either men or women when they are talking to men. When women are addressed, there are two separate forms depending on the sex of the *speaker*. A man would use a different form to a woman from what a woman would use to another woman (see table 4.3).

Douglas Taylor (1951) provides another example, this one from Island Carib from the Caribbean nation, Dominica. In this language, there is a tendency (apparently receding) for men to use the names of qualities, states, and actions as if they carried *feminine* gender while women treat them like *masculine* gender nouns. The expression 'the other day', for example, would be *ligira buga* if a woman says it, but *tugura buga* if spoken by a man. Interestingly, Taylor reports that 'perhaps a minority of men' regularly use feminine forms for non-concrete nouns, but that 'all women resort to this trick' when they are quoting conversations between men. Haas mentions that in Koasati narratives, women use men's forms to quote male characters and men use women's forms for quoting female characters.

Table 4.2 Two-way contrasting forms by gender in Kūṟux

Man speaking, any addressee; or woman speaking, man addressee	Woman speaking, woman addressee	Gloss
bardan	barʔen	I come
bardam	barʔem	We (my associates and I, but not you) come
barckan	barcʔan	I came
barckam	barcʔam	We (my associates and I, but not you) came
xaddar	xadday	children

Source: data from Ekka 1972

Table 4.3 Three-way contrasting forms by gender in Kūṟux

Man or woman speaker, man addressee	Woman speaker, woman addressee	Man speaker, woman addressee	Gloss
barday	bardin	bardi	you come
barckay	barckin	barcki	you came

Source: data from Ekka 1972

At the time most of these studies were done, linguists were most interested in sex-related linguistic features as a purely linguistic phenomenon, and secondarily as a possible clue about the historical development of the language. Interest in language as a possible cause and effect of the relation between men and women in a social and political sense was not to develop until some time later. Haas found internal linguistic evidence that at least some of the women's forms are older and more basic and the men's forms are derived from them historically. This is not always the historical order, though, since in data from Yana, a native American language of California, and Chukchee, a language of eastern Siberia, the men's forms seem to be more basic (Haas 1964:231). It might be worth noting, on the subject of historical change, that there are several reports of languages losing distinctions based on the sex of the speaker, addressee, and referent, and there are some languages in which such distinctions remain stable, but I do not know of any reports of languages in the process of *acquiring* these features.

Ekka speculates that in Kūṟux, forms that are fundamentally for use between men are accepted by women for use in cross-sex dyads. He suggests that the spread of the masculine forms is a consequence of the 'patriarchal' Kūṟux society. A citation from a 1911 grammar by a Rev. Frederick Hahn seems to indicate the motive was a sense of delicacy about sex. It seemed to him that the Kūṟux would think it 'rather indecent' if men were to talk about women or address a plurality of women using feminine forms, and that it would be 'very improper' for women to refer to themselves or other women as being of the feminine gender. If Hahn's perceptions were right it might mean that, among the Kūṟux, women are clearly of such lower social status that it would be almost embarrassing to remind a woman that she is female. Another possible explanation might be that the Kūṟux associate the female sex, but not the male sex, with the delicate aspects of biological reproduction.[3]

THE 'SOCIOLINGUISTIC GENDER PATTERN'

A description of the 'gender pattern'

Research that involves the quantitative analysis of social variables has taken sex differences into account from the beginning. There is one intriguing pattern by gender that is commonly reported. Male speakers are often found to use socially disfavored variants of sociolinguistic variables while women tend to avoid these in favor of socially more favored variants. We will be referring to male speakers' tendency to use forms that are generally considered 'correct' less frequently than women speakers do the *sociolinguistic gender pattern*. Perhaps the earliest example of this pattern was reported by Fischer (1958), who found that girls in a New England school used the '-in' variant of the '-ing' suffix less frequently than boys did. Since Fischer's study, the gender pattern has been reported with some regularity. For example, it has been reported for speakers on the Lower East Side of New York City (Labov 1966), for black speakers in Detroit by Wolfram (1969), for [1] deletion from certain pronouns and determiners in Montreal French (G. Sankoff 1975), for several variables in Norwich (Trudgill 1974b), and in Glasgow (Macaulay 1978) and Belfast (L. Milroy 1980, 1982).

In spite of this consistency, the gender pattern is not as robust as you might expect. Sometimes, differences by sex are slight. In Fischer's early study, the numbers of children whose speech was tabulated is small and the gender tendency, while noticeable, is not overwhelming. In fact, Fischer did not find it statistically significant. In other cases, men show a preference for the less acceptable variables in general but there are exceptions in some segments of the population. In other cases, the gender pattern does not involve *all* the socially sensitive linguistic features. I take it that there is nothing particularly significant about these exceptions; the gender pattern is probably weak enough to occasionally be obliterated by chance skewings in the data. In still other studies, the gender pattern failed to materialize at all. It may be that the consistency of the gender pattern has sometimes been overstated, but it would be a far bigger mistake to ignore the considerable amount of evidence from sociolinguistic research that demonstrates its existence. Although some have expressed skepticism about it, it is quite clear that the gender pattern needs to be explained.

A commonly reported version of the gender pattern shows female speakers avoiding socially disfavored linguistic features only in *formal* styles. In less formal styles, there is no substantial difference in the use of socially disfavored forms based on the speaker's sex. A caveat that is often made about the gender pattern is that it is only to be expected in Western societies. In a study of Swahili in Mombasa, Kenya, Russell (1982:140) found that 'it certainly looks as though it is women, rather than men, who are preserving the more obvious markers of this speech community'; by 'obvious markers of this speech community' she means vernacular, rather than standard, features. In some traditional communities, fewer women learn higher-status national and regional languages than men because they receive less formal education and have fewer opportunities to be in situations where the higher-status languages are needed. This does not seem to be a major factor in Mombasa, though, because all the subjects had considerable exposure to 'standard' Swahili.

A different and striking pattern involving sex has been reported independently by Cheshire (1982) for Reading adolescents and Schatz (1986) for Plat Amsterdams, the Amsterdam city dialect. In both cases, speakers of both sexes seem to agree on what the favored linguistic variants are, and also on most of the less favored, vernacular variants. But in both communities, female speakers used a few variants to mark local identity that male speakers did not use, and vice versa. In Plat Amsterdams, for example, long 'a' has raised and nasalized variants, both of which are stigmatized. The raised variant is seldom used by high-status speakers of either sex; both have index scores of about 2.5 where 15 would be the index if they always used raised long 'a'. Low-status men had a far higher index, 8.9, while the low-status women in Schatz's sample *never* used the raised variant in informal speech (figure 4.1). The results were reversed by sex for nasalized long 'a'. High-status speakers avoided nasalized 'a' almost entirely; both men and women had indices of less than 1. Low-status women, though, used nasalized long 'a' more than twice as frequently as low-status men did (the women's index was 7.4, the men's was 3.2: see figure 4.2). In both cases, the difference by sex showed up only among low-status speakers, and the pattern for both variants was statistically highly significant.

Cheshire found that four of the features she tabulated were highly sensitive markers of vernacular loyalty for the adolescent boys in her

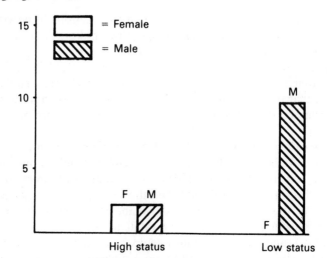

Figure 4.1 Use of raised long /a/ in Plat Amsterdams, by sex and status
Source: data from Schatz (1986)

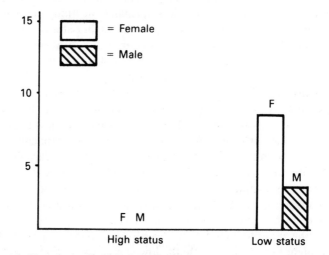

Figure 4.2 Use of nasalized long /a/ in Plat Amsterdams, by sex and status
Source: data from Schatz (1986)

data, but only three of them marked loyalty to vernacular values for girls; the fourth was a uniquely male loyalty marker. Two other features were less sensitive markers of vernacular loyalty in the boys' speech, but had no symbolic values for the girls. Another two features worked the other way around: they indicated vernacular loyalty for girls, but not for boys.[4]

In search of an explanation

A number of explanations for this gender pattern have been offered, most of them directed at explaining the linguistic behavior of women. In several places in her chapter on 'Status and standard/nonstandard language', Key (1975) suggests that women use favored linguistic forms as a way of achieving status through the use of linguistic features which is denied them in other aspects of life; for example: 'It would appear, then, that women have not universally accepted the position in the lower ranks, and that, out-of-awareness, and in a socially acceptable and non-punishable way, women are rebelling' (Key 1975:103). In his overview of linguistic sex differentiation, Trudgill (1983a:167–8) provides a series of related explanations:

Women are more closely involved with child-rearing and the transmission of culture, and are therefore more aware of the importance, for their children, of the acquisition of (prestige) norms.

The social position of women in our society has traditionally been less secure than that of men. It may be, therefore, that it has been more necessary for women to secure and signal their social status linguistically and in other ways, and they may for this reason be more aware of the importance of this type of signal.

Men in our society have traditionally been rated socially by their occupation, their earning power, and perhaps by their abilities – in other words, by what they *do*. Until recently, however, this has been much more difficult for women, and indeed women continue to suffer discrimination against them in many occupations. It may be, therefore, that they have had to be rated instead, to a greater extent than men, on how they *appear*. Since they have not been rated, to the same extent that men have, by their occupation or by their occupational success, other signals of status, including speech, have been correspondingly more important.

Working-class speech appears in our society to have connotations of masculinity.[5]

Some of the more recent research in sociolinguistics suggests a new approach and a new line of reasoning about the sociolinguistic gender pattern. An argument very much like the one I am beginning has been developed independently and in more detail by Coates (1986, especially chapter 5). Data that has been carefully analyzed by a group of sociolinguists in Belfast is the basis of a enlightening discussion by L. Milroy (1982). Of three neighborhoods in Belfast where data was gathered, one of them (called Ballymacarrett) is distinguished from the others in at least three ways. First, there are sharply different *network* patterns for males and females. Males have high network strength and women low. 'Network strength' is a measure of the number and kinds of social ties an individual has within a particular neighborhood. In Ballymacarrett, most men are employed in the local shipyard industry and do not have to leave the neighborhood to find employment. Women, most of whom hold jobs, are much more likely to be employed outside the immediate area. Men also spend their leisure time in local pubs and clubs. A second characteristic which is particularly pronounced in Ballymacarrett is that men's and women's activities are sharply polarized. The third fact is that it has the sharpest and most consistent gender pattern of the three Belfast neighborhoods. It appears that the community's linguistic norms – the ones that mark the local community, as distinct from more general, higher-status norms – influence most those with the most intense social involvement locally, and that these people are disproportionately likely to be men.[6]

Milroy (1980:79) reports that the association of network density and clearly defined sex roles, as in Ballymacarrett, is rather generally found in working-class communities, and that loosely-knit networks and blurring of sex roles also go together. Since the Belfast research was the first urban sociolinguistic survey project to use network analysis so extensively, no connection has been mentioned between the gender pattern and network density in other studies. If it is true that these two factors contribute to the gender pattern in Ballymacarrett and their coexistence is somewhat general, then we may have the basis for a new explanatory perspective.

The explanation that these facts suggest is well-illustrated by an anecdote from the East African nation of Tanzania (Abdulaziz Mkilifi 1978:142). In Tanzania, Swahili, the national language, symbolizes the country's traditional values in contrast with English, which is associated with technical innovation and outside values. Abdulaziz Mkilifi makes this comment about a response to one of his survey questions:

One of the respondents said that whenever he argued with his bilingual wife he would maintain Swahili as much as possible while she would maintain English. A possible explanation is that Swahili norms and values assign different roles to husband and wife (socially more clear-cut?) from the English norms and values (socially less clear-cut and more converging?). Maintaining one language or the other could then be a device for asserting one's desired role.

In the context of Milroy's description of Ballymacarrett, Abdulaziz Mkilifi's use of the terms 'more clear-cut' and 'less clear-cut' is quite striking. Assuming his interpretation of the bilingual argument is correct, could it be that women in Ballymacarrett and other communities with a clear gender pattern are using sociolinguistic variants within their languages the same way the Tanzanian woman is using English? In other words, by sounding *less* local, female speakers might be subtly and subliminally protesting traditional community norms which place them in a subordinate position to men in favor of a more egalitarian social order in which women are treated more nearly equal to men. If so, then we can understand how Key might be right when she suggests that women are 'rebelling' when they use standard linguistic variants more than men do.

Two difficulties arise in connection with this line of reasoning as I have developed it so far. First of all, the coexistence of distinctive sex roles and strong networks is said to be typical of *working-class* communities. To the extent that sharp sex-role distinctions and strong networks are not found in higher-status social groups, the explanation I have offered for the gender pattern is considerably weakened. In particular, the version of the gender pattern where women and men differ in the use of disfavored variants only in formal styles has not been explained very well since it seems to be a characteristically *middle-class* phenomenon. Second, Milroy emphasizes the *distinction* of sex-roles in Ballymacarrett, but never says that it works to the disadvantage of women. Logically, of course, the roles that are open to women might be equally desirable – or even more desirable – than those that are the prerogatives of men. If the proposal I am working towards is to work at all, we have to assume that sex-role distinctions in working-class communities discriminate against women.

Trudgill (1972, 1983a) discovered another phenomenon connected with the gender pattern. Trudgill's research in Norwich, in the main, uncovered typical patterns of class and style variation for linguistic variables and, as we have seen, typical examples of the gender pattern. When he went a step further and compared speakers' observed usage with what they *claimed* to say when questioned directly, he found a surprising difference by sex. If a speaker used a favored variable more than half the time, that person would be classified as using that variable. The Norwich speakers were also asked directly how they normally pronounced certain words that contained the same socially diagnostic variables. In this way, it was possible for a speaker to *over*-report use of a favored variant (by claiming it was typical of his or her speech when it was actually used less than half the time during the interview), *under*-report usage (by claiming not to use a favored variant that was actually used more than half the time) or *accurately* report use (by claiming to use a favored variant that was actually used more than half the time, or not claiming a favored variant used less than half the time). For several variables, Trudgill found that male speakers under-reported their use of socially favored variants far more frequently than female speakers did. Table 4.4 shows the results for the long 'o' variable, the vowel in 'moan' (but not in 'mown'). The local vernacular pronunciation of this variable would sound like 'moon' to an outsider. Notice than an absolute majority of the male speakers said they did not use the favored variant when they actually did. A majority of female speakers made accurate assessments of their use of these variants, but where they were different from their actual usage, women over-reported more often than under-reported. Trudgill, expanding on a term from Labov (1966), calls this phenomenon 'covert prestige'.

Table 4.4 Percentage of informants over- and under-reporting long 'o'

	Male	Female
Over-report	12	25
Under-report	54	18
Accurate	34	57

Source: data from Trudgill (1983a:176)

People who over-report present themselves as using a form they do not actually use, but over-reporting a disfavored variant generally contradicts what the same individual would say is 'good' and 'bad' speech; hence the sort of 'prestige' that emerges in this over-reporting behavior is 'covert' as opposed to the 'overt' evaluative comments someone would make to an interviewer under direct questioning. The covert prestige phenomenon, unlike the basic gender pattern, is evident only when speakers are asked what they *think* they say. In their actual recorded speech, Norwich speakers of both sexes demonstrate the usual patterns of class stratification and, for those variables that have it, style stratification.

Covert prestige of variants that class stratification patterns show to be disfavored is not limited to working-class men. For long 'o', for example, middle-class male speakers showed the same tendency to over-report their use of vernacular variants as working-class males did. The covert prestige of vernacular variants, then, sets both middle-class and working-class men apart from women.[7]

However attractive vernacular variants may be in general to male speakers at the level of awareness tapped by self-evaluation questions, the discovery of the covert prestige phenomenon in Norwich suggests a different approach to the gender pattern itself. Most discussions of the gender pattern, including this one so far, implicity assume that it is the *female* pattern which requires explanation, and that male usage is a kind of baseline to measure female usage from. In other words, it is as if the question to be answered were: 'Why do women use favored variables so much?' The covert prestige phenomenon makes it seem that *men* are dealing with socially significant variables in an unexpected way. Perhaps the question should be: 'Why do men use favored variables so little (or use disfavored variables so much)?'

If this is the question, the answer might be the exact reverse of the explanation I offered in connection with working-class women in Ballymacarrett and elsewhere. Perhaps men subliminally and implicitly perceive that in the context of the value system symbolized by local variants, they have the positional advantage. Like the Swahili-speaking husband in Abdulaziz Mkilifi's anecdote, men might use vernacular speech as a subtle way of endorsing the traditional values that have them in firmer control of everyday life than women are. To take Key's notion of rebellion a step further, it may be that the gender pattern represents as much a counterrevolution by men as a revolution by women. When we remember that Trudgill found covert prestige among middle-class men as well as those from the working class, the perspective I am suggesting – that men's treatment of the linguistic features requires explanation – would fit the gender pattern when it turns up in the middle class also. As far as the often-observed greater degree of style-shifting by women speakers is concerned, the approach I am suggesting would lead us to look at it as remarkably *less* style-shifting by men.[8]

Sex-based versus class-based differences

As we will see in chapter 8, sociolinguistic research on linguistic variation of the sort we have been looking at generally assumes that class and style are the fundamental bases for variation, with sex as a secondary influence. Class and style patterns, in fact, *define* what we consider 'favored' or 'correct' variants in the first place. Briefly, it is quite generally found that the forms used most by higher-status speakers in a community tend to be used the most by *all* speakers in more careful styles of speech, at least in the more developed variables. In English, for example, the pronunciation '-ing' for the suffix in 'going' would be more frequent for high-status speakers, and '-in' relatively more frequent for lower-status speakers. Speakers from all social levels will reduce their use of '-in' and increase the frequency of '-ing' as the speech situation demands more careful speech. From this we conclude that '-ing' is more socially favored than '-in'. It is in this context that we talk about men using less favored forms and women using more favored forms, and so on.

Suppose we have it backwards, however. Logically, it might be that there are ways of speaking which men use to emphasize their masculinity and other forms women use to symbolize femininity, and that this is more basic than social class. In some way we do not fully understand, perhaps men's speech became *derivatively* associated with lower social status and women's speech with high status, at least in many of the societies where sociolinguistic variation research has been done. We have already seen that male and female speech are distinguished even within the same social stratum in certain features of Plat Amsterdams and in the English of Reading, England. This idea has been explored by Coates (1986), Horvath (1985), and in a stimulating presentation by Lesley Milroy (1988a).

In the preliminary discussion of her work on the English of Sydney, Australia, Horvath (1985:64–5; cf. L. Milroy 1988b) reviews William Labov's pioneering work on the English of New York City (Labov 1966). Labov examined the pronunciation of the sound spelled (th) in words such as 'this' and 'there', which he symbolized as the sociolinguistic variable (dh). Labov's New York research will come up in more detail in chapter 8, but for the moment we only need to understand that he examined pronunciations like [ð] and [d] (the [d] variant makes 'there' sound like 'dare'), that he devised an index system such that speakers with the [ð] pronunciation in most of their 'th' words would receive a *low* index, and that he found that low indexes tended to correlate with higher social status. Horvath pointed out something that Labov had noticed but not developed; that a high proportion of female speakers, compared with male speakers, had low (dh) indexes, to some extent *apart* from social status. Horvath points out that sex explains the (dh) variable at least as well as class, perhaps better.

To see Horvath's point we need to understand a bit more about Labov's data. The data indicates that a (dh) index of 56 (out of a possible 150) was something of a natural cutting point on the scale. If we group the New York speakers into two groups for (dh) index (low index for those with indexes below 56 and high for those with higher indexes), two social class groups (middle class versus lower and working class), and the two sexes, Horvath's insight can be illustrated as in figure 4.3. The figure shows the proportions of speakers in each sex and class group who are also low-index (dh) speakers. Notice that *all* the middle-class women are low-index speakers. If we compare lower- and working-class female speakers with middle-class male speakers, we find that a substantially higher proportion of them are low-index (dh) speakers than the middle-class males are. This pattern would suggest that, although social class is undoubtedly an influencing factor, sex is more influential.[9] These results

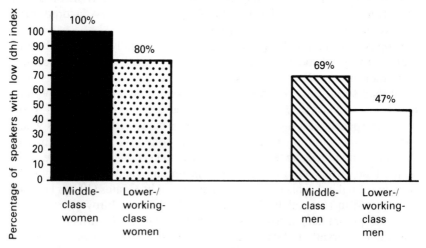

Figure 4.3 Percentage of speakers with high (dh) index, by sex and social class
Source: data from Labov (1966:280) and Horvath (1985: 65)

are only suggestive since the numbers of speakers is not very large (there are only 13 middle-class male speakers, for instance).

An even more striking case comes from unpublished research by L. Rigg, cited by L. Milroy (1988b), on the English of Newcastle-upon-Tyne in England. It is a feature of local speech that the stop consonants /p, t, k/ can be pronounced with a kind of 'catch' in the throat called glottalization. Figure 4.4 illustrates the pattern for the (p) variable, which is typical of the three consonants. This time, the percentages are based on the total number of words with (p) that receive the glottalized pronunciation in the data for speakers of a sex and class group, rather than a proportion of speakers with a high or low index. The striking fact is that male speakers almost *always* use glottalized (p). Female speakers use the variant much less. There is some tendency for middle-class women to use the glottalized variant less frequently than working-class speakers. For the male speakers there is scarcely room for more than a minuscule class effect, since they hardly ever *fail* to use the glottalized (p). It would not be unreasonable to say that working-class women of Newcastle-upon-Tyne symbolize their class status by using (p) like men do.

Further evidence comes from a study based in Dublin by J. R. Edwards (1979b). Edwards's study does not have to do with what people say so much as how they interpret what they hear. He asked listeners to try to identify the sex of children from tape-recordings. The children were young, so sex-related physiological differences had not yet developed. Yet the listeners could identify the sex of the speakers with considerable accuracy. The remarkable result, though, was in the pattern of *errors* in those cases where the listeners misidentified the speaker's sex. There was

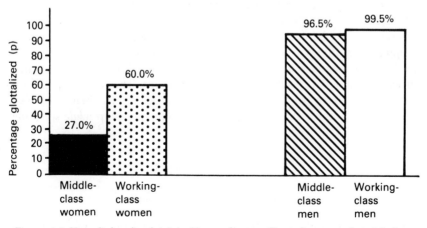

Figure 4.4 Use of glottalized (p) in Newcastle-upon-Tyne, by sex and social class
Source: data from Rigg as cited by L. Milroy (1988b:580)

a distinct tendency for the boys who were misheard as girls to be from the middle class and the girls who sounded like boys to be from the working class. It seems the listeners expected masculine speech to sound 'working class' and feminine speech to sound 'middle class'.

There will no doubt be more research on the relationship between sex and other patterns of sociolinguistic variation, including social status. At this point, it seems that the influence of gender is more fundamental than it has appeared to be so far, but that social status does play an independent role in linguistic variation as well. It will be fascinating to learn more about how the two work together.

As we leave our discussion of sociolinguistic research using sex as an independent variable, I am going to mention and endorse a distinction emphasized by Trudgill (1983a:164–7). In the main, the kind of linguistic variable used in the research I have just surveyed are what Trudgill calls *dialect and accent* variables. The sort of linguistic features we are about to examine he calls *language use* differences. Fundamentally, dialect and accent variables do not affect the content of what a speaker is saying, although they communicate other kinds of information. 'He's eatin' an apple' would not describe a different state of affairs from 'He's eating an apple', for example. One kind of language use analysis, on the face of it similar to dialect and accent feature research, is a study of the use of grammatical case conducted by Nancy Barron (1971). Using Fillmore's (1968) deep case theory, Barron found that women used greater proportions of explicit participative and purposive cases, while men used more instrumental, source, and objective cases. These differences, she concludes, rather than being markers of male and female as social categories, reflect differences in what people of each sex are inclined to talk about. Under Barron's analysis, women's selections of cases shows their greater concern with internal psychological states and the functions of objects for interpersonal use. The cases more used by men reflect interest in the implementation of action by means of objects and an emphasis on things acted upon. Barron's analysis of case, then, is an example of language use analysis with a view to discovering differences in what members of each sex want to talk about. The dialect and accent variables we have been looking at do not affect what is being said very much, but reinforce the speaker's sex-group membership *while* speaking.

SEX DIFFERENCES IN LANGUAGE USE

Language and women's place

The first widely influential study of language-use features was presented by Robin Lakoff, first in a journal article and later in a book, both under the title 'Language and women's place' (Lakoff 1973a, 1975). Lakoff's work led her to conclude that 'woman's language' – by which she meant both language used to describe women and language typically used by women – had the overall effect of submerging a woman's personal identity (Lakoff 1973a:48). With respect to the use of language, women's identities are submerged because they are denied the means of expressing themselves strongly, encouraged to use expressions that suggest triviality, and to use forms that express uncertainty concerning what they are talking about. She described six categories of language use that are sharply differentiated by the sex of the speaker: lexical distinctions such as color terms, strong versus weak expletives, 'women's' versus 'neutral' adjectives, tag questions, question intonation with statement syntax, and strength of directive speech acts.

Lakoff pointed out, for example, that for the most part, women are not expected to use 'strong' expletives, such as 'damn' or 'shit', but are encouraged to substitute weaker ones like 'oh dear' or 'fudge'. This difference in linguistic acculturation between men and women permits men the opportunity to express strong emotions with impunity, an opportunity that women are denied. To the extent that women are prevented from expressing themselves with feeling, their individuality along such lines is never publicly revealed. She was perhaps the first to notice the difference between 'women's' and 'neutral' adjectives. There is a set of adjectives in English which express approval and admiration in addition to their strictly literal meanings. Some of these, like 'great' and 'terrific', are neutral in the sense that they are readily and appropriately used by either men or women. Others of this set, such as 'adorable', 'charming', and 'divine', are expected in women's speech, but not generally in men's. The difference between 'a great idea', which either a man or a woman can appropriately say, and 'a divine idea', which would be cause for remark if a man said it, is that the second expression is a bit frivolous and expresses an idea that is important only for the speaker rather than the world at large. It might seem that women have the *advantage* over men since they are free to use either neutral or women's adjectives whereas men can only use the neutral ones but this, for Lakoff, is not the case. The existence of the women's words used only for trivial expression suggests, in a way, that what men have to say is *de facto* important, because a man says it. Linguistic provision is made for women – and *only* women – to express opinions that are seen immediately to be of no general consequence.[10]

A syntactic feature that Lakoff believes is more freely usable by women than by men is the tag question form. Tag questions are appended to statements by taking the tense-bearing element of the verb phrase, reversing its negativity, selecting the pronoun appropriate to the subject of the statement and making a question out of these elements, as in 'Howard wouldn't do such a thing, would he?' These constructions ask hearers to confirm explicitly that they agree with the statement. One reason speakers might use a tag question is to state a claim, when they are not fully confident that the person they are talking to will agree with that claim. Greater use of this form by women could mean that women, more often than men, are presenting themselves as unsure of their opinions and thereby as not really having opinions that count very much. Tag question usage, then, represents another example of the submersion of women's individualities. The use of question intonation with assertion syntax is quite similar. In answer to the question, 'When will dinner be ready?', women would tend to answer 'Around six o'clock?' Women would feel inclined, or perhaps obliged, to adjust dinner time to suit the convenience of other members of the family. On the other hand, if asked 'What time are we leaving for our trip tomorrow?', it would seem natural to expect a man to reply with something like 'At 7.30 and I want everyone to be ready.' In Lakoff's view, women would tend to avoid answering 'At six o'clock, and everybody better be here', and few men would answer 'At 7.30?'

Directives, things you can say to get someone else to do something for you, have a wide range of linguistic forms. The following range of possibilities is illustrated by Lakoff:

Close the door.
Please close the door.
Will you close the door?
Will you please close the door?
Won't you close the door?

These examples are listed in order of increasing politeness, in the sense that using the variants towards the end of the list leaves the addressee freer to refuse than using the ones at the beginning. For example, the last one is not only a question, implying that the response is not presumed, but it is negative in form, formally assuming a negative response from the addressee. Women seem to be taught to use the more polite, weaker, more self-effacing forms of directives.

In the years that followed the publication of Lakoff's work, a considerable amount of research was conducted in connection with Lakoff's hypotheses. A typical approach taken by researchers on this topic was to tabulate the features of female register or style – defined, more or less, by the list of linguistic features Lakoff discussed – in samples of speech from women and from men in an attempt to establish whether or not women used them more.

The net effect of this kind of research is that some results (Edelsky 1976; some results in Crosby and Nyquist 1977) support Lakoff's ideas. Other results (Dubois and Crouch 1975; Holmes 1986) seem to be counterevidence. Still other results (Brouwer, Gerritsen, and De Haan 1979; P. Brown 1980; other results in Crosby and Nyquist 1977) seem to indicate that Lakoff is on the right track, but that her ideas can be further refined and that the research needs careful interpretation. Part of Lakoff's work is based on differences involving elements in the speech of women that contrast with those in men's speech; but simply identifying the linguistic elements which belong to women's language and then tabulating samples of women's and men's speech to confirm that women use them more is just not adequate. As Lakoff makes clear in later work (for example, Lakoff 1977c), the individual linguistic elements are, in a way, artefacts of the overall interactional style differences that are developed and used by women and by men.

For an example of how simply counting features can be misleading, consider the case of tag questions. Lakoff suggested that tag questions might be a feature of women's style used to request confirmation that the hearer agrees with what she has just said. However, Dubois and Crouch (1975) found that only *men* used tag questions in the question and comment segment of a professional meeting. In the course of their discussion, they mention that tag questions have a usage in British English which is not common in American English. In British English, a speaker can use a tag question, with falling or terminal contour, appended to an assertion that the addressee presumably will *not* agree with, as a kind of ploy to force agreement. To an addressee who does not want the speaker to leave, for example, a speaker of British English might say:

```
                              have
                    now,      n't
      'I've got to leave          I'
```

Such an utterance, far from expressing uncertainty on the part of the speaker, is verbally aggressive. Cheshire (1982) presents a special case of the aggressive use of tag questions among adolescent boys in adventure playgrounds in Reading. These boys used a nonstandard, all-purpose tag structure involving the form 'in it'. One of Cheshire's examples is the following.

Roger: He might be taking Britt, he says.
Colin: Oh, what a thrill. What a name, Britt.
Puvvy: Who started calling her it?
Roger: It's her proper name, *in it*?

Colin and Puvvy apparently think 'Britt' cannot possibly be a real name. Roger asserts exactly what they are not prepared to believe, and forces their agreement with the 'in it' tag. As Cheshire (1982:165) explains: 'Again, the effect of Roger's tag question (in line 4) is aggressive: he conveys the impression that Puvvy is foolish not to know that "Britt" is a real name; and he is *telling* him that it is her proper name, rather than asking for confirmation.'

Of course, none of this has to have anything to do with Dubois and Crouch's data, which were collected at a professional meeting at an American university. Besides this, the British English usage I am talking about has falling intonation. All but two of Dubois and Crouch's 33 examples had *rising* intonation. In spite of this, I suggest that at least some of their examples might have involved a somewhat more mildly aggressive use of tag questions. It is my impression, at least in linguistics meetings, that male scholars in particular use the question and comment sessions to engage in what amounts to a kind of contest. If a question can be asked or a comment made which demonstrates that the questioner has noticed a flaw in the presentation, the questioner feels he has enhanced his reputation. If my impression is accurate, then question and comment periods would be the site of considerable antagonistic sparring between presenter and questioner. Dubois and Crouch do not say what academic field was the topic at the meeting where they obtained their data, and I have no way of knowing if scholars in that field have the same tendencies as linguists, or even if what I have said about linguists is right. Three of the examples Dubois and Crouch cite, however, look as if they could easily be examples of this sort of thing, although the immediate context of the examples is not given. These are the examples (Dubois and Crouch 1975:293).

You would miss it, wouldn't you?
They're going from a base of a so-called standard, aren't they?
Can't be very big, is it?

It seems quite likely that the speaker whose presentation drew the first comment would be reluctant to admit he would 'miss' something. The recipient of the second tag construction quite possibly would not readily endorse an assertion about a 'so-called' standard. If my conjecture is correct, it would tend to verify Lakoff's line of reasoning at a deeper level, while illustrating how merely tabulating linguistic items can be misleading. This point is also made by P. Brown (1980) and by Holmes (1986).

In other words, the question should not be, 'What features are used disproportionately more or less by women than by men?'; rather it is: 'What differences in interactional strategy between women and men are there, and how do they reveal the structure of society with regard to the sexes?' Linguists would make their contribution to the restated problem by discovering how language is used as the major tool for executing these strategies.

Some scholars – for example, Valian (1981) – take exception to Lakoff's work on gender in language on the grounds that she does not make a clear distinction between language and language *use*. Early in her original article, Lakoff (1973a:46) anticipates her conclusions in the statement:

'We will find, I think, that women experience linguistic discrimination in two ways: in the way they are taught to *use* language, and in the general way language *use* treats them' (emphasis added). It appears, then, that Lakoff is dealing with matters of language use. Towards the end of the article, though, she emphatically places the responsibility for dealing with sexism in language with 'nuts-and-bolts' linguists; the people who concern themselves with structures such as tag questions (Lakoff 1973a:77). In 1973, Lakoff considered a sentence like 'John is Mary's widower' as unacceptable in any context. Today, it seems no more than mildly unexpected. In her view, since society's changing attitudes play a crucial role in the statuses of the sentences of a language, societal attitudes – including those towards women – must be included in the linguistic analysis. We have seen that scholars like Givón and Hopper and Thompson have taken the position that grammar is derived from use (in discourse). From their perspective (and other linguists from within sociolinguistics would sympathize), Lakoff would be correct. But many syntacticians consider it of fundamental importance to abstract the study of syntax away from matters of language use. From their point of view, 'John is Mary's widower' may be *unacceptable*, but *grammatically* it is a perfectly good sentence. In other words, a formal grammar would declare that 'John is Mary's widower' is an impeccable English sentence; the fact that English speakers might not accept it would be explained in a separate study of language use.[11]

In any case, Robin Lakoff's disinclination to maintain a distinction between language and use has led to a criticism on methodological grounds. Her fundamental source of data is the one used in the analysis of abstract syntax. The data come from introspection based on Lakoff's own speech and that of her acquaintances. The introspective method works for syntacticians precisely because they assume that sentences are to be abstracted from language use. If language use is taken as an inherent part of linguistic scholarship, it is far from clear that the introspective method is still appropriate. Some of the work Lakoff's research has inspired was motivated by a desire to base conclusions on more systematically observed and rigorously analyzed data.

Conversations between men and women

Another productive avenue in the study of interaction has been the analysis of conversations between women and men. Using the 'simplest systematics' model of turn-taking developed by Sacks, Schegloff, and Jefferson which we are already familiar with, Candace West and Don Zimmerman (Zimmerman and West 1975; West and Zimmerman 1977) developed a definition of 'interruption' designed to distinguish between interruptions on the one hand, and overlaps and back-channels on the other. 'Minimal responses', like 'yeah' and 'um hmm' were correctly seen as supportive utterances and were not counted as interruptions. To avoid misidentifying overlaps as interruptions, Zimmerman and West (1975) tabulated as interruptions simultaneous speech that occurred together with the word *before* the last constituent that could qualify as preceding a transition-relevance place. West and Zimmerman (1983) developed the notion of *deep* interruption where simultaneous speech begins more than two syllables before or after the last syllable of a transition-relevance place. The earlier study was based on naturalistically collected data in public places, or in speakers' homes. In all cases, people in the same conversation were acquainted. In 10 conversations between two people of the same sex, there were just seven interruptions. In 11 cross-sex, two-party conversations, there were 48 interruptions and the male speaker was responsible for 46 of them.[12]

Their analysis of silences is just as striking. The silences that were counted were those between the end of one speaker's turn and the first utterance of the other speaker (within-turn silences were not counted). Silences were 'charged to' the speaker who had just stopped speaking. Ratios were computed by dividing the total number of seconds of silence 'charged to' the speaker with the least silence by the number of seconds of silence 'charged to' the speaker with the most silence. If each speaker in the dyad had the same amount of silence charged to him or her, this ratio would be 1.0. In the same-sex conversations, this was approximately the case; all the ratios were between 0.6 and 1.0 except for one conversation between two males. In the cross-sex conversations, though, the ratios were all *below* 0.5 except for one and, in *every case*, the woman had more silence 'charged to' her.

The interpretation for the silence patterns given by Zimmerman and West is that when the woman was developing a topic and came to a transition-relevance place, the man in the conversation would, far more often than the other way around, not take a turn where one was needed to continue development of the woman's topic. Often, after a silence 'charged to' the woman conversationalist had lengthened from a lapse to a gap of considerable length, the man would contribute no more than a minimal back-channel of the 'um hmm' variety. In their view, both interruptions and silences contributed to topic-control by the men. Either they intruded with their own talk where the 'simplest systematics' would have given them no right to speak, or they declined to offer support for topics the woman was developing.

In their subsequent study, West and Zimmerman (1983) replicated the experiment under laboratory conditions. This time, undergraduate students who were unacquainted were randomly paired and asked to converse in a laboratory room with microphones hung around their necks. This research design complemented the strengths and weaknesses of the earlier one. Although the conversations were 'unnatural' in the sense that would have not occurred without the experiment, it reduced the possibility that there were special factors in the relationship between the speakers which might have influenced the results. In addition, the conditions under which the data was collected were likely to *inhibit* interruptions, since people can be expected to avoid impolite behavior talking to a stranger, especially knowing their conversations were going to be analyzed. In spite of all this, the male speakers initiated 21 of the 28 interruptions observed. The result is an impressive replication of the earlier study.

Knowing what we do about high-involvement style, we need to consider whether these results might be an artefact of mistabulated interruptions. It is true that West and Zimmerman would have erroneously counted the elaborate support strategies of a high-involvement style speaker as interruptions, especially if the other person did not share that style. This would have misled them only if their cross-sex pairs systematically included more high-involvement males than high-involvement females. If that had happened, high-involvement male speakers would have been seen as interrupting their conversation partners when their intentions were supportive. The probability that that happened, though, is extremely small, especially given the replications using both naturalistic and laboratory methods.

Pamela Fishman (1980, 1983) found further evidence indicating women have less control than men in cross-sex conversations. Fishman gathered her data by placing tape-recorders in the homes of three couples and asking them to leave them running for a total of one to four hours. The subjects gave permission for this, and it was understood that they had the right to delete anything on the tape they wished to before Fishman heard it. Two of the women considered themselves feminists and the third woman and all three men said they were in sympathy with women's rights issues. Analysis of the data indicated a number of disparities in topic control in the conversations between these couples. Women used more strategies by far than men did to enhance the chances that what they said would be attended to. One such device is to ask questions. A question, as Sacks (1972) pointed out, is part of an *adjacency pair*; once it is asked, a 'slot' is created for the second member of the pair, the answer. Either the answer must be provided or it will be significantly absent. This puts some pressure on the nonturnholder to respond if the turnholder asks a question, and is one way for the current speaker to select the next. Robin Lakoff (1975) recognized that women asked more questions than men (and paid special attention to tag questions and statements with question intonation, as we have seen), but saw it as a reflection of general insecurity resulting from long-term oppression. Fishman interprets question-asking as one of the means women can use to try to compel attention to what they say; attention that they might not otherwise get from a male conversation partner. Perhaps both Lakoff's 'global' and Fishman's 'local' explanations have some merit. In any case, women in Fishman's data asked 263 questions to the men's 107, nearly 2½ times as many.

The other side of the coin, in a sense, to the use of questions as a way of increasing the chance of uptake on the speaker's topic, is the use of statements. Statements are not part of an adjacency pair; there is no structural reason they should induce a response. Yet the men in Fishman's data used statements more than twice as often as the women did, apparently secure that the women would contribute to their topics without special effort. This assumption was borne out; the women almost always responded to statements by the men.

Not only did the men not have to use special strategies to gain attention to their talk nearly as much as the women did, but they seemed to use minimal responses as a technique to *resist* contributing to topics under development by the women. Women used minimal responses largely as back-channels (that is, as indicators of attention and support during brief pauses within the men's turns). Men were more likely to use minimal responses as a *turn*. The minimal response, uttered before and after a lapse, is little more than a shadow of a turn; it does nothing to advance topic development. In fact, it is a rather formidable indicator of lack of interest in the talk under development.

In the end, the women were far less successful than the men in getting topics picked up. In the entire data set, 76 topics were introduced. In three cases, it was not clear whether the topic had been *successfully* introduced or not. The women introduced 45 of the remaining 73 topics and the men initiated 28. Of the 45 women's topics only 17 were successful. *All 28* of the men's topics succeeded (P. Fishman 1983:97). Fishman saw the force of her data as pointing towards a higher level of conversational support work being carried out by women. Men almost effortlessly raised topics for talk, which the women most often supported. Women's topics were not only less actively supported, but were frequently actively discouraged.

In another laboratory-style study of cross-sex conversation, Leet-Pellegrini (1980) investigated the effect of expertise along with sex differences. Same-sex and cross-sex dyads were set up among unacquainted college-student volunteers (as usual!). The conversationalists were asked to discuss the effects of television violence on children. Some of the participants were made 'experts' by being given information on the topic to read and think about in advance. These procedures allowed the possibility of dyads that were equal in expertise (both uninformed) and unequal (one informed and the other not). The conversations were measured for dominance in behavior (for example, which partner was more talkative). The participants themselves and four independent judges also judged the conversations afterwards for the degree of conversational control exerted by each member of the dyad.

Leet-Pellegrini found that expertise, taken as a main effect, had limited influence on conversational control. Sex, on its own, was even less of an influence. The most consistently significant results took both independent variables into account, with male experts found to be in control far more than female experts talking with males, and also more than either partner in same-sex pairs where both were equally uninformed. Just being male seemed not to be sufficient to motivate the men to take conversational control; the expertise factor was required to trigger the behavior. In general, the men who were made experts tried to hold their 'one-up' position by controlling their conversations. In dyads with other men, the uninformed partner would often respond by trying to recover from the disadvantage of being in the 'one-down' position by attempting to get control of the conversation as it progressed. This would account for the weakening of control effects in the male, unequally-informed pairs. Female experts reacted to their position quite differently. They would use their expert status as a resource for the uninformed partner, instead of as a competitive advantage. Particularly when the nonexpert was male, they used more supportive and collaborative strategies than usual. As Leet-Pellegrini (1980:103) put it: 'Whereas the name of the man's game appears to be "Have I won?" the name of the woman's game is "Have I been sufficiently helpful?".'[13]

TERMS RELATED TO SEX IN LANGUAGE

The second part of Lakoff's analysis has to do with the meaning of words referring to sex in the language. It is common knowledge, of course, that lexical items which are semantically male are traditionally used also for general reference, where the sex of the referent is not known and not relevant. This applies to the pronoun 'he', which traditional grammars prescribe in contexts like 'Each bicyclist must dismount and walk his bicycle across the intersection', where it is not known and it does not matter whether any particular bicyclist is female or male. It also applies to 'man', either alone or in compounds, as in the following examples.

Man has learned to control his environment to an astonishing extent.
The university's four-*man* crews won in both the men's and women's divisions.
The hospital emergency room is *manned* by a fully competent team of doctors and nurses.
This discovery will benefit all *man*kind.

Jane Johnson and her brother Howard both serve as chairmen of major committees.

There has been considerable discussion about whether or not this 'generic' use of masculine forms is really 'generic' (for example, see part III of Vetterling-Braggin 1981). Some of the apparently clearest cases of 'generic' uses can be seen as problematic, as a minor substitution in the following famous syllogism shows (Moulton 1981:109):

All men are mortal
Socrates is a man
Therefore, Socrates is mortal

If you substitute *Sophia* for *Socrates*, the result is disturbingly odd, despite the fact that it is obvious that the syllogism is supposed to lead to the conclusion that women are mortal as well as men. Generic statements about the definition of humans as mammals with respect to care of the young would also be strange; consider 'Like other mammals, man nourishes his young with milk.'

It is not necessary to examine our intuitive reactions to hypothetical generic statements, however. There has been a substantial amount of research on people's responses to supposedly generic uses of masculine forms, and the results overwhelmingly support the conclusion that this usage has the effect of excluding women (cf. Bodine 1975; Martyna 1980; MacKay 1983; and the references they cite). To take one example (McKay and Fulkerson 1979), the effect of generic 'he' was tested in an experiment involving 20 American university students, evenly divided by sex. They were asked to listen to a series of sentences and were asked to respond as quickly as they could about whether the sentence could refer to one or more females. To prevent the purpose of the experiment from becoming obvious, a number of 'filler' sentences were included that had nothing to do with generic pronouns. Given sentences like 'When a botanist is in the field, he is usually working', both the men and women students responded 'no' (the sentence could *not* refer to a woman) more than 90 per cent of the time. Assuming 'he' is generic in this case, as it should be since the sex of the botanist is neither known nor relevant, 'no' is the wrong answer. In one follow-up experiment, subjects were asked if the sentences could refer to *males* and 99 per cent said 'yes'. In another follow-up experiment, the pronouns were changed to 'she' and subjects were asked if males were excluded (97 per cent said 'yes').

In a third and crucial follow-up, the sentences were revised to eliminate the pronoun (the example above became 'A botanist who is in the field is usually working'). This would test the hypothesis that females were understood to be excluded because the subjects expected, based on their general experience, that a botanist would in most cases be a man. In this experiment, the errors (the response that the sentences could *not* refer to women) dropped to 43 per cent overall. Even when only those cases where the noun referred to an occupation associated with men were considered, the error rate dropped from over 90 per cent to 68 per cent. Where nouns that referred to occupations traditionally held by women were used the error rate was only 19 per cent (it was 42 per cent with neutral occupations).

These results are typical of what is found in this kind of research: when 'he' is used, regardless of the intent of the speaker or writer to use it in the generic sense, it will almost always be heard as excluding female referents. There is evidence that the exclusionary effect of ostensibly 'generic' masculine forms can have deleterious effects in real life. Martyna (1980) cites a study that indicated that women were much more likely to apply for traditionally male jobs if the advertisements were worded in a neutral way.

Apart from the problem concerning generic use of masculine forms, there are often-noticed overtones that are associated with sex-paired words. These words are supposedly semantically equivalent, except that one refers to men and the other to women. Robin Lakoff (1973a, 1975) makes a strong case for the euphemistic use of 'lady' as opposed to 'gentleman', as if 'woman' were an unpleasant term that ought to be avoided. Many other terms of this sort have worse connotations associated with the woman's term than the corresponding man's term. A 'bachelor' and a 'spinster' are both umarried, and one is a man and the other a woman. A bachelor, however, is seen as probably being unmarried by choice and living a happy and perhaps somewhat libertine life, while a spinster conjures and image of an old and unappealing woman living a drab and unfulfilled life in consequence of her failure to marry. A 'governor' wields considerable power as the executive of a political administrative unit; a 'governess' cares for small children while she is employed by their wealthy parents. Both a 'witch' and a 'warlock' possess evil supernatural power, but no one would think of indicating that some man they know is ugly and ill-tempered by calling him an old warlock.

Shockingly often, there is an imputation of sexual immorality to referents of the woman's term, with the man's term carrying very general, usually favorable implications. A 'madam' might be the manager of a brothel, but you would never call a pimp a 'sir'. A 'master' is an individual with great ability in some skilled endeavour; you would never use the word, as 'mistress' is used, to refer to someone's regular partner in adultery. In fact, there are far and away more words for prostitutes than there are for their customers. Schultz's (1975) sources list more than 500 English slang terms for 'prostitute', but only 65 for 'whoremonger'.

THE DEFAULT GENDER IN LANGUAGE AND IN
NATURE

Ignoring for the moment the well-established fact that 'generic' masculine forms do not work the way they are supposed to, consider what kind of reality a generic-masculine linguistic system would reflect. The meta-meaning of such a linguistic system would be that the default or unmarked sex is male. In other words, maleness is to be assumed except in contexts, especially those having directly to do with biological reproduction, where it is crucial to specify female sex. Exaggerating a little, but not very much, the world-view this sytem symbolizes is that everyone is male unless specifically designated otherwise. That human languages should so typically be organized this way is little short of astounding when it is abundantly clear that the relationship between the sexes in nature is *exactly the reverse*.

It is a fundamental fact of biology that maleness is, in a definite sense, nature's afterthought. A female child is conceived with the conjunction of two Y (female) chromosomes. A male child is the result of the combination of one Y (female) chromosome and one X (male) chromosome. Taking other species into account, there is a wide range of facts which demonstrates that female is the unmarked sex; I will cite three of the most dramatic examples.

1   There are a few species which have only female individuals and no males at all. Among these is a reptile species, the whiptail lizard of the south-western USA. Adult females conceive parthenogenetically and produce only daughters. An all-male species not only does not exist, but would be unthinkable.

2   In some insect species, such as the honey-bee and the leaf-cutter ant, many individuals serve special functions that do not involve reproduction. Among honey-bees, these are the workers that gather nectar and are distinct from the queen and (male) drones. Leaf-cutter ants, in addition to the queen and a few males, also have workers who cut sections of leaf from plants and bring them back to the hill. Besides workers, leaf-cutter ants also have soldiers with enlarged heads and immense jaws. Their function is to protect the colony from marauders from other species. These workers and soldiers are all sterile *females*. Since they do not reproduce, there is no reason for them to be one sex or the other, so they default, so to speak, to female.

3   In a few species, males become sustenance for the female immediately after they have fulfilled their role in reproduction. It is reasonably well known that praying mantis females eat the males right after or even during copulation. There is a species of north Atlantic Ocean fish in which the female is several times larger than the male. As soon as the male fertilizes the eggs, he attaches his small body to the side of the

female where it is gradually absorbed. There are no cases of females similarly nourishing males and you would not expect there to be.

In human societies, this natural order is so thoroughly reversed that the resulting perception of reality is built into language. If language reflected the natural relationship between the sexes, 'she' would be the generic pronoun and we would speak of 'the evolution of woman' and 'all womankind'.[14]

OTHER RESEARCH ON LANGUAGE AND SEX

There are a number of research reports on topics in the field that I have not mentioned. Several scholars have investigated the role of voice quality in the identification of the sex of a speaker (Sachs 1975; Aronovitch 1976). Other scholars have investigated the differences in intonation patterns between men and women; Brend (1975) and McConnel-Ginet (1983) are two examples. Sex-related differences in language use by children has been studied by Berko-Gleason (1978), Berko-Gleason and Greif (1983), Cherry (1975), and Goodwin (1980). Henley (1975) and the studies reported on in Mayo and Henley (1981) are examples of the investigation of sex differences in nonverbal communication. There is quite a large number of studies on attitudes to speech identified as women's or men's, including Elyan et al. (1978), Giles and Marsh (1979), Giles et al. (1980) and P. Smith (1980). Chapter 1 of this book is about the sociolinguistic significance of address forms in general; Kramer (1975) and Wolfson and Manes (1979) have looked at the relationship between address terms and the sex of the addressor and addressee. The interaction between sex and ethnic communicative styles, somewhat along the lines of the ethnography of communication research in chapter 2, has been examined by Tannen (1983a).

SUMMARY

Sex differences are a fundamental fact of human life and it is not surprising to find them reflected in language. There are a few languages which have certain phonological and morphological forms that are only appropriate for use by women and others that only men can use (unless a speaker of one sex is quoting a member of the other). In some cases, these kinds of difference depend not only on the sex of the speaker, but of both the speaker and the addressee. Sociolinguistic survey research has turned up a phenomenon I have called the 'gender pattern'. The gender pattern involves the differential use of certain status-marking linguistic forms by sex. In particular, those forms revealed as *disfavored* by overall patterns of class and style stratification are used more frequently by men than by women, especially in the more formal speech styles. This phenomenon seems to be a particular feature of Western societies. Recent research indicates that sex may be more fundamental as an influence on sociolinguistic variation than has been recognized so far. This may cause substantial rethinking about the significance of the sociolinguistic gender pattern.

Another emphasis in research on language and sex has to do with certain linguistic features that women use, apparently in response to dominance by men. Pioneered by Robin Lakoff in the middle-1970s, these features have been seen as reflecting 'female register'. Some recent research suggests that the emphasis should be on determining how certain linguistic devices are used to execute certain speech strategies. From this perspective, female register research is closely related to another area of language and sex study, the study of cross-sex conversation. These studies consistently show that men use various interactional means to seize and maintain control over the progress of conversations. Women, on the other hand, tend to use two other interactional strategies. More so than men, women use several devices to increase the probability that their contributions will be attended to and supported by their conversational partners. At the same time, they themselves tend far more to support the conversational agendas of the people they are talking with. To some extent at least, these results of conversational research provide explanations for the features of female register.

Another aspect of language and sex raised by Lakoff is the matter of how language *refers* to women and to men. A central issue in this area is the so-called 'generic masculine', in which masculine personal pronoun forms and the word 'man' alone and in compounds are supposed to refer to people of both sexes when the sex of the referents is not known or does not matter. Numerous psycholinguistic studies all agree that the generic masculine does not actually work; sentences with masculine forms, which by the dictates of prescriptive grammar ought to have generic reference, are usually taken to refer to men to the exclusion of women. Besides the supposedly generic use of masculine forms, sex-related differences emerge in the case of pairs of words that are denotatively the same, except that one term refers to a female and the other to a male. Almost always, there are connotations associated with the female-referring item that are either euphemistic ('lady' compared to 'gentleman'), or detrimental to women ('witch' versus 'warlock'), often imputing sexual immorality to the female referent ('mistress' versus 'master').

It is very difficult to tie together these strands of language and sex research into a unified whole. The gender pattern has resisted a really convincing explanation, although several have been offered. Lesley Milroy's work on language, sex, and social networks and Trudgill's discovery of the male covert prestige phenomenon suggests that an explanation of the gender pattern might be better if focused on male behavior. From this perspective, women's use of prestige features simply conforms to the ordinary sociolinguistic order, while men deviate from what is expected – probably below the level of consciousness – to endorse a social value system where their social control is not questioned.

A case can be made that the prescriptive use of the generic masculine runs counter to sex in nature. In nature, female is the basic, unmarked sex. There are a number of instances where males exist only to the extent that they are required for reproduction and in some species they are disposed of as soon as they fulfil that role. In language, the explicit reference to *female* sex tends strongly to have connotations of biological reproduction. This shows up in the dictum that male items are to be used unless explicit reference to femaleness is required, and in the frequent sexual connotations that are associated with the female-referring members of pairs like 'mistress'–'master'.

NOTES

1 A comprehensive study of these issues, partially paralleling my discussion, but in greater detail, is found in Coates (1986)

2 I find it much to Mary Haas's credit that her rules are very nearly informal versions of the kind of generative phonological analysis that would become common some 10 years later.

3 A thorough review and discussion of the literature on phonological and morphological differences between men's and women's speech is to be found in Bodine (1975).

4 The three features which were very sensitive markers of vernacular loyalty for boys and had a similar function in the girls' speech concern the use of 's' with present tense verbs when the subject is not third-person singular (the 's' with 'ignores' in utterances like 'I just ignores them'). Separate tabulations were made for regular verbs, for 'has' and for 'was' (Cheshire counted these as three features). Multiple negation was the fourth sensitive feature in boys' speech, but had no symbolic function for the girls. The two less sensitive markers of vernacular loyalty in boys' speech that were not markers in girls' speech were 'never' where standard English would have 'didn't' ('I never done it, it was him') and 'what' as a complementizer ('there's a knob what you turn'). For the girls, 'come' used in past contexts was a marker of vernacular loyalty, as was 'ain't'. These two features did not work as loyalty markers for boys.

5 Parts of this account are along the same lines as Key's suggestion.

6 I have stated the conclusion a little more strongly than Milroy does. She concludes that sex and network structure work together 'in a particularly intimate way', but that it is not yet possible to be very precise about the relationship between them (L. Milroy 1982:152).

7 For some variables, *younger* women (under 30) also demonstrated covert prestige for vernacular variables.

8 This point has been made before, see, for example, Frank and Anshen (1983:45). It is also implicit in much of the discussion in Coates (1986).

9 In fact the distribution of speakers by sex is significant by a chi-squared test ($\chi^2 = $

9.07, df = 1) at the 0.01 level of confidence; the distribution by class is not (χ^2 = 3.77, df = 1).

10 Lakoff points out that men in the upper strata of British society, and men in academia anywhere in the English-speaking world, may also use 'women's' adjectives. Her explanation is that men in these positions are seen somewhat as women are; they seem not to be part of the productive enterprises of society, and are engaged in unimportant pursuits while being supported by others.

A young woman in an introductory class I once taught agrees with Lakoff's analysis of these adjectives. She said that if she were going out and her mother told her she looked adorable, she would keep changing her clothes until her mother said she looked terrific.

11 Personally, I am on accord with those linguists who insist on a strict separation of language and use.

12 The two interruptions by a female speaker occurred between a woman teaching assistant and an undergraduate man. The woman clearly had more status. In spite of this, the male undergraduate interrupted her 11 times.

13 I have long had the impression that conversation is a competitive sport for men far more than it is for women. Leet-Pellegrini expressed the hope that her study would contribute to both men and women being released from their respective 'games'. Both men and women could then choose the strategy most appropriate to the task at hand. What she seems to assume, but I very much doubt, is that men and women will generally be able to agree on which strategy is appropriate.

14 The pipe-organ mud-dauber wasp is a more complex instance. Female wasps lay both fertilized and unfertilized eggs, both of which produce adult insects. The unfertilized eggs produce *males*. This may make the male sex seem to be the default in this species, but notice that female wasps are the ones to benefit from the genetic variation which comes from having two parents.

5

Linguistic Pragmatics:
Conversational Implicature

INTRODUCTION

Pragmatics, as a topic in linguistics, is the study of the use of context to make inferences about meaning.[1] The term 'pragmatics' has an interesting history in philosophy and linguistics and is undergoing rapid development. There is a wide range of linguistic topics that are addressed as problems in pragmatics, so it is not easy to define its scope. With its concern with context, though, it is not difficult to make the case that it is part of the sociolinguistics of language. Stephen Levinson, in his deservedly influential textbook *Pragmatics*, takes more than 50 pages to define the term 'pragmatics'. In the course of his discussion, he distinguishes between the 'Continental' and 'Anglo-American' interpretations of pragmatics (Levinson 1983:5). The Anglo-American interpretation is the more restrictive one and the one more closely associated with the traditional linguistic concern with sentence structure and grammar. The Continental interpretation is much broader and includes discourse analysis, the ethnography of communication, some aspects of psycholinguistics, and even such matters as the address terms topic in chapter 1 of this book.[2] The vigor of Continental pragmatics research is well documented in the *Journal of Pragmatics* and in the monograph series *Pragmatics and Beyond* (published by John Benjamins, B.V.).

Pragmatics will be treated here and in the next chapter, as it is in Levinson's book, mostly according to the Anglo-American tradition, although there will be a little discussion of the broader tradition. This is not to imply that only the restricted scope is correct. One reason for the decision is that many of the topics dealt with in the wider definition are treated in the preceding chapters. Another reason is that I find the philosophical issues which dominate this Anglo-American branch of pragmatics personally appealing.

The introduction of the term 'pragmatics' into the scholarly stream that has ultimately led to linguistic pragmatics is generally credited to the philosopher Charles Morris (1938). Morris was interested in *semiotics*, the study of systems of signs, whether linguistic or not. Morris saw a tripartite division of semiotics into syntax, semantics, and pragmatics. This trichotomy is still influential (for example, Parret 1983), especially with regard to the vexed question of the division between semantics and pragmatics. For theoretical syntacticians, the distinction between syntax and the other two is less difficult to maintain, as long as you take syntax to be about possible sentence structures, regardless of how they are used in utterances, and to some extent distinct from their meanings.[3] In chapter 3, though, we saw that linguists like Givón, Hopper, and Thompson take an approach that reduces the distinction between syntax and its use in discourse, a pragmatics topic in the broad sense. During the 1970s, the Generative Semantics school of American linguistics attempted to build both semantic and pragmatic meaning into a unified theory of syntax (for example, McCawley 1968; G. Lakoff 1971). This research program has since been abandoned (cf. Newmeyer 1980).

In this chapter and the next, we will be concerned with the issue of the relationship between semantics and pragmatics.[4] One fundamental question for philosophers of language has been *truth conditions*. It addresses the problem: given a sentence in any language, under what conditions is it true? In the most simple instances, an answer can be given that seems ridiculously trivial to the layperson. Taking the sentence 'Grass is green', one would say 'The sentence "Grass is green" is true if and only if grass is, in fact, green.' Of course, it remains to specify exactly what the property 'green' means and to determine the referent of the term 'grass' but, this done, we can say the sentence is true once we have checked the stuff we call 'grass' and determined it does have the property we call 'green'.

Where negation, connectives, quantifiers, and conditionals are involved, we need *rules of inference* in order to determine truth conditions. We have seen an example of a rule of inference in classical propositional logic in chapter 4. The discussion of the allegedly generic use of the word 'man' was illustrated with the classical example of a well-known rule of inference called *modus ponens*: 'All men are mortal. Socrates is a man. Therefore Socrates is mortal.' Leaving aside the sexist usage issue, we can determine the truth of the third proposition, once the truth of the first two are established, by inference using *modus ponens*. It is not necessary to inspect directly the individual called 'Socrates' for the attribute called 'mortal'. Of course, more complex truth determinations can be made by means of rules of inference, provided we first determine the truth of the relevant input propositions. For example, if we know that either 'Mildred's cat had kittens' is false or 'Mildred's husband

Harold is happy' is false, it is possible to prove beyond a doubt that 'Mildred's cat had kittens and Mildred's husband Harold is happy' cannot possibly be true. This is an example of one of two logical proofs that together are called De Morgan's Laws.

It might seem that if we had a complete and accurate lexicon such that we knew exactly what everything is called, and we had the right rules of inference, it would be possible to establish the truth of anything which might be expressed in the language that the lexicon goes with, without regard to who uttered the expression to whom under what conditions, or even if anybody ever said it at all. If this were the case, a truth-based semantics could be established completely independently of pragmatics. For better or worse, though, there are myriad problems with this idea. Some examples of these problems are discussed next.

REFERENCE

Presupposition

Establishing the truth of a proposition depends crucially on the possibility of identifying the referents involved. We can evaluate the truth of 'Grass is green' provided we can find out what 'grass' is and what 'green' means. What would we do with a sentence like 'The principal chief of the Kuikus delivered the petition'? Supposedly, we would have to find out who the Kuikus are and who their principal chief is, what petition is under discussion and then check to see if the individual delivered the petition. In putting it this way, though, I have *presupposed* that there is such a group as the Kuikus, that they have a principal chief, and that there was a petition. As a matter of fact, I made up the name 'Kuiku'; it would be an amazing coincidence if they exist and if they have a principal chief. What would we want to say about our sample sentence if there is no such principal chief? We surely do not want to say it is true, but there seems to be something wrong with saying it is false, too. It seems maddeningly pointless to talk about the truth or falsity of the principal chief delivering a petition if there is no such person in the first place. This would be a case of a referring expression ('the principal chief of the Kuikus') that does not refer to anything.[5] Not only does this raise the possibility that there might be *three* truth values (true, false, and neither), but it means that we have to be concerned with the truth of some other propositions, such as 'There exists a principal chief of the Kuikus', before we can evaluate the truth of the sentence under analysis. This turns out to be a century-old problem in the philosophy of language and linguistics that is still not completely solved. The hoary example used in much of this discussion is 'The present King of France is bald', which is like my example except that it is known that France does not now have a king.

For our purposes as people with an interest in sociolinguistics, a sentence like 'The principal chief of the Kuikus delivered the petition' is most interesting if we imagine someone uttering it. Does the speaker actually know of the existence of this principal chief? Do the other participants in the conversation have to know in advance that there is such a person? Are they likely to believe that there is a principal chief of the Kuikus after the utterance, even though the speaker did not actually say there is one? Imagine a man knows there is no such person as the principal chief of the Kuikus, but says this anyway. Suppose I am in the conversation and I later tell someone else 'There is a principal chief of the Kuikus' and that person corrects me. Do I have the right to accuse the person who made the utterance about the petition of lying to me? After all he did not actually say that there was a principal chief. Whatever solutions to presupposition problems as issues in semantics there might be, there are going to be other interesting issues for the sociolinguistics of language.

Deixis

Certain completely straightforward sentences present serious problems for an independent truth-based semantics. Consider the sentence 'I am the British Prime Minister.' Following the procedure for 'Grass is green,' we would check the referent of 'I' and see if the predication 'the British Prime Minister' were true of that referent. The trouble is, we can't locate the referent of 'I' until someone utters the sentence. What is referred to by 'I' depends on who says the word 'I' at a particular time. The sentence would be true at this writing if uttered by Margaret Thatcher, but not if uttered by anyone else. Not only is *who* utters the sentence important, but *when*. If Mrs Thatcher had said the same thing before she took office, or if she were to say it after leaving office, it would be false. There is a class of words whose referents depend critically on the time, place, and participants in the speech events in which they occur. These words are called *deictic* terms or simply *deictics* (the phenomenon in general is called 'deixis').[6] Besides the personal pronouns, deictics include references to location ('this', 'that', 'here', 'there') and time ('now', 'then', 'yesterday', 'tomorrow').

It might take a bit of thought in order to appreciate what is special about these words. We can talk about what 'grass' refers to without having any particular utterance including the word 'grass' in mind, but who is being referred to by 'she' depends very much on who says the word and who they are talking about at the time. Similarly we can evaluate the truth of a sentence such as 'Sheila Jones and Harold Crockett were married on 15 June 1982' without regard to any utterance of the sentence, but 'Sheila Jones and Harold Crockett were married yesterday' is only true if it is said on the day after their wedding. As a result, it is not obvious how an independent truth-based semantics can manage sentences that include deictics.

CONTRADICTIONS AND TAUTOLOGIES

Another famous problem with independent truth-based semantic theories involves contradictions and tautologies. An assertion like 'The sum of 1 plus 1 is the sum of 1 plus 1' seems totally vacuous, since it asserts that something is identical to itself. Such assertions (loosely called *tautologies*), considered out of context, ought to be meaningless.[7] Nevertheless, many tautological assertions are meaningful and fairly common, such as 'War is war'; or 'If he gets here on time, he gets here on time; if he doesn't, he doesn't; or the line attributed to baseball player and manager Yogi Berra: 'It's never over till it's over'. All three ought to be maddeningly pointless things to say, but of course they are not. However, in order to make 'War is war', or 'It's never over till it's over' meaningful, considerable background knowledge on the part of the hearer has to be assumed. In the first case, you have to assume that the hearer knows what war is like and knows that the speaker has a similar knowledge of what war is like and, further, that the speaker finds the concept so overwhelming that it seems impossible to say anything more than that war is what it is. Berra's quip has to be taken in the context of sports contests, in which one-sided scores near the end of the game can tempt participants and fans to assume the game is as good as over, but that teams which are far behind occasionally rally to win. In both cases, the explanation involves assuming a speaker, a hearer, and what they know about the world.

No such assumptions make sense unless the sentence is actually uttered by real people in a particular world-context. The case of 'If he gets here on time, he gets here on time; if he doesn't, he doesn't' is a little different. To make sense of this, it is necessary to assume that the speaker would *not* be so inconsiderate of the hearer as to say something completely pointless. The hearer will instead suppose that the speaker intended to convey *something* meaningful and will try to infer what it is. The inference is doubtless that the speaker proposes making no special concessions for the person referred to as 'he', such as waiting for him if he should not be on time. The idea that people in conversations assume that others in the conversation are trying to say something meaningful is essentially H. Paul Grice's *cooperative principle*, which will give us the foundation for a solution to this whole set of semantic problems. The mechanism will not work, though, unless there is a speaker and a hearer and both assume the other is trying to communicate. This entails that the apparently tautological sentence has actually been uttered by somebody to somebody.

Contradictions are involved in a similar effect. A statement such as 'The number 1 is not the number 1', since it denies that something is identical to itself, is contradictory, and hence false under any conditions. As such it would seem useless to assert a contradiction; it would fail even as a lie. But, like tautologies, contradictions are not uncommonly used and used meaningfully. An example I actually heard is 'Glenn couldn't sing even if he could'. This was said of a man assumed to have no particular talent for vocal music and who also found it necessary to clear his throat frequently. The speaker meant that even if Glenn had the necessary talent, his throat-clearing would prevent him from being able to sing. Quite often apparent contradictions, like this one, involve a proposition being false in one sense while it is simultaneously true in the other. The speaker leaves it to the hearer to select the appropriate senses, based on the assumption that the hearer will take it for granted that the speaker is trying to communicate something reasonable. Another example, 'Harold isn't himself today', is a contradiction that has become a conventional way of saying that a person cannot be expected to behave in the way he normally would. As with tautologies, in order for contradictions to be meaningful they have to be uttered in context.

Another problem arises in such cases as 'The evening star is the morning star', a much-discussed example. If you know that the morning star and the evening star are both manifestations of the planet Venus, and you consider only the *referents* to the terms 'morning star' and 'evening star' then the sentence 'The evening star is the morning star' is tautologous. Of course, someone can perfectly well use the sentence to inform someone who does not know that particular fact of astronomy. Even if the identity of 'the morning star' and the 'evening star' is known, it is possible as McCawley (1981:291) points out, to say 'The morning star is more beautiful than the evening star', meaning simply that the view of Venus in the morning is more esthetically pleasing than the view of the same planet in the evening. Somewhat similarly there is a problem evaluating the truth of 'Hubert knows that Mr Hyde has a successful medical practice.' If Hubert knows that Dr Jekyll has a successful medical practice, but does not know that Mr Hyde is really Dr Jekyll, is the sentence true? Other problems arise with such sentences as 'The Sheriff of Nottingham didn't know that Robin Hood was Robin Hood', supposing Robin Hood had fooled the sheriff with a disguise. Notice that this could be said even if the sheriff *did* know Robin Hood's identity but did not know that he was exceptionally clever or an excellent bowman or had some other characteristic essential to Robin Hood's nature.[8] It is difficult to think of solutions to problems like these without taking into account what the speaker knows and believes about who is the same person as whom and what personal characteristics are essential to someone's identity. Once more, this necessarily means we are talking about someone uttering a sentence at some place and time.

LOGICAL OPERATORS AND LANGUAGE EQUIVALENTS

Conjunction

Logicians have developed theories involving elements called *logical operators* which look very much like words in languages. For example, the logical operator of conjunction, symbolized $\wedge$, seems to mean the same thing as English 'and'. If we let p = 'Socrates was a philosopher' and q = 'Socrates is dead', the proposition p $\wedge$ q ('Socrates was a philosopher and Socrates is dead') is true only when both p and q are true. Crucially, it does not matter which way around we conjoin p and q; it would be nonsense to say: 'While it is true that Socrates was a philosopher and Socrates is dead, to claim that Socrates is dead and Socrates was a philosopher is completely erroneous.' But sometimes the order of conjuncts makes a very big difference in natural language. It makes perfect sense to say, 'It's true that Herman and Sarah got married and had a baby but it's slanderously false to say they had a baby and got married.' Notice that in both cases the individual propositions 'Herman and Sarah got married' and 'Herman and Sarah had a baby' could be indisputably true.

If what is said can possibly bear the interpretation, sentences including coordinate structures will be interpreted as stating that the first member of the conjunct occurred first and the second occurred subsequently. Furthermore, if the inference makes sense, there is even a tendency for what is said in the first conjunct to be taken as the *cause* of what is said in the second conjunct. If I were to say 'I stepped in a hole and broke my foot', you would no doubt think I was telling you that stepping in the hole caused my foot to break. If you were to discover that I had indeed stepped in a hole and later broke my foot, but breaking my foot was due to my dropping a brick on it, you would feel misled. It would be even worse if you found out that I broke my foot last week and stepped in a hole five minutes ago.[9] But there is still a sense in which the sequential interpretations are not an inherent part of the meaning. You *could* say, if you were given to slightly tasteless humor, 'Herman and Sarah had a baby and got married, but not, uh, in that order.' You cannot be accused of contradicting yourself, as you could be if you said 'Herman and Sarah had a baby first and then got married, but not, uh, in that order.' There seems to be a distinction between what an independent truth-based semantic theory would say about these compared to the meaning that is conveyed in the actual contexts.

Disjunction

Logicians recognize an operator that seems to be the same thing as the word 'or' in English. This operator is conventionally symbolized as $\vee$, so that p $\vee$ q means 'p or q' is true. In logic it is necessary to distinguish *inclusive* disjunction from *exclusive* disjunction. With exclusive 'or', the proposition 'Henry likes either apples or bananas' is *false* if it turns out that Henry is fond of both kinds of fruit. If inclusive 'or' is intended, the proposition is true if Henry likes either apples or bananas or both. In the case of assertions, people tend to take 'or' to be ambiguous. In our example, you would not be sure if the speaker means that Henry surely likes one fruit or the other and – for all the speaker knows – maybe he even likes both, or that Henry enjoys one of the two fruits but not the other, but the speaker cannot remember which. In fact, a *third* meaning is possible, in which Henry is not fussy; he would be happy to have either an apple or a banana. In other words, there is no doubt that he likes both apples and bananas. This reading seems to have the disturbing implication that 'or' can have the same truth conditions as 'and'.[10]

There is another problem for an independent truth-based semantics that involves disjunction. Given the utterance of 'Henry likes either apples or bananas', we have seen that it is possible to take it as meaning that Henry likes both kinds of fruit, or he likes only one or the other, but the speaker does not know which. Suppose I know that Henry likes apples, but dislikes bananas, and I still say, 'Henry likes either apples or bananas.' Logically, there is nothing wrong with the use of the disjunction, since one of the conjuncts is true. But my use of a disjunction seems to indicate that I do not know which conjunct is true, and if I do know and still use the disjunction, I could be blamed for misleading whoever I was talking to.

Quantifiers and other scalar phenomena

Some expressions, both in context-free truth-based semantic systems and in languages, refer to quantities. Such expressions include 'some', 'all', and 'every', and each of these has a logic symbol that is apparently the equivalent of the English word. But the similarity is flawed. For a speaker to say 'Some of the books are really expensive' almost unavoidably conveys the idea that not all of the books are really expensive. In logic, this inference is not valid; after all, if *all* the books are really expensive, it must be the case that *some* of the books are expensive, since some of the books is part of all of the books. This is an example of linguistic terms operating in a *scalar* manner (Horn 1972, 1973; Gazdar 1979). We can think of *all* and *some* as part of a *scale* (along with *most*, *many*, and *few*), in the following way:

$$\{all_1, most_2, many_3, some_4, few_5\}$$

An item on such a scale with a subscript of 1 is higher than the rest; an item with a subscript of 2 is lower than one with subscript 1, but higher than all the rest, and so on. In such scales, the assertion of an item from a lower position on the scale generally conveys the impression that, as far as the speaker knows, use of an item higher on the scale would not be appropriate. A speaker who says, 'Some of the books are expensive' is taken to be saying that not all of them are, at least as far as the speaker knows.

Numbers and certain sets of adjective expressions also form scales. A partial scale of the positive integers can be represented (somewhat confusingly, since higher numbers get *lower* subscripts) as:

$$\{n_1 \ldots 4_{n-3}, 3_{n-2}, 2_{n-1}, 1_n\}$$

In other words, the highest number under consideration is first on the scale, and 1, the lowest positive integer, is nth. Since we have a scale, we now expect that if a woman says 'I have four boys', she means she has no more than four, in spite of the fact that, if she has five boys, it is true that she is the mother of four, in the sense that you could easily line up four boys to whom she has given birth. There are many sets of adjectives that are scalar in this sense, for instance:

$$\{hot_1, warm_2\}$$

As a result, if I say 'The coffee is warm', I will be heard as saying that it is not really hot. Naturally, this is a problem for a truth-based semantics since what seems to be understood goes beyond what can be determined as true or false by means of logic.

Conditionals and 'invited inferences'

Geis and Zwicky (1971) pointed out a phenomenon involving conditionals that they called 'invited inferences'. The meaning of 'if–then', somewhat like the meaning of 'or', can be taken in two ways. The proposition 'If p then q', if true, entails that q will be true, if p is true, but says nothing about whether or not q is true if p is not true. A related conditional form is 'If and only if p then q' (sometimes written 'Iff p then q'). This relationship means that q is true if p is true and never otherwise. Geis and Zwicky pointed out that there is a tendency to interpret English 'if–then' constructions as if they were 'if and only if–then' statements. If someone says 'If you mow the lawn, I'll give you five dollars', where the proposition 'you mow the lawn' is p and 'I'll give you five dollars' is q, 'if p then q' logic would mean that q is true if p is true, and if p is not true, we have no way of deciding if q is true. That is, if you do mow the lawn, I will give you five dollars, but whether or not I will give you five dollars if you do not mow the lawn is an open question. Geis and Zwicky point out, though, that people tend to interpret such utterances as meaning the same as 'Iff p then q'. In other words, I will give you five dollars if *and only if* you mow the lawn (not otherwise). According to Geis and Zwicky, there is a tendency to 'perfect' conditional sentences of the form 'If p then q' to biconditionals of the form 'Iff p then q'. As a result the utterance of a sentence of the form 'If p then q' *invites the inference*, 'If not p then not q'.

In a response, Lilje (1972) pointed out that there were cases with the same structure as Geis and Zwicky's examples in which the predicted inference is *not* invited. For example, if you hear, 'If you scratched on the eight-ball, then you lost the game', it does not 'invite the inference' that you did not lose the game if you did not scratch on the eight-ball. Interestingly, it seems that the mistaken inference is not made even if you do not know the rules of pool. Lilje points out that Geis and Zwicky themselves mention context as contributing the invited inference:

Certainly, given our attitudes toward the exchange of money in our society, one would have some warrant for assuming that if someone says ['If you mow the lawn, I'll give you five dollars'] he will act as if he intended both ['If you mow the lawn, I'll give you five dollars'] and ['If you don't mow the lawn, I won't give you five dollars']. (Geis and Zwicky 1971:562)

But, of course, 'attitudes toward the exchange of money in our society' means that the interpretation depends on a 'society' with the specified 'attitudes'. Invited inference seems to be another phenomenon that cannot be analyzed by truth-based semantics alone. As Lilje (1972:542) puts it: 'I see little hope that this can be done by appealing to the logical form of utterances.'

GRICE'S SOLUTION: CONVERSATIONAL IMPLICATURE

This list of problems shows that there is a lot more to the meaning of what people say than can be readily captured by an independent system of truth-based semantics. Many of these problems have been addressed by an eminent philosopher of language, H. Paul Grice. It is scarcely an exaggeration to say that Grice's theory has become the hub of pragmatics research, with various scholars either applying, extending, or attempting to refute his ideas. In an article with the appropriate title 'Logic and conversation' (Grice 1975), Grice addressed the central problem I have been discussing; how to deal with the fact that natural language utterances do not convey the same meanings that the corresponding logical propositions would. Some philosophers conclude that natural language is inadequate for the precise, logical representation of meaning, and that it is necessary to devise ideal languages in which the problems we have just reviewed do not arise. Grice's judgement is that this approach is not necessary because the assumption that natural language expressions diverge from the formal devices of the logicians is itself faulty:

> I wish . . . to maintain that the common assumption . . . that the divergences do in fact exist is (broadly speaking) a common mistake, and that the mistake arises from an inadequate attention to the nature and importance of the conditions governing conversation. I shall, therefore, proceed at once to inquire into the general conditions that, in one way or another, apply to conversation as such, irrespective of its subject matter. (Grice 1975:43)

Grice seems to be saying that natural languages are just as good as special logic systems for making precise statements. The 'divergent' or 'extra' meanings that seem to crop up when certain kinds of natural language statements are made are due not to the syntactic or semantic rules of languages, but to rules and principles of *conversation*. To see if Grice is right about this, we will first examine the kind of conversational rules he proposed and check to see how sucessful they are at accounting for the problems we have just gone over.

The cooperative principle

The centerpiece of Grice's reasoning is what he calls the *cooperative principle*, which simply means that people engaged in conversation will say something suitable at that point in the development of the talk. For example, if I were to run my car into your parked car by accident, and you were to say 'Do you see what you've done? Just what do you intend to do about it?', it would be totally unsuitable for me to say 'The square of the hypotenuse is equal to the sum of the squares of the other two sides.' If I did say such a thing, you would be likely to doubt my sobriety, if not my sanity.

Grice has made the cooperative principle somewhat more explicit by subdividing it into a set of *conversational maxims* and submaxims. These maxims are as follows (Grice 1975: 45–7):

1 The maxim of Quantity
   Submaxim: Make your contribution as informative as is required (for the current purposes of the exchange).
   Submaxim: Do not make your contribution more informative than is required.
2 The maxim of Quality: Try to make your contribution one that is true.

Submaxim: Do not say what you believe to be false.
Submaxim: Do not say that for which you lack adequate evidence.
3   The maxim of Relation: Be relevant.
4   The maxim of Manner: Be perspicuous.
Submaxim: Avoid obscurity of expression.
Submaxim: Avoid ambiguity.
Submaxim: Be brief (avoid unnecessary prolixity).[11]
Submaxim: Be orderly.

Grice suggests five ways conversationalists can deal with these maxims. First, speakers can straightforwardly follow the maxims; that is, they can speak the truth, while giving just enough relevant information in a clear, unambiguous, succinct, and orderly manner. Quite possibly most people do just that most of the time. Second, someone may violate a maxim, as you would do if you told a deliberate lie. A third thing that can happen is that a speaker can 'opt out' of a maxim. This seems to be an uncommon occurrence; the example Grice gives is when someone has required information to contribute, but has an obligation not to divulge it and has to say something like 'I cannot say more, my lips are sealed.' The fourth possibility is the maxim clash; cases in which you would have to violate one maxim in order to fulfil another. The fifth and most intriguing way to deal with the maxims of conversation is to *flout* one of them. When a maxim is flouted, a speaker does not observe the maxim, but cannot be accused of violating it either, because the transgression is so flagrant that it is totally obvious that the speaker knows he or she is not observing it and realizes everyone else in the conversation knows it too.

The existence of the maxims makes *conversational implicatures* possible. Conversational implicatures allow a speaker to convey meaning beyond what is literally expressed. In order to see how this works, consider a few of Grice's examples:

A is standing by an obviously immobilized car and is approached by B and the following exchange takes place.
A: I am out of petrol.
B: There is a garage round the corner.

In this hypothetical conversation, all the maxims are being obeyed. The conversation is so natural that it is necessary to be relentlessly literal-minded to understand that something has been conveyed beyond what has been said. B's response is literally irrelevant; it simply states that there is a certain kind of place of business around the corner. But we are going to assume that B *is* being cooperative and that this statement is actually what is required at that point in the conversation. We will assume, as A would, that B's utterance somehow *is* relevant. The reasoning behind the derivation of the meaning is explained by Grice as follows: 'B would be infringing the maxim "Be relevant" unless he thinks, or thinks it possible, that the garage is open, and has petrol to sell; so he implicates that the garage is, or at least may be open, etc.'

Another example involves a clash between maxims. Grice's example for this is the following hypothetical exchange.

A is planning with B an itinerary for a holiday in France. Both know that A wants to see his friend C, if to do so would not involve too great a prolongation of his journey:
A: Where does C live?
B: Somewhere in the South of France.

Grice's 'gloss' of this example is:

There is no reason to suppose that B is opting out; his answer is, as he well knows, less informative than is required to meet A's needs. This infringement of the first maxim of Quantity can be explained only by the supposition that B is aware that to be more informative would be to say something that infringed the maxim of Quality, 'Don't say what you lack adequate evidence for', so B implicates that he does not know in which town C lives.

In general, it is possible to infringe any of the maxims if it is plausible that to do otherwise would involve a clash with another maxim, which is taken to be more important. A common sort of example is one in which the third submaxim of manner, 'Be brief' is not observed because the speaker expects the hearer to infer a clash with the first submaxim of quality ('Make your contribution as informative as required'). In other words, a speaker who is not being brief is implying that there is no shorter way to say what is required. People who abuse the cooperative principle in this way develop reputations as bores![12]

Some of the most interesting conversational implicatures in Grice's sense arise when a maxim is flouted. One of Grice's more amusing examples involves the flouting of 'Be brief', the third submaxim of manner:

Compare the remarks:
(a) Miss X sang 'Home sweet home'.
(b) Miss X produced a series of sounds that corresponded closely with the score of 'Home sweet home'.

A speaker who said (b) is obviously not trying to claim that there is a clash with the quality submaxim about providing sufficient information, since it is clearly possible to convey the fundamental message with something like (a). The implicature generated is that for some reason the word 'sang' has to be avoided, and the reader of (b), say in a review, would readily draw the conclusion that Miss X's performance, in the reviewer's opinion, was too poor to be called 'singing'.[13]

In general, a Gricean conversational implicature depends on a three-step process. First, a speaker says something that seems to involve a maxim violation, or at least it requires a little effort to understand how what was said conforms to the cooperative principle. Second, the speaker expects, nevertheless, to be interpreted as being cooperative and the hearer actually does assume he or she is being cooperative. Third, the speaker thinks, and expects the hearer to think the speaker thinks, that the hearer can work out what additional suppositions are necessary in order for the speaker's contribution to actually *be* cooperative. In the preceding example, the reviewer expects the readers to know that the obviously long-winded comment on the rendition of 'Home sweet home' could have been made more succinctly, but still expects the readers to take the comment as cooperative in Grice's sense. The reviewer is depending on the readers working out the supposition about Miss X's shabby performance that is required in order to see that the long-winded comment actually is cooperative, after all.

The notion of the cooperative principle and the conversational implicatures it makes possible seems to imply the following five characteristics (Kempson 1975:144).

1   Conversational implicatures depend on everyone concerned recognizing the cooperative principle and its maxims.

2   The implicatures will not be part of the meaning of the words in the sentence. It has to be possible to understand the sentence literally first and then to work out the implicature.[14]

3   The stress put on the cooperative principle by some utterances may be relievable by more than one implicature. As a result, the implicature generated is often indeterminate.

4   Working out an implicature depends on assumptions shared by the participants in a particular speech event. An exchange between one set of conversationalists might clearly generate a particular implicature. The same exchange in another conversation with different participants may result in an entirely different implicature.

5   Implicatures are cancelable. It is possible to say something following an utterance that generates an implicature which denies the implicature without contradiction. For example, if 'Miss X produced a series of sounds that corresponded closely with the score of "Home sweet home"' was followed by 'Yet her rendition was so exquisitely beautiful that it was difficult to believe she was singing such a simple, familiar tune', any inclination to draw the apparently obvious negative implicature would immediately evaporate.

If Grice is correct, it should be possible to resolve some or all of the problems that we have seen with independent truth-based theories of semantics. To test this idea, I will take each of the ones we have seen in turn and see if the problem yields to a solution involving conversational implicatures. Of course, our list is far from exhaustive, but it is representative. If a Gricean analysis fares well in giving a satisfactory account for these problems, it would be reasonable to hope it would also provide solutions to problems we have not raised.

Reference: presupposition

The paradigm case of presupposition failure involves propositions about entities for which there are no referents. As long as this problem is taken to be a problem about the truth-conditions of sentences whether they are uttered or not, it is obvious that a conversational implicature analysis has no bearing on it. If we limit ourselves to the relationship between the truth of the (possibly unuttered) sentence, 'The principal chief of the Kuikus delivered the petition', and the truth of the sentence 'There is a principal chief of the Kuikus', the question about anybody being cooperative simply does not come up. If we treat it as an *utterance*, however, it begins to look as if we have a possible violation of the maxim of quality, 'Try to make your contribution one that is true', if it turns out that there is no principal chief of the Kuikus. But this depends on what we understand by 'contribution' and 'true'. Does your 'contribution' include what you presuppose as well as what you assert? Is a contribution not 'true' if there is a presupposition failure? There is a chance that we would conclude that the statement about the petition is not true, but it is not exactly false either.[15] Presupposition failure means a presupposed proposition is false. It is interesting to consider whether or not the falsity of a *presupposition* constitutes a violation of the maxim of quality. It seems to me that it would be in the spirit of the cooperative principle to let the maxim of quality apply to presuppositions as well as assertions. To the extent that people come to believe in the truth of presupposed propositions on the strength of the presupposing utterances, and since Grice clearly finds it uncooperative to lead others to believe what the speaker believes to be false, it seems natural to claim a quality violation if a speaker deliberately utters a sentence with a presupposition that is false.

Reference: deixis

There seems to be no solution to the problem deixis presents for an independent semantics in the theory of conversational implicatures. One of Kempson's characteristics of implicatures is that they be cancelable. But the context-dependent nature of deictic expressions cannot be canceled. No one could say, for instance, 'It is absolutely true that I am the British Prime Minister, but I should inform you that when I said "I", I was referring, not to myself, but to Margaret Thatcher.' Nor could you say 'Harold is now eating a peach, but when I say "now", I mean a period of time that will start in 32 minutes and extend for 1 minute and 11 seconds after that.' Nor is it possible to cancel the meaning conveyed by any other deictic expression by explicitly denying it.[16] It seems clear that deixis is not a matter of conversational implicature and remains troublesome for the view that a semantic theory can be detached from pragmatics.

Contradictions and tautologies

Contradictions and tautologies lend themselves very well to analysis by Grice's principles. In fact, Grice himself uses the example 'War is war' as an example of the generation of an implicature by the flouting of the first submaxim of quantity, 'Make your contribution as informative as is required' (Grice 1975:63). Since tautologies are, taken literally, intrinsically uninformative, they will always infringe the quantity maxim, inducing people to look for an implicature that will save their faith in the cooperative principle. In the 'War is war' case, a plausible implicature is the one we have seen. It could be expressed something like: 'You and I both know how horrible war is, so horrible that I am at a loss to provide a description.' Remember, though, that implicatures can vary from conversation to conversation and are cancelable. A mercenary, for example, could say 'War is war. I don't mean to say it's horrible; what I mean is, for someone in my profession, it's simply a way to make a lot of money.' The same goes for contradictions. To salvage the cooperative principle, someone who hears something contradictory will conclude that there is a sense in which what the person has said is true and another sense in which it is not true. With 'Glenn couldn't sing even if he could', an implicature along this line was immediately and effortlessly generated in my own mind.

Cases like 'The evening star is (more beautiful than) the morning star', if said by one person to another, are no particular problem for an implicature analysis. If we decide that the literal meaning of the sentence is either tautological (with 'is') or is nonsense (with 'is more beautiful than'), then the cooperative principle is breached, and the intelligible meanings of these utterances become implicatures. It seems to me that the evident meaning of 'The morning star is the evening star' is cancelable as in an exchange like the following:

Humphrey: The morning star is the evening star.
Samantha: You mean they are both actually the planet Venus.
Humphrey: Are they really? I didn't know that. No, I meant they
             both symbolize my love for you equally. It burns just
             as bright in the evening as it does in the morning.

The same goes for cases such as, 'The Sheriff of Nottingham didn't know Robin Hood was Robin Hood.' The statement sounds contradictory, so we look for an implicature. The meanings involving Robin having successfully used a disguise or the sheriff having underestimated Robin's cleverness or bowmanship are simply alternative implicatures depending on the speaker's and hearer's background assumptions, as we would expect.

With 'Hyde has a successful medical practice', the problem is a little different. As an *utterance*, if the speaker knows (but the hearer does not) that Dr Jekyll and Mr Hyde are the same person, and if the speaker does not really expect the hearer to infer that, then I would want to say the speaker has *violated* the first submaxim of quality. What the speaker would communicate in that case is that one could go into a surgery somewhere and find the disgusting Mr Hyde making medical diagnoses and prescribing drugs. This is misleading to say the least. If the hearer *does* know of Jekyll/Hyde's two personas, we have an implicature generated on the basis of a strain on the first submaxim of quantity, 'Make your contribution as informative as required.' If the speaker is observing the first submaxim, he or she must regard it as necessary that the statement be made about Hyde, despite the fact that it would seem more natural to make it about Jekyll. An implicature would then result: for example, 'Isn't it a shame that someone with a successful medical practice would take on a despicable personality like this Hyde fellow has.' Again, the conversational implicature analysis appears to take us in a generally satisfactory direction, at least. But the analysis only makes a contribution if we take these examples as utterances, not sentences, as is to be expected. The problem involving the truth of the *sentence* 'Mr Hyde has a successful medical practice', or whether or not the *sentence* 'The evening star is the morning star' is tautological, apart from any such *utterances*, is little elucidated by a Gricean analysis. This is also to be expected.

Logical operators: conjunction

Sentences with 'and' conjunctions were a problem because the order of the conjunctions seem to be interpreted, if possible, as indicating that the first conjunct happened first and the second later. In a truth-based semantics system independent of the context of utterance, the order of conjunctions ought to be irrelevant. To repeat our example, to utter 'Herman and Sarah got married and had a baby' gives the strong impression that the baby came after the couple's wedding. We have already seen that the inference about the order is cancelable; reversing the conjunctions ('Herman and Sarah had a baby and got married') invites the conclusion that the baby was born out of wedlock, but this conclusion can be canceled by adding 'but not in that order'. This case seems to be a good place for the application of one of Grice's maxims, but which one? The fourth submaxim of manner, 'Be orderly' seems appropriate. It is reasonable that an obvious order for the presentation of information about events in time would be the order in which they occurred. In this case, the implicature arises by assuming that a speaker is *observing* the maxim of manner, rather than by flouting it.

The further meaning that commonly arises from the order of conjuncts, that the event in the first conjunct caused the event in the second (as in 'I stepped in a hole and broke my foot') has the property of being cancelable. I can say 'I stepped in a hole and broke my foot by dropping a brick on it. I've had nothing but bad luck today.' It is not quite so easy to appeal to the fourth submaxim of manner in this case, though. It is true that causes generally precede effects and if a speaker were to present a cause and an effect it would be orderly to present the cause first. The problem comes when inferring that the speaker is talking about a cause and effect relationship in the first place, since many things can happen before other things without causing them. Saying 'Horace brushed his teeth and cut himself shaving' would not mean that the tooth-brushing caused the shaving accident, for example. We might appeal to the first submaxim of quantity, 'Make your contribution as informative as required.'

If we can assume that the conversationalists tacitly agree that a cause–effect relation is important to what is being talked about, then if nothing explicit is said about cause and effect, a hearer would conclude that the speaker intends the cause to have been the event in the first conjunct and the effect in the second, assuming the cooperative principle. If the speaker is being cooperative, and cause and effect is necessary information, the hearer would conclude that the speaker believes he or she *has* given the information and that the hearer can readily find it. A completely plausible inference would be that the information is in the order of presentation. As Kempson (1975:36) has pointed out, conjunction is not even necessary. If someone says 'My left front tire blew out. Before I knew what was happening, the car swerved to the left', it is most natural to conclude that the blowout caused the car to swerve. Grice's approach seems to enable us to say that the order of conjuncts has nothing to do with the meaning of the sentence, as far as semantics is concerned, but the information about order of events and causation arises by conversational implicature when the sentence is uttered.

Logical operators: disjunction

The logic of disjunction is sufficiently complex that it bears a brief review here. If inclusive 'or' is intended, 'p or q' is true if p is true and q is false, if p is false and q is true, or if p and q are both true. In other words, as long as at least one conjunct is true, the whole expression is true. If exclusive 'or' is involved, then 'p or q' is true if p is true and q is false, or if p is false and q is true, but it is *false* if p and q are both true. We have already seen that it is possible to interpret 'Henry likes either apples or bananas' in three ways. Two of these correspond to the inclusive and exclusive interpretations of 'or'. You could say, for example: 'Henry doesn't like fruit much, but I know there is one fruit he does like. He likes apples or bananas, but I don't know which.' But the following context is equally possible:

Harvey: Henry likes apples or bananas.
Sandra: You're wrong, Harvey, he likes both.
Harvey: How does that make me wrong?

Harvey would have every right to be puzzled that Sandra takes her comment to be a contradiction, because Henry's liking both fruits would naturally be taken as included in Harvey's first statement. The third meaning is the one in which the speaker is saying that Henry likes precisely *both* fruits, and would be misunderstood if the listener takes it to mean he likes only one of them. We will have to return to this in the next chapter, where I will introduce the pragmatic principle of politeness (R. Lakoff 1973a; Brown and Levinson 1978) and the broader notion of hearer-option (Schiffrin 1987).

It is not difficult to think of contexts where the exclusive 'or' meaning is the most natural. To take Gazdar's (1979) example: 'John is either patriotic or quixotic.' It seems most natural to hear it as meaning: 'John is either patriotic or quixotic, but not both.' One way to explain the tendency to take this interpretation is to follow Horn's (1972) inclusion of 'and' and 'or' in the list of scalar items, and to exploit this analysis in conjunction with the first submaxim of quantity, 'Make your contribution as informative as is required' (Gazdar 1979:55–62, 1980; Levinson 1983). The two-item scale would look like this:

$$\{and_1, \text{ or } _2\}$$

If 'and' is higher on the scale, then the use of 'or' would convey the meaning that John is not both patriotic and quixotic, even though the meaning of 'or' would allow that interpretation. The reasoning is that if the speaker were ready to say John has both characteristics, he would have used the stronger 'and'. We are now in a position to say why this should be so. Since the first submaxim of quantity obliges a speaker to give as much information as possible without violating the maxim of quality, it must be that the speaker is not prepared to say that John is both patriotic and quixotic. This analysis allows us to retain an independent semantic analysis by which English 'or' has only the inclusive 'or' meaning with the apparently exclusive 'or' reading arising only when the sentence is actually uttered by a particular speaker, via the scalarity principle and the interaction of the maxims of quantity and quality. If this is the case, the implicature should be cancelable, and it is. There would be nothing wrong with saying 'John is either patriotic or quixotic, or maybe both.'

No speaker could cancel the exclusive implication if the concept of the world is such that both conjunctions could not simultaneously express true propositions. 'John is in the living room or in the library, or maybe both', or 'John is out driving the Toyota or the Mercedes or maybe both' do not work, but this has nothing to do with the semantics or the pragmatics of 'or'. Rather, asserting both conjuncts simultaneously conflicts with our assumption that the name 'John' refers to an ordinary person and with our assumptions about what is possible for ordinary people. Notice that it would be perfectly all right for a clergyman located in the USA, for example, to say 'God is both here with us and with our brethren in Nepal.'[17] At the same time, the first submaxim of quantity still leads the hearer to assume that the speaker who says 'John is either in the living room or in the library' has supplied all the information possible while observing the maxim of quality; that is, the person does not know which of the two rooms John is in. Or does it? Recall from our discussion of the Malagasy ethnography of communication in chapter 2 that a Malagasy could very well make just such an utterance, knowing full well which room John is in, without violating the Malagasy version of the cooperative principle. This is another issue we will come back to.

The conclusion of all of this is that the semantics of English 'or' is close to or identical with the inclusive 'or' of classical logic. The very strong tendency to interpret a sentence like 'John is either patriotic or quixotic' as excluding the 'or both' reading, making it seem to be a case of exclusive 'or' is the result of a modification of the semantic force of English 'or' by means of a conversational implicature. Semantic analyses that suggest that English 'or' is ambiguous between the inclusive and exclusive meanings, are considered mistaken by scholars who accept a Gricean treatment. In fact, Gazdar (1979) argues that there is no reason to believe that any natural language has an exclusive 'or'.[18]

Logical operators: quantifiers and scalars

The solution that was suggested for disjunction involves the interaction of Horn's idea of scalarity, the maxim of quality and the first submaxim of quantity. Take, for example, the sentence 'Some of the books are expensive.' 'Some' is lower on the same quantifier scale than 'all' is. If all the books are actually expensive, logically some of them are, as we have seen. In such a circumstance, though, saying 'Some of the books are expensive' does not give all the available information, and so does not conform to the first submaxim of quantity, 'Make your contribution as informative as is required.' However, if the speaker knows that not all the books are expensive, or does not have enough evidence that they are, he or she is obliged by the maxim of quality not to use the higher-scaled quantifier 'all'. Assuming, as always, that the speaker is being cooperative and is not violating the maxims, and in the absence of evidence that he or she is flouting them, the conversation participant who hears 'Some of the books are expensive', concludes that, for all the speaker knows, some of them are not expensive; if the speaker was sure all of them were expensive he or she would surely have said so. We would treat other examples in an analogous way. The mother who says she has four boys is heard as saying she has no more than four; if she has five, the first submaxim would require her to say so. Cooperatively saying 'The coffee is warm' means you cannot truthfully say that it is hot.

The last example suggests another level of use of a Gricean analysis. Suppose a woman sips coffee from her cup, winces, breathes in deeply, and with a distressed look on her face says 'Whew, this coffee is a bit warm!' Since it is obvious that she finds the coffee downright hot, it would seem that the cooperative principle has failed. But this would be wrong. The speaker has made it clear that she finds the coffee hot, so she is not violating the cooperative principle. Rather, she is flouting one of its maxims, thereby generating an additional conversational implicature. The coffee is obviously hot, but the speaker has only said that it is warm. The hearer has to look for a reason why. It may be that the speaker does not want to complain overtly about being served overly hot coffee, or may simply be taking pleasure in raising the hearer's involvement in the conversation (in Tannen's sense) by giving the hearer more of the work of interpreting the meaning of the utterance.[19]

As we have seen, one test of a Gricean analysis by conversational implicature is to see if the posited implicature is capable of being canceled. All of these are. There is nothing wrong with saying:

Some of the books are expensive; actually all of them are.
I have four boys; in fact I have five.
The coffee is warm; it's hot, in fact.

Compare these examples with, say, 'Some of the books are expensive; actually a few of them are', or 'I have four boys; in fact I have three', where the elaboration is heard as a correction of the original assertion rather than an implicature-canceling clarification.

Logical operators: conditionals and 'invited inferences'

At first blush, it appears that the tendency to 'perfect' conditionals noticed by Geis and Zwicky (1971) will be another routine case of the application of the maxims of quality and quantity to a Horn-scale. It turns out not to be so for two reasons. Crucially, in the invited inferences case, the scale runs in the wrong direction. 'If and only if' would be higher than 'if' on a scale. If it is true to say, 'If and only if you take your medicine, you will get better', it would also be true to say, 'If you take your medicine, you will get better', but not the reverse, since the second conditional sentence logically leaves open the possibility that you will get better even if you do not take your medicine. If we try to apply the reasoning we have used so far to Geis and Zwicky's example, 'If you mow the lawn, I will give you five dollars', we get the exact opposite implication from the one they get. Since the speaker has said only, 'If you mow the lawn . . .', we would reason, it must be that that person cannot truthfully say the more informative, 'If and only if you mow the lawn . . .'. Therefore the speaker must mean to convey that I might get the five dollars even if I do not mow the lawn. The actual result, I would agree with Geis and Zwicky, is the opposite.

Several scholars interested in linguistic meaning have mentioned this problem (Geis and Zwicky 1971; Boër and Lycan 1973:501–2; Gazdar 1979:87; Levinson 1983:146). We have already seen that Geis and Zwicky themselves and Lilje (1972) both mention 'attitudes toward the exchange of money in our society'. Boër and Lycan (1973) also refer to events that can be expected in a given society. Analysts seem to have difficulty talking about conditional perfection without also talking about a wider cultural or social setting, in addition to a speech event. Assuming people use sociocultural evidence to decide which of the maxims is appropriate, an analysis would go something like this (from the hearer's perspective):

> Someone has just said 'If you mow the lawn, I'll give you five dollars'. I take this to be, and I assume the speaker knows I will take this to be, a service-for-hire event. In a service-for-hire event the conditions to be met by the hirer and hiree are all that is relevant, or at least the most salient. I assume, in the absence of evidence of maxim-flouting, that the speaker is obeying both submaxims of quantity, 'Make your contribution as informative as is required' and 'Do not make your contribution more informative than is required', as well as the maxim of relation, 'Be relevant.' Therefore, his utterance contains no more or less than the service required (I mow the lawn) and the obligations of the employer (he'll give me five dollars). If there were some other service I could perform for five dollars, he is being uncooperative by not giving me the information about it.[20]

In Lilje's example, 'If you scratch on the eight-ball, you lose the game', something like the following Gricean analysis can be proposed:

> Someone has just said 'If you scratch on the eight-ball, you lose the game'. I take this to be, and I assume the speaker knows I will take

this to be, a rule-of-a-game explanation event. In a rule-of-a-game explanation event, not all the rules can be given in one utterance. Unless and until I am given a complete explanation, my understanding of what the rules of the game allow is necessarily incomplete. I now know that one can lose in pool by scratching on the eight-ball. I assume, in the absence of evidence of maxim-flouting, that the speaker is obeying both submaxims of quantity, 'Make your contribution as informative as is required' and 'Do not make your contribution more informative than is required', as well as the maxim of relation, 'Be relevant.' Therefore, in the absence of a complete explanation, I can only assume the information I have so far is relevant and necessary; there may be more information about the rules of pool that it is not necessary for me to know immediately. Consequently, there may be another way to lose at pool than the one way mentioned so far.

In short, the maxims are applied relative to the characteristics of the kind of speech event the participants know is ongoing. It seems that in the context of most speech events, the maxims of quantity and quality require a speaker to use a term from as high a position on a Horn-scale as possible, but no higher. In some cases it is possible to convey the information associated with an item higher on the scale by using one lower on the scale. One of the situations which allow this to happen might be due to culturally-defined properties of the speech event. Conditional perfection in the lawn-mowing example would be one such case.[21]

EVALUATION

I never gave a satisfactory Gricean account for deixis. We also have had to defer one or two problems connected with disjunction and with 'invited inferences' to the next chapter where the influence of cultural value systems will be discussed. Aside from these, though, the range of facts we have considered show considerable promise for Grice's contention that natural languages are not divergent from logic systems so far as truth-based considerations are concerned, as long as implicatures can be isolated in a principled way. This seems to open the way for associating semantics with the truth conditions of *sentences*, considered independently of their use, and pragmatics as being the additional meaning which results from the various implicatures that arise when *utterances* occur in context. This would give us a tidy separation of semantics and pragmatics, with pragmatics (but not semantics) as a topic in the sociolinguistics of language. There are two serious flaws with this conclusion, however. One has to do with the fact that many scholars seem unwilling to make such a strict distinction between sentences and utterances. Let us take Gazdar's (1979) work as one example. He offers the somewhat tongue-in-cheek formula: 'Pragmatics = Meaning − Truth conditions' as a crude definition of his concept of pragmatics. This would seem to translate into: 'Meaning = Pragmatics + Semantics', provided semantics is all about truth conditions.

This appears to allow a strict separation between semantics and pragmatics. However, Gazdar (1979:165–8) argues against the autonomy of semantics on the grounds that the truth conditions of a 'sentence' sometimes depend on the results of operations that are pragmatic. One example he uses is a case originally discussed by Wilson (1975:151): 'To have a child and get married is worse than getting married and having a child.' We have seen that it is possible to take the sequential interpretation of 'to have a child' and 'getting married' as an implicature derived via Grice's maxims, and Gazdar would agree that this is the correct general approach. Nevertheless, he takes Wilson's example to be strong evidence in favor of the necessity of determining the pragmatic properties of 'sentences' before it is possible to determine their truth conditions. Unless we interpret the clause about getting married and the one about having a child sequentially, we have no hope of deciding if the 'sentence' is true or not.

A way around this problem is to insist that Wilson's example, with the interpretation she (and Gazdar) intend, cannot be understood as a *sentence* but only as an *utterance*. As a sentence, it is complete nonsense, as much so as 'The number 1 is greater than the number 1', or 'To have blond hair and blue eyes is better than to have blue eyes and blond hair.' Since you cannot be following the cooperative principle and still utter complete nonsense, one cannot imagine anyone uttering the sentence without intending the sequential interpretation. But then the question of truth has to be asked about the proposition that is *conveyed* by the sentence that is uttered, namely: 'To have a child first and then get married is worse than getting married first and then having a child.' This strikes me as a reasonable solution. Apparently, however, it is not a move Gazdar would be willing to make, and perhaps most scholars in the field would agree with him.

Separating the sentences from utterances does not help at all where deictics or indexicals are concerned. Deictics, as you will remember, are items like personal pronouns, tenses, and time and space locators like 'here', 'now', and 'tomorrow'. The reference of these items can in principle never be determined until a sentence is uttered. As we saw, the truth of 'I am the British Prime Minister' cannot be determined until we hear someone make the utterance, so that we can discover what the referent of 'I' is. We also saw that the referent of 'I' (and of deictics in general) is not a matter of implicature. Telling evidence for this is that

we cannot cancel their meaning; I cannot say 'I' and successfully claim I
was referring to Margaret Thatcher when I said 'I'. Deictics would appear
to be a conclusive demonstration of the fact that even if semantics is
limited to matters of truth, it cannot only be about sentences understood
as divorced from context. Many, maybe most, scholars interested in
pragmatics would settle for an understanding of semantics as being at
least about truth, including truth that is dependent on the identity of
deictic referents. Pragmatics would then be about implicatures as they
arise in context via some notion related to Grice's conversational
implicatures, and a concept of semantics and pragmatics as heavily
intertwined.[22]

MODIFICATIONS OF GRICE'S APPROACH

Not all scholars of linguistic pragmatics have been willing to accept Grice's
analysis as he presents it. There are at least three current attempts to
streamline Grice's original concept of conversational implicature that are
promising, mostly because they involve the reduction of the number of
maxims. One of these is Horn's (1984) notion of the 'pragmatic division
of labor'. The basic idea is that the maxim of quality is to be maintained
as a special case but, of the others, only quantity and relevance are really
needed. The two surviving maxims lead to opposite kinds of implicatures.
Quantity leads to 'Q-implicatures' of the type 'I've said as much as I can,
you can't infer any more.' Relevance leads to 'R-implicatures' of the type
'I've said only as much as I must, I know you can work out the rest.'
One of Horn's (1984:15) examples is: 'It's possible John solved the
problem', which Q-implicates that the speaker does not know whether
John actually did solve the problem. This contrasts with 'John was able
to solve the problem' which R-implicates that he actually did solve the
problem. Of course, these two kinds of implicature lead to opposite
results and most of Horn's article is about how you know which one is
in force.

Levinson (1987) has developed a similar system, although he does not
think relevance is responsible for implicatures which go beyond what was
said. (He accepts a view of quantity-based implicatures that is essentially
the same as Horn's.) Instead, he posits an 'I-principle' ('I' for 'informativeness'), from which these principles are derived. Levinson deals with
the resolution of a clash between the two kinds of implicatures in a
somewhat different manner from the way Horn does, and extends the
analysis to apply it to problems in conversational analysis and syntax.

Sperber and Wilson (1986, 1987) have reduced the entire Gricean
mechanism to a matter of relevance. Their work required an entire book
to develop and cannot be summarized here. If they are found to be

successful, it would be a desirable outcome on the assumption that if a theory that can account for as much with fewer principles as a competing theory can with more principles, then it is the superior theory. In any event, all three of these developments seem certain to play a role in future discussions of conversational implicature.

SUMMARY

Since pragmatics is about making inferences about meaning based on *context*, it can be considered a topic in the sociolinguistics of language. It becomes clear, when we consider a range of cases, that the meanings that can be derived from a truth- and logic-based semantics of sentences out of context are only a part of the meanings that are conveyed if we imagine the same cases as utterances in context. The philosopher of language, H. Paul Grice, has taken the position that natural languages are as precise as artificially-created logic systems, but only when the meanings that emerge in conversations are factored out. To accomplish this, he has proposed the *cooperative principle* and associated set of conversational maxims by means of which *conversational implicatures* can be created in context which go beyond the literal meaning of sentences. Grice's approach is reasonably successful when it is applied to many of the problematic cases, and his work has been immensely influential in the study of linguistic pragmatics.

A few problems do not yield gracefully to a Grice-style analysis, particularly *deixis*. Most students of linguistic pragmatics would probably stop short of the total separation of semantic meaning and pragmatic meaning. They would prefer to see them as partly separable, but partly overlapping or intertwined. Some scholars, although they remain impressed with Grice's general insight, have tried to simplify and streamline his theory. Laurence Horn and Stephen Levinson are two pragmaticists who have attempted to do this, but perhaps the most comprehensive attempt – and the one currently receiving the most attention – is Sperber and Wilson's attempt to build a pragmatic theory on the concept of relevance.

NOTES

1   I am indebted to my colleague Deborah Schiffrin for suggesting this definition, one that summarizes what the diffuse field of pragmatics is about better than any I know.
2   Levinson would no doubt agree that there are British and American scholars of pragmatics whose work fits the Continental interpretation.
3   In the government-binding theory of Noam Chomsky (for instance, Chomsky 1981, 1988), for example, pragmatics issues are largely excluded and syntax and semantics are treated in separate modules (the semantics module is called 'logical form').

4 I have used McCawley (1981) as a reference for my discussion here. However, any errors or misemphases in the discussion are, of course, my sole responsibility.

5 As we will see in the next chapter, presupposition involves a lot more than reference.

6 Deictic terms are also commonly called *indexicals*.

7 Technically, a tautology is a proposition (for example, 'Jane is either at home or Jane is not at home') that is true regardless of the truth of its constituent propositions. The example I have just given does not fit the technical definition

8 For discussion of some of these issues, see McCawley (1981:288–96).

9 Notice that the temporal sequence inference seems natural only if verb phrases or whole sentences are conjoined. Take the following hypothetical utterances:

> Harry and Sylvia went to London.
> Hubert is sad and lonely.
> Sharon made telephone calls from home and from the office.

You would not infer that Harry went to London first and Sylvia went later (the most straightforward interpretation is that they went together), and you would not assume that Hubert became sad first and lonely later (it is more natural to take it that he is sad *because* he is lonely), nor would you feel misled if you discovered that Sharon made her phone calls from the office first.

10 There is, in addition, a well-known problem with inclusive and exclusive 'or' and negation, but it is too complicated to go into here.

11 The alternative expression of the third submaxim of Manner, 'Avoid unnecessary prolixity', has always struck me as rather an example of what it forbids, so much so that I often wonder if Grice had tongue planted in cheek when he wrote it.

12 Some people seem to think that members of my own profession, college professors, are especially prone to being guilty of this. Personally, I disagree, of course!

13 I am sure my readers would agree that (b) makes the review more enjoyable than if the reviewer had written 'Miss X sang "Home sweet home" so poorly that her performance cannot really be called "singing".' Perhaps part of the reason is related to the concept of high-involvement conversational style discussed in chapter 3. Since the reader has to draw the implicature, with some effort, from (b), the reviewer and the reader must both be involved in getting the message right. The reader can thus feel part of the construction of the review, instead of just absorbing the reviewer's opinion.

14 Grice says that this has to be *possible* for the analyst, not that conversational participants themselves necessarily go through the exercise.

15 Actually, most linguists agree that natural language semantics should be regarded as bivalent (that is, there are only two truth values, true or false).

16 An actor playing the role of the British Prime Minister in a play could felicitously say this, though. It is also true that if we regard tense as deictic, the time-reference of the present tense in historical present can be explicitly denied. Someone can say 'I'm sitting at my desk, see, I'm minding my own business, and she walks up to me and starts making all kinds of remarks. By the way, I'm talking about what happened yesterday morning.' In fact, it is possible to argue that the historical present arises as a conversational implicature. A speaker standing in your living room who says 'I'm sitting at my desk' is obviously flouting the first submaxim of quality, 'Do not say that which you believe to be false.' The force of a narrative in the historical present (something like, 'This narrative is being presented with the immediacy of an event that you are actually witnessing') could be said to be a conversational implicature. I have no explanations to offer for these facts. For a discussion of the historical present, see Wolfson (1979) and Schiffrin (1981).

17 Interestingly, it would be inappropriate for a devout person who believes in an

omnipresent God to say 'God is either here or in Nepal' precisely because a believer *should* be prepared to say God is in both places.

18   Whether to accept the conclusion that 'or' is necessarily inclusive, on the basis of a Gricean or other line of argument, remains controversial. Aside from Gazdar (1979), see Pelletier (1977), Horn (1985), Browne (1986) and the references they cite for further discussion. Cf. Schiffrin (1987:177–90) for some discourse advantages for interpreting 'or' as inclusive.

19   The stereotypical English understatement phenomenon, which might allow a full-scale riot to be described as 'a bit of unpleasantness', or a fabulously wealthy individual as someone who 'lives rather comfortably' is an example of the interaction of cultural values with Grice-type analyses. There will be more on this idea later.

20   Of course, I do not mean to say that a little boy with a lawn mower goes through all these explicit steps. These steps are for the *analyst* analyzing the hypothetical situation from the hearer's perspective.

21   Explanations based on the properties of the speech event are not sufficient, though. Such an explanation does not even cover Geis and Zwicky's first cited example, 'If John leans out of that window any further, he'll fall', which does not belong to any well-defined culturally relevant speech event. The issue of implicatures going in two directions has been addressed by Horn (1984) and by Levinson (1987).

22   My own present view is that semantics should be strictly about sentential meaning out of context and – here is the shocker – does not include deictic reference. Pragmatics is strictly about the meanings that result when someone utters something at some time and in some place. A textbook like this is not the place to defend this view, and it should not be taken seriously until it is defended.

6

More on Linguistic Pragmatics

INTRODUCTION

It is true that H. Paul Grice's work is of very great importance to linguistic pragmatics, but there are several other core themes, even within the so-called Anglo-American tradition of pragmatic scholarship. They also have a bearing on the question I am treating as central: the degree to which semantics and pragmatics can be separated. Among these themes are three that we will take up in this chapter: speech acts, politeness, and presupposition. Although I will not develop it to the extent it really deserves, there will also be an introduction to the broader Continental style of pragmatic research.

SPEECH ACTS

Properties of speech acts

In 1955, the philosopher John Austin delivered the William James Lectures at Harvard University. This series of lectures, later published as Austin (1962), were destined to have a profound influence on the study of language and meaning both in the philosophy of language and in linguistic pragmatics. Austin had noted that there were certain classes of sentences for which truth conditions seem to be simply irrelevant. These sentences were in the present tense indicative active, and had first-person subjects. They did not describe or report anything and it made no sense to speak of them as true or false. They had an additional, somewhat startling property: 'the uttering of the sentence is, or is part of, the doing of an action, which again would not *normally* be described as saying something' (Austin 1962:5).

Uttering such sentences, which Austin called *performatives*, is not so much *saying* something as *doing* something. An example of a performative utterance is, 'I promise to pay you what I owe next week.' Such an utterance would be reported as, 'She promised to pay me back next week', not, 'She said a promise to pay me back next week.' If you wanted to report the speech act using what grammarians call the pseudo-cleft construction, you would say 'What she *did* was promise to pay me what she owes next week', not 'What she *said* was promise to pay me what she owes next week.' Furthermore, if the promise is not kept, it would be very odd to say 'Her promise was not true', although you could say her promise was insincere or that she promised but did not mean it. Austin mentioned a number of verbs in English that can be used in just this way. In addition to 'promise', these verbs include 'bet', 'congratulate', and 'advise'. Not only are performatives, or *speech acts* as they are also called, not subject to truth conditions, but they can scarcely be analyzed at all without taking into account a speaker and a hearer and what they intend and understand by the use of these forms.

Dealing with performatives with Grice's approach would mean we would have to find a meaning for them in terms of truth or falsity and then detect some further meaning that a speaker means to convey, given the context. Performatives, in their *explicit performative utterance* (EPU) form mentioned by Austin, appear to make it impossible to take the first step. As a result, a Gricean analysis would be of no use where EPUs are concerned. EPUs are sentences that follow a particular formula. In their fullest form, they have (1) a first-person subject, (2) an explicit performative verb in the present affirmative indicative active, (3) a second-person pronoun which may be preceded by a preposition, and (4) a clause expressing the propositional content of the utterance, possibly introduced by a complementizer. The following are a few examples.

I promise you to mop the kitchen floor
1   2   3   4

I apologize to you for bumping into you
1   2   3   4

I request of you that you take your feet off my desk
1   2   3   4

The parts of the EPU formula that I have labeled 3 and 4 are optional for some speech acts. You can promise explicitly by saying 'I promise' or apologize by saying 'I apologize'. You cannot request by saying 'I request', but you can leave out 'of you'. A sentence in EPU form does not *necessarily* represent the performance of the speech act named by the performative verb. A woman could say to her husband, for example,

'Tell me again, what do you always do to make it up to me when I'm angry with you?' He could reply, 'I promise you to mop the kitchen floor' without performing a promise. Instead he is simply reporting his normal behavior under the circumstances, which happens to be that he makes a promise. The use of the word 'hereby' directly before the performative verb is a handy test of whether you have a speech act. If it does not distort your understanding of the sentence to insert the 'hereby', except to make the sentence stilted, you have a speech act in Austin's sense. If you can turn 'I promise you to mop the kitchen floor' into 'I hereby promise you to mop the kitchen floor' without doing any more damage than to distort the style, a promise is intended. If the husband in the example I just gave were to put 'hereby' into his answer, it would not be an answer to his wife's question.

Of course, such speech acts are not always performed by means of EPUs. In fact, they very seldom are. As we will see shortly, when performative force is conveyed indirectly, Gricean implicatures are very much in the picture. Explicit performative utterances, though, remain as a problem for an independent truth-based semantics.

Although it does not make much sense to say that a speech act is true or that it is false, things can go wrong with them. For example, I can say, 'I bet you sixpence it will rain tomorrow' (one of Austin's examples), or 'I sentence you to two years in jail', and the utterance will have these properties. Of course, it would be odd to reply to the bet by saying 'That's not true', or to the sentence by saying 'That's all too true.' Yet these speech acts can come out either well or badly in another sense. For example, if you reply to the bet utterance with 'Forget it, I've heard the weather forecast, too', the bet is not actually made. If the person who pronounces the jail sentence is not a judge, there really is no sentence.

Austin called the things that can and do go wrong with speech acts *infelicities* and proposed a set of six general *felicity conditions* which must be met if the speech act is not to go wrong. I give these in modified form below:

A.1   There has to be such a speech act recognized by the society.
A.2   It has to be performed by the right person under the right circumstances.
B.1   It has to be performed correctly.
B.2   It has to be performed completely.
Γ.1   The person or persons involved in performing the speech act has to have the thoughts and feelings connected with that speech act, if any.
Γ.2   The person or persons have to conduct themselves subsequently as if they had the right thoughts and feelings.

Austin switches from Latin A and B to Greek Γ for a reason. If there is a violation of an A or B felicity condition, the effect of the speech act simply does not come about. In the USA or Britain you cannot divorce your spouse by saying 'I divorce you' (although it is said that this is possible in Muslim societies) because, while these societies recognize divorce, it is not achieved by means of a speech act. If an American or British man tried to divorce his wife by means of this sentence, the divorce would not happen. There would be an A.1 felicity condition violation. If the speaker of the sentencing example above is not a judge, or if he or she is a judge and utters the sentence at a party, the addressee will not actually be sentenced; there is an A.2 violation. The conditions labeled B.1 and B.2 concern how the speech act is performed, not the surrounding circumstances. The bet that was not accepted in the example I gave is a case of an incomplete speech act and fails to go through because of the B.2 violation. If a will includes the speech act 'I bequeath my automobile to my nephew Humperdink' and the deceased did not own an automobile, the speech act was incorrectly performed and Humperdink does not get an automobile.

The Γ felicity conditions are different. If someone attempts a speech act but violates one of them, the speech act comes off, although there is something wrong with it. If I promise you to repay the loan you have just made me within a week, with no intention of carrying it out, and with a mocking smile on my face and a thinly disguised wink to my friend standing nearby, you may be quite convinced I will not keep the promise, but you cannot say I never promised to pay you back. I have committed a Γ.1 infelicity and no doubt a Γ.2 infelicity into the bargain, but I have made a promise anyway, even if it is a flawed one. If I apologize for stepping on your toe while grinning and giggling while I am speaking, I am no doubt guilty of a Γ.1 infelicity, but I have still apologized.

Fraser (1974) makes the distinction between *vernacular* and *ceremonial* speech acts. Vernacular speech acts are ones that can be performed by any member of a society in the normal course of daily interaction. Ceremonial speech acts, like christening, sentencing, and pronouncing people husband and wife, require that the speaker performing them has a special institutionally supported status and that the act be performed under the correct circumstances (hence, someone who is posing as a judge cannot really sentence you, even after a court trial, and neither can a real judge sentence you during a party). Much of Austin's discussion involves ceremonial speech acts. His A and B infelicities seem not to apply very well to vernacular speech acts. The A.1 felicity condition seems to be there so we have a way of saying what would be wrong if someone said something like 'I hereby sweet-talk you that you look lovely this evening.' You would not expect anyone to actually try a nonexistent speech act, either ceremonial or vernacular. The A.2 condition, as far as

I can see, applies only to ceremonial speech acts. Austin's examples of B.1 infelicities, where the speaker says the wrong thing, involve ceremonial speech acts, like the legacy example, or christening a ship with the wrong name. It is hard to imagine a credible scenario where a vernacular speech act was performed incorrectly, in Austin's sense. If you said 'I rejoice to you that I stepped on your toe', it would certainly misfire, as Austin puts it, if you intend it as an apology, but I cannot imagine anyone making a mistaken apology of that kind. Austin's example of the bet that is not accepted is an excellent example of an incomplete speech act, and betting is a vernacular speech act at that. But I am hard pressed to come up with another example, whether vernacular or ceremonial, short of an instance in which the speaker is struck on the mouth by a golf ball at mid-utterance, or something of the sort.[1]

A similar distinction is made by Bach and Harnish (1979), who distinguish *conventional* speech acts from those that are not. Bach and Harnish's conventional speech acts are essentially the same as Fraser's ceremonial speech acts. Their theory of the *speech act schema* is designed to cover roughly the same range of facts as the kind of analysis I am about to take up. It is important to note that their speech act schema theory is meant to apply only to nonconventional speech acts, roughly vernacular ones.

The Γ infelicities are much more important to vernacular speech acts and have been the subject of further analysis. John Searle (1969, 1975, 1979, 1983; Searle and Vanderveken 1985) has devoted a great deal of attention to speech acts. In Searle (1969), he proposed that speech acts are subject to four kinds of conditions on their use: propositional content conditions, preparatory conditions, sincerity conditions, and an essential condition. These differ from one speech act to another. The propositional content conditions specify aspects of what the act can be about. For example, requests are about future acts of the hearer and apologies are about past acts of the speaker. The sincerity condition, and perhaps the preparatory conditions, are related to Austin's Γ felicity conditions, particularly Γ.1. For example, Searle's (1969:67) conditions on *advising* are:

Propositional content condition	Future act of the hearer.
Preparatory conditions	Speaker has some reason to believe the act will benefit the hearer. It is not obvious to both the speaker and hearer that the hearer will do the act in the normal course of events.
Sincerity condition	Speaker believes the act will benefit the hearer.

Essential condition   Counts as an undertaking to
                                         the effect that the act is in the
                                         hearer's best interest.

For instance, if you say to me 'I advise you to eat lower-cholesterol foods', the propositional content, eating lower-cholesterol foods, is a future act that I, the hearer, am supposed to carry out. Before you can give the advice appropriately, you have to have a reason to believe that eating lower-cholesterol foods will benefit me, and it cannot be obvious that I would not control my diet in this way even if you did not give me the advice. For instance, the advice would be hollow if I am a strict vegetarian who never eats dairy products or eggs. You cannot sincerely give me this advice if you are not convinced it will benefit me. Finally, advice is 'an undertaking to the effect that an act [like eating lower-cholesterol foods] is in the hearer's best interest.'

One more important distinction made by Austin (1969:94–107) concerns the three kinds of action associated with any utterance. The first is *locutionary*, which is the simple act of saying something and meaning the things you say. By *perlocutionary* is meant the effect that you produce by saying what you say. A boy in an unattended class of rowdy children might produce the perlocutionary effect of alarming his classmates if he says 'The teacher's coming!' The *illocutionary* action or force is what is done in the act of saying something. Of the three, looking at some utterance as a locutionary act is the simplest; it is simply the act of talking. Of the other two, one way of thinking of the difference is that the illocutionary force is inevitable, if the act goes through at all (that is, if there are no A or B infelicities). As I mentioned, even an insincere promise is a promise. By contrast, convincing is a perlocutionary effect. No matter what I say, whether or not you are convinced is up to you. I may wish to convince you that I will keep my promise, and you cannot avoid being promised (short of stopping me from finishing the utterance of the promise), but you can decline to be convinced that I will do what I say. This is one difference between illocutionary force and perlocutionary force or effect. The upshot is that speech acts, in the sense used by Austin and Searle, are the same thing as illocutionary acts, and we can speak of their illocutionary forces.

Indirect speech acts

In everyday life, it is rare for someone to use an explicit performative utterance of the form 'I offer to you to help fix your car.' If offers are not made in this way, how are they made? One answer is that they are made by means of *indirect speech acts*. Gordon and Lakoff (1971/1975; cf. Searle 1975, 1979, chapter 2) propose a relationship between this kind of condition on speech acts and a way of conveying the same act indirectly. Briefly, it is possible to get across the illocutionary force of a given speech act by saying something involving one of its conditions. To take *advising* again: since a condition on a felicitous act of advising is that the speaker believes the act will benefit the hearer, a speaker can exert the same illocutionary force by saying, 'I believe you would be better off eating lower-cholesterol food' as he or she would by saying 'I advise you to eat lower-cholesterol food.' In other words, after hearing the former, I could justifiably report what had happened by saying 'That person advised me to eat lower-cholesterol food.'

Advice is not a particularly good example for illustrating indirect speech acts. A better example is apologies. It seems to me that there are the following conditions on fully felicitous apologies (I will not attempt to put them into Searle's categories):[2]

1   the speaker is responsible for the act for which he or she is apologizing;
2   the speaker regrets the act;
3   the act is detrimental to the hearer.

In principle, it ought to be possible to use any of the three to convey the apology, but one of the three lends itself far better than the rest, namely the second. When an apology is called for, the speaker would be disinclined to try to use 3, which focuses on the offense to the hearer. This becomes especially clear when we recognize that the most common response to an apology is not either to accept it or reject it, but to *deflect* it. Since deflection is the hearer's role, it is best to leave the third condition open so that the hearer can use it to deflect the apology by saying, 'It was nothing', or 'That's all right'; in other words to ritually deny condition 3. Still, in some cases, one might get across an indirect apology by saying 'Oh, did that hurt?' or 'Gosh, did I step on your toe? Gee!' The first condition is not usually open as a means for giving an indirect apology because it is usually obvious that the speaker is responsible. If you were to run into a woman shopping at a grocery store and make her spill her groceries, she would not be much mollified if you said, 'Oh dear, I made you spill your groceries.' On the other hand, I once caught myself using this very condition to apologize indirectly and the apology was successful. At a series of lectures, a linguist I know left the auditorium between lectures. I wanted to talk to the person she was next to, so I moved up to her seat. The next lecture started before I could return to my seat and, just as it was starting, the original occupant came back and sat in another seat. After the lecturer had finished, I turned to her and said, 'I took your seat.' She responded 'That's OK.' I have taken the liberty of relating this anecdote because I later had the opportunity to discuss the incident with my friend, and she told me that she took my remark as an apology, as I had certainly intended it. It was appropriate, because she could not be sure I recognized that she had a claim on the seat.

I am sure the overwhelming majority of apologies are conveyed indirectly by means of the second condition, 'The speaker regrets the act', and with the use of 'I'm sorry.' The second condition lends itself to the task better than the other two, because it involves the speaker's 'thoughts and feelings' which, unlike his or her responsibility for the act, are never self-evident. Furthermore, it is to do with the speaker, unlike the condition about detriment to the hearer. In fact, 'I'm sorry' is such a common way of apologizing that you may be surprised that I am calling it an *indirect* apology. I offer the following two hypothetical exchanges by way of illustrating that 'I'm sorry' *implicates* an apology, but *is not* an apology.

> My Aunt Sadie died last week.
> I'm sorry.

> My Aunt Sadie died last week.
> I apologize.

'I'm sorry' does not implicate an apology on the receipt of news that someone has died, since regrets are appropriate here, but not the acceptance of responsibility. Since 'I apologize' is a direct apology (although without the expression of the second person pronoun or the proposition), if it is felicitous, it conveys all three conditions, including the one about speaker responsibility. The speaker in the second exchange will be taken as accepting responsibility for Aunt Sadie's death (or maybe as showing he or she does not really know what it is to 'apologize')!

If it is possible to apologize, or perform other speech acts, by means of one of the conditions on its use, it looks very much as if we have a case of Gricean implicature. The hearer hears 'I'm sorry', but hears it as breaching the first submaxim of quantity 'Make your contribution as informative as is required', since an apology is required and an apology is more informative than an expression of regret (by at least two felicity conditions). Therefore the hearer infers that an apology was intended. In a context (like the one about Aunt Sadie's death) which does not require an apology, the expression of regret is all that is required, and the implicature is not generated.

Things are not that simple. In the first place, it would seem that the maxim of quantity would lead to the reverse inference, if felicity conditions work like scalar phenomena. A Horn-scale like the following seems reasonable since an apology includes regret, but not vice versa:

$$\{\text{apologize}_1, \text{express regret}_2\}$$

If so, if I say 'I'm sorry', it should lead to the implicature that I am in a position to do no more than express regret, because if I were ready to take the stronger step of apologizing, I would do it explicitly. This argument is parallel to the one by which we infer from 'The coffee is warm' that the speaker does not find that the coffee is hot. We also noted that the scalar implicature based on $\{hot_1, warm_2\}$ can be canceled by saying 'This coffee is warm, in fact it's hot'; but if you were to hear 'I'm sorry, in fact, I apologize' in a situation where an apology is called for, you would be a bit puzzled.

Another situation in which more information is inferred than is said is the phenomenon of 'conditional perfection' of Geis and Zwicky (1971). In connection with their example 'If you mow the lawn, I'll give you five dollars', I suggested that it might be the culturally shared structure of service-for-hire speech events which makes the implicature possible. The same factor might be appealed to here. If speakers and hearers are able to recognize the conditions under which apologies and other speech acts are culturally appropriate, they will infer that the speech act that is called for has been performed, even though what the speaker actually said is in some sense less than that speech act. This might work fairly well for apologies, which are understood to be needed whenever someone discerns that he or she is responsible for damage to someone else, but seems to me to be less convincing in the case of other speech acts, like promises or requests. I am not sure there are definable settings in which people are *expected* to make promises or requests, although once a person starts talking a hearer might find that the setting is at least congenial for interpreting what is being said as one of these speech acts. It is not clear to me that this is enough. In any event, an appeal to structured speech events will not be sufficient to explain all the cases in which more information is implicated than said (cf. Horn 1984; Levinson 1987).

I mentioned that the idea that 'I'm sorry' is an *indirect* apology might be surprising. It is so commonly used as an apology that it is initially hard to imagine it could be anything else. I have given reasons to support the idea that it is an indirect apology, but there is still something to the idea that English speakers simply tacitly agree that saying 'I'm sorry' is an apology. In the first place, I have suggested that 'I'm sorry' implicates an apology by a several-step conversational implicature. Searle (1979:46–7) gives a sequence of 11 steps by which a woman can conclude that someone who says 'Can you pass the salt?' intends to request her to pass the salt, not just to ask her whether she can, and he calls this a 'bare-bones reconstruction of the steps necessary'. Searle makes it clear, however, that he does not mean that hearers actually go through all these steps, even unconsciously (their food might get cold waiting for the salt if they did!), and I certainly do not mean that people go through a multi-step inferencing procedure when they hear 'I'm sorry'. What happens is that certain forms become 'conventionalized'.[3] When they do, hearers become immediately aware that a particular speech act is being performed and do not have to go through the inferencing steps. Evidence for conventionalization comes from the fact that near-synonyms typically differ markedly in the degree of ease with which they can be used in indirect speech acts. For example, 'I regret it' expresses regret at least as well as 'I'm sorry', but as an apology it does not work nearly so well.[4] Similarly, 'Can you give me a hand?' is readily available for use as a request but, as a request, 'Are you able to give me a hand?' is hard to imagine. This is true in spite of the fact that both are based on the condition on felicitous requests that the hearer is able to do what is being requested. With requests, this difference shows up in the possibility for inserting 'please' right before the verb in an indirect request. 'Can you please give me a hand' sounds perfectly acceptable, but 'Are you able to please give me a hand?' does not.[5] Bach and Harnish (1979:202) find convention an incomplete explanation for *please*-placement:

> We do not yet have an explanation of just when 'please' can occur and when it cannot. We could indulge in a bit of hand-waving and say that since certain forms have become standardly used nonliterally as requests, they have come to be able to take 'please' just as if they could be used to make literal requests. This is hardly an explanation.

Perhaps it is not, but it may turn out to be all that there is to say.

If this were the whole story, it would not be too bad. We could make a special case for implicatures that implicate more information than what is said, even if there is no culturally relevant speech event to appeal to, just in case a condition on a speech act is being used to convey that act. About conventionalization, we could say that some ways of doing this become common in a speech community and in a sense fossilize as a way of performing the speech act and inferencing is no longer necessary. But it turns out that some speech acts, particularly the class of speech acts which includes requests, can be conveyed in a whole range of ways, of which the following are only a few:

I request of you that you give me some help.
I want you to give me some help.
Can you give me some help?
Will you give me some help?
Could you give me some help?
Would you give me some help?
May I ask you to give me some help?
I'd like to ask you to give me some help.
I must ask you to give me some help.
I could use some help.
This sure is hard to do alone.
I've been running around like crazy all day and now here are all these dirty dishes!
Whew!

The first is a direct request using the explicit performative utterance formulas. Like many EPUs, it is hard to imagine a setting in which it would sound natural. The next three are easily understood as uses of conditions on requests; the next two may be, although there is no explanation for why they have 'could' and 'would' rather than 'can' and 'will', but the rest are not. The next is a request for permission to ask for help, but help is asked for before permission can be granted. The example beginning 'I'd like to' is literally an expression of a desire to make a request, the one with 'must' indicates an obligation to make a request, and the rest are decreasingly thinly-veiled hints. It appears that the implicature that the speaker is making a request of the hearer can be generated in lots of ways besides using conditions on requests.

Another issue that comes up is whether or not there is any relationship between performative verbs like 'advise' and 'apologize' and the speech acts that a society has. One problem is that of verbs which seem like performative verbs but can only be used to *report* speech acts, not in explicit performative utterances to make speech acts. Some examples are 'boast', 'insinuate', and 'allege' (you wouldn't say 'I insinuate that you are a fool', although there is nothing wrong with 'He insinuated that I am a fool'). But beyond this, there are 'thoughts and feelings' of speakers which can be conveyed with certain lexical items, but not necessarily by performative verbs. Fraser (1987) writes about some of these, ranging from 'frankly', as in 'Frankly, I don't like him', which expresses the feeling that the speaker is temporarily suspending the normal social obligation to speak politely, to the expletive in 'Where are the damned coffee filters', which expresses anger at the state of affairs. In fact, it is possible to convey all sorts of thoughts and feelings not far removed from those connected with common speech acts, but for which there are no words at all, let alone performative verbs. If, during a conversation, I 'happen' to mention to a male fellow-linguist that I have been invited to give a lecture at a conference in a foreign city when I know he has not been, on the surface all I have done is state a fact. But my true aim might be to convey the feeling that since I have been invited and he has not, I am a well-recognized linguist and he is not. But of course there is no performative utterance of anything like 'I hereby aggrandize my career at the expense of yours.' My fellow-linguist might later report my behavior as 'He aggrandized his career at the expense of mine', but I doubt that he would be understood as reporting a speech act, at least in the traditional Austin–Searle sense of the term.

Speech acts and the separation of semantics and pragmatics

So it is possible to consider 'illocutionary force', at least as applied to vernacular illocutionary force, to mean something like 'subsidiary speaker intentions conveyed along with the overt content of what is said', and a speech act as an utterance of whatever kind that succeeds, in its context, in getting these intentions conveyed. On this view, illocutionary force looks very much like a kind of conversational implicature like those we considered in the last chapter. It still seems, though, that speech acts made using an explicit performative utterance would not involve an implicature because the illocutionary force is part of the content of what is said, by virtue of the meaning of the performative verb. But even this is called into question by Bach and Harnish (1979:203–8). Contrary to what Austin originally argued, they contend that EPUs *are* statements. When you say 'I promise to pay you back next week' you are stating that you promise. Your hearer will *infer* that you are promising when you make such a statement, simply because there would be no other reason to make the statement. They conclude: 'Explicit performative utterances are indirect illocutionary acts . . . The explicit performative formula is standardized for the indirect performance of the illocutionary act named by the performative verb.' Remember, Bach and Harnish use 'standardized' to mean what I meant by the term 'conventional' in connection with saying 'I'm sorry' to apologize. What they mean is that saying 'I apologize' is a conventional (in my sense, not theirs) indirect performance of an apology, just as 'I'm sorry' is, although it is based on a slightly more direct inferential route.

All of this is beginning to get a little too technical for my purposes. I bring it up simply so that I can show how the speech act phenomenon can be related to the question of the separation of semantics and pragmatics. If illocutionary force is *not* part of the meaning of explicit performative verbs, then EPUs can readily be incorporated into an independent truth-based semantics, with illocutionary force arising in context by implicature. Neither is it necessary to agree with Bach and Harnish's analysis to come to this conclusion. Other scholars, including Levinson (1983, chapter 5) and Gazdar (1981) have concluded on independent grounds that sentences do not have illocutionary forces as part of their meanings. If these scholars are wrong, and the line of inquiry initiated by Austin and Searle is right, then we have a kind of meaning that is not truth-based but is not based on implicature either.

Before leaving speech acts entirely, I will briefly consider the status of assertions. Austin ultimately concluded that assertions are illocutionary acts. They can be performed directly by means of an EPU (such as 'I state to you that the Prudential Tower is in Chicago') or by means of declarative syntax ('The Prudential Tower is in Chicago'). They can also be performed indirectly in various ways such as 'I want you to know that the Prudential Tower is in Chicago.' Considered in this way, the two submaxims of quality could be restated as two of the conditions on the felicitous performance of assertions.

1 speaker believes the propositional content of the act to be true;

2 speaker believes the evidence for the truth of the propositional content of the act is adequate.

It is not clear to me what, if anything, would be gained or lost by restating the quality maxims as conditions on assertions.

POLITENESS

Politeness rules

Another central concept in linguistic pragmatics is politeness. It has been suggested (for example, R. Lakoff 1972, 1973b, 1977b; Brown and Levinson 1978; Leech 1980, 1983) that politeness is another level to conversational interaction besides the rules of the cooperative principle. Robin Lakoff (1977b) sees Grice's rules as essentially rules of clarity, and proposes that there are two prior rules of 'pragmatic competence'. These are: 'Make yourself clear' and 'Be polite'. She takes Grice's maxims as an approximation, at least, of how you conform to the rule 'Make yourself clear', and proposes her own three rules of politeness (R. Lakoff 1977b:88):

1 formality: don't impose/remain aloof;

2 hesitancy: give the addressee his options;

3 equality or camaraderie: act as though you and the addressee were equal/make him feel good.

Lakoff (1977b:89) elaborates the second rule as 'Permit addressee to decide his own options.' It is not difficult to see how the operation of this rule could lead directly to the troublesome inference in 'Henry likes apples or bananas' that we left unsolved in chapter 5. If we imagine, for example, that Henry's wife knows her host is about to serve fruit, she might well make this utterance, conveying and intending to convey that Henry is fond of both fruits; the host may select either option without fear of making a mistake. In such a case, Henry's wife can felicitously give the host the option only if either option will be successful, and that can only be true if Henry likes *both* fruits.

Leech's view of politeness involves a set of politeness maxims analogous to Grice's maxims. Among these are (Leech 1983:132):[6]

TACT MAXIM: Minimize cost to *other*. Maximize benefit to *other*.
GENEROSITY MAXIM: Minimize benefit to *self*. Maximize cost to *self*.
APPROBATION MAXIM: Minimize dispraise of *other*. Maximize praise of *other*.
MODESTY MAXIM: Minimize praise of *self*. Maximize dispraise of *self*.

These add up to 'an essential asymmetry in polite behaviour, in that whatever is a polite belief for the speaker tends to be an impolite belief for the hearer, and vice versa' (Leech 1983:169).

Frequently-cited examples first discussed by R. Lakoff (1972) are amenable to this general kind of analysis. Lakoff pointed out that a hostess would be seen as polite if she said, 'You must have some of this cake', but very impolite if she said 'You may have some of this cake.' On the face of it this is strange, since ordinarily you would think telling someone what they must do removes all other options, imposes on them, and is therefore impolite. On the other hand, granting permission, if one is in a position to do it, makes it possible for the hearer to do what he or she wants to do, and would seem polite, or at least considerate. The answer hinges on the fact that the hostess is responsible for the quality of the cake. Offering the cake by placing an obligation on the hearer conforms nicely to the modesty maxim. By implying that she cannot assume that the guest will want the cake is a way in minimizing praise to herself. If the hostess had offered the cake by saying 'You may have some of this cake', she would have violated modesty by appearing to assume that the cake is so good that the guest naturally wants a piece of it, and is only waiting to get permission.

Leech's politeness principle also seems to be applicable to the disjunction example in a natural way. One way that Henry's wife can conform to the maxim of tact, minimizing the cost to the host, is by making sure no one has to go to any special trouble to supply just the fruit Henry likes. Whichever of the two fruits can be supplied with minimum difficulty will be satisfactory. As I have said, this can only be really true if Henry likes both apples and bananas.

Brown and Levinson

Perhaps the most thorough treatment of the concept of politeness is that of Brown and Levinson (1978). They have set out to develop an explicit model of politeness which will have validity across cultures. The general idea is to understand various *strategies* for interactional behavior based on the idea that people engage in rational behavior to achieve satisfaction of certain wants. The wants related to politeness are the wants of *face*, 'something that is emotionally invested, and that can be lost, maintained, or enhanced, and must be constantly attended to in interaction' (Brown and Levinson 1978:66). The concept is directly related to the folk-expression 'lose face', which is about being embarrassed or humiliated. There are two kinds of face. One is 'negative face', or the rights to territories, freedom of action and freedom from imposition; essentially the want that your actions be not impeded by others. The other is 'positive face', the positive consistent self-image that people have and want to be appreciated and approved of by at least some other people. The rational actions people take to preserve both kinds of face for themselves and the people they interact with essentially add up to politeness.

A strength of the Brown and Levinson approach over the rule-oriented presentations of politeness by Robin Lakoff and by Leech is that Brown and Levinson are attempting to *explain* politeness by deriving it from more fundamental notions of what it is to be a human being (being rational and having face wants). There are two advantages of this over normative or rule-based approaches. First, norms are discoverable and valid within a particular culture and therefore not too useful in understanding a concept like politeness cross-culturally. Second, even to posit universal (not culture-particular) rules as arbitrary primitives is 'to invent a problem to be explained, rather than to explain it' (Brown and Levinson 1978:91). In other words, if you start with a set of rules like Leech's maxims of politeness, you can understand politeness phenomena in terms of these rules, but you do not learn very much about why there should be such rules in the first place. Granted, Brown and Levinson ask us to accept at the start that people are rational and have two kinds of face wants, but this is a much deeper starting point for explanation than starting with rules designed specifically for politeness itself.

Face wants become a problem if we assume that certain kinds of actions are intrinsically face-threatening. Such acts may threaten the hearer's negative face, like a request which, as an attempt to get someone else to do something that *you* want done, means that the recipient of the request is being impeded in pursuing what he or she wants to do. Others threaten hearers' positive face: for instance, a contradiction or expression of disagreement, which means the speaker thinks there is something wrong with an opinion held by the hearer. Even saying something irreverent or taboo threatens the hearer's positive face, since it reveals that the speaker does not care about the hearer's values. Face-threatening acts can threaten the speaker's face as well as the hearer's. The speaker's negative face is jeopardized when he or she makes an offer in somewhat the same way as requests threaten the hearer's negative face since, in carrying out the offer, he or she will be pursuing the hearer's aims, not the speaker's own. Confessions, admissions of guilt, and apologies threaten the speaker's positive face since they mean the speaker has done something the proper sort of person would not have done. Such nonspeaking acts as tripping or stumbling also threaten a person's positive face; they reveal a certain incompetence in carrying out a basic action like walking. None the less there are times when actions like this are going to occur and at times they may be desirable or necessary. In these cases, the rational person will look for ways of doing the act while minimizing the threat to face in one way or another.

Brown and Levinson (1978:65) show us five ways a person can deal with a 'face-threatening act' (FTA). The greater the risk, the more appropriate the higher-numbered ways of dealing with it are (see figure 6.1). But it will not do to minimize the risk too much, because that will imply that the act is more face threatening than it actually is. For example, if there is something that only someone else can do for you, and you really need it done, and you select 5, 'Do not do the FTA' by refraining from asking your best friend to do it for you, you will hurt your friend's feelings. Your friend could easily say, with a pained expression, 'Don't you think I would have done that for you?'

The meaning of the last of the five ways of dealing with a potential FTA is self-evident; you simply do not take the action that would threaten face. Doing an FTA 'off the record' is essentially dropping a hint, or otherwise trying to make the FTA salient while still keeping the possibility of denying that you ever intended an FTA more-or-less open. For example, if you say 'Gosh, I'm out of money. I forgot to go to the bank', your companion might take it that you want a loan. But if your companion responds by saying, 'Sorry, I'd like to help you out, but I'm a little short of cash myself', you could still say, 'Oh, I didn't mean I wanted *you* to lend me money!'

'On the record' FTAs with negative politeness redress are instances in which the FTA is undeniably made, but something else is said or done to show concern for the other person's freedom of action and right not to be imposed upon. One of the most straightforward ways of doing this is simply to express reluctance to impose: 'I hate to impose, but would you do something for me?' Brown and Levinson suggest that the use in many languages of the plural form of 'you' as a deferential form, as we saw in chapter 1, has its origins in negative politeness redress. One possible explanation, originally Robin Lakoff's and recapitulated by Brown and Levinson (1978:203–4) is that the plural form does not literally single out the addressee. If we assume that what the speaker has to say, or even the sheer fact that the hearer is obliged to listen, is a potential

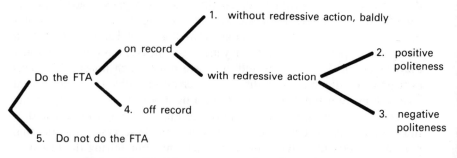

Figure 6.1 Possible responses to face-threatening acts

imposition on the hearer's freedom, then the use of the plural pronoun gives the hearer the option of taking it as being directed to someone else associated with him or her, not specifically to that person as an individual. Naturally, once this use of plural 'you' is conventionalized, like French *vous*, this option is not *really* there, but it still lets speakers represent themselves as desiring to give the hearer some such mitigating option.

An 'on the record' FTA with redress of the positive politeness sort makes the act less threatening by emphasizing in one way or another that the speaker shares the hearer's interests and desires. Brown and Levinson give 14 different examples of strategies of positive redress, of which perhaps the most direct is simply to include both the speaker and the hearer in the activity by using a first-person plural pronoun. The stereotype of the hospital nurse who says, 'Let's take our pill now, shall we?' is an example of this. The action is really at least a request, maybe even an order for the patient to take the pill, despite the use of 'let's', 'we', and 'our'.

A baldly executed FTA without redress would be, for example, simply to give a direct order like 'Shut the door' or to belch out loud without asking for pardon. It is at this point that the tie-in with Grice's implicatures comes. As Brown and Levinson (1978:99–100) see it, on-record FTAs without redress are enacted in full conformity with the maxims of the cooperative principle; they conform to quality by being transparent (if the speaker wants to make a request, he or she does not try to veil the fact that a request is being made); they conform to quantity by being sufficiently informative without being too informative; they are relevant, brief, and so on. At the opposite end of the scale, the nonconventional off-record FTAs depend heavily on the generation of implicature. As Brown and Levinson put it (1978:218): 'The basic way to do this is to invite conversational implicatures by violating in some way, the Gricean Maxims of efficient communication'.[7]

The relationship between an analysis in Grice's style and the on-record performance of FTAs with redress is a bit more complex. Take our example of the on-record request with negative politeness redress: 'I hate to impose but would you do something for me?' This can be seen as a violation of one of the submaxims of manner, 'Be brief', or maybe 'Avoid obscurity of expression.' The request has not even been made yet; the speaker has simply asked for permission to make a request, and has made the question hypothetical by saying 'would' instead of 'will', as if to say, 'under some unspecified set of conditions might it be the case that you would do something for me?' On the other hand, the component I wanted to focus on, the 'I hate to impose' part, could be taken as obeying the first submaxim of quantity since, given the fact that an FTA is in progress, it is essential information that the speaker hates to impose. The nurse's command example of an FTA with positive politeness redress seems something of a violation of the first submaxim of quality. Although it does not exactly say something that is not true, the literal meaning indicates the nurse will take a pill too, and that is not accurate.

It is important to note that the outcome of Brown and Levinson's approach does not contradict the conclusions we would draw by applying Lakoff's rules of politeness or Leech's politeness principle. Of Lakoff's three rules, 'Don't impose' and 'Give options' can without effort be seen as explications of politeness based on preserving negative face, while 'Make A feel good – be friendly' is just as clearly about positive face preservation. Whatever we have said on the basis of a rule-type approach can also be accounted for in Brown and Levinson's terms. For instance, the example 'Henry likes apples or bananas' is, in a sense, a case of negative face preservation from guest to host. Since Henry likes both fruits, the host's freedom of action in offering him fruit is maximized.

Furthermore, they point out throughout that preservation of face is not quite so simple as Leech's 'essential asymmetry in polite behavior', such that what is polite for the speaker is not for the hearer. Polite interaction is typically about preserving everyone's face, since causing loss of face for someone else may inspire him or her to do something to embarrass you in the future. Furthermore, it is not uncommon for the same event both to support and threaten face for both speaker(S) and hearer(H) at the same time. To make an offer, for example, supports positive face for S since S can display an image of him- or herself as the sort of person who helps friends. In one sense, H's positive face is preserved, because whatever H is doing that S is offering to help with is seen as worth getting involved in by at least one other person. In another sense, H has to accept a diminishment of his or her own positive face, since by accepting the offer there is an admission that H's own skills and resources are not fully adequate. S, meanwhile, has given up the freedom to pursue his or her own goals for as long as it takes to fulfil the offer, a diminishment of S's negative face. If H declines the offer, it may mean that he or she does not accept the idea that H cannot do whatever he or she is doing alone; hence S has insulted H by diminishing H's positive face and is at some risk of future retaliation. If the offer is accepted, H is now in S's debt and might be expected to help S at some future time, with the concomitant loss of H's own freedom of action. It is no wonder that bald, on-record offers of the form 'I offer to you to help you fix your car' are virtually never made!

Politeness and disjunction

Schiffrin's (1987:177ff.) work on 'or' as a discourse marker shows clearly that 'or' works precisely as a speaker's provision of options to the hearer. Several of her examples, taken from recorded interviews, illustrate how this use of 'or' gives options at a much more subtle level than the example I have given. One speaker, answering a question about where she would like to live, responds with:[8]

I'd like t'live in Huntingdon. [hhhhhhh] I was up there with my husband last week. There are some beautiful homes up there. **Or** I have cousins that live up in eh: Holland Pennsylvania, up past State Road? Up there are you familiar?

Here the speaker is presenting either Huntingdon or Holland as desirable places to live, allowing the hearer to take either or both as her response. Schiffrin points out that offering options is not exclusively a case of deferring one's own interests in favor of the hearer's; the speaker can derive benefits from giving options, too. Another interviewee, contending that movies present an unrealistic view of life, supports his position in the following way:

I'm – I'm speaking how kind everybody is on the movie. **Or** uh . . . how a poor working girl is out looking for a job, with a hundred and ninety dollar suit on her back!

By giving the two reasons conjoined by 'or', the speaker increases the chances that his point of view will be accepted. A hearer who does not think that movie characters are always kind might still accept the conclusion that movies are unrealistic on the view that they are likely to have a well-dressed actress playing a character who is poor. If the second scenario does not seem typical to the hearer, perhaps the excessive kindness argument will be persuasive (of course, if the hearer would accept both the proposed bits of evidence, that is all right, too). By presenting two pieces of supporting evidence (both of which, by the way, he himself would find valid) linked by 'or', he is giving the hearer options, but stands to benefit personally for doing so.

If we take it to be generally true that acting so as to benefit oneself is not polite, and acting to benefit others is, these examples seem to be problematic as polite acts, though they are clearly acts that give options. From Brown and Levinson's perspective, as I have said, politeness ultimately leads to a concerted effort on the part of everybody to maximize mutual preservation of face. One of the strategies of positive politeness exemplified by Brown and Levinson is to avoid disagreement. Although they do not give any examples that resemble the two cases from Schiffrin's interviews, these cases are quite clearly attempts on the part of the speaker to increase the likelihood that agreement will be reached. In the first example, the hearer has the option of selecting which of the two 'nice places to live' she finds a better example of her own concept of 'nice places to live', should she be disinclined to accept both. If the hearer happened not to think of Huntingdon as a nice place to live, perhaps she will agree that Holland is.

Similarly, the second speaker is maximizing the likelihood that his point of view about movies will not be an opportunity for disagreement by supplying a choice of evidence on the basis of which the other participants *can* agree with it. On one level, the giving of options by both of these speakers appears to be self-serving, but on further reflection their actions represent their contribution to the ongoing and mutual desire to preserve positive face by avoiding disagreement.

Coming back one more time to the problem in the last chapter about the 'or' that seems to have the truth-conditions of 'and', we can see how politeness ultimately leads to the inference that both members of a disjunction are valid without having to say that 'or' itself has this as part of its meaning. This result can be taken as support for Grice's contention that there is no divergence between the formal devices of logic and their natural language counterparts, at least as far as disjunction is concerned.

PRESUPPOSITION

The concept of 'presupposition' has a long history in pragmatics. Early controversies concerning the problem of reference failure were discussed by philosophers from late in the last century through to the middle of this century.[9] Sometime during the 1960s, linguists became interested in the concept and they gave it a lot of attention in subsequent years. The concept of presuppostion rapidly expanded beyond the reference problem in examples such as 'The principal chief of the Kuikus delivered the petition.'

The basic intuition behind the notion 'presupposition' is a relationship between something that is actually said (or could be said) and something else which has to be the case in order for the thing said to make any sense at all. A precise definition to capture this intuition was proposed. In order to understand the definition, it is necessary to understand a related concept, 'entailment'. A proposition p *entails* another proposition q if and only if whenever p is true, q is also true. The proposition 'Harry is a man' entails the proposition 'Harry is male.' As long as it is true that the individual we are calling 'Harry' is a man, it has to be true that 'Harry is male.' Notice that the reverse is not necessarily true. 'Harry is male' does not entail 'Harry is a man'; Harry could be a 6-year-old boy, or perhaps a bull. The definition of presupposition that seemed for quite some time to work well was this: 'A proposition p presupposes another proposition q if and only if p entails q and the negation of p also entails q.' In the case of definite descriptions like 'the principal chief of the Kuikus', any assertion about such a person entails the proposition 'There exists a principal chief of the Kuikus', but so does the denial of that same proposition. In the example we have used, 'The principal chief of the

Kuikus presented a petition' entails 'There exists a principal chief of the Kuikus', but 'The principal chief of the Kuikus didn't present a petition' entails the same proposition.

Levinson (1983:181–2) presents 13 examples from a list of 31 phenomena that have been called 'presupposition' originally collected by Lauri Karttunen. I have given just a few of them below, with the item taken to be responsible for the presupposition emphasized where necessary. You can test these cases against the definition by seeing if the example seems to you to entail the corresponding presupposed proposition and if the negation or denial of the example proposition also entails the presupposed proposition (see table 6.1).

The standard definition gives the right outcome in these examples and in many others. A problem arises with questions. Questions seem to share presuppositions with the corresponding assertions. For instance, consider the alternative question, 'Did the man who won the race get a medal or did he get a trophy?', said with something like the following intonation contour:

<pre>
                    dal
          ME   DID he
     get a   or   get a
                               TRO
                                  phy?
</pre>

The question presupposes 'There exists a man who won the race' and 'The man won the race'. But such questions also seem to presuppose that he got one of the two prizes mentioned, in that the question makes no sense (as an alternative question) if he did not get one of them. But

Table 6.1 Examples of constructions evoking presuppositions

Label	Example	Presupposed
Factive predicates	Harold *regrets* insulting Sandra.	Harold insulted Sandra.
Change of state verbs	Sally *stopped* smoking.	Sally had been smoking.
Iteratives	Hubert's rash came *back*.	Hubert had a rash earlier.
Temporal clauses	*After Samantha left him*, Humphrey became despondent.	Samantha left Humphrey.
Cleft constructions	It was Harrison who kissed Sigrid.	Someone kissed Sigrid.
Nonrestrictive relative clauses	The mathematician *who tried to prove the Goldberg Conjecture* failed.	The mathematician tried to prove the Goldberg Conjecture.

this presupposition does not holḍ under negation. In fact, it is not clear that it is possible to negate the question at all without having it lose its quality as an alternative question. You can imagine mechanically inserting a negative into each clause, and you would get 'Didn't the man who won the race get a medal or didn't he get a trophy?' If you say this sentence forcing yourself to use the same intonation pattern, it is not exactly clear just what is being asked, to say the least. The more stilted negation, 'Isn't it the case that the man who won the race got a medal or he got a trophy?', again forcing the alternative-question intonation is no better (it is perfectly all right as a yes–no question). The negative entailment test, then, cannot be made to work.

A special auxiliary procedure will enable us to test for the particular presuppositions that are associated only with questions. If a proposition p is entailed by every answer to a question q, then p is a presupposition of q (Keenan 1971:48; cf. Levinson 1983:184).[10] In our example, if the winning racer got a medal, then it is also true that he got a medal or a trophy; similarly if he got a trophy. If we are dealing with an alternative question, these are the only two legitimate answers. It turns out that this test works as well for yes–no questions and WH-questions as it does for alternative questions. The yes–no question, 'Do you know that Harvey realizes that Sarah is his daughter?' presupposes 'Sarah is Harvey's daughter'. This second proposition is entailed whether the answer to the question about whether you know it is 'yes' or 'no'. Similarly for a WH-question like 'Where did Hank bury the loot?'; this presupposes 'Hank buried the loot somewhere', whether the answer is 'Hank buried the loot in his grandmother's attic' or 'Hank buried the loot on Assateague Island' or any other legitimate answer to the question.[11]

Linguists with rather a more sociolinguistic bent have suggested extending the notion to cases in which 'presuppositions' were propositions that are assumed valid when a particular utterance is *appropriately* used. Take an example involving a T/V pronoun contrast in a language like French, such as:

Vous êtes le professeur
You (V form) are the professor

or

Vous n'êtes pas le professeur
You are not the professor

Using *vous* can be said to 'presuppose' that the addressee is either non-solidary with or more powerful than the speaker, regardless of whether the assertion or denial is being made. However, you get a different result if this kind of 'presupposition' fails. Recall that a presupposition failure in the cases we have considered so far makes it problematic whether or not the sentence should be called true or false. If I say 'Hal realizes that he's going to recover', we do not know what to say about the truth of the sentence if Hal is not going to recover. But if someone were to say to a child, in French:

Vous êtes mon enfant
You (V form) are my child

it would sound strange that an adult addresses a child with the V form, but it would still make perfect sense to say that it is either true or false that the addressee is the speaker's child. Even in a case that does not involve social relationship distinctions, like 'My neighbor has hurt herself' (McCawley 1981:237) the same problem comes up. This utterance can be said to presuppose that the neighbor is female, but if he is male (a male transvestite, perhaps, taken for a woman by a speaker, or if the utterance is made by a speaker with an imperfect control of English gender distinctions), it still makes sense to try to determine whether or not he has hurt himself.

This led some linguists – for example, Keenan (1971) and McCawley (1981:236–7) – to suggest that there are two kinds of presupposition: *semantic* presuppositions which are subject to tests like entailment under assertion and negation, and *pragmatic* presuppositions based on the concept of appropriate usage. More recently, though, the idea that there can be any notion of semantic presupposition at all has been given up by almost all linguists. The most devastating argument against the definition based on entailment under both negation and assertion is that the definition can be shown to lead to a very undesirable conclusion. Under the double entailment definition, only propositions that are true no matter what can be presuppositions. The argument, stated informally, goes like this.[12]

1 Definition: p presupposes q if and only if p entails q and not-p entails q.
2 As a starting point, assume not-q (the presupposition is false).
3 If p entails q as the definition of presupposition requires, and q is false, then p has to be false, too (by a rule of inference called *modus tollens*). Consider our example of entailment: if Harvey is not (even) male, he cannot possibly be a man.
4 If not-p entails q as the definition of presupposition also requires, and q is false, then not-p has to be false (again by *modus tollens*.)
5 If not-p has to be false, then p has to be true (by another rule of inference called negative elimination).
6 Step 3 proves that p has to be false and step 5 proves that p has to be true, so p has to be both true and false, if we want to maintain the definition and the assumption that q is false.

7   Since p cannot simultaneously be true and false, then if we want to keep the definition, we have to give up the assumption that q can be false.
8   No presupposition can ever be false.

This would mean, for example, that 'Homer has come before' cannot possibly be a presupposition for 'Homer is coming again' since it is certainly possible to imagine that the proposition 'Homer has come before' could be false. In this way, the definition leads to the exclusion of the very cases it was designed to handle.

There are other, more interesting, reasons why the proposed semantic definition of presupposition, or any other semantic account, is going to run into severe problems. Keep in mind that if an explanation is semantic, at least if we are talking about an independent truth-based semantics, nothing should be affected by the context of an utterance. The work of many linguists, including Wilson (1975), Kempson (1975), and Gazdar (1979), has revealed numerous situations in which the entailments that we would need if we are to keep the definition do not hold true. To take one example, 'know' is one of the 'factive verbs' (Kiparsky and Kiparsky 1971) which are supposed to presuppose their complements. If the subject of 'know' is in the third person, the definition seems to work satisfactorily. If I say 'Herb knows that the winter solstice is next Sunday', it seems to have to be the case that the winter solstice actually occurs next Sunday, even if I am wrong about Herb knowing about it. But I can perfectly well say 'I don't know that the winter solstice is next Sunday' with the exact purpose of challenging the claim that it is. A little reflection shows why there is a problem. If I talk about what Herb knows, I can fully well presuppose that something other than what Herb knows is true. When I talk about what *I* know, on the other hand, I cannot be taken for a sane person if I overtly deny knowing what I am supposedly presupposing is true. It would be just as bad as saying, 'Of course it's true that the world is round, the problem is that I don't know it.'

One of the temporal clauses that are said to generate presuppositions are ones introduced by *before*. To say 'Sue turned 30 before she finished her thesis', presupposes 'Sue finished her thesis'. Suppose, though, that someone says 'Sue moved to Australia before she finished her thesis.' If we know that Sue was writing her thesis at Oxford, we will not be quite so sure that 'Sue finished her thesis' is true. It might be the speaker's point that moving to Australia prevented her from ever finishing her thesis. If someone says 'Sue became incurably schizophrenic before she finished her thesis', we can be almost sure that the alleged presupposition is *not* true; if someone says 'Sue died before she finished her thesis', we can be dead sure (sorry!) that it is not.

To all these problems with a semantic concept of presupposition, we have to add what is called the 'projection problem'. It is one thing to say that a certain simple sentence has a certain presupposition. But what happens if we embed that sentence in another one, to get a more complex sentence? It turns out that sometimes the presuppositions of the simple sentence become part of the set of presuppositions of the complex sentence. The predicates of the main clauses of sentences like this have been called *holes* in an influential discussion of pragmatic presupposition by Karttunen and Peters (1979). Others seem to block the presuppositions of embedded clauses; these are called *plugs*. Under a third set of circumstances, the presuppositions are blocked under specified conditions. These are *filters*. Factive verbs are one kind of 'hole' predicate. In 'Harrison knows Sheila regrets going to the party', the presupposition of 'Sheila regrets going to the party' is 'Sheila went to the party' and it is also a presupposition of the whole sentence. Verbs of saying and believing and the like are plugs. In 'Harrison believes Sheila regrets going to the party', 'Sheila went to the party' is not presupposed because Harrison's belief could be totally wrong. Not only might it be wrong in what it states, that Sheila regrets going, but in what it presupposes, that she went. Conditional expressions with 'if–then' are filters. Normally presuppositions of clauses embedded in the parts of conditionals become presuppositions of the whole sentence. For example 'Harrison left the party before Sheila arrived' presupposes 'Sheila arrived'. In 'If Harrison left the party before Sheila arrived, he regrets not staying longer', the same presupposition is still valid. In cases in which a presupposition of the 'then' clause is made hypothetical in the 'if' clause, then it is 'filtered out'. If someone says 'If Harrison left the party before midnight, then he regrets it', since 'regret' is factive, it presupposes its complement (whatever 'it' means; in this case 'Harrison left the party before midnight'). But this is exactly what is made doubtful by appearing in the 'if' clause, so it is not a presupposition of the whole sentence.

The pragmatic theory of presupposition involving plugs, holes, and filters has many technical problems. In addition, other linguists have presented cases in which the plugs do not plug very well and the holes and filters become clogged. Trying to repair the theory to account for these counterexamples makes the technical problems worse.[13]

A more promising alternative was proposed by Gazdar (1979). Gazdar attempts to solve both the problem involving the contextual canceling of presuppositions and the projection problem by introducing the idea of 'potential presuppositions'. Potential presuppositions are automatically assigned to simple sentences and parts of complex sentences whether the result makes sense or not. Furthermore, potential presuppositions are not stated as entailments of sentences, but as propositions that the speaker knows. In order for a potential presupposition to become an actual presupposition, it has to be tested against the information that is already in the context. If it does not contradict something already in the context, then it becomes one of the actual presuppositions of the sentence. If it becomes an actual presupposition, this counts as being in the context where it would have the power to cancel further potential presuppositions. There is a parallel mechanism in Gazdar's system for conversational implicatures.[14] Some idea of how it would work would come from an informal description of Gazdar's treatment of an example such as 'I don't know that the winter solstice is next Sunday.' Gazdar has a potential presupposition function for factive verbs that automatically assigns 'the winter solstice is next Sunday' to the sentence as a potential presupposition. Potential presuppositions (or actual ones, for that matter) are not strictly entailments for Gazdar, but are propositions attributed to the set of things the speaker knows. So the potential presupposition, once automatically assigned, means 'the speaker knows that the winter solstice is next Sunday.' Of course, the sentence as a whole denies precisely that. What a sentence actually states is considered to be in the context before any potential presuppositions are taken up. As a result, the potential presupposition is canceled since it is contradicted by something that is already in the context.   Whatever the merits of Gazdar's particular approach, a consensus has developed that no context-free concept of presupposition can be maintained. If only pragmatics is allowed to refer to context, most of the instances of what linguists have treated as presuppositions are pragmatic. This can be taken to mean that whatever problems with presuppositions there are, they are not semantic problems, so Grice's idea that the elements of natural language semantics are not divergent from the corresponding elements of logic systems is not refuted by the fact that presupposition is pragmatic.

Nevertheless, even if we agree that presupposition is a pragmatic matter, are there different ways in which that can be interpreted? It turns out that there are. One of the ideas of theoretical linguistics has been that there is a distinction between 'competence' and 'performance' (for example, Chomsky 1965). Competence is what a speaker knows about his or her language and about language in general, in an abstract and unconscious sort of way. Performance is what happens when speakers put their competence to work in actual language use. This is often taken to mean that anything to do with context is a matter of performance, since competence is taken as independent of context. A natural way to view the matter of the distinction among syntax, semantics, and pragmatics is to say that syntax is certainly a matter of competence, semantics almost certainly is, but that pragmatics is part of performance. On this view, presupposition becomes part of the study of performance and linguistic competence theories of syntax and maybe semantics are entitled to ignore it. Kempson (1975) and Katz (1977) are two scholars who have taken this position. Gazdar (1979), on the other hand, despite the fact that his system requires context to be considered, describes his own work, in contrast to Kempson's, as 'unrepentantly competencist' (Gazdar 1979:3). Assuming that linguistic theory is responsible for everything that is a matter of competence, Gazdar's view would mean that presupposition, although not a matter of semantics, still has to be included in linguistic theory. Would this mean that Grice is wrong about there being no disjunction between the appropriate logic system and natural language semantics? The answer is 'no', I would think, as long as Grice and linguists could agree on a definition of semantics. Whether linguistic theory should then include pragmatics as well as semantics would presumably be of only passing interest to Grice, who is, after all, a philosopher and not a linguist.

CROSS-CULTURAL ISSUES IN PRAGMATICS

In chapter 5, I raise the issue of the influence of cultural context on implicature in connection with Geis and Zwicky's example of conditional perfection. When pragmatic inferencing in cultures other than Western ones is investigated, the issue is magnified. The difference in implicatures that would be made among the Malagasy of Madagascar and what would be the case in Western culture was so great that Elinor Ochs Keenan (1975/1983) concluded that Grice's first submaxim of quantity, 'Make your contribution as informative as is required' did not apply. As we know, if a Malagasy villager who had gone to the market and returned to the village was asked 'What's new at the market?' he or she could respond 'There were many people there' (Ochs Keenan 1975:264–5). In a sense, the maxim can be seen as violated, since the answer gives no information (there are always many people at the market), and the questioner would really like to know what had gone on at the market. In another sense, if we understand Grice's term 'required' to mean 'what is required of a person during a conversation in this culture', it is possible to claim that the quantity maxim *is* being fulfilled. Since information in the society is a valued commodity, someone who has been to the market and accumulated a supply of information is not really expected to 'spend it all in one place' so to speak. Perhaps, over a period of days, the villager will tell people the interesting events observed there. The point for our purposes here is that no implicature is generated.

The corresponding question and answer in a Western setting is likely to cause one of several reactions. First, a Westerner who answers by saying 'There were many people there' might be seen as having actually *violated* the first maxim of quantity and has therefore been rude not to supply information he or she obviously has and which the questioner is entitled to have. Second, the answer could be seen as a *flouted* maxim, generating an unuttered implicature. The questioner might conclude that the returning villager had had some unfortunate experience at the market and did not want to talk about it. (Probably, one would check out that hypothesis with someone who knows the person better.) Alternatively, the questioner might take it as a lead-in to further discussion about the topic 'people at the market'. The inferencing might go something like, 'He's said that there were many people at the market, which he knows I already know. He's being cooperative, so he intends to give the "required" information. Therefore, he wants me to ask for more information and he has given me a hint about the topic.' He goes on to ask if the other had seen anybody *special* at the market, and perhaps hears about a chance encounter with someone that had worked with the man's grandfather as a young man, or something of the sort. The point is, none of these conclusions would be drawn by the Malagasy precisely because, it could be argued, the apparently uninformative answer is all that is required.[15]

A similar contrast with English usage, this time compared with Polish, is discussed by Wierzbicka (1985). Most languages have imperative forms that allow speakers to give 'directives': speech acts by which a speaker gets a hearer to do something directly and without using EPUs. In English, it is possible to say 'Mop the floor' instead of 'I command you to mop the floor' or such like. In English, however, both forms are avoided in favor of attempting to generate an implicature that a directive is intended by indirect means, as we have already seen. In Polish, the imperative form is far more commonly used, so that it was possible for the representative of a Polish organization in Australia to offer a distinguished guest a seat by saying 'Please! Sit! Sit!' without being rude, because that is how such a directive would naturally be made in Polish. As a matter of fact, the flat imperative is rather mild in Polish; a really angry or stern individual would use the bare infinitive, like a phrase that would be translated literally 'To take oneself off from here!', but means something more like 'Off with you!'

Furthermore, even if one were to try to use the indirect devices commonly used in English, they would not generate the same implicatures. To say, 'Why don't you close the window?' in English would implicate a mild suggestion. The equivalent in Polish would generate quite a different implicature, along the lines of 'I can't see any excuse for your failure to have closed the window long before this!' On the other hand, 'Won't you close the window?', translated into Polish, is not likely to be heard as a directive at all, but as a real question meaning something like 'It seems you're not going to close the window. That's strange; I wonder why?' The question implies surprise on the part of the speaker, and not criticism of the hearer's lack of action. Wierzbicka goes on to question whether some of the conventional (standardized) indirect means for performing directives in English any longer serve their original purpose.

In the discussion of politeness, I suggested that there are several layers of potential FTAs connected with making offers. The same line of reasoning can easily be extended to directives. This would seem to explain why speakers of English would tend to use an indirect directive: to mitigate an FTA. But this is just what Wierzbicka questions. She has found examples like the following in dialogue written by Australian writers:

Can't you shut up?
Will you bloody well hurry up?
For Christ's sake, will you get lost!

Here we find conventional indirect directives in utterances that in other ways look like bald, on-record FTAs. It is almost as if it is more impolite in English to use an imperative than it is to say 'shut up' or swear at someone! Wierzbicka goes on to account for these differences in performing speech acts in terms of cultural values and differences between English-speaking communities and other communities, like Polish speakers. It is important, quite evidently, to keep in mind that cultural values have a critical bearing on what implicatures are generated by a particular utterance. Other studies in which the same point is emphasized include Hakulinen (1987) and Olstain and Weinbach (1987).

THE TRUE SCOPE OF PRAGMATICS

I have given an overview of pragmatics by treating it as an effort to deal with a particular limited issue. I began with Charles Morris's division of semiotics into syntax, semantics, and pragmatics, and added H. Paul Grice's professed motivation for developing his immensely influential theory of conversational implicature (to demonstrate that natural language logical devices do not diverge from those used by logicians). I then took up the question of whether we can view pragmatics, in a principled way, as the study of the meaning of what people utter in context. The remainder, what a piece of language structure means whether anyone uses it to communicate or not, would be semantics. I have concluded that the research program initiated by Grice gives reasonable promise of defining the line between semantics and pragmatics in this way, provided there is some other way to deal with deixis. Whatever the merits of the discussion of this theme, or of the conclusion I reached, I am convinced that in the process I have at least touched on the major themes to be found in the Anglo-American style of pragmatic research.

However, as I indicated at the outset, there is more to pragmatics than this. There is the Continental approach, which is much broader (and, by the way, includes many British and American scholars). Scholars who do research in both kinds of pragmatics have conducted a series of international conferences and have formed an international association, The International Pragmatics Association (IPRA). An insightful discussion of pragmatics from the point of view of a Continental scholar is given by Jef Verschueren (1987) in his introduction to the papers from the 1985 conference. Noting that 'pragmatics is a large, loose, and disorganized collection of research efforts', he finds the diversity that this implies a strength, but one that threatens to become the weakness of fragmentation 'in the absence of a more or less coherent framework' (Verschueren 1987:4). Interestingly, Verschueren calls for a return to the view of pragmatics espoused by Charles Morris: that pragmatics is about everything human in the communication process, psychological, biological, and sociological. Taking this point of view leads to a very different concept from the one I have presented here:

if our starting point is to be situated at Morris's level of generality, pragmatics cannot be viewed as another layer on top of the phonology-morphology-syntax-semantics hierarchy, another *component* of a theory of language with its own well-defined object . . . Nor does it fit into the contrast set containing sociolinguistics, anthropological linguistics, psycholinguistics, neurolinguistics, etc. Rather, pragmatics is a *perspective* on any aspect of language, at any level of structure . . . One could say that, in general, the *pragmatic perspective* centers around the *adaptability of language*, the fundamental property of language which enables us to engage in the activity of talking which consists in the constant making of choices, at every level of linguistic structure, in harmony with the requirements of people, their beliefs, desires and intentions, and the real-world circumstances in which they interact. (Verschueren 1987:5)

This makes any aspect whatsoever of linguistic interaction a legitimate topic for pragmatic research. The range of topics studied under the auspices of Continental pragmatics extends from more philosophical issues such as conversational implicature, presupposition, and speech acts to such subjects as the pragmatics of the mass media (Verschueren 1985; Jucker 1986; Schmidt and Kess 1986) and the political implications of language use (Haberland and Skutnabb-Kangas 1981; Mey 1985). Among the most fruitful of current topics in pragmatics is 'developmental pragmatics', the study of how children develop the ability to use language to interact effectively. The studies in Ochs and Schieffelin (1979) are one source of research of this type; others include Nemoianu (1980), Camaioni (1981), DeGelder (1981), Streeck (1983), Franco and D'Odorico (1987), and Ervin-Tripp (1987). In fact, any topic in this book could easily be treated from the pragmatic perspective.

SUMMARY

Several themes are important in the study of linguistic pragmatics besides Grice's theory of language and conversation. One of the most-discussed is *speech acts*. As described by Austin, these are sentences, or utterances, that involve *doing* something more than just *saying* something; they are neither true nor false; and they can be conveyed by the syntactic formula for EPUs. Although they do not seem to have truth value, they can go wrong, or be infelicitous, if conditions on them are not met. Some violations of conditions cause the *illocutionary force* of a speech act to fail. Other violations, like insincerity in making a promise, make the speech act faulty, but the illocutionary force is still exerted. Searle has developed a theory of speech acts which, among other things, accounts for how speech acts can be performed *indirectly* by making assertions or asking questions about the conditions on them. In ordinary interaction, illocutionary acts are usually performed indirectly. In the view of some linguistic pragmaticists, speech acts can be performed very indirectly with no reference to conditions on direct speech acts, and speech acts exist for which there are no EPUs at all. The idea that indirect speech acts are instances of Gricean implicatures has been thoroughly explored, and at least one study, by Bach and Harnish, concludes that *all* speech acts are conveyed by implicatures, even those performed by means of EPUs.

The properties of *politeness* have been explored as a way of understanding pragmatic phenomena in language, including indirect speech acts. Besides rule-based theories of politeness, like those of R. Lakoff and Leech, there is a well-known comprehensive theory of politeness by Brown and Levinson that tries to derive politeness phenomena from human universal needs to save face. Much of the theory has to do with FTAs and how they can be mitigated. Their ideas on politeness, together with Schiffrin's work on the use of 'or' as a discourse marker that can be used for giving options, provides a possible solution to one problem with the meaning of 'or' in ordinary conversation.

A third theme in linguistic pragmatics is presupposition, a topic with a long history in philosophy and linguistics. Presuppositions are propositions that have to be true in order for some sentence or utterance to be meaningful, or perhaps appropriate. The search for a definition of presupposition within context-free truth-based semantics appears to have failed. It now seems that all presuppositions are related to context, in the sense that they depend on what people know or believe about the world. Presuppositions have an interesting and potentially powerful property. They seem to have the potential to convince hearers of the truth of a proposition more effectively than assertions.

In spite of the fact that some scholars who have worked on problems in linguistic pragmatics are reluctant to talk about *cultural* contexts, it is fairly obvious that notions like implicatures and indirect speech acts have to be interpreted in relation to the cultural values of communities of speakers. Those who take the broader Continental view of pragmatics are quite at home with this idea. They see pragmatics as the study of the entire pheonomenon of human communication, at whatever level of analysis. This approach to pragmatics, by no means limited to scholars on the European continent, and admittedly under-represented in my chapters on linguistic pragmatics, has stimulated a great deal of vigorous research and ongoing scholarly activity.

NOTES

1   A *bid* at an auction that is not recognized by the auctioneer might be another example. You would probably report such an incident as 'I tried to bid on the green sofa, but the auctioneer didn't hear (see) me' rather than 'I bid on green sofa, but . . .'. Hancher (1979) mentions a class of speech acts including *barter* and *contract* that involve more than one agent and are therefore subject to one agent performing his or her part and the other not. I find it difficult to see the members of this class as speech acts in Austin's sense, at least in English.

2   I am not inclined to include other conditions that have been suggested to me by students. Some suggest that another conditon is that the speaker will not allow the act to happen again, but it seems to me that this follows as an inference from the condition that the speaker (sincerely) regrets the act. People given the task of suggesting conditions on apologies usually state 1 as 'Speaker did the act', but you can felicitously apologize for your dog's having dug up the neighbors' garden, or for your husband's rude behavior at last night's party.

3   Bach and Harnish (1979), having used 'conventional' to apply to the speech acts I am calling 'ceremonial', use the term 'standardized' for what Searle calls 'conventionalized'.

4   On the other hand, the formula for cancellation of scalar implicatures works much better: 'I regret what I have done, in fact, I apologize' sounds more natural than the corresponding example with 'I'm sorry'.

5   The split infinitive is not the reason. 'I want you to please take out the garbage' sounds much better than 'Are you able to please give me a hand', in spite of the split infinitive in both.

6   I have simplified these maxims somewhat.

7   If Brown and Levinson had wished to preserve Grice's distinction between 'violating' and 'flouting' maxims, they would have used 'flouting' instead of 'violating' here.

8   The transcription has been somewhat simplified.

9   For a clear, succinct summary of this controversy see Levinson (1983:169–77).

10   As Keenan points out, exactly what counts as an answer to a question in terms of logic is not easy to specify. The usefulness of this test for question presuppositions depends on it being possible, however.

11   It is cheating to say that an answer such as 'Hank hid the loot only in his dreams' proves the test wrong because it does not presuppose that he hid the loot somewhere; in fact it indicates he did not really hide any loot at all. It is cheating because 'only in his dreams' is a constituent of the whole sentence 'Hank hid the loot' and the

presupposition only holds on the reading of the question in which 'where' questions a constituent of the verb phrase 'hid•the loot'.

12 This argument assumes a bivalent semantics. I base it on Gazdar (1979:90–1).

13 Critical discussion of Karttunen and Peters's proposed solution to the projection problem is found in Kempson (1975) and Gazdar (1979), to cite just two. Levinson (1983) provides a nice summary discussion.

14 Further details can be found in Gazdar (1979) and in the summary of Gazdar's theory in Levinson (1983).

15 Cf. Horn (1984:16–17).

7

Pidgin and Creole Languages

INTRODUCTION

Among the thousands of languages in the world, there are two related kinds of language that linguists have usually treated as special, called pidgins and creoles. Several books have been devoted to the study of pidgin and creole languages, including Hall (1966), L. Todd (1974, 1984), Adler (1977), Mühlhäusler (1986), and Romaine (1988). In spite of the attention pidgins and creoles have received, the two most recent of these books begin with statements on how difficult it is to define them. Roughly, a pidgin language is generally understood to be a 'simplified' language with a vocabulary that comes mostly from another language, but whose grammar is very different. Pidgins, in the stereotypical case, are formed when speakers of one language engage in trade with speakers of another, or work on plantations managed by speakers of another, and neither knows the other's language.[1] Pidgins are no one's mother tongue. They are used primarily in trading or plantation situations. In plantation settings, their main function is to enable workers to communicate with each other, since plantation laborers very often do not speak the same language. Pidgins are also used, to some extent, by overseers for directing manual labor.

Pidgins

Pidgins are 'simplified' most noticeably in certain aspects of grammar and pronunciation. For example, pidgins will not have grammatical gender in the noun system and do not have noun-verb agreement endings. Tense and aspect are expressed, if at all, with separate words rather than by endings. Pronunciations tend towards a pattern of consonant followed by vowel and clusters of more than one consonant tend to be avoided. I have used quotation marks around the word 'simplified' to try to avoid a misunderstanding. Many creolists, including Mühlhäusler (1986:4), argue that pidgins are full of irregularities and in consequence are far from simple (although they may be called 'impoverished' because expression in a pidgin is difficult in some ways). As pidgins develop, they become simpler in a more valid sense, by becoming more regular.

The best way to get an impression of what a pidgin language is like might be to see some examples. The following letter was written by a Rarotongan man, a teacher on the island of Mataso in the New Hebrides. It was written to a European missionary named Mr Comins and eventually was given to one of the first linguists to study pidgins and creoles, Hugo Schuchardt. Schuchardt used it as an example in an article that he published in 1889.[2] The pidgin in question got most of its vocabulary from English (its *lexifier* language).[3] It seems that there are no pidgin languages being formed at the present time. Furthermore, there are few written records of their formative stages because pidgins and creoles have always been disparaged as hopeless corruptions of their lexifier languages. Mühlhäusler (1986:140), however, finds this text a reliable example of a pidgin at an early stage of development. Although we are looking at an English-lexified pidgin, an English speaker will not understand it. I have supplied an interlinear translation, adapted from Schuchardt's:

Misi kamesi Arelu   Jou no kamu ruki me
Mr   Comins, How are you? You no come look me,

Mi no ruki iuo Jou ruku Mai Poti i   ko Mae tete
me no look you. You look my   boat he go Mae today.

Vakaromala mi raiki i   tiripi Ausi   parogi iou i
Vakaromala me like   he sleep house belong you he

rukauti Mai Poti mi nomea   kaikai me angikele nau
look-out my boat. Me no-more kaikai, me hungry now.

Poti mani Mae i   kivi iou Jamu Vari koti   iou kivi tamu
Boat man Mae he give you yam   very good. You give some

te pako paraogi me i   penesi nomoa   te Pako
tobacco belong me he finish. No-more tobacco.

Oloraiti
All right

Even with the interlinear translation, it is difficult to make out what is meant, although it was probably easier for Mr Comins, who knew the writer and what he was likely to want to talk about. This is a typical situation where pidgins are involved; speakers and listeners have to rely on extralinguistic aspects of the immediate speech situation to a considerable degree. Schuchardt did not supply a connected translation, neither did Mühlhäusler along with his citation of the same text. Although I am not a creolist and I am only somewhat familiar with pidgins or creoles, I am supplying my guess (no doubt foolishly) as to what the letter might have meant:[4]

Dear Mr Comins,

How are you? We haven't seen each other for awhile. Please watch for the boat from here that is going to Mae today. I would like Vakaromala, who will be looking after my boat, to sleep at your house. I have nothing more to eat and I'm hungry now. The fellow on the boat to Mae will give you some very good yams. The tobacco you gave me is all used up; I don't have any more tobacco.

Sincerely,

It is very likely that I have mistranslated the letter in several spots. For instance, the discussion about the yams and tobacco might be about a trade of yams for tobacco. But I have little doubt that a more accurate connected translation would have to be fleshed out at least as much as has been done in my attempt. In particular, a smooth English translation would require tense markings, plural suffixes, forms of 'to be', and relative clause constructions that are actually not present in the original text.

A second example comes from Hawaiian Pidgin English as spoken in the early part of this century (Bickerton 1981:13). In this case, the connected translation is supplied by Bickerton and I have inserted the interlinear one:

samtaim   gud rod get, samtaim, olsem   ben   get
Sometimes good road get, sometimes,all-same bends get

enguru get, no? enikain seim. olsem   hyuman laif,
angles get, no? anykind same. all-same human life,

olsem.   gud rodu get, enguru get, mauntin get – no?
all-same. good road get, angles get, mountain get – no?

awl, enikain, stawmu get, nais dei get – olsem.
all, anykind, storm   get, nice day get – all-same.

enibadi, mi olsem,   smawl taim.
anybody, me all-same,small time.

Sometimes there's a good road, sometimes there's, like, bends, corners, right? Everything's like that. Human life's just like that. There's good roads, there's sharp corners, there's mountains – right? All sorts of things, there's storms, nice days – it's like that for everybody, it was for me, too, when I was young.

Creoles

Creoles, according to the most general account, arise when a pidgin language becomes the native language of a new generation of children. One way in which this can come about is when a man and woman who speak different languages marry, both know a pidgin, and neither learns the other's language. The pidgin then becomes the shared home language and becomes the mother tongue of the children. A setting in which this has happened occurred during the bleakest days of slavery in the Western hemisphere, when efforts were made to separate African slaves with the same native language in order to forestall insurrections. Only pidgin languages were available as common languages and they became the basis for the mother tongues of new generations.[5]

Once a pidgin language becomes a mother tongue, it must support all the interactive needs of its speakers, since they have no other language to fall back on. A creole becomes simpler (in the sense of more regular) and expands its grammatical machinery, as well as stabilizing and expanding its lexicon. If a creole is in touch with its lexifier language, it may 'decreolize' and develop varieties increasingly like the lexifier language. If the less decreolized varieties fall out of use, the decreolized remnants of the old creole may be seen simply as substandard dialects of the lexifier language. As we will see, this has been proposed as the origin for US Vernacular Black English (VBE).

The following is an example of an English-lexified creole; it is an excerpt from a West Cameroon folktale told by Solomon Ndikvu and recorded by Gilbert Schneider in 1963. The transcription and connected translation are taken from G. Schneider (1966:218–20). The creole is called Cameroon Pidgin English by Hancock (1977), although Schneider calls it West African Pidgin English. In spite of its name, it is a creole, not a pidgin. A number of creoles have pidgin as part of their names, with Hawaiian Pidgin and Tok Pisin ('Talk Pidgin') of New Guinea as two of the better-known examples. The folktale is titled 'The Hungry Leopard'.

wan dey, taiga i   don tey hongri lak tu   dey. so i
one day, tiger he done stay hungry like two day. so he

na bat meyk miting   ha   dem gow kas   bif.   wen dat
and bat make meeting how them go   catch beef. when that

dey i   bi kom, dem meyk som ples we   taiga i   bin
day he be come, them make some place where tiger he been

silip lak i don dai. bat i bin   gow fo ntop
sleep like he done die. bat he been go for on-top

sitik fo bigin kol bif dem fo bus wan-wan fo dem
stick for begin call beef them for bush one-one for them

neym fo kom beni taiga. i bin   bigin witi antilop.
name for come bury tiger. he been begin with antelope.

wen antilop bin   hia i   neym, witi i long-long fut
when antelope been hear he name, with he long-long foot

i   bin   ron kom kwikkwik. wen i   kom fo ples
he been run come quick-quick. when he come for place

we   taiga i bin   silip, taiga i wekop an i
where tiger he been sleep, tiger he wake-up and he

kas-am.   i bigin chop-am.
catch-him. he begin chop-him.

The Leopard had been without food for two days so he and Bat decided how they could catch some animals. On the appointed day Leopard came to the chosen spot and played dead. Bat went up in the tree to start calling out the name of one animal after the other to come bury Leopard. Bat began with Antelope. When Antelope heard his name, he ran swiftly with his long legs and came quickly to the place where Leopard was laying. Leopard leaped up, caught him and began to eat him.

Compared to the connected English translation, the Cameroon Pidgin English may seem grammatically sparse to a speaker of English. But it is substantially enriched compared to the pidgin samples. The pidgin samples have no complement clauses, but the creole story has several (*meyk miting [ha dem go kas bif]*, . . . *bigin kol bif . . . [fo kom beni taiga]*). There are rather complex adverbial phrases ([*wen dat dey i bi kom*], *dem meyk som ples*). Time previous to the current point in the narrative can be marked with *bin* or *bi*, and *don* indicates completed action. There is an agreement marker for subject noun phrases (*i*), and transitive verbs take the suffix *-am*.[6] There is much more to a typical creole grammar than there is to a pidgin.

The examples I have given might leave the impression that pidgins and creoles are always lexified by English, but that is not true, of course. The most widely-studied creoles are those that have been lexified by European languages. A listing of the world's pidgin and creole languages has been compiled by Hancock (1971, 1977) and his two lists have been collated by Romaine (1988). Besides Cameroon Pidgin English, some of the best-known English-lexified creoles from these lists are Hawaiian

Creole (the successor to Hawaiian Pidgin, and still popularly called Hawaiian Pidgin), Gullah (an apparently receding creole spoken in coastal areas of the south-eastern USA), Guyanese Creole, Jamaican Creole, Sranan, and Tok Pisin. Some of the more widely-studied creoles lexified by French are Haitian Creole, Louisiana French Creole, Seychellois, Mauritian Creole, and Réunion Creole (these last three spoken on Indian Ocean islands). Of the Portuguese-lexified creoles, two of the better-known are Saramaccan and Cape Verdean Crioulo. There are surprisingly few creoles lexified by Spanish on the lists, but Palenquero and Zamboangueno are perhaps two of the best examples. Papiamento, a creole with a considerable number of speakers on Curaçao, Bonaire, and Aruba has a Spanish-influenced lexicon, but it no doubt derived from an earlier Portuguese-lexified creole. Pachuco, a mixed language spoken along the US–Mexico border, and Cocoliche, an italianized Spanish spoken in Buenos Aires, are listed and have received considerable attention from linguists, but whether they should be considered creoles is dubious.

Possibly the best-known Dutch-lexified creole is Negerhollands, once spoken in the Virgin Islands, but now almost extinct. A Dutch-lexified creole is reported for the interior of Guyana. The variety of German spoken by immigrant laborers in Germany, sometimes called 'Gastarbeiter Deutsch' has some features of pidginization and might be considered a German-lexified pidgin (Klein and Dittmar 1979). Mühlhäusler (1986:222) has discovered a creole of Papua New Guinea called 'Unserdeutch' which was lexified by German. Sabir, a trade language that may have been a pidgin, was spoken in the Mediterranean basin at the time of the Crusades and is important to adherents of the *monogenesis* theory of creole origins. By the monogenesis theory, the majority of the existing creoles of the world are derived from the same original language, and Sabir is often proposed as this source language. There are creoles that are not extensively lexified by European languages, possibly some that are not known except to their speakers. Two that are rather widely known are Chinook Jargon, widely spoken along the Pacific north-west coast of North America in the late nineteenth century, and Sango, a pidginized language of central Africa known largely through the work of William Samarin (for example, Samarin 1967). Another is an Assamese-lexified creole spoken in north-eastern India, Nagassamese or Naga Pidgin (Sreedhar 1977, 1979).

Pidginization and creolization

The sketch of pidgin and creole languages I have just given is, in broad outline, the most generally accepted concept of these linguistic types. Yet everything I have said has been challenged by someone at some time or another. The study of pidgin and creole languages is inherently controversial, partly because their unique properties are usually taken to be related to their historical origins and their historical origins are so hard to trace. It seems that pidgin languages are not being formed today. Furthermore, there are few written records of their formative stages because pidgins and creoles are almost always disparaged as hopeless corruptions of their lexifier languages. Another basis for controversy is the combination of language mixture and reduction that is typical of these kinds of language. This aspect has inspired a great deal of debate about how many of the properties of pidgins and creoles can be attributed to the languages available at the time of their formation and how much should be attributed to general principles of linguistic reduction. Not having specialized in pidgin and creole linguistics, I am in a poor position to evaluate the conflicting opinions in most of these controversies. Instead I will present what I take to be 'conventional wisdom' on most issues. Readers should be aware that almost any issue in creolistics (as the study of pidgins and creoles is sometimes succinctly called) is a controversial one.

It is true that having native speakers is perhaps the most common defining criterion for a creole; it is also true that creoles are structurally enriched compared to pidgins. On the other hand, there need not be a leap from the earliest pidgin stages to a creole, although the abrupt appearance of a creole is common and perhaps typical.[7] In some cases, a pidgin expands and becomes more stable with continued use during the period before it acquires native speakers. Mühlhäusler (1986:5) presents the following development pattern from early pidgins through to creoles that would represent these cases:

jargon
↓
stable pidgin
↓
expanded pidgin
↓
creole

When pidgin development takes place along these lines then some pidgins are more similar to creoles than others; specifically, an expanded pidgin would be more creole-like than a jargon.

Considerations like this have led most creolists to the idea that pidgin and creole language phenomena should be examined in terms of processes and not in terms of types of languages. For example, Dell Hymes (1971b:65) has suggested the study of *pidginization* and *creolization*, 'not as unique and marginal, but as part of our general understanding of linguistic change.' His suggested definitions of the terms have been rather widely accepted (Hymes 1971b:84):

Pidginization is that complex process of sociolinguistic change comprising reduction in inner form, with convergence, in the context of restriction in use.

Creolization is that complex process of sociolinguistic change comprising expansion in inner form, with convergence, in the context of extension in use.

Pidginization is usually associated with simplification in outer form, creolization with complication in outer form.

Hymes's definitions involve reduction, simplification (not in the sense of regularization that was suggested much later by Mühlhäusler), and restriction in use for pidgins, and the opposite – expansion, complication, and extension in use – for creoles. By 'outer form', Hymes refers to matters of linguistic structure, like inflectional endings and word order. In his view, simplification (in his sense) and complication of outer form are usually associated with pidginization and creolization, respectively, but are not part of the definition. One advantage of these process terms is that pidginization, for example, can be applied to trade languages, or *koinés*, without precipitating controversy about whether languages like the trade varieties of Swahili, Malay, or Hindi actually are or were pidgins.

The pidginization and creolization processes have been applied to various phenomena in addition to the study of the languages called pidgins and creoles. 'Baby talk' and 'foreigner talk' (for example, Ferguson and DeBose 1977) is one example; second language acquisition (for example, Schumann 1978 and discussion in Romaine 1988 and in Adamson 1988) is another. For our purposes here, the aspects of pidgin and creole linguistics that are most directly related to issues in sociolinguistics will get the most attention. Creolistics has influenced sociolinguistics perhaps most profoundly in the analysis of linguistic variation and change. An important issue in variation analysis and one of the early forces in the development of variationist sociolinguistics concerned the linguistic history of US VBE. During the mid-1980s, the history of VBE again became an issue, and I will discuss it in some detail. Another major issue in creolistics, the Bickerton bioprogram hypothesis (Bickerton 1981, 1984), is usually seen as a matter for theoretical grammar or psycholinguistics. In my view, however, Bickerton's hypothesis about the role of pidgins in revealing the details of the innate human capacity for language makes a critical contribution to an important issue for sociolinguistics: namely, the relationship between sociolinguistics and traditional linguistics.[8] Because of this, and because of its inherent interest, I will include a discussion of the bioprogram hypothesis.

Negative attitudes towards creoles

Before we can begin any discussion of variation analysis, it is important to say something about the universal point of view among linguists about language variation. This 'linguist's viewpoint' is one that I take for granted throughout this book, and particularly from this point onwards. I need to mention it because the linguist's assumptions are directly opposed to those of nonspecialists, even well-educated people. To a linguist, all varieties of language are to be treated as subject matter for analysis, without prejudice about their adequacy or esthetic value. The contrast between the approach of linguists and the reactions of many other people is never clearer than it is with regard to pidgins and creoles. If you are a reader of this book who has not studied linguistics, you may have a rather negative reaction to an excerpt from a creole. Consider, for example: 'when that day he be come, them make some place where tiger he been sleep like he done die' (the English word-for-word translation of one sentence from the Cameroon Pidgin English story). The thought that such a sentence is a woeful corruption of English may have at least crossed your mind. You might be able to understand why a Cameroonian would use the word 'tiger' to mean 'leopard', since tigers are found in India, not Africa. But why does the narrator not say 'lie down' instead of 'sleep'; the leopard is obviously not asleep since he leaps up and kills the antelope? Why would a Pidgin English speaker refer to a 'day' as 'he' (or use any pronoun at all in this position), and where do such verb constructions as 'be come', 'been sleep', and 'done die' come from? If a linguist is to take any interest in this kind of talk, you may be thinking, it should be with the goal of correcting it. In actual fact Gilbert Schneider, from whose work I took this excerpt, received a PhD in linguistics after submitting a doctoral dissertation analyzing the creole based on this text and others like it. His research involved painstaking effort to record the creole material exactly as it is spoken and his analysis would have been ruined if he had tried to 'correct' the creole texts.

What many people are inclined to do and linguists never do is compare any speech or writing that seems to be English with the rules of grammar they have studied in school. It is not surprising why this should be so, since people are ostensibly taught grammar rules for the purpose of improving their spoken and written use of language, and their written compositions have been scrutinized and downgraded over their school years for grammar and usage errors. Linguists take a different view, partly because they have studied the structures of other languages. Chinese, for example, is structured very differently from English (in some ways, in fact, Chinese grammar is reminiscent of creole grammars), yet the Chinese have a more ancient civilization than the European ones. The Mayan languages of Central America have yet another structure that is different from both English and Chinese. Nevertheless, European explorers found impressive civilizations built by speakers of Mayan languages. If a grammatical structure like those of the European languages is necessary for logical thinking or for the advancement of civilization, then Chinese civilization would not have been ahead of European civilization for so long, and neither would the Mayans have been able to achieve what they achieved independently of Old World influence.

Apparently the whole range of the grammatical structures of human languages are able to support the best of human achievement. With this in mind, linguists approach any language with the assumption that its grammar falls within this range, and take it as their job to discover the details of that grammar, more or less the way a biologist approaches a newly-discovered species. When the new language is a pidgin, a creole, or a rural or urban working-class lect, linguists take the same appproach. They investigate the linguistic system on its own merits rather than comparing it to its disadvantage with the standard or lexifier language. Schneider's dissertation on the grammar of a creole – the source of the West Cameroon Pidgin folktale – is just one example of the way linguists work.

Highly negative attitudes about pidgins and creoles were very common when they were discussed in published accounts by Europeans. Mühlhäusler (1986:26–7) cites examples in which creoles are referred to as: 'adaptions of French or English to the phonetic and grammatical mentality . . . of a linguistically inferior race', or as 'a debased mongrel jargon', or 'a crude macaronic lingo'. It is less likely now that one would find such blatantly racist and contemptuous descriptions of pidgins and creoles in print, but they are still commonly held in very low regard, the research of linguists notwithstanding. Just a few weeks before I wrote this, I was told by a friend from Honolulu (who did not know my views on the subject), that Hawaiian Creole was a miserable language, and although she realized her children had to speak it among their friends due to peer acceptance, she would not allow them to speak 'Pidgin' in the house. The structures of creoles are different from the structures of their lexifier languages, but not because the lexifier grammar has been debased. Figueroa (1971) points out that poets such as Derek Walcott and novelists like George Lamming have written in creole languages. Writers like these present a creole as a rich language resource, rather than a 'problem'.

CREOLISTICS AND LINGUISTIC VARIATION AND CHANGE

The creole continuum

A bit of a sermon that, I know, but my background assumptions, I think, are now clear. For linguists, pidgins and creoles have considerable value as a site for the study of language change. A creole can develop from a pidgin within a generation or two. This represents a considerable amount of change in a very short time. Studying creole development holds out the promise of allowing language change to be observed as it is happening. Changes of similar magnitude in other languages would span the lifetimes of several linguists. In addition, the various stages of development of a creole tend to be preserved as reflections of social status levels. Similar reflections of social factors appear in noncreoles in a more subtle way, suggesting that variation in more commonly-studied languages might also be indicative of historical change, as we will see in the next chapter. The study of variation and change in creolistics has had considerable influence on variation analysis in general.

A typical pattern for variation in a creole that is in contact with its lexifier language is for there to be a variety that is maximally different in structure from the lexifier language, called the 'basilect'. The local variety of the lexifier language is called the 'acrolect'. Between the basilect and the acrolect there will be myriad ways of using language, some of which are rather more like the basilect and some of which are more similar to the acrolect. This series of graded varieties are called 'mesolects'. This kind of variation is called the *post-creole continuum*.[9] One of the most influential contributions to the study of the creole continuum was made by David DeCamp (1971). DeCamp noticed that the Jamaican Creole continuum seemed to fall into an *implicational scale*. He selected six paired features with one member of the pair from the acrolect (indicated with a plus sign) and the other from the basilect (with a minus). The features were the following:

+A child	−A pikni
+B eat	−B nyam
+C /θ ~ t/	−C /t/
+D /ð ~ d/	−D /d/
+E granny	−E nana
+F didn't	−F no ben

The features represent three lexical items (A, B, and E), a grammatical feature (F) and two pronunciation features (C and D). The notation /θ ~ t/ for feature C means that the speaker alternates between /θ/ (the *th* sound) and /t/ in words like 'thing'. The notation /t/ means that only this variant is used. Feature D represents the analogous situation for /ð/ and /d/ in words like 'those'. For seven speakers interviewed by DeCamp from a survey of 142 Jamaican communities, the combinations of the six features were as shown in table 7.1. The data shown in table 7.1 mean that Speaker 1 used all six acrolectal variants and Speaker 7 used all the basilectal ones. But for Speakers 2–6, the use of the variants is ordered *implicationally*. This means, for example, that the use the acrolect form

Table 7.1 Implicational scale for six features of Jamaican Creole

	Feature					
Speaker	B	E	F	A	C	D
1	+	+	+	+	+	+
2	+	+	+	+	+	−
3	+	+	+	+	−	−
4	+	+	+	−	−	−
5	+	+	−	−	−	−
6	+	−	−	−	−	−
7	−	−	−	−	−	−

Source: data from DeCamp (1971)

'child' for feature A *implies* that the same speaker used the acrolectal forms of features B, E, and F, the three features to the left of it on the scale in table 7.1. Similarly, the use of the basilect form for A, 'pikni', implies that the basilectal variants of features C and D, to the right of A on the scale, will also be used by the same speaker.

It seems as if all the variants are not equal. The basilect variant of feature D is apparently 'not so basilectal', since a speaker who uses acrolect variants of all the others might use the basilect variant for D. Feature C is a little 'more basilectal', since a speaker who uses it will not avoid the basilect variant of D even though he or she retains the acrolect in the remaining features. Using 'nyam' instead of 'eat' is apparently the most basilectal of the six, since Speaker 6 avoids using the form although using basilect variants for all the other features. The orderly march of minus signs from left to right is quite impressive, since there are a large number of other logically possible orders in which the pluses and minuses would appear in no particular pattern.

Of course this is not so impressive with only seven speakers. DeCamp might have selected just these seven because they happened to be placed in the order in table 7.1. In fact, DeCamp says he has a Speaker 8 whose array of pluses and minuses would be:

B	E	F	A	C	D
+	−	+	−	−	−

Features E and F are out of order for Speaker 8. If they were reversed, Speaker 8 would fit the pattern of table 7.1 as would Speakers 1–6, but Speaker 7 would not. DeCamp indicates that Speaker 8 is deviant, since he had 'many more informants who agree with 7 than who agree with 8' (DeCamp 1971:357).

The fact that there was a Speaker 8 raises one of the problems with implicational scaling. DeCamp's comment suggests that deviant speakers would be in a small minority. But how small a minority is tolerable? One answer is given by Louis Guttman (1944) who had earlier proposed implicational scaling for data in sociology.[10] Guttman provided as a rule of thumb that 85 per cent scalability would be a sufficient approximation of a perfect scale. This means that 85 per cent of the pluses and minuses would have to be in the proper place in order for the data to scale acceptably. To see how this would work, imagine that we added Speaker 8 to table 7.1. Speaker 8 has one deviation; if we could change the plus for feature F to a minus, Speaker 8 would be just like Speaker 7, who has no deviations. Now we have to ask how many pluses and minuses we have altogether. This is easy to calculate. We have six columns of features and we now have eight rows of speakers, giving six times eight or 48 *cells*. One of these 48 cells is a deviation, so 47 of 48 are in the correct order. The equivalent of 47/48 is 97 per cent, so the data on the eight speakers easily meets the requirements of Guttman's rule of thumb. Of course, we would really like to see the data for all DeCamp's speakers to see if it is acceptably scalable with a larger number of speakers.

A fascinating aspect of implicational scales is that they often give you usable information 'for free'. The speakers in table 7.1 were ordered in rows and the features in columns so as to maximize the scalability of the entire data set. We have already seen that the resulting order of features can be interpreted as reflecting degrees of 'basilect-ness' or 'acrolect-ness'. The speaker order also comes out in an interesting way. Speaker 1, who has acrolect variants for all six features, has the social identity qualities associated with acrolect speakers. He is a young well-educated proprietor of a successful radio and appliance shop. Speaker 7, with all basilect variants, is an illiterate peasant in an isolated mountain village. The social identities of the speakers in between 'are roughly (not exactly) proportional to these informants' positions on the continuum' (DeCamp 1971:358). For example, Speaker 3, with four acrolect features and two basilect features, has a responsible job as a market clerk and has had some formal schooling and a relatively high income.

Bickerton (1971, 1973) has used implicational scaling at several points in his analysis of Guyanese Creole. Bickerton (1973:17) sees little value in 'reading off' social status differences or degrees of acrolect–basilect quality from the axes of implicational scales. Instead, an implicational scale is 'an abstract measuring device' which, if it reveals data that scale successfully, will have found a case of 'a succession of rule-changes [that have] spread fairly evenly and consistently through the community as a whole' (Bickerton 1973:202). He is much more interested in the structure of a creole continuum as it reveals grammatical change than as a way of examining the social structure of creole communities. One of his most striking analyses involves the changes accompanying the introduction of forms of 'to be' into Guyanese Creole.

Bickerton's scale is designed to elucidate the linguistic change by which the English copula forms 'is' and 'was' (*iz* and *waz* in their Guyanese Creole spellings) move into the language. To see this, he distinguishes several *linguistic environments* in which these forms would be required in English. The form before which English would have 'is' or 'was' is underlined in the examples, except for the cleft and impersonal constructions where the entire construction is underlined.[11] The fact that Guyanese Creole grammar is not English grammar is emphasized by the wide variety of forms that are all symbolized by '1' on the scale. These are basilect forms, and Guyanese Creole grammar requires a different 'equivalent' for the English 'to be' form, depending on the construction. The first environment is the continuative verb construction. There are two Creole constructions for this; the first one, *a* plus the verb, is more basilectal than the V*ing* (verb + -ing) form with nothing preceding. In locative or existential constructions, *de* is used where English has a 'to be' form. What would be predicate adjectives in English seem better analyzed in Guyanese Creole simply as attributive verbs (hence the quotation marks around 'P(redicate) A(djective)'. Attributive verbs are unmarked in present contexts and are preceded by *bin* in past contexts. In other words, *yu tal* 'you are tall' is not a pronoun followed by an adjective with a 'missing' copula verb, but a pronoun subject followed by an attributive verb, parallel to *yu wok* 'you work'.

The rows in table 7.2 are labeled with letters designating *isolects*, not individual speakers. The term 'isolect' was introduced by Charles-James Bailey (1973a) and refers to a linguistic variety which is minimally different from other varieties. In this case, the isolects differ by the environments in which one or more alternative forms appear. Bickerton sees isolects as levels of style in a creole continuum. Each isolect can be, and generally is, represented in the data by a different speaker, or by two or three speakers who were recorded speaking in the same style. It would be possible for the same speaker, if he or she changes speech styles, to provide data for different isolects, but in practice data are not usually collected that way. The speakers in Isolect H, for example, have all three possibilities – *de*, Ø, and *iz/waz* – in locative or existential environments.

We are now in a better position to interpret the scale. The general tendency is for the copula forms *iz/waz* to enter Guyanese Creole from the right and proceed through the environments from right to left. This means the environments on the right are somehow more hospitable or favorable to the introduction of *iz/waz* than the ones on the left. This requires an explanation beyond just saying that some environments are

Table 7.2 *Implicational scale for the introduction of the English copula in*
Guyanese Creole

			Linguistic environments				
Isolects	$V_{cont.}$	*Loc./Exist.*	*'PA'$_{pres.}$*	*Cleft*	*'PA'$_{past}$*	*NP*	*Impersonal*
A (2)	0	1	1		1	1	1
B (1)	1	1	1		1	13	
C (2)	1	1	1	1	13	23	3
D (1)	1			13			
E (3)		1	1	3	3	3	1
F (2)	1	1	13		3	3	
G (2)	1	12	13	3	3	3	13
H (3)	13	123	13	3	3	3	3

Environment examples:
$V_{cont.}$: mi a *kom* back haptanuun – 'I'm coming back in the afternoon'
    mi *livin* a sevntiwan – 'I was living in Seventy-one' (name of a village)
Loc./Exist.: dem de *aal oova di plees* – 'they were all over the place'
'PA'$_{pres.}$: yu *redi* fi sliip – 'you are ready to sleep'
Cleft: a *da* me tel dis bai – 'that's what I told this boy'
'PA'$_{past}$: da taim ting bin *haad* – 'things were hard then'
NP: dooz pleesiz *terribol rapidz* – 'those places are terrible rapids'
Impersonal: a *hau* dem pak tre hiip – 'how is it that they made three stacks?'
Variable forms:
0: *a* + V
1: Various basilectal forms; verb + -ing (no auxiliary) in $V_{cont.}$, *de* in Loc./Exist.,
    Attributive verbs ('predicate adjectives') in 'PA'$_{pres.}$, equative *a* in Cleft, NP
    and Impersonal, *bin* in 'PA'$_{past}$
2: Ø
3: *iz/waz*
The number of speakers recorded from each isolect appears in parentheses.
Source: data from Bickerton (1973)

more or less 'basilectal' than others. Bickerton's (1973) article provides a linguistic analysis designed to give just this explanation, but we need not be concerned with the technical details.

Another thing to notice about table 7.2 is that it has four symbols in the cells, not just the pluses and minuses in DeCamp's scale. These symbols, of course, represent various options for these constructions, not basilect or acrolect alternatives of unrelated linguistic features. The 0 in the upper left corner simply shows that the *a* + V form appears only in the most conservative isolect and the most conservative environment. The 2, indicating Ø in an environment in which the basilect would have a form like *de* or *bin*, appears in environments along with, or after one of the forms indicated by 1 and before 3 takes over. Again, unlike table 7.1, the scale is not perfect. With four values it is not so easy to see what should count as a deviation, but in general a 2 should not occur above or to the left of a 1 and a 3 should not occur above or to the left of a 1 or a 2. If a 3 appeared above a 1, it would mean that the new form *iz/ waz* had come into the same environment in a more conservative lect before a less conservative one. If a 3 appeared to be left of a 1, it would mean that the new form *iz/waz* had moved into an environment that is supposed to be less favorable before it moved into a more favorable environment. There are two such cells in table 7.2, both in the impersonal environment. In isolect E, a 1 has several 3s to the left of it and a 3 above it. If this 1 were a 3, the scale would be corrected in both directions, so this counts as one deviation. In isolect G, another 1 appears, this time along with a 3 in the same environment, and again with 3s to its left and a 3 above it. If this 1 could be removed, the scale would be correct. But, of course, the speakers actually used these forms, so they cannot be removed and must be counted as deviations. Since in this scale a row may represent more than one speaker, the total number of cells must take this into account. You cannot just multiply the rows by the columns. I will not go through the arithmetic here, but these two deviations mean table 7.2 is 95.5 per cent scalable, well above Guttman's suggested limit.[12]

The final scale we will examine, in table 7.3, is another one from Bickerton (1973). In this analysis, Bickerton is interested in the appearance of Ø forms in Guyanese Creole where the basilect has pronounceable form. He uses two such environments, Loc./Exist. and NP (along with $V_{cont.}$ and 'PA'$_{pres.}$) to show how the appearance of Ø forms relates to the general change introducing *iz/waz*.[13]

In general, the instances of Ø (symbolized by 2) occur roughly between the creole forms symbolized by 1 and *iz/waz*, symbolized by 3 in those environments where the basilect has some pronounceable form in that environment (Loc./Exist. and NP). There are one or two technically deviant cells. One troublesome one is the appearance of Ø in the NP environment of isolect B, which is several isolects before it becomes common. It turns out that this deviation represents only two utterances and there seem to be explanations for why these particular deviations occur (Bickerton 1973:32). Otherwise, Ø does not appear until *iz/waz* is well established in the NP and 'PA'$_{pres.}$ environments. Notice that this means that the Ø copula makes its appearance in the mid-mesolect isolects. In other words, the Ø copula is not a part of the Guyanese Creole grammar itself, but is introduced into the mesolects due to a clash between existing basilect rules and the incoming acrolect system. Notice that in both the NP and Loc./Exist. environments both the acrolect and the basilect require *some* form. It is only the mesolects in which Ø is possible. I am going into some detail on this issue because it has ramifications for two other topics, the history of VBE and the 'developmental' theory of linguistics.

A central notion in developmental linguistics is the notion that linguistic systems (roughly 'languages') are distinct from each other. According to the theory, a language may change in certain ways without being influenced by another language, but will not generally become a new linguistic system unless there is contact with another system. Within-system variation and change leads to a continuum. By contrast, the pattern of change in progress where there is contact between systems should be viewed as a *gradatum* since change is not smoothly continuous, but has definite boundaries – or *discontinuities* – within it. C.-J. Bailey (1973a, 1974) used an abstract version of Bickerton's data in table 7.3 to illustrate one way this can happen. This scale, in modified form, appears as table 7.4.

In table 7.3, isolects E–K are the true mesolects since only they (ignoring the problem with the NP environment in isolect B) have Ø, the feature 'peculiar to the mesolect' corresponding to Y in table 7.4. The Guyanese Creole data depart from the ideal pattern in table 7.4 in that the acrolectal *iz/waz* enters the earliest environment (NP) before the mesolectal Ø appears at all and, when Ø does appear, it appears first in Loc./Exist., not NP. As Bickerton (1973) explains in some detail, there are good reasons for the situation in Guyanese Creole.

Notice that an implicational scale can be seen as a reflection of changes over time. In tables 7.2 and 7.3, for example, we can see the isolects towards the top of the scale as earlier and the ones towards the bottom as representing a later state of affairs. The initiation of a new feature, such as *iz/waz*, gains a toe-hold in the most favorable environment early in the process, and then spreads more widely through the language as

Table 7.3 Implicational scale for the spread of zero copula in Guyanese Creole

Isolects	$V_{cont.}$	*Loc./Exist.*	*'PA'*$_{pres.}$	*NP*
A (1)	1	1	1	13
B (2)	1	1	1	23
C (3)	1	1	1	3
D (2)	1	1	13	3
E (2)	1	12	13	3
F (1)	13	12	13	23
G (4)	13	123	13	3
H (1)	13	13	13	23
I (2)	13	3	13	23
J (1)	13		3	23
K (1)	3	23	3	3

Environments and variable forms as in table 7.2.
Source: data from Bickerton (1973)

Table 7.4 Abstract scale for mixing systems in a trisystematic decreolizing gradatum (Modified from C.-J. Bailey 1974:90)

Linguistic environments	Most recent	Next	Earlier	Earliest
Acrolectal system	Z	Z	Z	Z
Mesolectal gradatum (Y is	Z	Z	Z	YZ
peculiar to the mesolects)	Z	Z	YZ	Y
	Z	YZ	Y	XY
	YZ	Y	XY	X
	Y	XY	X	X
	XY	X	X	X
Basilect (X is basilectal)	X	X	X	X

time goes on. This sort of interpretation of the patterns revealed in implicational scales is present in Bickerton's work and is systematically exploited in developmental linguistics, as we will see in the next chapter.

As I have said, the notion of a creole continuum (or gradatum) and the associated implicational scaling technique have had considerable influence on the analysis of linguistic variation by sociolinguists. But, like almost everything else in creolistics, it is controversial. Excellent, detailed discussions of the criticisms of the creole continuum notion are to be found in Rickford (1986) and Romaine (1988) and in the references they cite.[14] I will take up here three of the major criticisms. One of these has to do with whether an unidimensional basilect-to-acrolect model can do justice to the actual facts of language use in creole communities. Robert LePage (1980b; LePage and Tabouret-Keller 1985) is the most eloquent critic from this point of view. In LePage's theory of language, communities have a range of variation at their disposal, and the variants are capable of symbolizing social identities. Speakers attempt to project who they are relative to the community and relative to other participants when they engage in speech acts (hence the title of LePage and Tabouret-Keller's book, *Acts of Identity*). If a relatively similar sort of identity is enacted by most community members most of the time, the individuals and community will be *focused*. If there are several conflicting but valued kinds of identity, the community will be *diffuse*. Over time, people's linguistic behavior can become more diffuse, more focused, or become refocused in new directions. It is easy to see how the notion of a creole continuum would seem too restrictive from this point of view. A continuum with speakers lined up on only one dimension would not fit the facts. It seems to leave no room for diffuseness and to imply that there is always only a single focus (on the identity represented by the acrolect). The data from creole communities of Belize and St Lucia indicate no such singularity of focus, and it seems the creole continuum notion would fail there.

One response to this objection has been made by Rickford (1986). After reaffirming the apparent usefulness of the continuum model for Guyanese Creole, he suggests that it might be possible to analyze the Belize and St Lucia data with a series of overlapping unidirectional continua.[15] This would allow for diffuseness without giving up the simplicity of the continuum concept. If the linguistic situation in some communities is truly multidimensional, with multidirectional interactions (in a technical statistical sense), then the series-of-continua solution would not work.

Another way to respond is to hold that the continuum model is not designed to model the social structure of a community with regard to language, but only as a tool for understanding how linguistic features of the acrolect interact with the existing creole grammar during decreolization. It is indisputable that there are varieties within creoles, such as Guyanese creole, that are rather more like English and still others that are less like English. The continuum notion can be used, from this point of view, to find out what happens in grammars, rather than in communities, as these changes happen. A linguist like Bickerton, for example, concentrates on the structure of grammars and is convinced that members of communities subsequently and indirectly make use of what happens in the structure of languages. He makes his perspective quite clear:

> In fact, the creole continuum is first and foremost a LINGUISTIC and not a SOCIAL phenomenon. Assignment of social values to language is something that takes place at a conscious level . . . The development of the language itself, which must have predated any assignment of social value, is a very different matter . . . Such pressures [to avoid the basilect or acquire the acrolect] do exist, on the social level, but they do not CAUSE changes in language, they merely EXPLOIT such languages. (Bickerton 1980:124–5, emphasis in the original)

Developmental linguistics holds itself responsible for both of what C.-J. Bailey (1982) refers to as the neurobiological and sociocommunicational aspects of language, but the two are to be kept somewhat distinct. As Bailey (1982:10) puts it: 'the study of language . . . ought to proceed with some sort of unity (but not *confusion*) among pragmatics, rhetoric and grammatical (and lexical) analysis' (emphasis in the original).

LePage's approach to linguistics is the opposite. For him, there is no such thing as a grammar independent of social life. His point of view is clearly expressed:[16]

> Over the past few years I have suggested a number of ways of looking at language which have allowed me . . . to have a general linguistic theory which was, I felt, both psychological and sociological in nature. That is, it related the individual to society, and sought to explain the properties of linguistic systems in terms of that relationship. It is not, however, a *grammatical* theory. A grammatical theory

requires that one keep a particular social artifact, 'the language,' a constant. But
. . . the relationship between the social artifacts, 'language,' or 'language variety,'
and 'language community' is in fact a variable. Neither of these can be kept
constant or internally self-consistent except by a process of idealization which is
bound to distort the sociolinguistic model. (LePage 1980b:331–2)

Behind the controversy about the creole continuum, then, lies a more
fundamental controversy within the field of linguistics. This disagreement
comes out all too often in the shadow of another controversy, such as
this one concerning the creole continuum. Much of the research in
sociolinguistics has been motivated by the view that linguistics has in the
past greatly overstated the distinction between language and its use. Many
would agree with LePage that linguistic theory is precisely the discovery
of regularities in the use of language in its social setting. William Labov,
perhaps the leading scholar in sociolinguistics, takes an intermediate view
(Labov 1980a). In discussing LePage's work on Belize Creole, he approves
of LePage's study of language in its social context and of his use of
quantitative and longitudinal data. His own work in Philadelphia indicates
that black speakers and white speakers are members of different speech
communities, to a significant extent, based on substantial differences in
the linguistic systems they have. This suggests a description of speech
communities that is 'not . . . far from the characterization of the
community put forward by LePage', and Labov believes 'that we may
find that "continuum" is a slightly misleading term' (Labov 1980a:384).
On the other hand, Labov's description is of a cline of linguistic systems,
some of which are 'structurally more united than others' with transitional
zones of which speakers have less consistent and partial knowledge. It
seems to me that this leaves open the possibility that the principles of
variation and change that have been revealed through the continuum
model might apply at least within these 'structurally united' systems.[17]
My own inclination is to see, as Bickerton does, a sharp difference
between linguistic structure and the principles of language use in social
settings.

A second criticism of the creole continuum is not really about the
continuum concept itself, but about implicational scaling (cf. Romaine
1988:186–7). Commonly-mentioned problems concern scalability and
variable cells. We have already seen that Guttman's 85 per cent rule of
thumb is commonly appealed to, but this value only represents Guttman's
impression based on general experience. There may well be established
tests of statistical significance, at a given level of confidence, for
implicational scales but, if so, linguists do not use them. There is
considerable freedom for manipulating the data in an implicational scale,
since the environment can be rearranged in any order that gives the best
results, and the rows of isolects of speakers can likewise be reordered.
Nevertheless, in whatever order the environments are ultimately placed,

it must work for (virtually) all the isolects. At the same time, the ordering of isolects that is finally chosen must give the right results for (virtually) all the environments. Obviously the data for a given environment cannot be moved into a different environment, and neither can a speaker's utterances in one environment be assigned to a different isolect from that person's utterances in another environment, so there are built-in restrictions on the freedom to manipulate data in constructing a scale. Romaine (1988:187), for one, finds implicational scaling 'far too powerful' in spite of these restrictions on data manipulation.

A third problem has been pointed out by Anshen (1975) and discussed by me (Fasold 1975). In many implicational scales in the published literature, especially on matters of grammar rather than phonology, the data in a given cell is likely to be sparse. In an interview of an hour or so, a speaker might not have very many occasions to use the constructions represented by the environments in tables 7.2 and 7.3. An isolect with a 3 in an environment signifies that *only iz/waz* was used in that isolect in that environment. But it might well be the case that only one or two utterances occurred in that environment. Suppose the interview had gone on for another quarter of an hour and during that time one of the speakers from that isolect had used the construction in question with one of the basilect forms represented by the number 1. If that had happened, the cell would have 13 in it. Even if the interview had continued for four hours beyond that point and the speakers from that isolect used *iz/waz* exclusively, the cell would still contain 13. In other words, once a cell becomes variable, it cannot become invariable with the addition of data. On the other hand, the more data we have, the greater the opportunity there is for speakers to use an alternative form, which would make the cell a variable one. Conceivably, virtually all the cells could become variable so that we end up with a table with 13 or 123 in every cell. Technically, this scale would be perfectly scalable, but would be totally unrevealing. Of course it can be argued that if speakers provide variable data when larger amounts of recorded speech are investigated, it means that they have switched styles within the recording session, and therefore different parts of the interview should be assigned to different isolects. But this argument would be far more convincing if the data in each cell were based on, say, 15 or more utterances from the same part of an interview, rather than on one or two. As Romaine points out, information on the number of instances in each cell is often not provided.

In spite of these objections, data displayed as shown in table 7.2 or 7.3 appears to be 'trying' to reveal the patterns that Bickerton is claiming. We might want to withhold final judgement pending data with more filled cells and with more generously-filled cells, and we might wish for more statistical rigor in deciding when an implicational scale is a satisfactory approximation of a perfect scale, but I personally find Bickerton's analyses reasonably well supported and far more precise than any alternative proposal with which I am familiar. Unfortunately, scholars who are disinclined to agree with analyses supported by implicational scales have the option of raising objections along the lines I have just discussed.

'Grammaticalization' in creoles

So far, I may have left the impression that the creole continuum and associated implicational analysis is the only contribution to variation analysis made by creolistics. It is true that this strand of research has had a substantial influence on the study of linguistic variation, particularly within developmental linguistics. Nevertheless, there are important influences from other directions. One of the most important is the tracing of the development of grammatical markers from lexical markers within discourse structures in the process of decreolization. In broad outline, this line of research shares the outlook on language that we have already seen in Hopper and Thompson's work on text analysis. Perhaps the best-known example of this kind of analysis was carried out by Sankoff and Brown (1976/1980). Their data on Tok Pisin, the New Guinean English-lexified creole, shows that the most common way to mark relative clauses is by 'bracketing' them with the word *ia*, as in this example from Sankoff and Brown (1980:213):

Na pik *ia* [ol ikilim bipo *ia*] bai ikamap olsem draipela ston

'And this pig [they had killed before] would turn into a huge stone'

The Tok Pisin word *ia* is derived from the English word 'here' and seems originally to have been used as a locative adverb as in *Yu stap ia*, 'You stay here', although such a use is now rare. It is more common for *ia* to have a deictic function, specifying the noun after which it comes, as in the following example about the purchase of a type of cloth (Sankoff and Brown 1980:223):

Disfela *ia*, ol ikosim em haumas?

'This one, how much do they charge for it?'

As Sankoff and Brown point out, the use of an adverb of place as a general deictic element is not an exotic sort of phenomenon that happens only in creoles. The nonstandard English expressions, 'this here one' and 'that there one' are examples, as would be the more elegant English usage exemplified by 'the issue here is' (which strikes me as on the border between locative and deictic force), and the standard French *celui-ci* 'this one' and *celui-là* 'that one' (from the French adverbs *ici* 'here' and *là* 'there').

A further use for *ia* is to call attention to the noun phrase it follows as one that is about to receive further identifying or descriptive material, in order to help the hearers find the referent. For example, a woman describing a movie with two main male characters says (Sankoff and Brown 1980:226):

na em, man *ia* [lapun man *ia*], stap autsait ia

and this man, [this old man], stayed outside.

The noun phrase between the square brackets, meaning 'old man' serves to identify the referent as the older of the two main characters in the movie. It is then just another step to extend the use of *ia* to identify a noun phrase that is about to receive a more extensive descriptive construction, a relative clause, as in the example above about the pig. The form becomes 'grammaticalized' as a relative marker as its deictic function fades in favor of a status as a formal marker of relative clauses of any kind. Sankoff and Brown's point, of course, is that this sort of development can be illustrated by reference to a creole, but is a typical example of the relationship between discourse phenomena and syntactic marking in any language. It probably is not actually a creolization process at all, since this kind of clause-bracketing is not found in other creoles.[18] Romaine (1988:241–51) provides an interesting comparison of Sankoff and Brown's analysis and other analyses of creole relative clauses and her own work on the acquisition of relative clause structures by children.

THE BIOPROGRAM HYPOTHESIS

Derek Bickerton's (1981, 1984, 1986, 1988) 'bioprogram hypothesis' has received a great deal of attention in creolistics and has considerable implications for the study of language beyond creoles themselves. According to Bickerton's hypothesis, human beings have a biological program for language that is distinct from whatever general learning resources they may have. In other words, a human being comes into the world with a capacity for acquiring a language and this capacity is of no use for learning anything *but* language. So far, this idea is not unique to Bickerton. Chomsky (cf. a rather lucid recent argument for this position in Chomsky 1988) and many who have followed him (for example, Lightfoot 1982) have argued that people have a biological 'organ' for language that can be compared to a bird's capacity to learn to fly.

Bickerton sees his hypothesis basically as an enhancement of Chomsky's version of the innateness hypothesis.[19] In Bickerton's initial proposal (Bickerton 1981), linguistic innateness is different from Chomsky's view. In his view, the details of bioprogram grammar could be overridden by the influence of 'cultural language' (Bickerton 1981:296). In Bickerton's more recent thinking, there is one fundamental set of syntactic principles that is valid for all the world's languages, whether creole or not. This basic syntax can be derived from principles that Chomsky and other syntacticians have developed. The differences among the grammars of different creoles (or among the grammars of languages in general) come from properties of the *words* that a language has.[20] Chomsky's view of the innate language capacity of humans is essentially structural and deals with what structural configurations are possible and which element can refer to the same entity as another element. For example, the binding theory component of Chomsky's theory of linguistics is designed to account – in addition to other syntactic facts – for an interesting property of the following two sentences:

His$_i$ psychologist says the patient$_i$ can't accept himself$_i$.

He$_i$ says the patient$_j$ can't accept him$_i$.

The subscripts *i* and *j* are intended to indicate sameness and difference in reference. In the first example, the pronoun 'his' can refer to the same person as the noun phrase 'the patient'; in fact, that would be the most natural interpretation if the sentence were uttered. Furthermore, the reflexive 'himself' *must* refer to the same person as 'the patient'. It would not occur to anyone to think the sentence might mean that the patient cannot accept *the psychologist*. In the second example, the man referred to by 'he' is *not* the same person as the one meant by 'the patient'. At the same time, 'him' *could* be the same individual as the pronoun 'he' refers to, and it is certain that 'him' cannot possibly mean 'the patient'. The difference between the first parts of the two example sentences has to do with the fact that the pronoun 'his' in the first example is *part of* a noun phrase construction with 'psychologist' as its head. In the second example, the pronoun 'he' *constitutes* the noun phrase which has no complex internal structure. The difference in the second parts of the examples is related to the difference between plain pronouns and reflexives. Reflexives *have to* refer to something mentioned in the same clause (where 'same clause' means everything after the word 'says' in our examples), and plain pronouns *cannot* refer to anything in the same clause.[21]

Chomsky would argue that this sort of thing could not be deduced from language children hear as they grow up, partly because children would not have sufficient evidence to learn it: sentences exhibiting the relevant distinctions are not often spoken to begin with, and in any case are not the sort of thing you say to small children. Furthermore, there is no evidence that children make mistakes along these lines. Youngsters apparently do not say things like: 'She says Jenny hid my doll' where 'she' refers to Jenny. Indirect evidence that this is not an expected error comes from the fact that grammar books never contain rules that say anything like, 'Never use a pronoun subject to refer to the same person as the subject of the complement of its verb', no doubt because it never occurs to authors of grammar books that anyone would have the slightest inclination to do so.

To show how lexical differences can produce a difference between creole grammars, Bickerton (1986:229–30) compares English-lexified creoles with early French Haitian Creole. Because of certain pronunciation features of reflexives in English compared with French, English creoles, at an early stage of development, take at least one plain pronoun form from English, and also a form of *self* as a reflexive, but French creoles take only pronouns at a comparable stage. Since the French-lexified creoles do not have separate words for pronouns and reflexives at this stage, the restrictions that the innate bioprogram theoretically place on pronouns and reflexives do not apply. As a result, these creoles allow sentences like:

li_i bat li_{ij}.
He hit him(self)

Here, the second *li* (from French *il*), can refer either to the same person as the first *li*, or to somebody else; the sentence is potentially ambiguous. This does not mean that particular structural principles of the bioprogram do not apply to early Haitian Creole, it is just that the language does not have the words that they would apply to.

Bickerton's earlier thinking about differences between the grammars of languages was quite different. His idea then was that the bioprogram effects can be suppressed if children learn a 'cultural language', like English. Chomsky's theory calls for certain *parameters*, or choices that are made differently in different languages. For example, in Spanish, but not in French or English, personal pronoun subjects need not appear, although what the pronoun would be is indicated by the endings on the verb. Chomsky would say that children are born with a kind of 'expectation' that they will have to select either a grammar that requires an explicit pronoun or one that does not, depending on the language they hear. He would *not* want to say that the innate linguistic capacity stipulates there has to be pronouns, but that children learning Spanish simply ignore that part of it because they hear so many Spanish utterances without subject pronouns.

This creates a substantial difference between Chomsky's view and Bickerton's earlier view of the status of what you might find in an actual language. For Chomsky, if a given structure occurs in some language, it must either be called for by the innate human language capacity, or by one of the choices it allows. In Bickerton's initial thinking, if you find, say, time distinctions indicated in a certain way in given language, it may be a consequence of the bioprogram; however, it is more likely to be the consequence of the linguistic structure of a 'cultural language' that has little or nothing to do with the bioprogram, but which has over-ridden what the bioprogram would have specified if 'left alone'. This would seem to mean that we would want to find out what kind of language children would speak if they never heard any language at all. This does not work though, because in the rare and tragic cases in which children grow up in isolation, they do not learn any language at all. Instead, we need a case in which children get linguistic input, but input that is so poorly organized that the child-learner simply does not get the material needed to develop a grammar. In such cases, Bickerton argues, there is nothing to rely on but what the bioprogram calls for, and a bioprogram grammar results. What children would receive this kind of input? Bickerton's response is: children who acquire their first language from speakers of an unexpanded pidgin, say a 'jargon' in Mühlhäusler's terminology. This situation is extraordinarily rare.

Two creole cases that are particularly helpful are the development of Hawaiian Creole from Hawaiian Pidgin early in this century, and the evidence from Saramaccan, a largely English-lexified creole spoken in Surinam (Bickerton 1981, 1984). What is special about Surinam, Bickerton argues, is that it changed from English to Dutch control before the pidgin English spoken by the slaves there had a chance to expand. With only a rudimentary pidgin English available, and with those in control of the country speaking a totally different language, Dutch, new generations of slaves would have had to rely heavily on the bioprogram. Saramaccan is the result following this line of reasoning. Hawaiian Creole, of course, developed in contact with English, but its development happened sufficiently recently for creolists to have been able to study speakers who represent some of the early stages. Saramaccan and some of the data on Hawaiian Pidgin, Bickerton finds, represent close approximations of the bioprogram, but its effects are present, to a greater or lesser extent, in other creoles as well (Bickerton 1984). Today, Bickerton would explain the critical role of creoles in figuring out what the bioprogram is like on the basis of *lexicon*. Creoles, especially Saramaccan which developed with such limited contact with its original lexifier language, just do not get very many of the grammatical words – prepositions, for example – that allow the grammatical differences that exist between most languages to come out.

The bioprogram hypothesis has come under considerable scrutiny and criticism. Mühlhäusler (1986) makes references to it, mostly negative. Romaine (1988) devotes a whole chapter to the hypothesis, in which she examines a rather wide range of evidence on the issue and remains unconvinced, although apparently regards the question as still open. The 'open peer commentaries' to Bickerton's 1984 article in *The Behavioral and Brain Sciences* include both supporters and detractors and a typical range of reactions to the proposal.

The similarity among creole grammars is one fact that might be explained by the bioprogram hypothesis. It can be explained another way, according to an earlier proposal, by *monogenesis* and *relexification* (cf. Mühlhäusler 1986:107–13; Romaine 1988:86–91, and the references they cite). By this reasoning, most of the creoles lexified by European languages are ultimately derived from the same original pidgin, perhaps the medieval Mediterranean trade language, Sabir. Since these creoles are now lexified by various languages, this hypothesis requires that monogenesis be accompanied by relexification: the rather startling idea that a creole can lose its original lexicon and replace it with another one. As radical an idea as relexification might seem to be, Mühlhäusler (1986:108–10) presents several case studies which seem to show that relexification has taken place in some Pacific creoles, and the idea is not usually rejected by creolists, at least not on the grounds that it could not have happened. Bickerton's response here is to argue that Hawaiian Creole, at least, could not have been influenced by the descendants of this original pidgin (if it existed), given the historical facts; yet he would argue that the development of Hawaiian Creole provides clear evidence of the bioprogram at work.

It is easy to see how the issue can continue to be argued inconclusively since so much depends on the condition of the inputting pidgin at the time of the original formation of any given creole and this, it seems, can never be established beyond dispute. One way around this, as one of the respondents to Bickerton (1984) seems to suggest, would be to observe children who are currently learning creoles with only unexpanded pidgin input. But Bickerton points out that it is three-quarters of a century too late to conduct any such research, since this kind of creole-formation is not going on anywhere in the world. This led Bickerton, in collaboration with Talmy Givón, to propose the following somewhat audacious experiment (discussed in Bickerton 1979; Mühlhäusler 1984:93–4). They proposed placing 16 volunteers, including couples with young children, on an uninhabited Pacific island. These volunteers should be speakers of different languages, historically unrelated and structurally different from each other. They would be given all necessary social and medical facilities, and a vocabulary of about 200 essential words. Aside from that, they would be left alone. Bickerton and Givón predict that within a year the adults would develop a rudimentary pidgin and that the children would later develop a creole based on the pidgin. The proposal was submitted for funding, but did not receive it, and so was never carried out.[22] It seems that the historical or experimental evidence required to decide the validity of the bioprogram hypothesis is so difficult to get that the hypothesis is doomed to continuing inconclusive controversy until linguists eventually lose interest in it.

Amid the din of the scholarly conflict over the bioprogram hypothesis, one of its implications is almost totally overlooked. Bickerton once openly proposed an innateness hypothesis according to which the outcome of unrestricted application of the innate mechanism can be over-ridden by an aspect of the context in which learning takes place, namely the 'cultural language' that the vast majority of children learn. The Chomskyan hypothesis tacitly assumes that the innate mechanism cannot be over-ridden, although the language being learned can determine which parameter settings emerge. Beyond that, contextual factors, it is assumed, can only influence the choices allowed by the grammar of the speaker's language, or cause people to produce utterances that the grammar would not allow (that is, make mistakes in speech). Bickerton's current view is that grammatical differences come from properties of the words that different languages have. This idea is much easier to reconcile with the idea of parameters in current syntactic theory. In spite of Bickerton's modification of his thinking, I still think it would be worth putting his earlier idea under scrutiny. Perhaps it is possible that languages end up with fully acceptable constructions, considered unexceptional by speakers, which *replace* some of the constructions that are specified by universal grammatical principles of the sort explored by theoretical syntacticians. As we have seen in the preceding chapters and will continue to see, sociolinguists tend to take language to be entirely a social phenomenon that has reality only (or mostly) in the context of people communicating with each other. Research in syntactic theory by and large takes it as given that communicational behavior can safely be ignored. Conceivably, the idea that the innate can in part be over-ridden by the cultural can be shown to be generally valid. If so, it would demand a whole new way of looking at the relationship between the various kinds of sociolinguistic research and the investigation of abstract grammatical structure. It would also demand much more mutual respect between practitioners of the two kinds of linguistics than we have today.

CREOLE AND US VBE

Features of the VBE verb system

An examination of the considerable research that has surrounded the relationship between US VBE provides a reasonable connection between this chapter and the next one. Part of the research has been concerned with the hypothesis that VBE is a substantially decreolized linguistic descendant of a Plantation Creole spoken in the USA before the Civil War, with linguistic ties to English-lexified creoles spoken in the Caribbean and West Africa. At the same time, the study of variation in VBE supplied a lot of the data and inspiration that led to a period of great growth in variation analysis.

It will be useful at this point to review some of the aspects of VBE which seem to distinguish it from other kinds of American English. These features have been summarized by Wolfram and Fasold (1974, chapters 6 and 7), and more recently by Baugh (1983). It is the features of the verb system that are the most remarkable, and I will go over some of these here.

1   Habitual or distributive 'be'. One of the most-discussed features of VBE is the use of uninflected 'be' as a main verb, in such sentences as (Baugh 1983:70–1):

When they get caught stealin – they *be* talkin bout how innocent everybody is.
But the teachers don't *be* knowing the problems like the parent do.

This form is used in the context of repeated events, as indicated in the first example by the adverbial 'When they get caught stealin'. The protestations of innocence are presented as a typical response to getting caught stealing. The use of 'is' is appropriate in talking about the innocence of the alleged thieves. To use 'be' here would suggest that they were only intermittently innocent. There are instances of uninflected 'be' that occur in other varieties of English as well as in VBE which are sometimes mistaken for this VBE form (cf. Fasold 1972b), and this has generated some baseless controversy about the form. Habitual 'be' can be distinguished in negative sentences like the second one above from all other uses except the imperative, because it is takes the auxiliary 'don't'. Imperative uses of 'be' are usually clear from the context.[23] The second example may not appear to be 'habitual', but it is iterative in the sense that the speaker is saying that any teacher you encounter at any time will not be as familiar with children's problems as a parent would be.

2   Remote time 'been'. We have seen that *bin* is often a marker of past time in English-lexified creoles (in Guyanese Creole, for example). In modern VBE, when 'been' appears in a verb phrase construction, often with a past participial form, it has the meaning, according to Rickford (1975), of placing the initiation of the action in the remote past. Most often, perhaps we would want to say always, the form 'been' is stressed. According to Rickford and Baugh (1983:81), it contrasts with unstressed 'been' which indicates simply a prior state of affairs, but not necessarily one that was initiated remotely prior. In any case, VBE allows 'been', both stressed and unstressed, in constructions in which they would never occur in other kinds of English, for example:[24]

I *béen* knowing that.
'I learned that a really long time ago, why would you think it's new to me?'

They *béen* called the cops, and they're still not here.
'They called the cops a long time ago; they've had plenty of time to get here.'

He *béen* been in jail.
'He was put in jail a long time ago and he's still there.'

I *been* had it there for years. (Note: 'been' is unstressed)
'I have kept it there for years.'

You won't get your dues that you *been* paid. (Unstressed 'been')
'(If you give up the club membership) the dues that you had paid will not be returned.'

3   Completive or perfective 'done'. The form 'done', with the force of a completed action, can be used in constructions with past or past participle forms, as in (Baugh 1983:76):

I *done* forgot to turn off the stove.
if Pop'd catch us, he say, 'Boy – you *done* done it now'.

Some English-lexified creoles, including Guyanese Creole (Bickerton 1975) have *don* as a verbal particle. But other English lects have it as well (Wolfram and Christian 1976; Feagin 1979). Baugh (1983) doubts that the VBE usage is exactly parallel to the construction in other English lects.

4   Future completive or future perfective 'be done'. The use of the future completive is potentially one of the most dramatic possibilities in VBE. Preceding a past form of a verb, it signifies that the future completion of the act is assured.[25]

We *be done* washed all the cars by the time JoJo gets back with the cigarettes. (said at a church-sponsored car wash)

I'll *be done* bought my own CB waitin on him to buy me one.

I'll *be done* killed that motherfucker if he tries to lay a hand on my kid again.

The last example was said (by the parent of a youngster who had been pushed into a swimming pool by a white lifeguard) as a threat against the lifeguard. Although the speaker probably was not literally contemplating murder, anyone who understands the verbal system of VBE would find it a particularly chilling threat, since the father is presenting 'be done killed' as an act already complete in the future if the child is threatened another time. In other words, retribution is guaranteed.

5 Aspectual 'steady'. The form 'steady' occurs with verb + *ing* constructions to indicate intensive continuation (Baugh 1983:85–9).

your mind is *steady* workin.
'You are thinking continuously and intently.'

Them fools be *steady* hustlin everybody they see. (Note: this usage is in construction with distributive *be*)
'Those fools hustle everybody continuously and they work at it.'

6 Semi-auxiliary 'come'. A use of 'come' before verb + ing constructions for the purposes of expressing indignation about the action being spoken about was analyzed by Spears (1982). For example:[26]

We sitting there talking, and he *come* hitting on me for some money.
'We were sitting there talking and he had the nerve to pressure me to lend him money.'

She *come* going in my room – didn't knock or nothing.
'She had the nerve to go into my room without knocking.'

7 Absent forms of 'be'. Many linguists who have worked on VBE have noticed that 'be' can be absent where one of its forms would be required in other lects of English, with studies by Wolfram (1969, 1974a), Labov (1969, 1972a), and Baugh (1980) being among the most thorough. Some of the examples recorded by Wolfram (1969:165) include:

She ⎯ real nice.

They'll probably say that they ⎯ the boss.

He ⎯ not German.

If we ⎯ fighting and we ⎯ getting beat . . .

No semantic distinction between these kinds of sentence and the corresponding sentences of standard English is claimed.

8 Absent verbal 's'. In standard English, the suffix 's' is required on verbs in the present tense if the subject is in the third person singular. In VBE it is a variable, with both 's'-suffixed and unsuffixed forms being observed, but the frequency of unsuffixed forms is very high, approaching 100 per cent in the most thoroughly vernacular speech collected by Labov (1972a). This phenomenon has been well-documented (Wolfram 1969; Fasold 1972b, Labov 1972a). Some examples include:

He walk ⎯ to school every day.

She like ⎯ chocolate the best.

Derrick do⎯n't know nothing.

The creole origin hypothesis

The language of black Americans was given scant attention before the early 1960s. It was generally taken for granted that the kind of English used by most American blacks was comparable to the language of white Americans of the same geographical region and social status (for example, McDavid and McDavid 1951). During the mid-1960s, the creole history hypothesis was presented in articles by Beryl Bailey (1965) and (more forcefully) by William Stewart (1966, 1967, 1968). The hypothesis became more widely known with the publication of J. L. Dillard's (1972) book on Black English.[27] The presence of Gullah (cf. Turner 1949; Hancock 1980; Jones-Jackson 1986; Mufwene and Gilman 1987), a language spoken by black speakers on the Sea Islands off the South Carolina and Georgia coasts, an unmistakable creole, was treated as exceptional by McDavid and McDavid and others, but taken as evidence of an earlier creole stage within US borders by proponents of the creole origin hypothesis. The idea was strongly resisted by many during the 1960s and 1970s (for example, Williamson 1971), but gradually received increasing acceptance over the years. Part of the argument in favor of the hypothesis is that so many of the verbal features of VBE, including many of the ones I have just summarized, either do not occur in lects spoken by whites or are used differently or with sharply lower frequency. At the same time, the majority of these distinctive linguistic features strongly resemble features of English-lexified creoles.

We have seen that *been* and *don* occur as creole verbal markers, at least in Guyanese Creole, although the case for *don* is a bit muddied because of its use in white lects. The absence of the present tense marker 's' matches the typical creole unmarking of nonanterior tense. The absence of inflected forms of 'to be' before adjectives arguably reflects creole attributive verbs (translated as adjectives, but with no form of 'to be' necessary in the creole). Similarly, as we saw for Guyanese Creole, one form for continuative verbs is verb + *ing* without any form of 'to be'. In other environments, mesolectal Guyanese Creole develops a Ø form where English would have 'to be'. Habitual 'be' is harder to trace to creole origins, but Rickford (1974) has made the most convincing case. Although Baugh (1983) and Spears (1982) suspect that a creole origin for 'steady' and 'come' might eventually be found, there is no known evidence yet. The future completive 'be done' seems to be a VBE innovation.

In Fasold (1981), I summarized the research up to that time on differences between black and white speech in the USA, and found the creole history hypothesis the most likely explanation as the source for these differences. Labov (1982b:192) lists the creole origin hypothesis as one item of consensus on Black English: 'It [Black English] shows evidence of derivation from an earlier Creole that was closer to the present-day Creoles of the Caribbean.' In fact, at least where the absence of 'to be' is concerned, objections have been raised to claims that VBE has *de*creolized as much as some analyses would suggest. In a classic article, Labov (1969) argued that present-day VBE 'to be' absence is an extension of English contraction, by allowing the remnants of contraction ('s' and 're' but not 'm') to be deleted after contraction had taken place. Although I tried to argue (Fasold 1972a) that Labov's analysis might be the outcome of very late stages of decreolization, Bickerton (1973) and Romaine (1988:167–72) are doubtful that contraction is involved in 'to be' absence in VBE at all; in other words, it is more of a creole than Labov's analysis would imply.[28] By the early 1980s, the only issue in the history of VBE seemed to be how far it had decreolized; the creole history hypothesis was well-established.

The divergence controversy

Since then, three strands of research have appeared to open up new challenges to the idea that the linguistic ancestor of VBE was a creole. In a recent article, Labov and Harris (1986:20) came to a startling conclusion: 'The Philadelphia speech community is separating into two distinct speech communities: white and black. They share a large part of the general English language, and a number of local words as well . . . But the number of differences between them in grammar and pronunciation seem to be growing steadily greater.' Some of the data they base this conclusion on has to do with sound change in the vowel system, which is seldom involved in the creole origin issue. A morphological feature they use to support their conclusion, which has come to be known as the *divergence* issue, is the 's' suffix on present tense verbs. As we have seen, the absence of this suffix has been explained as a residue of the posited earlier creole stage of VBE. Based on data collected by Myhill and Harris (1986), Labov and Harris conclude that 's' is being acquired by core groups of VBE speakers, not as a grammatical marker of person, number, and (present) tense, but as 'a mark of the narrative past' (Labov and Harris 1986:16); that is, it appears during the course of narrations of past events. No such use of verbal 's', Labov and Harris report, has been discovered in the speech of any white dialect.

Independent and parallel research by Guy Bailey and Natalie Maynor (1985a, 1985b, 1987), particularly that presented in the most recent article, indicates the same thing is happening in black speakers' language in Texas. In the use of habitual 'be', which they call be_2 following an earlier practice of Labov, they find that old black adults in a rural area use very little be_2, especially compared to a sample of children aged 12 or 13 from the same general social and geographical background. The greater frequency of be_2 used among the younger speakers was almost exclusively before verb + *ing*, as in 'He always be fighting'. In other cases, for example before adjectives ('she be mean sometimes'), or locatives ('They be out on the street'), the frequencies for the older and younger speakers are similar. This leads Bailey and Maynor to the conclusion that the children are not just increasing their use of be$_2$, but giving it a new grammatical significance.[29] At the same time, the younger speakers show markedly greater frequency of inflected 'to be' absence where 'is' is expected than the older speakers do, although they have less absence than the old people where 'are' is expected. This is important, because it is regularly noted that white lects of Southern States American English quite commonly have Ø for 'are' while Ø for 'is' is generally rare or nonexistent. This means that the youngsters are increasing their use of the Ø copula precisely where it makes their speech *less* like the surrounding white lects than the speech of the old people. In sum, Bailey and Maynor have presented serious, carefully analyzed empirical data in support of the divergence hypothesis.

The divergence hypothesis, as you might expect, has not gone unchallenged. At a conference at Georgetown University in 1985, a panel discussion of the divergence issue was held (*American Speech* 67(1), 1987). Labov and Bailey were both on the panel and they presented and supported their position that the evidence indicated divergence was taking place. Four other linguists, Walt Wolfram, Fay Vaughn-Cooke, Arthur Spears, and John Rickford, commented on the idea.[30] Of the four, Wolfram and Vaughn-Cooke were the most critical. In their discussions, a number of points were made.

In the first place, Bailey and Maynor's data relies implicitly on the 'apparent time' method of sociolinguistic research. By this method, the speech of older and younger speakers in the same community is compared. The sample from older speakers is taken to represent the facts at the time they were learning their language, while the younger speakers are taken as representatives of the current state of affairs. But apparent time studies have a built-in hazard: the effects of age-grading. Age-grading means that people might use language in a particular way when they are young and change their use as they grow older, and that this pattern might repeat generation after generation.[31] In the Texas data, it might conceivably have been the fact that the old speakers used VBE just as the young adolescents are now doing when they were that age, but changed as they grew older. If so, we might expect the younger speakers to use be$_2$ and Ø for 'is', just as the old speakers are now doing, when they reach the age of 70 or so. Bailey and Maynor are aware of this danger, and deliberately chose children who were at least 12 years of age, since earlier reports have indicated that age-graded phenomena in VBE tend to diminish at around the age of 8. This cut-off age, however, is of questionable reliability, and age-grading remains a potential flaw.

Still, other facts in the Texas research make it an unlikely explanation, at least in my own view.

Another factor has to do with the method of data elicitation. The use of be$_2$ becomes very frequent when people who use the feature are asked to describe what happens in their everyday life. For example, when one asks children how they play games like tag and hide-and-go-seek (this is a common kind of question in sociolinguistic interviews), the description is probably part of their everyday life and the question creates a very favorable setting for the use of be$_2$. The same question asked of an adult has to framed as, 'How did you play tag when you were a child?' The response is about an earlier period in the respondent's life and creates a much less favorable context for be$_2$. This might create the illusion of an age difference when be$_2$ might be just as common in the older speakers' interviews, had the interview question created an equally favorable context.

Labov and Harris's case does not depend so heavily on the apparent time method. Labov has been carrying out research in VBE for decades and their data can be compared with data collected about 20 years earlier. In this connection, though, another problem arises. Not only has understanding of VBE increased over the last 20 years, but techniques of data collection have improved as well. Labov in particular has shown great and increasing skill and creativity in tapping subjects' *vernacular* linguistic systems: that is, their everyday language use when no one is around observing them. If the emergence of 's' as a marker of narrative past only emerges, or emerges most reliably, in 'core' vernacular narratives, and if it has only been fairly recently that the techniques for eliciting good vernacular narratives have been developed, the failure to find narrative 's' in the earlier data might reflect this difference in field methods. The feature might have been present 20 years earlier but the methods used did not elicit it. Wolfram (1987) also noted that the use of narrative 's' patterned very much like the 'historical present' in Schiffrin's (1981) analysis of the speech of white Philadelphians. To the extent that this is true, it would not be a very good example of divergence.

There is a good deal of other evidence, some of it presented by members of the 1985 panel, of convergence with American English in some features of Black English (see especially Vaughn-Cooke 1987). In response to a conference report of still other data showing convergence (Butters 1987), Labov clarified his view of divergence by making the following three points: divergence is a matter of *qualitative* changes in the VBE linguistic system, not changes in frequencies of variants; divergence applies only to the Black English *Vernacular*, the speech of the most ethnically isolated blacks (other black speakers are converging); and only certain important features of VBE are diverging, not the entire grammar. This sharpened version of the divergence hypothesis would not be vulnerable to most of the evidence showing general convergence.

Another objection, not of an academic nature, is the effect of the divergence hypothesis on people who have no interest in matters of linguistic analysis. The hypothesis has received considerable attention from the US communications media, both broadcast and print. Much of the coverage has involved Labov himself. His motivations for making general presentations of the hypothesis are impeccable. He feels that he has evidence for increasing rifts in US society and for increasing educational problems in communities of poor black people, and wants the potential problems to get the attention that might lead to their amelioration. The actual effect, as Vaughn-Cooke (1987) pointed out, might be quite different. Given popular prejudices against nonstandard lects, the average newspaper reader or television viewer might not come away with the message: 'Black and white communities are separate and getting more so. We have a problem that needs a solution.' The message they get instead might be: 'Black people use very bad English already and their English is getting worse.'

I have reviewed two independent strands of research, the studies in Philadelphia described by Labov and Harris and the analysis of the central Texas data by Bailey and Maynor. Before we get to the third, it should be pointed out that even if the conclusions drawn by Labov and Harris and by Bailey and Maynor are correct in every detail, it would still detract very little from the creole origin hypothesis. The evidence presented could easily represent a new divergence trend involving a creole that had already reached an advanced stage of decreolization. In the case of verbal 's', it would mean that, in the course of adding an element from the acrolect, VBE speakers had put it to a different use from the use it has in the acrolect. We could even argue that that is what *usually* happens in creoles. To take an example, 'been' is a past participle of 'to be' in English, but *bin* is a particle marking anterior tense in Guyanese Creole and other English-lexified creoles. Assuming a creole origin for be$_2$, an interpretation could be that VBE speakers in central Texas, and perhaps elsewhere, are retaining and developing a creole feature instead of losing it. If be$_2$ is an innovation in VBE, as Bailey and Maynor tend to think, then it can be seen as a case like 's' as a narrative past marker: that is, a new use for English 'be'.

From a creolist perspective, there would be nothing new in this. LePage's approach, for example, leads the analyst to expect multiple focus and refocusing. If VBE has begun to diverge, it could be seen as an instance of a community refocusing in a new direction, away from the acrolect. The older focus on the segment of the society symbolized by the acrolect would have caused a very advanced state in the decreolization process, while the new focus leads the speech community in a different direction. In fact, a good bit of Labov and Harris's description of the conditions under which divergence has taken place in Philadelphia could readily be reinterpreted in LePage's terms. Even without a full commitment to LePage's approach, something like divergence would not be totally unexpected; recall the objection raised to the continuum model on the grounds that it seems to imply a unidirectional movement toward the acrolect. Among segments of the British black population (British-born descendants of immigrants from the West Indies) in the UK, a phenomenon which Romaine calls *recreolization* is taking place, as a result of which some younger speakers are moving towards more basilectal speech, in spite of the fact that they live in the original English-speaking country and have been educated there (cf. Romaine 1988:188–203 and the references cited there). Rickford (1987), the only creolist on the 1985 panel, in fact made the precise point that the post-formation development of a creole is not a steady, unbroken move towards the acrolect, but a series of changes in a variety of directions.

Of itself, then, divergence is far from incompatible with the hypothesis that US VBE has its origins in a creole. In order to cast doubt on that, it would be necessary to find evidence that VBE was no more like a creole earlier in history than it is today. As you can well imagine, this would not be easy to do. It is always possible to point to Gullah, which is no doubt a creole, and say that it represents an earlier stage in the development of VBE, as Dillard and Stewart, who sparked the current interest in the creole hypothesis, have done. But the objection can be raised that Gullah is the result of special circumstances and has nothing to do with inland Black English. Stewart and Dillard have also appealed to general descriptions of black speech from the southern States before the Civil War by travelers and others as support for their hypothesis. This sparks a new controversy about the reliability of such data. Detractors argue that such accounts are invariably written by whites with low regard for blacks and who would therefore portray their speech in a way that would make them seem unintelligent. Dillard (1972:18) responds that if the writers were making up Black English, it is surprising that their various accounts are as uniform as he finds them to be.

Another source of information is to be found in the slave narratives collected by the US Federal Writers Project designed to provide employment for news reporters and other writers during the Great Depression in the early 1930s. Many of the narratives were taken from former slaves who would have been about 100 years old in the 1930s. If we use their data as apparent time evidence, their speech would represent the Black English as it was during the middle of the nineteenth century. In fact several linguists have done analyses of these narratives, myself included (Dillard 1972; Brewer 1973, 1979; Fasold 1976; E. Schneider

1983; Pitts 1986). In some ways the language of these narratives is like an English-lexified creole, in some ways it is not. Recently, however, Bailey and Maynor have found evidence which shows that the narratives were fairly extensively edited before being archived and the language in them might be very different from what the ex-slaves had actually said.

However, these materials were collected at a time when sound-recording technology was just being developed, and there are a handful of actual *recordings* of slave narratives. The quality of some of them is poor and some of them are recordings of songs, but G. Bailey (1987) has conducted an analysis of copula deletion for some of them and found that the absence of 'to be' resembles the data from the present-day rural speakers he has analyzed. In other words, these data from people who were acquiring their language in the mid-nineteenth century show little evidence that Black English was more like a creole then than it is now.

Perhaps the most dramatic evidence on the creole origins and divergence controversies has come from the analysis of data from a community of slaves liberated from the USA located in the Dominican Republic. This community, called Samaná, is populated by descendants of slaves who had been liberated and enabled to emigrate under the auspices of American church and philanthropic organizations beginning in the early 1820s (Poplack and Sankoff 1987; Tagliamonte and Poplack 1988). The community is currently undergoing a shift to Spanish by the most recent generation, but has maintained English up until now. Data has been collected from some of the older English-speakers of Samaná and subjected to painstaking quantitative analysis for those features that seem most likely to reflect creole origins.

What is unique about the Samaná data is that English has been maintained apparently in the absence of significant contact with any outside variety of English. This would have left the community without any contact with English to serve as an impetus for decreolization. Except for influence from Spanish, which seems to have been slight, any changes that may have occurred would seem to be only those changes that any other language would undergo. There would be no reason to suppose that it would become more like a standard variety of English than it had originally been. In a sense, we might compare the Samaná data to finding the intact remains of a woolly mammoth frozen in an iceberg in the state it had been in when it died. The results of the analyses by Poplack and her associates demonstrate that present-day Samaná English is no more like a creole than are various samples of modern VBE speech collected in the USA. If we can take the Samaná data to be representative of US Black English from the early nineteenth century, then the most straightforward conclusion would be that Black English had already decreolized to modern-day levels by then, or else it had never been a creole in the first place.

There can be no doubt that the analysis of the Samaná data conclusively demonstrates that it is no more creole-like than present-day VBE is. The data collection and analysis procedures were exemplary. It is possible to argue that the Samaná data are not representative of vernacular black speech in the USA when Samaná was settled. It is well-known that the Samaná immigrant population did not all come from the same kind of background. Some had been living in Philadelphia or other areas in the northern states before emigrating, but others had apparently recently been emancipated from slaveholders in the south. Of these, many may have been field slaves, who might have had little contract with relatively standard English lects, but others may have been house slaves with a much better opportunity to hear the regional standard English. If there *had* been a Plantation Creole at the time, the Samaná immigrants would have included speakers of various mesolect levels as well as the basilect. It is not necessary to assume that all these varieties would have survived, even if they were present at the beginning. In a community of only a few hundred or a few thousand, a few individuals might have had a disproportionate influence on the ultimate community speech norms. This is a possibility that has been pointed out by Samarin (1984) in another connection.

The case of Pitcairn Island is a possible example. Pitcairn Island was settled by nine mutineers from the HMS Bounty, their Polynesian wives, and nine other Polynesians (Tahitians and Tubuaians). They remained isolated for more than 30 years. Yet the creole that developed is an English-lexified language. This happened despite the fact that half the Englishmen died in the first four years and all but one within ten years, most in disputes over women (Romaine 1988:64–5,259; Mühlhäusler 1986:93). Under a similar scenario, the Samaná community would have become focused on the social identity represented by speakers of the upper mesolects in the community. These 'upper mesolects' would correspond roughly to the level of decreolization to which historical forces eventually have brought the rest of VBE in the mid-twentieth century.

An account like this would 'explain away' the Samaná data, but it involves a great deal of speculation and would have nothing to say about the recorded slave narratives that G. Bailey found to be comparable to his present-day VBE data. (After all, the ex-slave narrators would never have been influenced by anything that went on in the Dominican Republic!) The actual speech data that are available, however problematical, point to the conclusion that VBE either has a separate history from the Caribbean Creoles and Gullah, or it had decreolized and stabilized as a language that looks very much like contemporary VBE by the mid-nineteenth century at the latest.

SUMMARY

Pidgins and creoles have been seen and studied as 'special' languages. Typically taking most of their vocabulary from a particular language (their lexifier language), they have grammars which are generally very different from that of the lexifier language. Pidgins are typically formed in trading or plantation situations in which speakers of one language need to communicate with speakers of other languages in a limited way. Pidgins are conventionally taken not to have native speakers, by definition. Their grammars are 'impoverished' since they lack grammatical devices that other languages have, and are often very erratic in form, especially near the time of their formation. When pidgins gain native speakers, again according to the conventional definition, they become creoles. Creoles are grammatically distinct from their lexifier languages. The source of these differences is a source of intense controversy. The differences may be due to languages other than the lexifier that contributed to the formation of the creole, or to universal psycholinguistic tendencies, or a combination of the two.

Many creoles have been lexified by European languages and most of the languages of European countries that had overseas colonies have lexified one or more creoles. Creoles lexified by European languages have been the most extensively studied, but there are a number of creoles which have other languages as lexifiers. Confronted with a creole, speakers of the language that has lexified it will almost inevitably see it as a corrupt and degenerate treatment of their own language. Linguists, who are familar with the wide variety in linguistic systems around the world, see creoles as functioning linguistic systems on their own, which should not be compared – especially unfavorably – with their lexifier languages.

Creolistics, the study of pidgin and creole languages, is fraught with controversy. Many creolists have tacitly agreed to avoid controversies over whether a given language is 'really' a pidgin or a creole by accepting Hymes's (1971b) suggestion that the processes of pidginization and creolization should be the topic of study. Not only does this avoid the problem of labelling particular languages but, more importantly, it opens up the possibility of studying these processes as part of general linguistics.

A major contribution from creolistics to the sociolinguistic study of language variation has come from the creole continuum model (and from criticism of it!). The creole continuum is a model used in the analysis of various subsystems found in creole-speaking communities. The model was devised for situations in which the lexifier language is present as an acrolect, along with the basilect – the variety of the creole most distinct from the acrolect – and various mesolects between. The implicational scale is commonly used as a way of revealing the structure of the continuum. The general insights of the continuum model and the order revealed by implicational scales have been used in developmental linguistics, which can explain these phenomena and others in terms of waves of change through time and by other principles. Other linguists, like LePage, have criticized the continuum model as distorting the social structure of creole communities. Some supporters of the continuum concept defend it as a way of understanding linguistic, rather than social, dynamics.

Another contribution to variation analysis from creole studies is the study of the 'grammaticalization' of certain linguistic elements as creoles develop. Sometimes items originate in an advanced pidgin or an early creole as an ordinary word but, under the pressure of discourse requirements, become grammatical particles. A detailed and often-cited study of this type was carried out by Sankoff and Brown (1976/1980) on the development of *ia* (English 'here') in Tok Pisin from a locative item to a particle marking the beginnings and endings of relative clauses and a few similar structures. The point of view in these grammaticalization studies, relating grammar to discourse, is quite similar to the approach taken by Hopper and Thompson that we saw in chapter 3.

Another important concept from creolistics is the bioprogram hypothesis of Derek Bickerton (1981, 1984, 1986, 1988). The bioprogram hypothesis posits a biological capacity uniquely organized for language in the human species. In that respect, it is similar to the innatist theory of Noam Chomsky (for example, Chomsky 1988) and scholars in theoretical syntax who have followed Chomsky's general approach. The bioprogram differs in that it involves semantics and makes predictions about certain grammatical markers, rather than limiting itself to structural relationships as conventional innatist linguistic theories do. A crucial difference, to my mind, is the idea than the details of the bioprogram can theoretically be entirely over-ruled when 'cultural languages' are being learned. (This view is no longer part of Bickerton's thinking, however.) In conventional theories, the particular language being learned can at most determine which of a set of well-defined options will be taken by language learners. If this idea from an early version of the bioprogram hypothesis can be defended, it would create a new relationship between sociolinguistics and traditional linguistic theory.

Controversies about the history and future of US VBE have involved creolistics. The suggestion that VBE might have its origins in a creole was much disputed during the 1960s and 1970s, but seemed to be widely accepted by the early 1980s. At that time the divergence hypothesis was proposed on the basis of research by William Labov and associates, and independently by Guy Bailey and Natalie Maynor. In principle, both the creole origin hypothesis and the divergence hypothesis can be true at the same time. However, some of the evidence that has come to light in the research on the divergence hypothesis has created a new challenge for the creole origins hypothesis. Regardless of the merits of these hypotheses, it seems clear that VBE is no more an unworthy approximation of English than English-lexified creoles are. In fact, the verb system of VBE seems to be noticeably richer than the verb systems of socially favored English lects.

NOTES

1   According to LePage (1977:222–3) every time anybody talks to anybody else, the result is an 'instant pidgin', the resulting talk being the product of the linguistic competence of one or more persons. In the case of conversations among people who speak the same language, the linguistic competence that is shared among them is considerable, so the resulting talk has considerable resources to draw on. In the situations in which pidgin languages develop, the shared linguistic competence is severely restricted and the resulting talk is consequently impoverished in some ways.

2   The version I am citing is the translation of some of Schuchardt's work on pidgins and creoles by Glenn Gilbert (1980:26–7).

3   Traditionally, the lexifier language has been called the *base* language. A creole or pidgin lexified by English, for example, would be called an *English-based* creole or pidgin. As Mühlhäusler (1986:5) points out, quoting Dennis and Scott (1975), there is no good reason to consider the vocabulary of a pidgin or creole to be any more of a 'base' than the semantics, syntax, or pronunciation.

4   Schuchardt indicates that the phrase *paraogi mi*, 'belong me', in *te pako paraogi mi*, 'tobacco belong me', is to be taken as a dative.

5   What I am outlining is the traditional account of creole development. I find Bickerton's (1986, 1988) account both more sophisticated and more compelling but, like almost everything in creolistics, it is controversial.

6   Although *i* has English 'he' as its source and *-am* comes from 'him', they have become grammatical markers in Cameroon Pidgin English.

7   As Bickerton informs me in personal communication. He sees the development of Hawaiian Creole as virtually such a leap from Hawaiian Pidgin. This historical event provides crucial evidence for his 'bioprogram' hypothesis, as we will see.

8   The general hypothesis that human beings are born 'wired for language' in an important sense is widely (though not universally) accepted by linguists; less widely by psychologists.

9   LePage (1980a) and later Romaine (1988) point out that the concept of the linguistic continuum is an old one and is implicit in the writings of Hugo Schuchardt.

10   DeCamp became aware of Guttman's work only after he had independently seen it as a way of dealing with creole continuum data.

11   The cleft construction would have 'it' plus a 'to be' form in English; a more direct structural equivalent of the example would be 'It's *that* that I told the boy'. Impersonal constructions in English have a semantically empty 'it' followed by the 'to be' form, as the translation indicates.

12   Some cells are blank, meaning that *none* of the variants of this form were used in a particular environment in a particular isolect. Blank cells are left out of the scalability calculations entirely.

13   The isolects in table 7.3 represent some of the same speakers as those in table 7.2, but include different ones as well. There is no match between the isolects in the two scales.

14   Interestingly, Rickford emerges cautiously approving of the concept, and Romaine rather skeptical.

15   Rickford, by the way, is Guyanese by birth and a native speaker of Guyanese Creole.
16   Interestingly, LePage and Bickerton's statements appear in the same collection, but neither seems to have read the other's contribution before publishing his own. At first I was inclined to consider this a pity, but I now think that LePage's and Bickerton's background assumptions about language are so different that there would be very little to gain from a dialog between them. However, Washabaugh (1980) does respond to Bickerton's article in the same volume from a general perspective similar to LePage's.
17   Labov's statement is also reminiscent of Bailey's decreolizing gradatum.
18   As Bickerton has pointed out to me.
19   In his most recent work, Bickerton (1986, 1988) proposes a theoretically elegant and simple way of relating his bioprogram hypothesis to some of the basic principles in Chomsky's theory.
20   The differences between grammars that Bickerton has in mind would be called *parameters* by Chomsky.
21   If you have studied syntax, you know that there is more to it than this. What I have said here will be sufficient for our purposes.
22   You might think about whether you would be willing to serve as a volunteer if the experiment were ever to be funded!
23   Recent research on 'be' by John Myhill (1988) has indicated that habitual meaning might not be the only or even the main significance of this form. Other research by Elizabeth Dayton and Ann Houston suggests that the semantics of uninflected 'be' in infinitives, imperatives, after modals auxiliaries, and elsewhere in VBE might be the same as in the kind of constructions I have cited and different from the corresponding constructions in white dialects.
24   The second and third examples are from Baugh (1983:80–1). The fourth was spoken by one of the Detroit informants whose speech was analyzed by Wolfram (1969). The first and fifth are my own observations.
25   The first two examples are from Baugh (1983:78); the third is from Labov (1982b:191).
26   The standard English translations are quite loose ones.
27   Schuchardt (1914:97–8) seems to have considered the language of American blacks to have been a creole, or related to creoles, at least the coastal variety called Gullah, but possibly the inland varieties as well. He distinguishes and discusses both varieties in the context of a survey of Western hemisphere European language-lexified creoles, but does not quite assert that US blacks spoke a creole or the descendant of one. Gilbert (1985:83), who has translated Schuchardt's work into English, has no doubt that Schuchardt believed the language of blacks in the USA originated as a creole. Schuchardt's work, however, was not widely known to linguists working on VBE in the 1960s and 1970s.
28   Labov originally proposed that deletion of the remnants of contraction is unique to VBE and that this explained 'are' absence in white lects that do not have [r] in 'are', since 'are', being represented only by a vowel, would be entirely removed by contraction in these lects. This was conclusively shown to be incorrect by Wolfram (1974a). Romaine (1982a, ch. 8) presents rather telling counterarguments to other aspects of Labov's analysis. In spite of all this, it is my opinion that contraction-deletion is part of modern VBE.
29   This is not the place to go into it, but I want to point out that Bailey and Maynor's interpretation of the data, while a reasonable one, is not the only one it will bear.
30   I served as moderator of the panel.
31   The age-grading factor was pointed out in another context in the companion volume to this book (Fasold 1984a:283–4).

8

Linguistic Variation

INTRODUCTION

One of the major topics in sociolinguistics is the study of language variation and change with its inevitable relationship to social forces. In the earlier part of this century, the orientation of structural and generative linguistic theories discouraged the quantitative analysis of observed language behavior. Linguists did not try to find out about the principles of language variation or how it might be related to linguistic change and to the social setting, so very little was known about it. An early study by John Fischer (1958) demonstrated that variation between '-ing' and '-in' (as in 'talking') in a group of children was influenced by social factors such as sex and social status. But most of the advances in studies of variation and change were inspired by the work of William Labov.

Many of the concepts and methods that were to influence linguistic studies of change and variation originated with Labov's classic *The Social Stratification of English in New York City* (Labov 1966). Labov used audio-recordings of the speech of residents of New York's Lower East Side. He knew quite a lot about the social characteristics of the speakers because they had participated in an earlier study by a team of sociologists, so that rather sophisticated comparisons between linguistic and social data were possible. The basic elicitation tool was the *sociolinguistic interview* in which the investigator asks the respondent a series of questions that have been designed to inspire connected speech and to encourage the use of particular linguistic forms. The sociolinguistic interview method has been developed considerably since that time (for example, Labov 1984; L. Milroy 1987, chapters 3 and 4).

CLASS AND STYLE STRATIFICATION

One of the concepts that Labov developed was the *sociolinguistic variable*. A sociolinguistic variable is a set of alternative ways of saying the same thing, although the alternatives will have social significance. For example, '/ɖ ~ d/', one of the features DeCamp used to construct his implicational scale for Jamaican Creole, can be treated as a sociolinguistic variable. Recall that this notation means that the speaker alternates between [ɖ] and [d] in words that begin with 'voiced "th"', like 'then' and 'those'. When a speaker uses [d] so that 'those' sounds like 'doze', he is not really saying 'doze', of course, but he intends the same word as when he says [ɖoUz]. In fact, Labov did analyze this feature as a sociolinguistic variable in his New York City research. The alternatives that belong to a sociolinguistic variable are called *variants*. DeCamp took two variants, [d] and [ɖ] into account. For New York City, Labov recognized three variants: [ɖ], [d], and [dɖ], an affricate pronunciation of voiced 'th' that is in a sense between [ɖ] and [d], both phonetically and socially. The convention Labov introduced for symbolizing variables, placing them between parentheses, has been used ever since. He designated this variable (dh), to distinguish it from (th), the variable involved in words like 'thing' and 'third'. Labov's (th) variable would correspond to DeCamp's '/θ ~ t/'.

The analysis resulted in a pattern that has been replicated many times since, called *class stratification*. If a variable shows class stratification, certain variants are used most frequently by the highest-status class, least frequently by the lowest-status class, and at intermediate frequencies by the classes in between, with the frequency matching their relative status. Figure 8.1 represents the results for (dh) in Labov's data.

The vertical axis of figure 8.1 represents an index for the variable (dh). The index is a slightly complicated calculation that results in higher scores the more frequently a speaker or group of speakers uses [d] and lower scores for [ɖ] usage. Using [dɖ] contributes an intermediate value. If we ignore styles B and C for the moment, we see that the highest index belongs to the lower class, the working class has the next highest, and the middle class the lowest. The classes come out in order, just by using this one sociolinguistic variable. Furthermore, the indexes are associated with classes in just the way you would expect. The middle class apparently uses the most [ɖ] and the least [d], the lower class seems to use the most [d] and the least [ɖ] and the working class is in between. This might be the result of chance if (dh) were the only variable that worked this way, but it is not. Labov found class stratification with five sociolinguistic variables in New York City and class stratifications with equally intuitively satisfying patterns have been discovered in numerous other studies.

Two things need to be stressed in connection with the class stratification of sociolinguistic variables at this point. First, the variants are not associated exclusively with one class or another. Middle-class speakers use some [d] and [dɖ] and working-class and lower-class speakers use some [ɖ]. It is only the relative frequencies that are stratified by class.

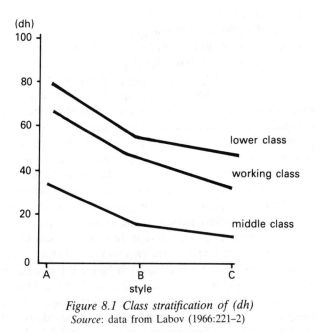

Figure 8.1 Class stratification of (dh)
Source: data from Labov (1966:221–2)

Just as we saw in the creole studies, class stratification studies do not suggest that efforts should be made to get everyone to use [đ] all the time. Actually, lower- or working-class speakers might well be considered too 'posh' or 'snobbish' if they used [đ] too frequently. The same might be true of middle-class speakers in casual style.

The second point has to do with the assignment of social class. Labov had the advantage of access to a class stratification system developed for the population he wanted to study by professional sociologists. Subsequent sociolinguistic studies of a similar kind have had to adopt and adapt other class determining methods, and it is rare for two sociolinguists to use the same method. In general, the methods all use a status characteristic indexing approach, in which status characteristics like occupation, education, residence, and income are assigned numerical values so that a given individual can be assigned a position on a status scale. Status indexes are then grouped into classes. Linguists have usually used such schemes uncritically and somewhat naively, from the point of view of sociology. It is a testament to the robust nature of class stratification that it has been so readily replicated in spite of the flaws in the treatment of the concept of social class.

Figure 8.1 also illustrates another concept from Labov (1966), *style stratification*. The horizontal axis in that figure is marked off in three *styles*, labeled A, B, and C. These styles are designed to reflect increasing formality or awareness of *how* an individual is speaking in addition to *what* is being said. Style A is 'casual style'. One way casual style comes out in the sociolinguistic interview is in speech by the respondent to someone other than the interviewer (for example, an aside to a family member). As variation analysis developed, Labov has put increasing emphasis on this sort of speech as representing the vernacular. Labov has found the vernacular, speech which people use in their everyday lives and which does not show the effects of observation by the analyst, to be the most regular and systematic of any speech style. Style B is 'careful speech', represented in the interview by most of the speech addressed to the interviewer. Here, the speaker must give considerable attention to the content of the answer, but is aware at the same time that he or she is talking to a relative stranger and someone associated with higher education.[1] Style C represents reading style, where the respondent is asked to read a connected passage. The content is provided, so more attention can be given to pronunciation, but there is still some emphasis on content since the reading material is a connected story. There are two still more formal styles, not represented in figure 8.1 since they were not used to study (dh), which Labov labels D and D'. Style D is the reading of a list of words that contain some pronunciation feature the investigator is interested in, and D' consists of paired lists of words which focus on the contrast between two variants of a variable. If D' had been used to investigate (dh), 'those' and 'doze' would have made a good minimal pair.

Returning to figure 8.1, notice that the three classes are ordered not only in style A, but in styles B and C as well. Furthermore, each of the three lines representing a different social class slopes downwards; the index for style B is lower than the one for style A and style C is lower than style B.

While the patterns of stratification by class and style are prominent in Labov's work, there are a number of other influences as well. We saw some of the issues connected with the influence of the sex of the speaker (and addressee) on sociolinguistic variables in chapter 4, including whether class stratification really is more fundamental than variation by sex (Horvath 1985; L. Milroy 1988b). The discussion of US VBE in the last chapter illustrated the critical role of ethnicity in variation and change in language. Both these social factors are discussed at some length by Trudgill (1983b, chapters 3 and 4).

VARIATION AND LANGUAGE CHANGE

The embedding problem

As important and interesting as the relationship between language and social forces is at any particular point in the life of a speech community, this is only part of the story. The patterns of linguistic variation are critical for a full understanding of language change over time. Labov has contended, contrary to previous theory and practice in linguistics, that sound change in progress can be observed, but only by studying language in its social context. Labov and his colleagues isolated five 'problems' in the study of linguistic change (Weinreich, Labov, and Herzog 1968; Labov 1972a). To a great extent, variation analysis in the last two decades has tacitly been concerned with one of these, the *embedding* problem. The embedding problem is to find the continuous matrix of social and linguistic behavior in which the linguistic change is carried out. Another of the five problems, perhaps the most recalcitrant one, will come up from time to time as we proceed. It is called the *actuation* problem, or actuation 'riddle', and it is to do with what sets a linguistic change in motion in the first place.

Before the development of variation studies, research on linguistic change meant research on *structural* linguistic change. Once an analysis based on the linguistic structure had been completed, perhaps a few comments about the social setting where the change occurred might be made, but the two were kept separate. Labov's formulation of the embedding problem takes account of social facts about the speech community, as well as pressures from within the linguistic system. In a classic study of vowel change on Martha's Vineyard, an island off the coast of Massachusetts, he demonstrated that both linguistic influences and social change had their effect (Labov 1963). The vowel change involved was the raising of the vowel [a] in the diphthongs /ay/, as in 'light' and 'line', and /aw/, as in 'out' and 'town'. The two sounds are related in phonological space, as the vowel chart in figure 8.2 shows. After pronouncing the vowel nucleus [a], the speaker 'glides' towards [i] to produce /ay/ and towards [u] to produce /aw/ ([i] and [u] are conventionally written as [y] and [w], respectively, in diphthongs). Both diphthongs start with the same vowel and glide upwards in phonological space. Therefore, a process that affects one may well affect the other.

This turned out to be part of the story on Martha's Vineyard. The diphthong /ay/ was raised first, with [a] moving toward [ə], as indicated in figure 8.2. Later, the [a] in [aw] began to be raised as well, partly under pressure from the change in /ay/. Furthermore, both changes were favored in words of a particular phonological configuration, particularly words in which the diphthong was followed by a voiceless obstruent, like [t] or [s], as in 'out' or 'rice'.[2] But these influences were intricately connected with social forces. Raising of /ay/ began in a particular social subgroup, the Yankee descendants of the island's original settlers. It began with unsystematic fluctuations between relatively raised and relatively lower pronunciations of the [a] in /ay/. As Martha's Vineyard became an increasingly popular holiday spot, the Yankee natives developed

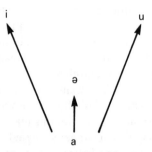

*Figure 8.2 The relationship between /ay/ and /aw/ in phonological structure,
showing raising of [a]*

an unconscious need to distinguish themselves as natives from the visitors. Raising in /ay/ began to take on this social meaning. Raising spread from /ay/ to /aw/, from the favored pre-voiceless obstruent environment to less favored phonological environments, to new generations and to different ethnic subgroups native to Martha's Vineyard in an intricate but systematic manner.[3] In Labov's terms, the sound change was *embedded* in both the phonological system and the social milieu.

Labov found the same kinds of embedding patterns in a number of sound changes that took place in New York City (Labov 1972a). Generalizing from the changes in these two communities, Labov (1972a:178–80) proposed several steps that a sound change in progress can be expected to go through. I will summarize the more salient ones.

The change originates out of irregular linguistic fluctuation in the speech of a social subgroup who, for one reason or another, unconsciously see a weakening of their separate identity within the community.

When the change spreads to all members of this subgroup, it is called an *indicator*. The speakers who are moving the change forward are not aware of it, and the incipient variable does not show style stratification.

The change spreads to other subgroups in the larger speech community to the extent that the values of the original subgroup are adopted by new groups. In LePage's terms, the originating group and its indicator variable become a target of focus.

When the change reaches the outer limits of its expansion and has become adopted by the larger speech community, it is called a *marker*. It begins to show style stratification, but is still below the level of speakers' conscious awareness.[4]

The original change affects other elements in the linguistic system, as the raising of [a] in /ay/ began to affect the [a] in /aw/ on Martha's Vineyard.

All these stages are part of *change from below*, meaning below the level of conscious awareness.

If the change did not begin with the highest-status group (subsequent research indicates that change seldom does begin in this group), and if they do not tacitly ratify the change by adopting it themselves, the changed form becomes *stigmatized*; that is, not considered a 'correct' way to speak.[5]

Stigmatization initiates *change from above*; that is, change from above the level of conscious awareness. Speakers now sporadically change their use of the variants endorsed by the highest-status group, especially in more highly-monitored styles. The variable shows increased style stratification as well as social stratification.[6]

If stigmatization is sufficiently extreme, the form might become a topic for discussion. Forms like this are called *stereotypes*. The form may disappear, or it may remain stagnant; that is, remaining variable, but not undergoing further change (cf. Fasold 1973). If the change originates in the highest-status group in a community, it is not stigmatized and may become a *prestige* model and will be used more in careful, monitored styles than in causal speech, and more by higher-status groups than by lower-status ones. If it is tacitly accepted by the highest-status group, I would add, it loses its stigmatization and may acquire prestige.

Given these stages, you can see how variation itself and patterns of style and class stratification result from and interact with language change. Variation and change are related, but in a single direction. All change involves variability, but not all instances of variability involve change (Weinreich, Labov, and Herzog 1968:188).

The measurement of phonological change

Newer techniques have allowed variation analysts to examine phonological change, particularly in vowels, at a more detailed level. In order to do this, computational and acoustic phonetics equipment and methods are used. It is not possible to give a lot of background in acoustic phonetics here, but a few basics are necessary to understand the applications in variation analysis. Sounds can be analyzed by a device called a sonograph using a technique called *sound spectrography*. Vowel sounds are characterized in sound spectrography by intermittent concentrations of energy at different frequency levels. These energy concentrations show up on the patterns a sonogram draws as more or less wavy dark horizontal stripes, with white areas in between. The dark stripes represent *formants*. The acoustic characteristics of vowels are largely captured by two of these formants, the first and second formants (often designated by F_1 and F_2).

It is possible to create a grid with F_2 on the horizontal axis, with lower frequencies to the right and higher ones to the left, and F_1 on the vertical axis, with lower frequencies at the top and higher frequencies at the bottom. If this is done and the appropriate frequency ranges are selected for the two axes, when the F_1 and F_2 frequencies for vowels are plotted on this grid the result is very much like the traditional vowel chart found in articulatory phonetics books. A major difference is that vowels on vowel charts in phonetics books are positioned at a particular *point* on the chart. In the two-dimensional displays by F_1 and F_2, vowels are located in elliptical *envelopes*. These envelopes are essentially created by plotting several utterances of words with the same vowel in them on the grid, and then drawing an ellipse so as to include them all. When this is done, we find out that there is considerable variation in how a particular vowel is pronounced, and that the envelopes for various vowels overlap each other. A typical example of this can be seen in figure 8.3, showing part of the vowel distributions for a 73-year-old resident in New York City (Labov, Yaeger, and Steiner 1972, Volume 2:1).

Notice that 'iy, as in 'beat', appears where /iy/ would appear in charts of English phonemes. Likewise 'ey' is roughly where /ey/ would appear on phoneme charts. But these and all vowels are represented by elliptical envelopes, and there is *overlap*. For example, some of pronunciations of words with 'ey', like 'bait', have formant values in the same range

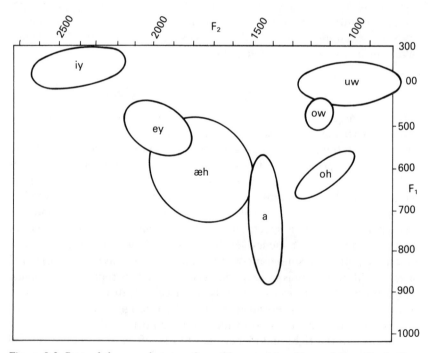

Figure 8.3 Part of the vowel system for a 73-year-old resident of New York City
    Source: adapted from Labov, Yaeger, and Steiner (1972, Volume 2:1, figure 1)

as some pronunciations of words with 'æh', representing the raised pronunciation of /æ/ in such words as *bad* in New York City and in other English lects. Similarly, the envelope for 'a' at least touches the one for 'æ'.

But there is no requirement that only the phonemes of standard phonemic analyses of English be represented, if a different subdivision of vowel sounds would show the variation and change patterns in a more revealing way. Alternative subdivisions of vowels are actually more typical in these studies. In Figure 8.4, for example, 'ehr' as in 'bear' appears, although that would be considered two phonemes in most analyses. Similarly 'ihr' ('ear') and 'ahr' ('cart') are represented as units. Furthermore, 'a' and 'ah' are given separate representations, where 'a' represents the pronunciation of the standard phoneme /a/ before voiceless consonants, and 'ah' represents the slightly different pronunciation in other positions in words. There are also separate envelopes for 'æ' and 'æh', with 'æh' standing for a raised pronunciation of the sound, and 'æ' an unraised pronunciation. These two sounds would standardly be called allophones of the same phoneme.[7] Labov and his colleagues are not presenting the

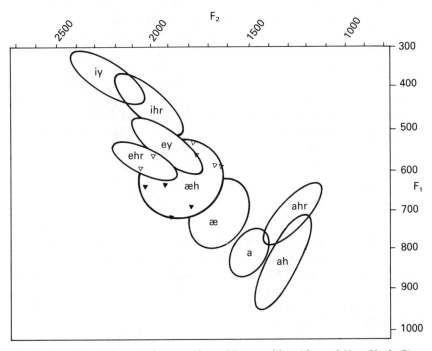

Figure 8.4 Part of the vowel system for a 57-year-old resident of New York City
Source: adapted from Labov, Yaeger, and Steiner (1972, Volume 2:2, figure 2)

data this way to be perverse; they have evidence to indicate that these vowels are undergoing *split*; that is, what have been allophones of the same phoneme are becoming separate phonemes.

Figure 8.4, part of the vowel system for a 57-year-old New York City man reveals another value for this kind of research, the possibility of examining a vowel by the surrounding sounds. In the figure, those pronunciations of 'æh' that occur before the nasal consonant /n/ are indicated by a filled-in triangle. Occurrence of 'æh' in other phonological environments is indicated by an open triangle. Notice that where 'æh' occurs before /n/, the values of the two formants place it near the front edge of the envelope for 'æh'. This turns out to have considerable significance, since it shows the favoring effect of a following nasal consonant for peripheral movement of the vowel. Speakers from different social groupings, ages, and sexes are also compared to determine how the sound change is embedded in the social setting (for example, Feagin 1986).

Using acoustic phonetic and computational techniques is difficult because of the skills and equipment needed. There are numerous technical problems, even if the investigator knows how to do sound spectrography and has good quality recordings. One major problem is the limitation to detailed analysis of only relatively few speakers, because of the large amounts of computer memory required to digitize only a second or two of speech. With the solution to the technical problems, and technological advances, analyses of this level of sophistication – and higher levels – may become commonplace. Partly based on the techniques I have been describing, in spite of the problems, Labov and his colleagues have proposed that there are strong general tendencies in vowel shift phenomena, at least in the type of change historical linguists call *chain shifts*, where movement in one vowel seems to influence movement of others. The three chain shift generalities they have proposed are (Labov, Yaeger, and Steiner 1972:264):

1 long or tense vowels rise;
2 short or lax vowel nuclei fall;
3 back vowels move to the front.

Labov (forthcoming) later showed how these principles work with others to produce three chain-shift patterns that are at work in English lects today in various parts of the English-speaking world. The principles have inspired research by other linguists attempting to confirm or modify Labov's proposals, including Feagin (1986), Yaeger-Dror (1986, 1989), and Wolfram (forthcoming).

The capacity for automatic speech *synthesis* as well as speech *analysis* was exploited in some fascinating experimental research reported by Graff, Labov, and Harris (1986). Advanced technical skills, largely of the first author, enabled the investigators to insert machine-generated vowels, with the values of F_2 carefully controlled, into words within naturally-occurring recorded speech. Listeners were asked to make judgements about the white or black ethnicity of speakers where the only difference was the vowel with the controlled second formant value. The results confirmed hypotheses that very subtle differences in vowel sounds are used systematically by Philadelphia speakers to make racial judgements. Adjusting one formant of a single vowel in an utterance was enough to make a white speaker sound black, and vice versa, to people from Philadelphia.

The location of incipient change

In research conducted in Philadelphia and reported in 1980, Labov combined the spectrography methods with a statistical method called regression analysis in another approach to the embedding problem. The details do not belong in this book, but the general procedure was to use social factors like age, sex, and social class to attempt to predict the formant values of vowels known to be undergoing change. For two of the changes, the upper part of the working class turned out to be the speakers leading the change at statistically significant levels, with both lower and higher classes trailing behind. This would be a surprising result to anyone who finds the traditional conception of language change by class to be plausible. The traditional idea is called 'the flight of the elite' and, according to this notion, the highest strata in a community change their speech patterns to distinguish their speech from lower strata. As soon as the lower strata notice that this is happening, they attempt to imitate the new way the elite are talking.[8] When the high-status speakers realize that the 'common folks' are trying to talk like they are, they change again, and this process perpetuates. But Labov's results do not fit this idea. Not only are the higher-status speakers not the initiators of the changes, but they trail the real initiators, the upper working class, by a wider margin than the lower class does.

The Philadelphia results are not an exception. Trudgill (1974b) had found exactly the same pattern in several variables in his research on variation and change in Norwich. In Norwich, the variable (e) is the vowel in words like 'tell' and 'better'. The newer variants are centralized pronunciations, and more centralized variants get higher index scores. Figure 8.5 is the class and style stratification display for (e) in Norwich.

At first glance, figure 8.5 looks like a typical class and style stratification pattern, where the high-index variants of (e) are stigmatized. Except for one class, the middle working class in casual style, the index values increase as we move from the highly monitored word list style to the nearly vernacular casual style. This means that speakers generally try to

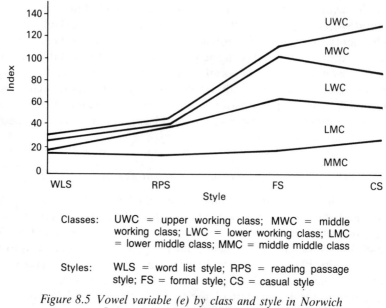

Classes: UWC = upper working class; MWC = middle
working class; LWC = lower working class; LMC
= lower middle class; MMC = middle middle class

Styles: WLS = word list style; RPS = reading passage
style; FS = formal style; CS = casual style

Figure 8.5 Vowel variable (e) by class and style in Norwich
Source: data from Trudgill (1974b:105)

avoid the centralized variants of (e) when they are paying closer attention
to how they sound. Class stratification seems to bear this out; the middle
classes have the lowest values in all styles and the working classes have
the highest.

Within the working classes, we might expect the upper working class
to have the lowest values, the middle working class somewhat higher
values and the lower working class the highest values. But this is not the
way it comes out. The middle and upper working classes have the highest
values, with little difference between them, except in casual style. Here,
the upper working class has the highest values of any group. The lower
working class has higher values than the middle classes, but the lowest
of any working class division. This shows, as Trudgill (1974b:104) says,
'In the vanguard of this change . . . are the upper members of the WC.
The LWC and LMC are also participating in the change, but at a lower
level, and the MMC *is not participating at all, or very little*' (emphasis
added). Not only are highest-status speakers not leading the change, they
show no evidence that they are even aware of it! The (e) variable is not
the only one like this; two other vowel variables that are undergoing
change display the same pattern.

This is exactly the same pattern as Labov found for the two vowel
changes in Philadelphia, where the change seems most advanced in the
working class with the lower class trailing somewhat and the middle class

very much behind. One possible answer is that Labov and Trudgill have shown us stigmatized innovations. If we could only see data for prestige innovations, the 'flight of the elite' hypothesis might come out right. But a moment's reflection will show that this line of reasoning is not very helpful. The innovation is showing the style stratification it does *because* it did not begin with upper-status speakers. We still need an explanation for why at least some innovations do not begin with high-status speakers since the 'flight of the elite' hypothesis seems to predict that all innovations begin with them.

Kroch (1978) noticed that there were *no* cases in which the highest social group initiated a systematic linguistic change. Labov (1980c:253) was able to confirm this on the basis of studies set in nine different cities, and involving several langauges, including French, Spanish, and Farsi, as well as English. If this is the case, then some other principle is needed. One possibility might be a tendency of languages to become simpler, or easier to speak in some sense. Bloomfield (1933:385) speaks of many sound changes that 'lessen the labor of utterance' but he does not find it a satisfactory general explanation. Furthermore, it is difficult to see how a simplification principle would predict that sound change would begin in any particular social stratum.[9]

SOCIAL NETWORK ANALYSIS

The issue of whether or not members of lower social groups imitate speakers with more social privilege is related to some of the criticism of the creole continuum idea that we saw in the last chapter. Some of the earlier studies by Labov and sociolinguists who followed him seemed to emphasize a unidirectional pattern of variation, with an orderly correlation of stigmatized linguistic variables from high to low as we look at social strata from low to high, and the opposite pattern for prestige variables. LePage's principle of focus allows speakers to adjust their speech in various directions and at different times and there seemed to be no room for this kind of latitude in a social stratification model. Variation analysts working in Britain – for example, Romaine (1982b:13–14) and J. Milroy (1982:38–9) – have found the idea of a single social dimension correlating with a unidimensional linguistic variable less than adequate for much the same reasons that were used in criticisms of the creole continuum.[10]

One outcome was the development of the *social network* concept (L. Milroy 1980; Milroy and Margraine 1980).[11] This approach does not require large surveys or the grouping of speakers by status indexes of any kind. Rather, you examine the character of the network of social interactions the speaker has. Two aspects of social networks are particularly important, *density* and *multiplexity*. A dense network simply means that the people a given speaker knows and spends time with know each other as well. L. Milroy (1980) illustrates the difference between high and low-density networks in figure 8.6.

In both parts of figure 8.6, the individual indicated by X has four other people in her network. In figure 8.6(a), these people are also acquainted with each other; in figure 8.6(b), the only connection they have to each other is through X. In other words, if the focal individual in 8.6(a) was at a party where two of her friends were also present, she would not have to introduce them; the focal individual in 8.6(b) would. Multiplexity refers to more than one basis for a tie among individuals. For example, if a man owned a business which employed his brother-in-law and both sang in the same church choir, their network tie would be three-ways multiplex; via their employment relationship, family relationship, and shared choir membership. L. Milroy was able to develop a means of measuring *network strength*, designed to reflect the degree to which a speaker has a dense and multiplex network structure. The method was applied in major sociolinguistic variation analysis research in Belfast, Northern Ireland, with the hypothesis that: 'even when variables of age, sex and social class are held constant, the closer an individual's network ties are with his local community, the closer his language approximates to localized vernacular norms' (L. Milroy 1980:175).

The reason is that strong network ties within a community have the effect of reinforcing the norms of that community, including speech norms. This only makes common sense. If almost everyone you associate with talks and acts the same way, you are under powerful motivation to talk and act that way, too. Notice that it is *vernacular* norms which are reinforced in this way. Now it is possible to see why there are people who would have little inclination to pursue 'the elite'. These 'elite' are not among the people who are important to them in everyday life. It is much more important to conform to what people in your personal network expect of you than to what you are taught in school or hear on television. Labov gives very much the same explanation for the role of the upper

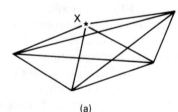
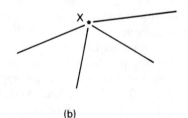

(a)   (b)

Figure 8.6 (a) High density and (b) low-density social network structures where X is the focal point of the network
Source: adapted from L. Milroy (1980:20)

working class in the Philadelphia vowel changes when he speaks of 'local prestige' which not only allows a focus on norms that are not associated with the highest strata of society, but is even 'powerful [enough] to *reverse* the normal flow of influence, and allow the local patterns to move upward to the upper middle class and even to the upper class' (Labov 1980c:262, emphasis added).

I think we can now understand how an innovation, if it were part of the vernacular norm of some community with strong social networks, could survive and spread even if that community were not from the higher social strata of a wider community. I have not yet made it clear why such a community is rarely, if ever, from the higher strata. As we saw in our discussion of language and gender in chapter 4, working-class communities quite typically have strong network structures (Milroy and Margraine 1980:48–9 and the references they cite). So here is a promising connection. If strong social networks are a means of enforcing vernacular speech norms, and if strong social networks are found precisely in traditional working-class communities, then working-class communities are exactly the place to look for systematic linguistic patterns that are different from those reinforced in school and by other institutions of society. Middle-class sections of societies, at least Western societies, tend to have weaker, more open networks and as a result would not have the means to enforce speech norms that differ from official ones.[12]

The question still remains about the lower strata within working classes where both Labov and Trudgill found innovations less advanced than in higher strata of the working class. It will be easier to address this problem if we first try to answer another unanswered question: why do upper levels of the working class have strong networks in the first place? One answer that has been offered is that communities like these are able to meet their own needs at a personal level, rather than having to turn to the detached and impersonal institutional service-providers of the large society. A good way to illustrate this, rather than from the sociolinguistic or sociological literature, is from humorist Garrison Keillor's description of the mythical town of Lake Wobegon, Minnesota. Loyalty inspires the residents of Lake Wobegon to shop at Ralph's Pretty Good Grocery rather than the supermarket in the nearby city of St Cloud where better quality food is available at lower prices. As Keillor (1985:95–6) describes it:

Lake Wobegon survives to the extent that it does on a form of voluntary socialism with elements of Deism, fatalism, and nepotism . . . You need a toaster, you buy it at Co-op Hardware even though you can get a deluxe model with all the toaster attachments for less money at K-Mart in St. Cloud. You buy it at Co-op because you know Otto. Glasses you will find at Clifford's which also sells shoes and ties and some gloves . . . You should think twice before you get the Calvin Klein glasses from Vanity Vision in the St. Cloud Mall. Calvin Klein isn't going to come with the Rescue Squad and he isn't going to teach your children about redemption by grace. You couldn't find Calvin Klein to save your life.

Keillor, it seems to me, has captured the essence of a typical strong-network community, although Lake Wobegon is a rural setting rather than the urban one usually studied by variation analysts. There is no ambulance service paid for by the government, but you can rely on the Rescue Squad staffed by volunteers. There are public schools, but if you want your children to gain the central moral and religious values that you cherish, you need to depend on volunteer Sunday School teachers from the community. A voluntary, informal system of rights and obligations is in place and, to share in its benefits, community members have to adhere to its norms of behavior. In a more scholarly vein, Milroy and Margraine (1980:69), citing sociological research, suggest that strong network structures are common in poorer social settings because 'the maintenance of strong solidary relationships is necessary for survival.'

The middle classes, it seems, rely on their personal resources, and on services provided by institutions to a greater extent, and so they would not get the same benefits from a strong solidarity, strong network social structure. But what of the lowest classes? Members of this group have perhaps less chance of surviving on the basis of their own resources and ready access to institutional services than the upper working class does. This question is not so easy to answer, but I would like to point out that the lowest classes in Philadelphia and in Norwich were not nearly so far behind in the advancement of innovations as the middle class was. This might indicate that the most underprivileged strata do have relatively strong social networks, and that they take their cue from the people just above them. Second, at least in comparison with the situation in the Ballymacarrett neighborhood in Belfast studied by Milroy, many members of the lowest class would not have jobs in a large industry, like the shipyards of Ballymacarrett. Instead, many would be unemployed, or have occupations such as domestics or janitorial workers where they might work in relative isolation and have less chance to develop social ties with other members of the community. Their greater poverty might make it harder for them to develop social ties through such leisure time activities as visiting the neighborhood pub. Still, neither of these observations counts as a fully convincing explanation and the second one is pure speculation.

THE INITIATION OF CHANGE: THE 'ACTUATION RIDDLE'

There is one more question I have to deal with. We have seen that it is typical for at least the upper strata of the working class to have the means to maintain speech norms that are different from the ones supported by formal education. We have also seen that the middle classes typically do not have the required strong network structures to do the same thing. This would explain why the upper working class might *maintain* different speech norms from those that guide the usage of the middle classes, but it says nothing about how the differences get there in the first place. Two answers have been offered by variation analysts: introduction of new norms from outside the community, and the relatively sudden exaggeration of an existing difference between the local community and surrounding speakers of the same language. We have already seen an example of the second in Labov's research on Martha's Vineyard. Here, the group with the strongest loyalty to the local community, the Yankee fishers, pressed the unsystematic local tendency to raise [a] in /ay/ as a response to the increasing influx of off-islanders. This eventually precipitated a sound change that successively involved other subgroups and the linguistically analogous diphthong /aw/. The key was the increase in tourism, which Vineyarders began to see as a threat to control of their home area.[13] In order to resist the perceived threat, the local people felt a need to reaffirm the local social network that they rely on implicitly for dealing with problems.

Labov finds similar explanations available in his work in New York and Philadelphia. In Philadelphia, for example, ongoing sound changes that have marked the city for some time are currently accelerating. Again, there is an incoming group that is seen as a threat, this time the mid-twentieth century move of black people from the rural south to cities in the north. In Labov's (1980c:263) words: 'The renewed emphasis on local identification is accompanied by a strenuous reassertion of local rights and privileges by the ethnic groups who hold them, and a continued resistance to the pressure from black citizens of Philadelphia for their share of the jobs, housing, and political priorities in the city.' Labov's research suggests that this might be one answer to the 'actuation riddle' (why sound changes start up and continue in the first place). The Philadelphia case, incidentally, places the divergence hypothesis discussed in the last chapter in a new perspective, especially with respect to the fact that white speakers are emphasizing local Philadelphia sound changes and black speakers are not participating in the changes at all.

Another source of change is influence from outside the community, either from speakers of other languages or from speakers of the same language with different linguistic norms. Since strong social networks are mechanisms for norm enforcement, any influence from outside the community must come through people who are accepted in the community but whose networks are open enough to allow influence from other communities. As Labov (1980c:261–2) describes these innovators:

It appears that the speakers who are most advanced in the sound changes are those with the highest status in their local community, as the socioeconomic class patterns indicate. But the communication networks provide additional information, discriminating among those with comparable status. The most advanced speakers are the persons with the largest number of local contacts within the neighborhood, yet who have at the same time the highest proportion of their acquaintances outside the neighborhood. Thus we have a portrait of individuals with the highest local prestige who are responsive to a somewhat broader form of prestige at the next larger level of social communication.

Geography becomes an issue when the community that supplies the new influence is some distance from the one receiving the innovation. These cases involve a concept in spatial dialectology known as *focal points* or, in the terminology Trudgill (1974a) uses, *central places*.[14] It is quite often the case that an innovation spreads from a city or large town to another substantial-sized town in the same region, but has no effect at all on speakers in the countryside between them. This can be understood as the result of people in the smaller town having business or social contacts in the larger town, but not in any of the territory around either of them. In their face-to-face dealings in the other 'central place', people will begin to *accommodate* their speech by convergence towards the speech of their interlocutors.[15] When they return, the others in the local community will begin accommodating to their speech and a new linguistic form enters the community as an innovation.

Sometimes the innovation is led by a segment of the population that has the least contact with the other community. One such feature is the variable merger of /θ/ and /f/ in London English, so that 'thin' sounds like 'fin' and 'both' sounds as if it is spelled 'bofe'.[16] This feature is spreading into East Anglia, an area north and east of London (Trudgill 1986:54–6). Striking features about this spread are that it is rapid (the merger was totally absent in the speech of people born in Norwich, an East Anglian city, in 1957 but common in the speech of working-class Norwich youth born after 1967), and that *adolescents* are the leading innovators. They have this merger variably in their speech, while it is less common among young adults, and for speakers over 30 it is not found at all. It is true that the /f/–/θ/ merger is associated with the street-smart toughness of Cockney speakers in London, and that these are values that are particularly appealing to adolescent working-class males. It is also true that there are several television programs in which the main characters speak Cockney, so the model is available. If these factors on their own were enough to produce the innovation, then the /f/–/θ/ merger should be spreading everywhere in Britain. After all, the kind of people Cockney speakers are supposed to be is known all over the country, and television programs are available nationwide. But it is only in East Anglia that the merger is progressing.

Trudgill suggests two somewhat related solutions. One explanation involves youngsters who leave the community where they were born, live for a year or two in a different city, and return to their birthplace. At their age, they are capable of acquiring certain aspects of the speech in the place they moved to. When they return, they are not outsiders, since they can reactivate (as it were) their old networks. Once back in their former strong networks, they are in an excellent position to introduce new speech forms. The drawback is that there are presumably relatively few such cases. On the other hand, if they had temporarily lived in a place like London, their speech might have an appeal out of proportion to their numbers in a smaller city in East Anglia. People like this were called 'language missionaries' by the Norwegian scholar Anders Steinsholt (1962, cited in Trudgill 1986:56).

The other possibility offered by Trudgill is a quite startling phenomenon in its own right, especially since it was independently observed in a community in the USA. Trudgill (1986:35–6) discovered that distinctions in saying certain words that are characteristic of the English of the city of Norwich are not mastered by young people, even if they themsleves were born in Norwich, unless their *parents* have been born there. Part of the evidence was a test sentence, 'Norwich City scored an own goal', referring to the Norwich City football team. For most English speakers, the vowels in 'own' and 'goal' sound the same. In Norwich, the vowel in 'own' sounds more or less the way most English speakers would expect it to sound. The word 'goal', by contrast, would sound like 'ghoul' (it has the vowel [u:]). Twenty Norwich youngsters were asked to pronounce the test sentence with 'a proper Norwich accent'. All 20 understood exactly what they were supposed to do. Ten of them had parents who were born in Norwich and every one of them used the two different vowel sounds in 'own' and 'goal'. Of the ten who did not have Norwich-born parents, *none* distinguished the vowels in the two words; they used the vowel sound of 'own' in 'goal' also. It was not because they had not learned to speak with a Norwich accent; the rest of the sentence was pronounced by all of them with a perfect local accent.

Payne (1980) discovered the same phenomenon independently in research with children of families who had moved to a suburb of Philadelphia. The pattern of use for short 'a' in Philadelphia (the vowel in 'ran') is distinctive and differs from what is found in other areas of the north-eastern USA. The situation is analogous to the 'own' and 'goal' vowel sounds in Norwich. There are two pronunciations of short 'a', tensed and lax. One unique aspect of Philadelphia speech is that Philadelphia speakers, unlike speakers of other American English lects, make a distinction between the vowel in three adjectives – 'mad', 'bad', and 'glad' – in which short 'a' is tensed, and all other short 'a' words ending in 'd', where the vowel is lax. As a result, a Philadelphia speaker would say 'I was *mad* [mɛəd] yesterday but today I'm just *sad* [sæd].' Payne's research shows that unless a child's parents are born and raised in the Philadelphia area, a child's chances of learning this aspect of the short 'a' pattern is 'extremely slight' even if the child is actually born there (Payne 1980:174).

This idea that a child born in a particular speech community will not learn some parts of local speech patterns is a phenomenon that has to be accounted for in theories of first language acquisition. The phenomenon is quite unexpected and would not have been discovered without the kind of careful, quantitative analyses of recorded speech data that only variation analysts do. To serve as an explanation for the /f/–/θ/ merger, it would mean that a number of London families who have the variable merger would have moved to East Anglia and raised children there. The East Anglian categorical distinction between /f/ and /θ/ would have to be one of those features that children would not acquire unless their parents came from a community that had the distinction categorically. As a result, there would be a certain number of East Anglian children who had a fully local accent and were fully accepted as members of the speech community, but would have a few unusual speech features, including the inability to consistently distinguish 'fin' and 'thin' and 'mown' (which has the vowel in 'own') and 'moan' (which has the vowel in 'goal'). As fully-fledged members of local networks, they would be in a position to serve as innovators of the /f/–/θ/ merger, even if they had been born in an East Anglian community and never left it. Neverthless, as Trudgill himself points out, there is no evidence that this is the correct explanation. I would regard the introduction of an innovation from one central place to another by young speakers who are not geographically mobile to be one of the unsolved questions in variation analysis. Perhaps it should be regarded as a part of the actuation riddle, which remains largely a riddle in spite of recent insights into the problem.

THE LINGUISTIC MARKET

It seems that research based on correlations of sociolinguistic variables with social status can be fruitfully related to research based on social network analysis. There is reason to believe that we can benefit from the insights of both approaches without discarding the results of either. I had occasion in chapter 7 to refer to an article by Labov and Harris (1986) in connection with the VBE divergence controversy. In the course of their efforts to find social forces that went together with certain important linguistic differences *within* the group of black speakers they interviewed, Labov and Harris constructed social networks with Harris, an established member of the community, as the focal point. They examined the absence of possessive 's' (as in 'Derek car' for Standard English 'Derek's car') and several other linguistic features of VBE in the speech of members of this network structure. It turned out that several speakers rarely used this 's', while others used the suffix quite frequently. Although speakers with high-frequency possessive 's' absence showed some tendency to be concentrated in two dense, multiplex sections of this network, there were several low-frequency speakers in these networks. At the same time there were high-frequency speakers in other parts of the network where all the other speakers were low-frequency speakers. This use of network analysis is a little different from its use in the Belfast research. There, each individual's network strength in the community was measured by means of an index number so that statistical analysis could be carried out. Here, Labov and Harris examined the actual network interrelations of a few individual speakers, and did not assign an index score.

When the speakers were grouped on a different basis, the results seemed to be more consistent. A core group of seven young speakers who had been raised in North Philadelphia and who did not have much contact with whites was identified along with four other speakers who were 'not socially very distant' from them (Labov and Harris 1986:9). All of them except one were very heavy possessive 's' absence speakers. Two other groups of a few speakers, one consisting of Puerto Ricans whose social life was in the black community and the other consisting of three people born in the south, were also high-frequency speakers.

Among the remaining speakers was a group of four whites who had friends in the North Philadelphia black community. As is typical of such white people, they accommodated their speech to VBE in the use of lexical items and some pronunciation features, but showed no familiarity with grammatical features of VBE such as the possessive (cf. Ash and Myhill 1986). The remaining black speakers were either isolated from the rest of the black community, or had interests that made considerable interaction with whites necessary. None of these speakers used a high degree of possessive 's' absence except one man, a musician. The white speakers and the isolated black speakers are plainly not sufficiently part of the community to respond very strongly to community linguistic norms. But the other black speakers seem to be very much part of community life. What seems to be common among these groups is a need to deal with white speakers on a regular basis. In this regard, they seem to exemplify another way of seeing the relationship between sociolinguistic variables and social factors, the *marche linguistique* or 'linguistic market'.

The linguistic market concept was developed by Sankoff and Laberge (1978; cf. Sankoff et al. 1989). They find correlations based on social class membership not very well motivated, since this forces the analyst to ignore the fact that people such as teachers or receptionists have to conform to 'official' speech standards more than other members of the same socioeconomic strata do. With this in mind, Sankoff and Laberge constructed a linguistic market index which was designed to measure 'specifically how speakers' economic activity, taken in its widest sense, requires or is necessarily associated with, competence in the *legitimized* language' (Sankoff and Laberge 1978:239). They then applied this index to the analysis of several sociolinguistic variables in Montreal French, with illuminating results.[17] Labov and Harris did not attempt to assign a linguistic market index to these three groups of speakers, but it seems reasonable to assume that they would have received a higher index than the speakers in the core group and the other high-frequency speakers. It is not clear whether some concept such as the linguistic market should replace either social class based analyses or social network analysis, or if it should supplement them in some way.

VARIABLE RULES

Categorical, optional and variable rules

Most of what I have said so far is connected with the social setting aspects of the embedding problem and I have touched on the actuation riddle, which seems to be fundamentally a matter of the social setting of linguistic change. We have mentioned the influence of the linguistic system in connection with vowel change, where socially stimulated changes in one part of a vowel system seem to stimulate change elsewhere. A substantial amount of work in variation analysis, however, involves variation and change in its 'nuts and bolts' *linguistic* context, and most of it has centered around the *variable rule*. The variable rule was introduced by William Labov in a classic analysis of the copula/auxiliary in VBE (Labov 1969). I have already mentioned this article in connection with the hypothesis about the creole origin of VBE. In it, Labov proposed an analysis in which the present-tense forms of 'to be' could be removed in VBE by a rule that deleted the consonant remaining after contraction had applied. As you may recall, this analysis stimulated several studies on the implication of this analysis for the hypothesis that 'to be' absence was related to 'to be' absence in the mesolectal levels of Caribbean creoles. The contraction and deletion rules were analyzed as phonological variable rules.

Until that time, rules of phonology were of two kinds, obligatory or *categorical*, and *optional*. A typical categorical rule in classical generative phonology would be (Chomsky and Halle 1968:85,245):

$$\begin{bmatrix} -\text{stress} \\ -\text{tense} \\ \text{V} \end{bmatrix} \rightarrow \text{ə}$$

This rule says that a vowel (V) that is unstressed (−stress) and lax (−tense) will become the mid-central vowel [ə]. We can take a rule which operates on the output of the above rule as an example of an optional rule (C.-J. Bailey 1973b:224–7):

$$\begin{bmatrix} -\text{stress} \\ -\text{tense} \\ \text{ə} \end{bmatrix} \rightarrow (\emptyset) \;/ \;\underline{}\; r$$

I have oversimplified this rule considerably compared with the detailed description given by Bailey and it will not actually give the correct results in all cases. The rule takes an unstressed, lax [ə] and deletes it (rewrites it as ∅) *optionally* before /r/. The optionality of the rule is represented by the parentheses around ∅. The notation '/ _____ r' means 'in the environment before r'. In other words, any unstressed, lax [ə] can be deleted provided it comes before r, but it need not be. This rule is designed to account for the fact that you can pronounce any of the words: 'hist(o)ry', 'gall(e)ry', 'cel(e)ry', 'sal(a)ry', or 'scull(e)ry' either with or without the vowel in parentheses. The point, for our purposes, is that you can say either [hɪstʰri] or [hɪstəri] for 'history' and still get an English pronunciation.

Variable rules are more like optional rules than categorical rules. A variable rule would likewise indicate that the result conforms to the phonological pattern of the language whether or not it is applied. But variable rules are different from optional rules in two important respects. They allow social factors to be included in the constraining environment, and they use both social and linguistic environmental features to specify at least the relative likelihood that the rule will actually be applied in a particular environment. In other words they say, in effect, 'the rule may be applied in environment A or in environment B; either way the result is in the language, but the rule is more likely to be applied in A than in B.'

Constraint hierarchies

Perhaps the most thoroughly examined variable phenomenon in linguistics is the deletion of a final [t] or [d] in English. Final 't', 'd' deletion has almost always been examined in nonstandard kinds of English such as VBE and the English of Puerto Rican speakers in north-eastern US cities, but there is no doubt that it is a general variable process in anyone's English.[18] One of the most detailed studies of 't', 'd' deletion was done by Wolfram (1974b). He presents detailed quantitative data on part of the overall picture for 't', 'd' deletion, the deletion of 'd' after vowels. Although the speakers providing the data were young men of Puerto Rican ethnicity from New York City, other research indicates that the variable constraints Wolfram confirmed have nothing to do with these speakers' Spanish-speaking background, but would be generally valid for

English. He tested three pairs of *variable constraints*. Variable constraints, if they are present, have an effect on the likelihood that the rule will be applied. If the variable constraint favors the rule, its presence increases the likelihood that the rule will be applied; a disfavoring constraint decreases the likelihood of application. However, their presence or absence neither guarantees that the rule will apply nor absolutely prevents it from applying.

In Wolfram's rule, the symbol '#' is a 'morpheme boundary' and means the following [d] is *grammatical*; that is, it represents the '-ed' suffix.[19] The three sets of constraints are shown below.

1   Whether the following word began with a vowel or not.
Examples: The *food* [fu:d] is wonderful.
            The *food* [fu:d] smells wonderful.

2   Whether the syllable containing the final [d] is stressed or not.
Examples: We *agreed* [a'gri : #d] on that.
            We *carried* ['kʰæri : #d] a box.

3   Whether the final [d] was grammatical or not.
Examples: That's the wrong *side* [saˡd].
            I wonder why he *sighed* [saˡ#d].

We have three groups of two possibilities, consisting of the presence or absence of one of these constraints. These three groups of two *constraints* generate 2^3 or 8 potential *environments* (it is important to keep the distinction between constraint and environment in mind), by combining the possibilities in all the logical ways. The resulting eight environments can be arranged in a sideways tree structure, such as figure 8.7. This striking pattern is quite typical of data on variable phenomena. It is generally possible to arrange environments in order by percentage of rule application, with each successive environment equal to or greater than the next, and a hierarchical pattern emerges.

A successful cross-product display like this one shows a *hierarchy* of constraints. In figure 8.7, the two-way major branching shows that a following vowel is the strongest constraint. This is clear because every environment without a following vowel has a greater percentage of application than every environment with a vowel. The next level of branching shows that [−stress] is the second strongest constraint. Nongrammatical [d], at the third level of branching in figure 8.7, is the third strongest constraint. Figure 8.7 allows the following variable rule to be written:

$$[d] \longrightarrow \langle \emptyset \rangle \, / \, \langle [-\text{stress}] \rangle \, \langle -\# \rangle \underline{\qquad} \#\# \, \langle -V \rangle$$

As before, we are using '#' to indicate a morpheme boundary, meaning that the deletable [d] is grammatical if '#' is present. The angled brackets around ∅ indicate that deletion of [d] is variable. The angled brackets

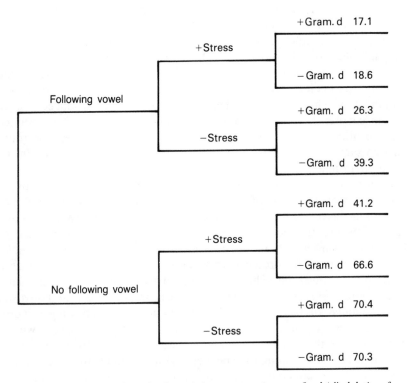

Figure 8.7 Cross-product display of three constraints on final 'd' deletion for New York City Puerto Rican male adolescents (effect on deletion in per cent)
Source: data from Wolfram (1974b:122)

around features to the right of the environmental slash (/) mean that these are variable constraints. The absence of angled brackets around '##' means it is *not* a variable constraint. As Wolfram analyzed [d]-deletion, [d] must be word-final to be deleted by this rule. The minus signs before '#' and 'V' mean that the rule is favored by the *absence* of these constraints. The minus sign with [stress] indicates an unstressed syllable. A plus sign, of course, would have indicated a stressed syllable.

It is also possible to add social factors, creating a combined sociolinguistic 'environment'. For example, if we had a final [d] in the topmost environment of figure 8.7, and that speaker were a young, middle-class male, we could add the features [+young], [+MC] and [−female] to the environment, along with following vowel, [−stress] and grammatical [d]. When compared with data from other speakers with other social characteristics, we might be able to assign positions in the hierarchy to these characteristics as well. In the original variable rule proposal, Labov placed social factors outside the system of variable constraints, but in a manner which allowed them to interact with the linguistic constraints to predict relative frequencies. There is considerable evidence that this is the most fruitful way to deal with social constraints, since social constraints tend to affect variable frequencies differently from the linguistic constraints. In particular, social constraints, called *external* constraints, commonly *interact* with each other. For instance, female gender might promote the use of a particular variable, but only in the working class, not in the middle class. This is precisely the case in Amsterdam city dialect, as we saw in chapter 4. Linguistic constraints, also called *internal* constraints, tend to affect a rule *independently*. This means that a given constraint has the same force, regardless of what other constraints might be in the same environment.

It turns out, however, that a great many variable rules cannot be constructed on the basis of a cross-product display like Wolfram's. For one thing, cross-products can give a reliable hierarchy only when constraints are treated as binary, as in the presence and absence of something. This is not always appropriate. In figure 8.7, for example, Wolfram treated the presence and absence of a following vowel as a single binary constraint. This was a valid analytical decision for his data, since there were no substantial differences in the effect of nonvowel environments. In fact, though, if there is no vowel following a word, there are *two* other possibilities. The next word might begin with a consonant, or there may not even *be* a next word; the word ending in [d] might be the last thing the speaker says at the time. In some variable rules, the three possibilities – vowel, consonant, and pause – all make distinctly different contributions to the likelihood that the rule will be applied. In analyzing these variable processes, the sideways tree would have three branches on the far left, not two. An instance of ternary branching makes it impossible to decide if the second strongest effect, say, in a three-way branching is stronger or weaker than the strongest constraint in a two-way branching in the next lower level of the tree. (I realize that it will be hard to understand what this means without considerable reflection.) Where three-way or greater branching is appropriate in the analysis of a particular variable phenomenon, cross-product analysis fails.

A second problem with cross-product displays is that the mechanical assembly of all possible constraints into environments might call for an environment that is impossible. Imagine a rule in which vowel versus consonant and nasal versus oral quality were both constraints. These two binary constraints combine in four ways, oral consonants, nasal consonants, oral vowels, and nasal vowels. If the language lacks the distinction between oral and nasal vowels, there will never be data for environments that call for nasal vowels. Yet these environments may well be crucial in deciding which of the two constraints is the stronger. In such cases a cross-product display will not allow a satisfactory analysis.

Varbrul analysis

In 1974, Henrietta Cedergren and David Sankoff proposed a mathematically-based solution that solved both problems. In addition, their solution resolved some difficulties in the mathematical interpretation of Labov's original model of the variable rule. Their method involves assigning probabilities, or *weightings*, to each of the constraints by a procedure called maximum likelihood. The analysis is performed using the data on rule applications in various environments as input. The method of calculation assumes that the constraints are independent of each other in their effects. Fortunately for me, and I daresay many of my readers, it is not necessary to know how to do these calculations; it is not even essential to understand them fully. The mathematical calculations are performed by a computer and the program has by now been adapted for a range of mainframe, mini and microcomputers, including the IBM Personal Computer. It is important to be able to interpret the results, but this is not too difficult.

There are at least five versions of the *Varbrul* program. Cedergren and Sankoff (1974) described the first two versions, which were variations on Varbrul 1. Varbrul 1 proved unsatisfactory and has fallen into disuse, although there are several articles published in the 1970s where it was used. The third version is called Varbrul 2. This is the one I will describe because it is currently the most commonly used. The fourth version is Varbrul 2 with an enhancement. It has been used in some research in the literature, but space prevents a description of the enhancement here. Varbrul 3, the fifth version, is considerably more powerful than the others but, for the moment at least, it requires the computer resources of a mainframe computer and is seldom used.

In a Varbrul 2 analysis, the constraints are grouped into *factor groups* (the constraints themselves are called *factors*). A factor group consists of just the constraints, or factors, that would be placed in the same branching in a cross-product display. In figure 8.7, for instance, 'following vowel' and 'not following vowel' would make up one factor group; [−stress] and [+stress] would make up another; and 'grammatical [d]' and 'non-grammatical [d]' would be a third. If the difference between a following consonant and nothing at all, or pause, had been appropriate to Wolfram's analysis, the first factor group would have consisted of three factors, 'following vowel', 'following consonant', and 'following pause'. The factors that go into the same factor group must not be capable of occurring in the same environment. Environments, just as in the classical model of the variable rule, consist of selecting one factor from each factor group. If the result produces an impossible combination, like nasal vowel in a language without nasal vowels, that environment is simply not part of the input. The program will produce interpretable results anyway.

Varbrul 2 generates quite a bit of information, but only two parts of it are really critical. One is a Varbrul weighting (or probability) associated with each of the constraints or factors. These weightings range between 0 and 1. A factor that receives a weighting greater than 0.500 is shown to favor the rule. A factor with a value less than 0.500 disfavors the rule (makes it less likely that the rule will be applied when this factor is in the environment). The second kind of value that is provided by the program is an *input weighting* (usually called an *input probability*). It also ranges from 0 to 1, and its value is interpreted exactly like the factor probabilities. The input weighting is best understood as the propensity of the rule to be applied, 'on its own', apart from the influence of the environment. Wolfram's data, analyzed by Varbrul 2, give the results shown in figure 8.8.

The conventions for writing variable rules when Varbrul is used is to place the variable constraints in angled brackets in the rule and to put the input and variable constraint weightings in a table. The input weighting indicates that the rule would be somewhat unlikely to be applied if there were no variable constraint effects. Among the variable constraints, the following vowel constraint (at a weighting of 0.725) is by far the strongest favoring constraint, with its absence as a correspondingly strong disfavoring influence. In the other two factor groups, the absence of stress, at 0.555, favors the rule slightly, with its presence a slight disfavoring factor. The results for grammatical [d] are similar, with application slightly favored when the deletable [d] is not 'grammatical'. The fact that these two factor groups are so similar points up another advantage of the Varbrul programs over cross-produce analysis. The cross-product analysis allows us to place the three favoring constraints in a hierarchical order, but it is not easy to see that the following vowel influence is very much greater than the effect of the other two. Nor would we know that the other two constraints had virtually equal effect.

External or social factor constraints are included as factor groups just like the internal constraints in figure 8.8. There might be a factor group for gender, with female and male as factors. These two constraints would

$$[d] \longrightarrow <\emptyset> \ / \ <[\pm stress]> \begin{pmatrix} \# \\ \emptyset \end{pmatrix} \underline{\qquad} \begin{smallmatrix} \# & \# \end{smallmatrix} \begin{pmatrix} v \\ \sim v \end{pmatrix}$$

Input Weighting: .410

Following vowel		Stress		Grammatical [d]	
Present	.275	+	.445	Present	.451
Absent	.725	−	.555	Absent	.549

Figure 8.8 Varbrul 2 analysis of three constraints on final 'd' deletion for New York City Puerto Rican male adolescents

Table 8.1 Results for ten hypothetical speakers with opposite categorical deletion in vowel and nonvowel following environments

Speaker	Before vowel	Not before vowel
1	5/5	0/5
2	5/5	0/5
3	5/5	0/5
4	5/5	0/5
5	5/5	0/5
6	5/5	0/5
7	5/5	0/5
8	0/5	5/5
9	0/5	5/5
10	0/5	5/5
	35/50	15/50
	70%	30%

be assigned weightings like the ones in table 8.1. A class factor group might have four factors, like upper middle, lower middle, upper working, and lower. Each of these would also receive a weighting, with the lower-status classes typically being assigned higher probabilities if application of the rule created a stigmatized variant. A difficulty here, as I have pointed out, is that it is typical for external constraints to interact, while internal constraints usually show an independent effect. The Varbrul computer programs make their calculations under the assumption of independence. This might seem to make the use of the programs inappropriate for use with external contraints. However, it is generally easy to detect when there is an interaction between factors and a skilled variation analyst will not be misled if an interaction appears. The assumption of independence is a computational expedient, not a theoretical principle.[20]

Problems and issues with variable rules

In spite of the substantial discoveries of regularities in variable patterning that variable rule analyses allowed, the variable rule concept came under almost immediate criticism. One early criticism was that if variable rules were written on the basis of group results, categorical behavior of individuals could be masked. To take a simple example, suppose we had ten speakers, each of whom had ten utterances of words ending in [d] after a vowel. Suppose further that seven of them always deleted [d] before a vowel and three of them always deleted [d] before a non-vowel. The results could be displayed as in table 8.1.

What would look like a variable constraint on [d] deletion for the group would actually be the result of mixing two distinct groups of speakers. One group would consist of a minority for whom following nonvowels *prevented* deletion and the other of a majority for whom a following nonvowel *required* deletion. At the individual level, there would be no variability to write a variable rule about. But the data used by variation analysts is never like this and this criticism was easily refuted, most elegantly by Gregory Guy (1980).

The place of variable rules in linguistic theory has been attacked as flawed both as an expansion of theoretical phonology and syntax and as an illuminating part of sociolingusitically oriented linguistic theory. Some of the early work on variable rules led several scholars (for example, Kay 1978; Kay and McDaniel 1979; J. Milroy 1982; Romaine 1982b) to the conclusion that variable rule analysis implied a 'variable rule speech community'. In a variable rule speech community all members of a community would have the same rules with the same constraints and the same constraint orders. The variable rule speech community concept is fatally flawed, and Sankoff and Labov (1979:202–3) point out that linguists who have used variable rules never really intended it. Instead, they have assumed that individuals participated in 'over-lapping and intersecting speech communities', similar to the concept developed in chapter 2. This would easily allow differences in the details of the variable rules for speakers from the same larger community who may be members of different smaller speech communities. On the other hand, the idea of a variable rule as part of a phonological or syntactic theory seems to contribute little to our understanding of language use in social contexts. This is true only of the variable rule notion itself, not the data analysis which variable rules are based on. These analyses have led to substantial advances in our understanding of variation and change.

Early misgivings expressed by Bickerton (1971) and by Berdan (1975) about how well variable rules could be incorporated into the line of linguistic theory-building initiated by Chomsky (1957, 1965) have never been satisfactorily laid to rest.[21] Kay and McDaniel (1979) were two among several scholars who pointed out that the concept of language assumed in the dominant phonological and syntactic theories of the last 30 years conflicted with that of variation analysts and with the variable rule. The leading theories have set about specifying what constructions are *possible* in a given language, or in languages in general, versus what must be ruled out. An optional rule serves just this purpose. As I pointed out earlier, the optional rule of unstressed [ə] deletion results in a perfectly acceptable English pronunciation whether it is applied or not. Both [hIstəri] and [hIstʰri] are perfectly good English pronunciations of the word *history*. Labov analyzed contraction as a variable rule, but any variable rule would be an operational rule in traditional generative phonology, with the variable constraints removed. The interpretation of the optional rule would be that both 'she is' and 'she's' are part of English. A variable rule attempts to make a statement about the conditions under which these alternative forms are more or less likely to be *used* by speakers of a language.

To see the difference, imagine that there is a family which owns two cars, a Mercedes-Benz and a Toyota. Two survey studies are being conducted, one by a research team that is interested in automobile ownership patterns, and the other by a group interested in the distribution of automobile use in families with more than one car. The first group need only determine that the family are proper owners of the Mercedes and the Toyota; they can then continue the survey with the next owner. The second team must interview or observe the family to see what leads them to drive the Mercedes instead of the Toyota, or vice versa. The data collected by the first team would be necessary, but insufficient for the second team. The data the second team gathered might be of passing interest to the first team, but irrelevant to their purposes. The reactions in linguistics are similar. Practitioners of the major theories have shown very little interest in variable rules since variable rules seem irrelevant to what they see as their task: namely, finding out what variants a given language 'owns'. Variation analysts have insisted that no theory without variable rules, or more accurately, no theory that cannot account for variable linguistic phenomena, can be considered adequate, since they care about how variants are 'used'.

Attempts to extend the variable rule into syntax by modifying the syntactic transformations of Chomsky's 'standard theory' and 'extended standard theory' – both of them theoretical orientations which have since been abandoned – were never successful and the attempts were only half-hearted. Unlike phonological optional rules, the syntactic transformations of the older theories typically did not convert a possible structure into another structure that was also possible in the same language. Rather, they rearranged an underlying, but unutterable, structure so that it became more nearly sayable. Most studies of syntactic variability involved the selection of approximately equivalent grammatical morphemes or constructions. For example, Romaine (1982b) has examined variation among three possible occupants of the complementizer position in English relative clauses, a WH-word, 'that', or nothing at all, as in these examples:

He is the one *who(m)* I promoted.   (WH-word)

He is the one *that* I promoted.   ('that')

He is the one ___ I promoted.   (nothing)

Another example is the variation among question forms in Montreal French (Lefebvre 1981, 1989). Examples of the possible options would be:

Qui vient?
Who is coming?

(C'est) qui qui vient?   or Qui   (c'est) qui   vient?
(It is) who who is coming?   Who (it is) who is coming?

/kiski/ vient?
Who   is coming?[22]

A third example is the variation between the agentless passive and indefinite active examined by Weiner and Labov (1983). The difference is the one between these two sentences:

We had a robbery last night and they took my new television.

We had a robbery last night and my new television was taken.

The pronoun 'they' in the first example is to be taken as indefinite in reference, meaning something like 'the robber(s), whoever he or they were', not in the sense that the speaker has particular individuals in mind. Weiner and Labov take these two constructions as alternatives a speaker might choose between if he or she needed to say something about an event without knowing or wanting to say who it was that did the activity.

One issue in the analysis of syntactic variation that has been hotly debated is whether or not the variants of a syntactic variable are really different ways of saying the same thing, as the phonological alternatives clearly are (for example, Labov 1978; Lavendera 1978; D. Sankoff 1988). The examples I have given seem to make only a stylistic difference: for instance, it would be hard to see a difference in meaning between 'He's the one I hired' and 'He's the one whom I hired', although the first sounds more colloquial. David Sankoff (1988) argues that some forms that mean different things when they are examined closely and out of context are 'neutralized in discourse', in the sense that people are not thinking of the subtle differences in meaning when they are in the act of talking. One variable that is said to be so neutralized is the difference between *on*, 'one', and *tu/vous*, 'you (in the impersonal sense)', in the kind of French sentences that would be translated 'One never knows what might happen' compared to 'You never know what might happen' (cf. Laberge 1978). This phenomenon is usually presented in discussions of syntactic variation, although it is actually a choice among lexical forms. Lavendera (1984) argues that the careful, instance-by-instance examination of the analogous usage between *uno* and *vos/usted* in Spanish in recorded discourses reveals that the choices between them are motivated precisely by a desire to make subtle meaning distinctions. The issue of what should count as the kind of 'sameness' that justifies treating two or more forms as variants of a syntactic variable has yet to be resolved to everyone's general satisfaction.

Apart from the sameness issue, there is a problem with trying to analyze most instances of syntactic variables as the consequence of syntactic variable rules. There seems to be little reason to suppose that most of these variants are related by the application or non-application of a rule of any well-defined kind. Romaine (1982b:188–217) experimented with a variable rule analysis of the occupants of the complementizer slot in relative clause constructions. The rule systems she used called for the WH-word to be rewritten as 'that', but there are convincing arguments that 'that' in these constructions is the same complementizer as the 'that' in 'I suppose that he is competent' and has nothing directly to do with relative pronouns. In any case, Romaine found the variable rule analysis unsatisfactory on other grounds. Lefebvre (1989) argues explicitly that the alternatives for question formation in Montreal French are structurally distinct and should *not* be related by variable rules. Weiner and Labov use Varbrul 2 in their analysis, but only as a statistical analytical tool; they do not propose that the indefinite active and agentless passive are related by the application or nonapplication of a variable rule and presumably do not believe that they are.

The quest for explanation brings us back to phonology where variable rules once seemed to be successful. Rules that raise vowel heights and delete consonants seem to make sense as variable rules. However, shortly after variable rules were first proposed, Kiparsky (1971) raised the objection that just saying that a constraint favors the application of such and such a rule with such and such a weighting does not explain anything. Why do the constraints that favor have a favoring effect, and those that inhibit have an inhibiting effect? For example, Labov's (1969) variable rule for contraction indicates that a major favoring factor is whether the preceding word ends in a vowel. If we think about what contraction does, this turns out to make articulatory sense. In general, it is easier to pronounce things if consonants and vowels alternate. The mouth can come to a more or less closed position for the consonant then open for the vowel, and then move to a different closed position for the next consonant. If more than one vowel or more than one consonant has to be pronounced in a row it is a little harder. It is far from impossible to pronounce vowel (V) or consonant (C) clusters and languages commonly have them, but we can see why it would be nice to have vowels and consonants alternating as much as possible.

Consider the following two examples of potential contraction:

The man *is* going to leave.
  C VC
The guy *is* going to leave.
  V VC

In the first example, we already have the favored CVC pattern and contraction would only disrupt it. Therefore it is not surprising to learn that contraction is disfavored in that environment. In the second example, we have two vowels in a row. Contraction would remove the second one, creating a favorable VC pattern. This fact did not escape Labov; he pointed it out quite carefully in the original article. The problem is that there is nothing in the variable rule as a theoretical concept which would lead us to say that preceding vowel is a favoring factor. A perfectly well-formed variable rule could be written that said a preceding *consonant* favored deletion. Of course, the data would prevent us from making that mistake, but the fact remains that an accurate variable rule simply displays patterns for us; it does not provide any explanation for them, and neither does it do much to distinguish spurious patterns from significant ones.

At the same time, phonological theory has moved beyond the generative phonological model which was originally supposed to be modified to accommodate the variable rule. Newer theories attempt to develop explanations to replace the descriptions of certain processes taking place in particular environments, as in Chomsky and Halle's (1968) theory. In syntax, not only is it difficult to see syntactic variation as related to syntactic transformations in most cases, but transformations themselves have far less prominence in syntactic theories than they once did. In fact, the current version of Chomsky's syntactic theory (for example, Chomsky 1981) allows only one transformation – roughly 'Move anything anywhere you like' – with strict conditions on which of the outcomes of applying this rule are to be accepted. It would be difficult, and I think pointless, to attempt to graft syntactic variable rules on to this theory, or on to any of the currently competing syntactic theories, for that matter.

In current work in variation analysis, the variable rule as a part of linguistic theory has quietly been abandoned. This is not to say that the investigation of linguistic variability or even the Varbrul 2 computer program are no longer useful; quite the contrary. Varbrul 2 continues to function as a statistical tool for the analysis of variation. It is rather common to see studies such as a recent one by Cedergren (1986) in which tables with factors and weightings are given, but no associated rules are written. Some studies (for example, Myhill 1984; Wolfram 1989) use the program profitably to investigate cases of variation which make no sense as variable rules in the original sense. Wolfram's study involves the acquisition of the distinction among the three final nasal consonants in English, [m], [n], and [ŋ], by children learning VBE. Among other things, he learned that [n] is the last consonant to be learned, following the other two, but with no difference between acquisition of [m] and [ŋ]. Part of the evidence that [n] should be opposed to [m] and [ŋ] instead of there being a three-way opposition was that the Varbrul 2 weightings for [m] and [ŋ] were very close to each other (especially for 36-month-old children) and contrasted sharply with the weighting for [n]. But these weightings emerged from an application of Varbrul 2 that treated nasal consonant acquisition as if the children started out knowing all three consonants, but gradually stopped deleting them. Such a rule seems very implausible. Still, the numerical results that come from the Varbrul 2 analysis which assumes it are readily interpreted in more reasonable terms. It seems that nothing terribly crucial is lost if the variable rule as a part of linguistic theory is given up, as long as the insights we get from the quantitative analysis of variable linguistic phenomena continue. This is what seems to have happened in the practice of variation analysis.[23]

DEVELOPMENTAL LINGUISTICS

The demise of the variable rule as a component of linguistic theory accompanies a certain reluctance among the leading variation analysts to attempt to construct a full-scale formal theory. William Labov, without doubt the leading figure in the research on linguistic variation, has repeatedly acknowledged the contributions from the formal theories in syntax and phonology. It is true that his proposed principles of vowel shift, the progress his work has made and inspired towards the solution of the actuation problem, and his careful, closely reasoned description of the relationship between sound change and variation and the notion of 'speech community' (Labov 1989) could no doubt provide the building blocks for a fully developed general theory including variation. Yet Labov has not made general theory construction a high priority. The closest thing to an attempt at a comprehensive formal theory of linguistics which includes variation and change is the developmental theory pioneered by Charles-James Bailey (1973a, 1980, 1981, 1982, 1987, forthcoming).[24] As such, it is worth presenting in some detail in this overview of variation analysis.

Like most variation analysts, Bailey recognizes two sides of language, which he calls the 'sociocommunicational' and the 'neurobiological'. By the sociocommunicational, he means all the factors that shape language which are due to its use by people when they talk to each other. This includes the influence of ethnicity, gender, social status, and style: the sorts of social influence I have said so much about in this chapter. It also includes pragmatic and discourse patterns, at least to some extent. Generally, as you might suspect from the word 'sociocommunicational', this aspect covers most of the sociolinguistics of language. The 'neurobio-logical' is to do with the capacities human beings bring to the task of language learning, and with the physiological development of the human language facility. This contrast is recognized at least implicitly by variation analysts who have followed Labov's work, and explicitly by Labov himself.

A recent statement by Labov (1989:1) indicates that analysts are faced with something of a choice between the 'system of social control' (roughly, Bailey's sociocommunicational aspect) and the 'physiological system' (roughly, Bailey's neurobiological aspect).

There is general agreement that language is an instrument of communication that depends jointly on an underlying physiological system and a system of social control. The question is where to find the most systematic view of the linguistic system – in the individual who carries the genetic mechanism, or in the community that exerts the stimulus and control.

In Bailey's view, languages tend to maintain a balance between the two and this is a fundamental part of its nature. For him, unlike for Labov, the individual speaker is the site for linguistic patterns of both types. Furthermore, the nature of language is to be sought in its *development*, since you can understand why language is the way it is by understanding how it got to be that way. Development, for Bailey, encompasses language change over time: first language acquisition by children, then pidginization and creolization processes, and language death. All of these processes involve *time*, the basis for developmental theory. Bailey looks for evidence of the neurobiological in patterns of change that repeat themselves from language to language and seem clearly to be independent of sociocommunicational considerations.

A difference, at least in emphasis, between developmental linguistics and other work on linguistic variation is the idea of *system*. In developmental linguistics, there is great emphasis on putting together the patterns of variation into overall systems. Developmentalists see much of the research on variation as too involved with the details of individual variables, instead of an overall view of linguistic systems.

A key notion in developmental linguistics is *marking*. In essence, an unmarked element is one that is to be expected, in the absence of good reasons for it not to appear. An example given by C.-J. Bailey (1981:48) is that apical stops and nasals – the consonants usually spelled 't', 'd', and 'n' – are most expected (that is, least marked) at the beginning of a syllable. Velar stops and nasals – the stop consonants spelled 'k', 'g', and the nasal [ŋ] – are least expected (that is, very much marked) at the beginning of a syllable.[25] At the end of syllables, the situation is the other way around. The apical stops and nasals are marked at the ends of syllables, where the velar stops and nasals are much less marked.

This does not mean that it is impossible to find a velar stop at the beginning of a syllable or an apical stop at the end of one. In fact, the English word 'cut' [kʰət] has both a velar and an apical stop in their respective highly marked positions. Markedness is not discovered in the presence or absence of marked forms, but in relationships of change and in implicational relationships. C.-J. Bailey (for example, 1982:51–2) defines markedness by both relationships. To simplify his definitions a

Linguistic Variation 259

bit: as a general rule, x is more marked than y if x connaturally changes to y (the developmental linguistics notions of *connatural* and *abnatural* change will come up shortly). Furthermore, generally if a language has some more-marked x, then it will also have the less-marked y, but not necessarily the other way around. The marking relationships for apical and velar stops and nasals can be illustrated with several changes in the Indo-European languages, by children's language-learning mistakes (as when a Chinese child says *tuk* instead of *kut* meaning 'bone'), and in the change of syllable-final 't' to 'k' in English-lexified creoles, giving forms like 'fraikn' for 'frighten'. In fact, the data on the acquisition of syllable-final nasal consonants analyzed by Wolfram (1989) is striking confirmation of what these marking directions would predict. Recall that the children who supplied Wolfram's data were more likely to have [m] or [ŋ] at the end of a syllable than [n].

Another central idea in Bailey's thinking is the distinction between *connatural* and *abnatural* development. *Connatural* developments are to be expected when development proceeds within a language system with no contact with other systems, or from hypercorrections that result when people begin speaking the way they think they 'should' (for example, saying 'off-ten' for 'often'). Generally, connatural changes result in less marked outputs over time within a language. However, allowances have to be made for increased lower-level marking caused by unmarking at a higher level, and for markedness-reversal; these are theoretical details that are important, but ones we have to leave unexplored. *Abnatural* changes come from conscious attention to speech, and from the contact between languages. Abnatural changes *may*, but need not, lead to an increase in marking. Abnatural change is not a derogatory concept; it is very common and contributes to the balance that developmental theory emphasizes.

Bailey is in principle never content with simply stating what is more or less marked. Ultimately, developmental linguistics would like to find an explanation, here in neurobiological terms. Apparently (C.-J. Bailey 1981:49) there is evidence to indicate that the brain sends information to the speech mechanism in syllable-sized (or perhaps measure-sized) chunks. Velar sounds are made by moving the back of the tongue or dorsum; apical ones are made with the tip or apex. As you can easily test with your own tongue, the apex is far more supple and easier to move quickly than the dorsum. If the instructions for a whole syllable or measure arrive at once, the most efficient syllable would have the apex moving first and the dorsum last. That way, the apex could enact its instructions while the dorsum was enacting its directions. Since the apex can act faster, it would be finished while the dorsum was still completing its movements and the syllable would be completed in the correct sequence. If the velar consonant were at the beginning and the apical one last, the instructions to the apex would have to 'remain on hold' while the slower dorsum finished its assignment for the syllable to come out right. Of course, speech is so automatic and rapid that speakers are not aware of any greater difficulty in saying the word *cut* than in saying *tuck*; nevertheless, the evidence from language acquisition and change indicates that the explanation Bailey offers may be correct.[26]

Developmental linguistics allows for binary distinctions where they are appropriate, so that a phonological feature like [nasal] can be assigned a + or a −. But developmental phonology (or 'phonetology' as it is called in this theory) allows for more than binary distinctions. Frequently, rules are written with feature specifications of +, −, or ×, where × is an intermediate value. In some cases, like [stress], the intermediate value is understood as a *gradient* sequence of more or less stress, so that [+stress] indicates full stress, [−stress] indicates unstressed, with the notations [>stress] and [<stress] for gradient mid-stress. A > would indicate that a rule is sensitive to increasing stress, a < similarly refers to decreasing stress. Not only phonological, but also syntactic and semantic categories can have gradient values. I am going to illustrate gradience in a grammatical category a bit later. Even marking itself is a gradient concept in the sense that we are to think of elements as more or less marked, rather than just marked or unmarked.

A variable rule in developmental phonetology is different from variable rules in other kinds of variation analysis. Consider once more the variation between fuller and briefer pronunciations like 'history' and 'hist'ry'. C.-J. Bailey gives a rather complete version of this rule in Bailey (1981:58–61) and a much briefer version in Bailey (1987:276–7). A somewhat simplified version of the more complete rule would look like this:

$$
\begin{bmatrix} +\text{nucl} \\ \text{x turb} \\ >\text{defl} \\ A \end{bmatrix} \xrightarrow{>} \emptyset \ / \ [+>\text{x turb}]\_\_\_\_ \begin{bmatrix} -\text{nucl} \\ \text{x turb} \\ \text{defl} \\ A \end{bmatrix} \begin{bmatrix} -\text{segm} \\ ->\text{xwd.b.} \end{bmatrix} \begin{bmatrix} -\text{turb} \\ <\text{stress} \end{bmatrix}
$$

The rule looks quite formidable, I know, but there are only a few aspects of it that I want to explain. Instead of the weightings of Varbrul, the developmental rule has features that take > or < as part of their specification. For example, the symbols +>x before [turb.(ulent)] in the first part of the environment means that the rule is more favored if the segment preceding the deletable one is [+turb.] (an obstruent) than if it is [xturb.] (a sonorant). This turns out to mean that, if everything else is equal, we expect that 'robb'ry' from 'robbery' is favored over "chol'ra' from 'cholera'. The −>x specification for the feature [wd.b.] (word boundary) would have an analogous interpretation. The feature [stress] in the final environment position is specified as <.

Since [stress] has gradient mid-values, rule-application becomes increasingly likely the less stress there is on the vowel. To illustrate, C.-J. Bailey (1987:276) presents the forms 'cooperative', 'cooperate', and 'cooperation' with these stress patterns:

còóp[ə̂r]ative
còóp[ə̂r]àte
còóp[ə̂r]átion

The stress on the vowel spelled 'a' is least in 'cooperative', so the rule predicts that 'coop'rative' would be the most favored reduced form of the three. 'Cooperate' has greater stress on 'a', so 'coop'rate' is less favored than 'cooperative', but more favored than 'coop'ration', where the 'a' has the greatest stress of the three.

The symbol > over the rule arrow means the rule as a whole is favored by a faster tempo of speech and a reduction in self-monitoring (that is, attention to how you are saying what you are saying).

We can see that the rule in developmental phonetology can express the same variable constraints as can be expressed by Varbrul weightings, but with the added advantage that the gradience of the stress constraint can readily be expressed.[27] If the values +, −, and x were converted to marking values – as they would be in a still more technical version of the rule – and if explanations along the lines we illustrated earlier can be found for these marking values, then the severest criticism of variable rules, that they state hierarchies without explaining them, is overcome.

The rule is to be taken as a rule of the English *language* community. Simply put, it is a rule of English and is relevant to any speaker of English, regardless of *speech* community membership. This accents another feature of developmental theory: it is *polylectal*. In other words, the rules of the grammar of a language are valid for any lect within that language, even if there are no speakers who use all the forms that the rule allows. Since the theory is developmental, the rule is considered valid as long as it allows valid natural *developments* in the language. For example, suppose there are no speakers of English who would say 'coop'ration', but there are speakers who say 'coop'rate'. The rule would not have to be modified, since it shows that the next natural development in the language would be for the rule to extend to the environment that includes 'cooperation', even if this development never actually takes place.

The polylectal nature of developmental grammars has been a matter of controversy in a couple of respects. Since the rules may well not apply to the linguistic behavior or capabilities of any speaker, the question arises about what a polylectal grammar is a grammar of. Bailey has in the past replied that while a polylectal grammar may not correspond to any one speaker's *production*, it comes close to speakers' *understanding* capabilities, especially a speaker who had been exposed to a wide variety (even if not all) English lects. Further, a properly-written polylectal grammar is *learnable* if not actually learned. Besides this, Bailey would want to say there is a sense in which the speaker of a language 'knows' what future natural developments are possible in the language, even if they are never actuated, and the polylectal grammar reflects this. Another problem has to do with the boundaries of what should be considered a *language*. For Bailey, each language is a different system, and languages typically develop when 'discontinuities' develop within systems. A discontinuity, I take it, would be something like the boundaries between acrolects and mesolects, and again between mesolects and basilects, in table 7.4 of the last chapter. Discontinuities result when there are abnatural changes, and language contact is a frequent trigger of abnatural changes. When discontinuity produces a new system, Bailey considers it a *daughter* language of the system where the discontinuity occurred. At an early stage in developmental theory, Bailey (1973a:65) expressed a lack of knowledge about where the boundaries of systems are to be found. It may be that the problem has since been solved.

I have mentioned that variable rules sometimes include social forces as factors included in variable rule environments, so that a weighting can be assigned to a factor like 'female' or 'upper middle class' as well as to [+stress] or 'noun phrase'. This is not done in developmental theory. While language is seen as a balance between the sociocommunicational and the neurobiological, linguistic rules of the kind we have seen are written only for the neurobiological aspect. Abnatural changes are the result of social and communicational forces. The causes of abnatural change are entirely different from the causes of connatural change; so much so that abnatural patterns are often the mirror-image of connatural ones. Connatural patterns themselves are accounted for by the neurobiological part of linguistic theory, but the forces that *assign* these patterns to different styles, social groups and geographical regions are completely different from the forces which produce the patterns themselves. These assignments could have a lot to do with future developments of the language, at least in a particular speech community, and so are part of developmental theory. However, because their causes and effects are different, developmental linguistics treats linguistic patterns and the influencing social forces separately. The distribution of social interpretations of connatural patterns are *superadded* to the grammar (Bailey 1987:273). The grammar is held responsible for the patterns themselves, but not for their social interpretation.[28]

Developmental theory is not limited to matters of phonology. Considerable developmental work on morphology has been conducted by Mayerthaler (1981, 1988). The theory can also be used in syntax. Bailey has given one or two sketches involving morphology and word-order in

German, but Ross (1973) has argued that even a fundamental syntactic category like 'noun phrase' (NP) seems to be gradient.[29] In particular, concrete NPs are the 'best' kind, NPs referring to forces of nature are 'worse', event NPs are worse still, and abstract NPs are even worse. Most constructions are capable of taking any quality noun phrase, but some are quite sensitive. For example, a verb like 'prevent', especially when passivized, gives increasingly less acceptable results when its surface subject is lower-quality NP. The following examples show this, where * indicates 'unnacceptable', ? indicates 'doubtful' and *? indicates 'really doubtful':

The wall was prevented from falling by the support struts.
? The storm was prevented from causing too much damage.
*? The concert was prevented from beginning.
* Prosperity was prevented from spreading.

Ross's analysis was done before developmental linguistic concepts had advanced very far, and he does not suggest any explanation for this gradient. It does have a clear intuitive appeal which suggests that an explanation in terms of a natural perception of the concereteness of nominal referents can be found.[30] It looks as though Ross's example would depend on a rule of passivization and then only when the main verb is one of a few verbs like 'prevent'. This would make it appear that gradience in noun phrases has to be associated with a particular rule, raising some of the same problems that make syntactic variable rules virtually impossible. Using a developmental linguistic approach, I can imagine that we might want to say that *all* references to noun phrases in grammars would refer to an entity like the following (cf. C.-J. Bailey 1981:55):

NP
>

This would mean that the construction referred to is more natural the higher the quality of the noun phrase. In most constructions, the effect of lower-quality noun phrases would not be sufficient to create doubtful acceptability but, in some constructions, perhaps differing for different speech communities, the sensitivity to degrees of 'noun phrasiness' might come out as it does in Ross's examples. A solution along these lines would not require reference to particular rules.

As I have tried to show, developmental linguistics represented by Bailey's work from this perspective has a number of advantages when compared to other work in variation analysis. Yet there are still reservations about developmental linguistics on the part of other linguists. Some would be more impressed if the principles he has proposed were to be more thoroughly tested than they have been (some of Bailey's predictions, mostly in phonology, have actually been tested and confirmed). There has been a good deal of work in phonology from the developmental perspective, but work at other levels of linguistics, with the exception of Mayerthaler's recent research on natural morphology, has been rather sparse. The few examples concerning syntax are difficult to relate to the issues that interest researchers in the major syntactic theories. Many sociolinguists seem to resist the separation of the 'neurobiological' and the 'sociocommunicational', despite the fact that Bailey argues quite cogently that the degree of division in developmental lingusitics prevents confusion among unlike phenomena. These sociolinguists would be happier with a theory which put most of the emphasis on the sociocommunicational. At the same time, several innovations in the developmental approach, such as the emphasis on the polylectal aspect of grammar and the role of language contact in historical developments, contrast so sharply with traditional concepts in linguistics that resistance is probably inevitable.

SUMMARY

The study of linguistic variation has been deeply influenced by the work of William Labov. He introduced the concept of the *linguistic variable*. Linguistic variables are sets of other ways of 'saying the same thing'. The choices among the variants of a linguistic variable are influenced by both social and linguistic forces. A commonly-discussed pattern of social-force influence is *class and style stratification*, in which the distribution of variants of a variable in a speech community according to the class status of the speaker and the style of the speech situation falls out in a sensible pattern. Linguistic variation and change are related, since change means there is variation, although there can be variation without change. Labov and his colleagues have tried to understand how language change happens by examining how it is *embedded* in a social and linguistic context and what might *actuate* the change. His classic study of phonological change on Martha's Vineyard (Labov 1963) illustrates how these problems can be investigated. Using the results from this research and later research in New York City, Labov and his colleagues proposed a series of steps which sound change in progress can be expected to go through.

Greater precision made possible by the use of instrumental techniques in the analysis of vowel change, and techniques of speech synthesis, has made new discoveries possible. Partly on the basis of instrumental techniques, Labov has proposed three very general rules of vowel shift. Speech synthesis experiments done in Philadelphia suggest that very subtle variations in vowel pronunciation can have quite consistent effects on social judgements about a speaker.

A range of research results have converged towards the conclusion that the higher social strata are typically not the site where linguistic change begins, contrary to what had been supposed earlier. Instead, the lower to lower-middle strata are almost always the location for linguistic innovations. A possible explanation for this is related to *social network* analysis, pioneered in sociolinguistics by Lesley Milroy and her colleagues. Strong social networks seem to be associated with locally-oriented working communities. These networks have the effect of enforcing norms of behavior, including how people should talk. Furthermore, if a group with strong networks finds itself in a situation (perhaps due to outside pressure of some kind) in which it feels the need to emphasize its own identity, the group might fix on a variant of its local speech as a symbol of its identity. If other groups adopt this variant as their own, it may become an innovation in the language as a whole. This process may be part of the answer to the actuation riddle. Another source of change is the introduction of a new feature from some other community of speakers of the same language.

The *linguistic market* concept is another way of understanding variation in language. Here the emphasis is on a speaker's need to use socially approved forms of language for economic reasons. This concept has been used in sociolinguistic research, especially in Montreal.

In the late 1960s and in the 1970s, attempts were made to account for linguistic variation in terms compatible with theoretical linguistics by introducing *variable rules*. Variable rules were designed to replace or supplement optional rules in generative linguistic theories. Variable rules, unlike optional rules, allowed the influence of social constraints on the choice among alternative forms to be expressed. The early version of variable rules, which depended on more–less relationships, was replaced by more sophisticated versions in which weightings could be assigned to constraints by means of computer analysis of frequency data. For a number of reasons, variable rules as a theoretical concept has not been generally successful, although the 'Varbrul' computer programs are still widely used as analytic tools.

Developmental linguistics, an approach led by Charles-James Bailey, may be the most comprehensive attempt to develop a complete linguistic theory that includes variation and change. Developmental theory is concerned with explaining the nature of language by explaining how it came to be as it is. Time, then, is seen as a basic force in explaining developments. Both sociocommunicative and neurobiological influences on language are taken into account. Since the principles behind these two aspects and their results are seen as different, they are treated separately. Neurobiological developments are *connatural*; they are in confirmity with the fundamental nature of language. Sociocommunicative developments are *abnatural*. Abnatural developments are not undesirable.

New languages develop as a consequence of abnatural change, and a balance between the two is essential to the health of a language. The notions of markedness and gradience are central to developmental linguistics, and contribute to its attempt at explanation and prediction. Various patterns of change and development, for the developmentalists, must be related to each other in overall *systems*.

There are many unifying themes in linguistic variation research. It now seems clear that variation in language is patterned, that it is related to language change, and that it depends crucially on the interaction with the social setting. Scholars of linguistic variation take it as established that there is nothing pathological, like 'illogical thinking', associated with language varieties that are not the same as the most socially approved varieties. There is no doubt that the study of linguistic variation will be a permanent part of lingusitic research for the foreseeable future.

NOTES

1 Usually the respondent is not aware that speech and language is the subject of the research.

2 Remember that we have encountered the notion 'favored environment' in connection with the creole continuum and associated implicational scales.

3 The details of the sound change on Martha's Vineyard have been summarized very nicely by Downes (1984).

4 The difference between *markers* and *indicators* seems to depend on Labov's definition of speech community as a group which shares normative values about language. This definition allows him to distinguish a speech community from its subgroups. As we saw in chapter 2, 'speech community' is a difficult concept to define and Labov's general views on linguistic change are more widely accepted than his definition of speech community.

5 The notion that the highest group might ratify a change by accepting it themselves is not in Labov's original discussion, but is my own interpolation.

6 The terms *change from below* and *change from above* are sometimes mistakenly taken to mean 'change originating in the lower social strata' and 'change originating in the higher social strata'. Since stigmatization is the basis for change from above, and stigmatization is the prerogative of the higher social strata, this misunderstanding can go undetected.

7 I am comparing the practices I am describing to 'standard' phonemic analyses, because I think phonemics might be the most widely-known kind of phonological analysis. There are several other phonological theories that are actually inspiring most of the current research in phonology.

8 Bloomfield ('1933:477) takes a rather guarded version of this position: 'No person and no group acts always in one or the other capacity, but the privileged castes and the central and dominating communities act more often as models, and the humblest classes and most remote localities more often as imitators.'

9 However, if the notion 'simplification' is replaced with the developmental linguistics concept of *connatural change*, it is possible to go much farther towards an explanation of the role of the lower to middle social strata in initiating changes. Developmental linguistics and connatural change will come up later in the chapter, but we will not be able to pursue this explanation.

10 J. Milroy (1982:35) is not interested in sweeping away Labov's work which he regards as 'an extremely important methodological innovation which has, moreover, a considerable potential for theoretical advances'. This viewpoint seems to be judicious since, as we have just seen, Labov does not now work with a concept of social structure where values correlate in a single direction from bottom to top.

11 This is an idea which, incidentally, Labov (1972c) had used in a limited way in his work on VBE.

12 Lesley Milroy (1980:179–80) suggests that the *upper* class in British society is characterized by strong network ties for reasons analogous to those that encourage strong networks in the upper working classes. The linguistic result is a stable speech norm, RP.

13 Why should newcomers be a threat? I have no information about Martha's Vineyard, but a newspaper story about a similar small community on the western shore of the Chesapeake Bay in the state of Maryland might provide some insight. A long-time resident told the reporter that he would not mind the newcomers if they did not try to tell him how to live. As an example, he mentioned that a new neighbor from another part of the state had called the local police to complain about his dogs barking and had confiscated a 'frisbee' that had landed on the neighbor's roof. I think it is significant that the outsider solved both 'problems' in impersonal ways, either appealing to institutional authority, or exploiting the personal advantage that came from owning the property the frisbee landed on. It apparently never occurred to him to discuss the problems with the local man, which would be the first thing a person in a strong-network community would do.

14 Some important work in this field has been done by Trudgill (for example, Trudgill 1974a, 1975a, 1983a).

15 *Accommodation* is a concept introduced and developed by the sociolinguist and social psychologist Howard Giles and his associates (for example, Giles 1973; Giles and Smith 1979).

16 This merger also occurs in VBE, but only at the ends of words and before 'r'. You would not hear 'fin' for 'thin' in VBE.

17 I have some reservations about the method of constructing the linguistic market index which, originally at least, involved a team of sociolinguists evaluating the extent to which speakers participated in the linguistic market on the basis of a 'socioeconomic life history' of the speaker. The judges were explicitly instructed not to try to use explicit or objective criteria.

18 If you doubt that 't', 'd' deletion ·is a process in your speech, try saying 'west side' three times rapidly without deleting the 't' in 'west'! Even to say 'west side' once, slowly with the 't' intact strikes many speakers of English as somehow *too* correct.

19 A fourth constraint, whether a 'grammatical *d*' was past tense or not, was difficult to analyze because there was so little data. It appears to be a weak constraint at best.

20 As Sankoff and Labov (1979:203–6) point out and illustrate.

21 Interestingly, Bickerton and Berdan came to opposite conclusions on how to resolve the theoretical disparity. Bickerton called for the abandonment of variable rules, Berdan for the adaptation of Chomskyan theory to accommodate them.

22 Lefebvre treats *kiski*, from *qui c'est qui* or perhaps *qui est-ce qui*, as a single complex form. The variation between *qu'est-ce que* and *ce que* in indirect questions and other constructions in French (Kemp 1979) is another much-discussed instance of grammatical variation in Montreal French.

23 On the other hand, Adamson (1987, 1988) is one investigator of language acquisition who finds the variable rule a promising way to model certain aspects of language acquisition.

24 The most complete overview of developmental linguistics is to be found in C.-J. Bailey (forthcoming).

25 These marking relationships apply only to single consonants. In consonant *clusters*, markings are quite different, but again for very good reasons.

26 It might be instructive to say 'tick-tock' five times in rapid succession, then do the same with 'kit-cot' and see if you notice a difference in effort.

27 The little-used Varbrul 3 computer program will allow different weightings to be assigned to gradient levels of stress.

28 Bailey has discussed and exemplified the relationship between implicational patterns and historical and geographical linguistics in Bailey 1980.

29 Gradience in grammatical categories, as well as cognitive categories in general, is a central theme in G. Lakoff's (1987) theory of language and cognition.

30 Remember that Hopper and Thompson, in work we discussed in chapter 3, found a kind of gradience in 'nouniness' and 'verbiness' in a discourse context.

9

Some Applications of the Sociolinguistics of Language

INTRODUCTION

Research in the sociolinguistics of language has always been accompanied by a strong emphasis on applications of the results to social problems. The first set of problems sociolinguists tried to help solve was in education. Since then, sociolinguistic research has been applied to other professions, including the law, medicine, advertising, and even interpersonal interaction. My own interest and experience has been in the field of public education, so a large part of this chapter will be about that particular application. Fascinating work on applications of sociolinguistics to the other fields has been done, though, and some of it will also be illustrated.

One reason why so much early variation analysis was on US VBE (Stewart 1967; Labov et al. 1968; Wolfram 1969; Fasold 1972b) was a desire to use linguistic analysis to work towards a solution to shortcomings in education where poor black youngsters were concerned. There was considerable general awareness at the time that young people in poor neighborhoods, most of them black, were not getting expected benefits from public education. A lot of attention was paid to reading and literacy in particular. Since reading involves language, it seemed a good place for linguists to make a contribution. In Britain, linguists with similar motivations tried to apply what they knew to issues in the education of working class youngsters and the children of immigrants (for example, Trudgill 1975a).

SOCIOLINGUISTICS AND LANGUAGE ARTS TEACHING

Language differences or language deficits?

Some research, not by linguists, on language and education in the 1960s and 1970s led to what was called the *deficit hypothesis*. Basil Bernstein (for example 1961, 1972) is a sociologist whose research was prominent in this area. It is not at all clear that Bernstein himself intended the deficit hypothesis, at least in its strongest forms, but some of his proposals were interpreted in that direction. Bernstein wrote that two kinds of English 'code' could be distinguished: 'elaborated code' and 'restricted code'. Restricted code is used by everyone, but some children also acquire the elaborated code, which Bernstein saw as essential for success in school. In earlier work, Bernstein indicated that children from working classes were likely to be limited to restricted code, while middle-class children would also have the elaborated code, but he later modified this. In his later work, he associated the acquisition of both codes with families, of whatever social class, that had a certain interactional style which he called 'person-centered'. Children in families with a different style of interaction, called 'positional', were more likely to learn restricted code only. So far Bernstein might be accused of overstating the case, or perhaps of a bit of mistaken emphasis, but what he says is plausible enough. In particular, there are striking parallels between some aspects of elaborated and restricted codes and the low and high dialects of diglossia, a topic discussed in this book's companion volume (Fasold 1984a) and a very common sociolinguistic phenomenon. Whatever the merits of Bernstein's research, he has been criticized – sometimes severely – by sociolinguists (for example, Dittmar 1976).

It is fair to say that Bernstein's work has also been misunderstood.[1] The idea of a 'restricted code' suggested to some educators in the USA that there could be children from economically poor homes and neighborhoods whose language was severely *deficient*. Children like this are said to have such an incomplete sort of language that they do not have the cognitive tools to think rationally. The cure for these deficiencies is to place the youngsters in special programs where their language learning can be completed, at which time they would be ready for school. In some cases, the suggestion is that young children should be taken from their homes for large parts of the day, since home is supposed to be where the problem starts.

At times, VBE is taken to be a kind of Bernsteinian restricted code, but it is ridiculously easy to show that it is not. By definition everyone, economically advantaged or disadvantaged, uses restricted code on some occasions. Almost *no* speakers of favored lects of English have more than the most rudimentary capacity to speak or even thoroughly understand VBE. It is clear that VBE is not a 'deficient' code either. We saw in chapter 7 that the verb system of VBE is arguably substantially richer than the verb system in the standard varieties of English, in the sense that fine distinctions of verbal aspect can be made succinctly and efficiently. Furthermore, sociolinguists who have recorded samples of speech from people who are supposed to have these deficits, and have analyzed recordings made by members of the communities themselves, get a very different picture. This kind of evidence reveals the existence of finely-honed verbal skills which are valued as well as practised. When youngsters from the same communities are interviewed by adult investigators in school offices or other formal surroundings, they become very unsure of what is expected of them and deal with the situation by giving the briefest responses they can get by on. This is no doubt one source of reports of 'deficient language'. On the other hand, Labov presents an inner-city youth's well-reasoned discussion of the character of God and the existence of heaven, delivered in fluent VBE.[2] Many people have found it a cogent demonstration that the ability to conduct a reasonable discussion does not depend crucially on the ability to use 'correct' grammar.

A tidy demonstration of the differences between nonstandard lects and 'restricted code' was given by Trudgill (1975a:93), using nonstandard linguistic features of British English (showing that the point applies to 'restricted code' and nonstandard language in general, not just VBE). Trudgill compared these two sentences:

The blokes what was crossing the road got knocked down by a car.
The gentlemen were crossing the road and a car knocked them down.

The first of the two is obviously nonstandard, but it illustrates *elaborated* code. It contains a relative clause and a passive clause, both examples of syntactic elaboration. The second uses standard English forms, but is syntactically more like what you find in *restricted* code, with both clauses in the active and conjoining used instead of subordination.

It has always seemed to me that Bernstein's distinction is more related to certain concepts in sociolinguistics that we have looked at than nonstandard language. In particular, the network analysis concept discussed in the chapter on variation analysis is a good background for understanding what 'restricted code' might be about. Dense and multiplex networks, where an individual's friends and relatives are likely to be friends or relatives of each other, are common in working-class societies. Conversational participants do not have to actually say a lot of what will be understood with people they know well and with whom they share a lot of the same background. Much of what would have to be explained to an outsider can simply be assumed within a tightly-knit group. If this is true, then dense, multiplex networks like these would be a natural environment for 'restricted code' and not a very good one for 'elaborated code'. There would be a good deal less need for lengthy verbal explanations of things that everybody understands anyway. Nonstandard language varieties are also associated with working-class and lower-class communities, but for different reasons. First of all, the association between nonstandard language and social status almost has to be true by definition (the language features used by people in a position to set the standards are almost certain to *be* the standards!). Besides, we have seen that innovations almost always originate in the upper levels of the working-class. Again, almost by definition, an innovation is a departure from overt standards. Standards are usually based on admired literary works of the past and are therefore based on established usage.

To see how this works out, we will compare two narratives which I personally recorded at about the same time (in 1968 and 1969), given by two boys of about the same age, both black and both born in Washington, DC. One was from a disadvantaged, black inner-city neighborhood. The other was from a professional family – his father is a surgeon and his mother is a pediatrician – and he was attending a prestigious private school. As you would expect, the youngster from the inner-city neighborhood tells his story, a description of a 'Western' movie, in what I take to be typical 'restricted code'. The other boy retold an episode from the television series 'Star Trek' in what I assume Bernstein would agree is 'elaborated code'. The restricted code narrative was as follows:

He . . . he rode in town. So . . . this fat man, he had killed his sister and his mother. And his father. They took his father and . . . took his father and his sister and cut they hair off. So when they came back home and this . . . see, coming back where everybody looked at him and he went ho . . . home and he saw three, three of they g . . . graves. So he went back. It was a fat man had this hair . . . put the hair on his head . . . he was bald-headed. He took his sister hair and put it on his head. He kind of fat. And the other man . . . gunslinger. And then the other one . . . It was about . . . ten mens. So . . . he went into . . . he was looking for all of them.

Later, the narrative becomes much more animated, but no easier to follow:

He kept throwing things and snucked in the back door and then got one of the mens, one of the mens. They was scared, he got to the door. He throwed a rock in there, 'terrr'. And then they say, 'Let's get out of here, Frank.' 'Aw, you scared, go on.' So he went through the door. He say . . . Kicked the door open, 'Boom boom'. He fell out the d . . . one of the mens kept trying to get away like way down there. Well, he took a, uh, one of his rifles and the, 'Ch-khhh'. He fell off.

The speaker is a fluent speaker of VBE and uses several of the salient features of VBE in this excerpt (absence of possessive marking in 'they graves' and 'his sister hair'; absence of 'is' and 'are' in 'he kind of fat', and 'you scared'; the hypercorrect plural 'mens', possibly based on the optionality of plural morphology in VBE). But these grammatical features are really beside the point. The story is scarcely comprehensible (the full narrative is no more so!), but not because of the grammatical features. The principle protagonist is not identified in any detail and the pronominal references are very hard to sort out. After a couple of rereadings, you might be able to infer that the 'fat man' had killed the father, mother, and sister of the man who 'rode in town', but this is not made explicit. Possibly the 'other man . . . gunslinger' is the character who 'rode in town', but after all these years I am still not sure! The story is not told in the temporal order in which it occurred in the film. First, one character rides into town, then the murderers cut off the victims' hair, though this apparently had happened much earlier. After this, we find the hero looking at his family's graves, then we discover the motivation for the earlier hair-cutting. One of the murderers, the fat man, was bald and was using the victims' hair as a toupée. Eventually, I am still not sure exactly where, we get to the point in the narrative where the protagonist is looking for the murderers.

This narrative very much reminds me of the description of lower-class narratives collected in the 1950s by Schatzman and Straus (1955), whose work is cited by J. R. Edwards (1979a:31–2) as an early study of the 'deficiencies' of lower-class speech. The interviews produced narrative descriptions of a tornado that had struck in Arkansas. As Edwards summarizes Schatzman and Straus's description:

There was little attempt to set the scene, as it were, for the interviewer, and the respondents were apparently able to do little more than reconstruct the event as it has appeared to them personally . . . it proved difficult for the interviewer to obtain a rounded picture of what had happened. People were mentioned in the narrative . . . whose roles were unclear, and yet little attempt was made properly to identify and integrate such persons.

The conclusion that Schatzman and Straus (1955:336) came to about these narratives was that the lower-class speakers 'literally cannot tell a straight story or describe a simple incident coherently'. This comment is too judgemental for my taste, but I have no doubt that Schatzman and Straus would also have applied it to the movie narrative above. What should not be overlooked is that the movie account and no doubt the tornado narratives would have been perfectly adequate under one condition: that is, that they were being told to someone who had already seen the film or had experienced the tornado. In fact, listening to the movie narrative, I found myself with the vague wish that I had seen the movie so that I could enjoy what was unfolding as a very enthusiastically-told story.

The story told (in elaborated code) by the son of the two doctors was very different.

Once the Klingons . . . ahhh, uh, declared war on . . . the . . . Enterprise, that's the name of the ship. And the Fed . . . and the Federation . . . uh . . . they had a treaty . . uh, the Federation and . . . uh . . . the . . . Klingons thought that the people of the Enterprise had . . . uhm . . . had broken this treaty. But it really wasn't the . . . people . . . it . . . of the Enterprise, it was . . . this . . . life-form that fed on hate. He tried to make them hate each other. And as they hated more, he got stronger and stronger. And he took over both ships. But soon they found that this was happening, so . . . they . . . kept . . . they . . . made him feel that . . . there was no more hate and there was just friendliness and he left.

   This story was told under some duress. I had arrived at the boy's home by appointment to conduct the interview, but it turned out that he needed to spend time studying that evening (the school he attended was very demanding). As a consequence, it was to his advantage to tell the story as succinctly as possible. In spite of this, and in spite of a number of disfluencies, the participants are all well-identified, their actions follow the natural temporal order, and each action is explicitly motivated. In fact, most of the disfluencies arise specifically where the narrator was concerned that the identification of a participant be adequate for a stranger. For instance, when he began, 'Once the Klingons . . . ahhh, uh,' he hesitated while he searched my face to establish whether or not I knew who 'the Klingons' were (I had just mentioned that I was a 'Star Trek' fan). When I nodded affirmatively, he continued; I have no doubt he would have explained who they were otherwise. Later on, there is a hesitation when he decides he has *not* made a proper identification when he says, 'it really wasn't the . . . people . . . it . . . of the Enterprise, it was . . .'. It seems he started to say 'it really wasn't the people, it was this life-form', but decided in mid-sentence that he had to say *which* people. All of this distancing of the narrator from the story for the benefit of an outsider leads naturally to features of 'elaborated code' like subordination ('life-form that fed on hate') and impersonal constructions ('there was just friendliness').

   It should be clear that the most important differences between the two narratives have nothing to do with stigmatized linguistic features, but how each young man constructed the story. The second story is far easier to follow, but the narrative *performance* was rather bland compared to the exuberant retelling of the Western movie. The most serious problem with the 'restricted code' story from the point of view of an educator is that it would communicate so little to an outsider (someone who had not also seen the movie). School, of course, is a place where people (teachers) inform other people (pupils) about things that the teachers know and the pupils do not. The ability to use language to get things across to 'outsiders' is crucial in school. It is not crucial in the playgrounds and streets of inner Washington, DC, or, I daresay, in Ballymacarrett and working-class neighborhoods in general.

   I am going into this much detail in an effort to give a different perspective from the observations of Bernstein, Straus and Schatzman and many others. Some youngsters who come to school simply have not had to use language in ways it is used in school, while other children have. It is a 'deficiency' of sorts, but the same 'deficiency' that people from England, however naturally athletic, would have the first time they came to North America and tried to play softball, or that even athletically gifted North Americans would have in their first cricket game. Neither set of players would have had the occasion to develop the specific skills the new sport demanded. The 'deficits' of children without 'elaborated code' skills are quite possibly analogous. They have not had occasion to learn what the new game (school) demands, and they are being compared to children who have. Of course, the English people who played softball badly the first time they tried the game *may* not have been very good athletes, but it would not be fair to come to that conclusion based on their performance in that first softball game.

Reading

In general, linguists have not found the arguments in favor of the deficit hypothesis at all convincing. They would agree with Edwards and Giles that linguistic research 'rather undercuts the philosophy of intervention and compensatory language programmes for the pre-school child since there is, in effect, nothing for which to compensate' (Edwards and Giles 1984:122), at least where nonstandard language is concerned. Where the 'restricted code' phenomenon is concerned, I have just suggested that a deficit approach might be seriously misleading. Instead, some sociolinguists have pointed out the similarities between children who come to school speaking nonstandard lects like VBE and children in other parts of the world who speak vernacular languages different from the national or regional language used in school.

In this book's companion volume (Fasold 1984a, chapter 11), one proposed solution to this problem was discussed in some detail: vernacular language education. According to this proposal, children would receive early education and reading instruction in their native vernaculars while they were being taught the regular school language, and gradually be switched to the school language. Although some research indicates that this approach might sometimes work, there are substantial problems with it. In particular, it has not been possible to demonstrate *conclusively* that vernacular language education works, and it is very expensive, especially for developing countries. Furthermore, parents and community leaders sometimes see the national school language as the only path to advancement and take vernacular language education to be attempts to block that path.

The same solution has been proposed for speakers of VBE and other minority languages and language varieties, with very much the same results. It is not difficult to show that VBE spoken by a 6-year-old urban black child, for example, is systematically and extensively different from both the language spoken in the classroom and the language of the written educational materials; much more so than the differences faced by children of the same age from middle-class backgrounds. It is equally easy to argue that the VBE speaker faces not only the same new challenges and experiences that any 6-year-old faces in the early years of school, but that he or she faces a gap between pre-school and school language experience that the middle-class child does not face. (It should be clear by now that 'gap' means a *difference*, not a *deficit*.) A clear conclusion from this line of reasoning is that the youngster speaking VBE can be spared a major obstacle if early reading experience, at least, is with primers written in VBE. When the reading skill itself is established, it would be transferred to reading material in standard English.

Implicit in this line of reasoning is the relationship between spoken and written language which linguists have endorsed in the past. This traditional point of view, taking spoken language as primary and written language as derived, is nicely summarized by Stubbs (1980:23–8). For decades, the viewpoint succinctly stated by the famous American linguist Leonard Bloomfield (1933:21) went unchallenged: 'Writing is not language, but merely a way of recording language by means of visible marks.' The argument usually given in support of this view is developed in more detail by Stubbs, but the main points are these.

1 Spoken language came first in the history of the human race. In comparison with speech, writing is a recent event in history.
2 Spoken language comes first for individuals. The vast majority of people learn speaking without very much explicit instruction, but learn to read only with formal teaching.
3 Spoken language is biologically based. Most linguists take at least some grammatical principles ultimately to be properties of the brain, although this is controversial among psychologists. It furthermore seems that the human upper respiratory and digestive systems are modified for speech. No such biological adaptations specifically for reading and writing are apparent.
4 Spoken language is highly resistant to conscious control. Writing is markedly less so.
5 Spoken language comes first for individual societies. There are no human communities without 'spoken' languages (where 'spoken' is meant in a broad sense which includes sign languages used in communities of deaf people). Many of these languages, perhaps still a majority, do not have writing systems.
6 Literacy as a widespread phenomenon is a very recent historical event.
7 People speak much more than they read or write.
8 Spoken language is used in a much wider range of functions than written language.

If writing is 'merely a way of recording language by visible marks', then if the marks do not match the language of the learner, learning to read would be much more difficult. This trail of reasoning leads quite naturally to the dialect reader proposal. However straightforward the line of reasoning might seem, the proposal has fared *less* well than the vernacular language in education proposal has fared in developing countries, at least where VBE in the US is concerned. One reason is that Bloomfield's statement is an overstatement.[3] It is now well recognized that written language is much more than just spoken language marked down on paper, a point Stubbs makes immediately after presenting the above arguments (Stubbs 1980:29ff.; see also Goody and Watt 1963; Ong 1977; Tannen 1982b, 1982c; Stubbs 1986:202–23). One difference is that people in literate societies generally have a special respect for written language. A result is that the idea of teaching children to read from books written in a stigmatized speech variety like VBE is distressing to most people on the face of it. Teachers and educational administrators see it as a lowering of language standards. Parents of speakers of VBE and community leaders suspect that the dialect reading materials are a means of limiting opportunities for children in the community. The idea that the ultimate goal is skill in reading *standard* English and that the goal might be reached more efficiently if the beginning of reading is taught through VBE is difficult to get across and is generally treated with deep suspicion.[4]

Due to strong resistance towards the use of any stigmatized language variety in education, there has been very little research to show whether or not this 'dialect reader' approach would work. As in the case of research on vernacular language education, the few research efforts that have been made have research–design problems and their conclusions are mixed (cf. Leaverton 1973 for one of the few research reports). J. R. Edwards (1979a:120–3) has summarized many of the reservations that scholars have raised about the value of dialect readers. He cites William Labov (1972a:241), a linguist who had done more than anyone else to promote respect for the integrity of VBE:

Some writers seem to believe that the major problem causing reading failure is structural interference between these two forms of English. Our research points in the opposite direction . . . The number of structures unique to BEV [Black English Vernacular] are small, and it seems unlikely that they could be responsible for the disastrous record of reading failure in the inner city schools.[5]

A rather cogent argument along these lines was raised by Joshua Fishman (1969), who pointed out that there are many populations with very high literacy levels, including rural Japanese and the citizens of German-speaking Swiss cantons, where the vernacular language is about as different from the school language as VBE is from the school language in the USA. The 'dialect reader' approach, once advocated with some vigor (for example, some of the articles in Baratz and Shuy 1969), is seldom mentioned now.

Earlier, Wolfram and I (Wolfram and Fasold 1974) mentioned three other strategies which might be used in teaching reading to children who speak VBE. These were to teach the school language before teaching reading, to provide reading materials that simply avoided areas of difference between VBE and standard English, and to use traditional materials, but allow children to read them orally in their own speech variety. It is now clear that the first two of these are even less feasible than dialect readers. There is no evidence to encourage the expectation that teaching spoken standard language in classrooms would be successful (cf. Edwards and Giles 1984 for some discussion). Even if it were, it would mean that reading instruction would be delayed intolerably long. The second suggestion means simply that only constructions that are the same in the nonstandard and standard lects would appear in the reading primer. For children who speak VBE, this would mean, for example, that the generic present tense ('the little girl eats lunch every day') could not be used, since VBE does not have the standard grammar '-s' suffix on present tense verbs. It seems that so many fundamental constructions would have to be avoided that you could not write a story for children that sounded at all natural.

We would still offer the last suggestion (with the concurrence of Edwards and Giles 1984:147) as valid as far as it goes. That is, if a VBE child sees '"Nobody is home", said the little pig' and reads 'Nobody home' or even 'Nobody not home', the teacher should realize that the child has read successfully, as far as understanding what he or she is reading is concerned. Both of these are possible ways of saying 'Nobody is home' in VBE. You could even argue that you can be *more* confident that the child understands than if the child had said 'Nobody is home.' If he or she had read exactly what was written, the child might have just been 'calling the words'. If the sentence has, in effect, been translated into the child's own grammar, the child must have understood what he or she was reading to get the 'translation' right. The trouble with this suggestion is that it assumes that the youngster has acquired enough reading skill to read aloud in the first place. If it is actually true that the difference between the community language and the language of the reading book is preventing some youngsters from working out how to read, they will never get to the place where they would benefit from being allowed to read orally in the vernacular.

We will probably not find out in the near future how many children there are for whom language differences are substantial because the research needed to find out would be so controversial. At the moment, it seems that language differences are not the greatest problem in teaching reading. Labov (1987:10,12) would agree, although he is convinced that black and white vernaculars are diverging. In his discussion of the divergence issue, he said, 'I can see that the primary cause of educational failure is not language differences but institutional racism.'⁶ Later in the same article, though, he also said, 'And we as linguists have yet to make a significant contribution to the school curriculum that will put our linguistic knowledge to use.' In his opinion, there are ways in which linguistic information can contribute to better school curricula.

Writing

Analogous issues arise where teaching writing is concerned. If there are children who enter school with a community language different from the school language, it will show up in their written work. There is a great deal of recent research to show that there are substantial differences between spoken and written language. Yet, in a real sense, speaking is primary and writing is a kind of addition. Especially when written skills are first being acquired, learners will tend to try to write what they would say. A youngster who is socially and economically privileged who does this, since his or her community language is only a little different from the school language, will be seen as someone on the right track who needs instruction in matters of style, punctuation and so on, and perhaps a little more maturity. Teachers are likely to see a child with a stigmatized community vernacular who writes the way people speak in the vernacular as scarcely able to write at all, since their writing seems to be so full of 'grammatical errors'.

It is not hard to show that neophyte writers include stigmatized forms in their writing. The following paragraph, for example, was written by an inner-city black elementary school child in Norfolk, Virginia, who was asked to write a paragraph about a television program she had seen (stigmatized sociolinguistic variables are italicized):

it was about this cuntry boy he did *not know nothing* about city school. So *them* people *keep* telling him to do soming and he though it was right.

This excerpt is from a composition written by a sixth-grade youngster in an elementary school in a small town in Pennsylvania:

I walked inside and *seen* crates. I opened one and there were *them* things that guy had pitched. So i took to crates and went to play. Then i started to throw the things. When they *got all* i went home to go bed.⁷

Not only do socially disfavored forms appear in writing, but also exceptionable features that seem to be inspired by an effort to avoid disfavored forms, a phenomenon called *hypercorrection*. An example from the written work of children in Reading, England, who typically have the verbal '-s' suffix with all persons (for example, their grammar calls for 'I goes' as well as 'he goes'), is given by Cheshire (1984:552): 'It *taste* all rich and creamy.' It appears that the writer is avoiding all verbal '-s' suffixes since so much of his natural use of the suffix exposes him to criticism. Notice that the same absence of '-s' in the paragraph by the Norfolk, Virigina, child is *not* hypercorrection, since the grammar of her spoken lect calls for an uninflected verb form. Similarly, hyper-correct plural suffixation is reported by V. Edwards (1984:567) in the writing of speakers of British Black English. Examples such as 'They picked up sacks of *golds*' are hypercorrections that appear next to instances such as 'The headlight are *thing* you put on at night to look out for *thing* like *dog* or *cat*.' The latter sentence has unmarked plurals, no doubt because plural marking is not demanded by the child's spoken language grammar. The hypercorrection in the former example appears to be motivated by a desire not to leave a noun unsuffixed in written work a teacher will evaluate. A particularly telling case is cited by Reed (1981:148), where a speaker of US VBE wrote 'my reason ~~are is~~ are that some people have children to soon.' A feature of VBE is that number concord in forms of 'to be' is not required, so that 'they is' and 'he is' are both grammatical. Not willing to risk a use of 'is' that would sound natural to her, but might not be correct in written English, the student finally settles on 'are', which unfortunately is no more correct in written English than it would be in spoken VBE.

On the other hand, it is also clear that written infelicities which can be traced to disfavored features of spoken language are far from the only problems a composition teacher would see, even in the examples I have presented here. There are numerous unconventional spellings (some of which, like 'cuntry', would yield the appropriate pronunciation of the word by general spelling rules of English), punctuation errors, omissions, capitalization problems, and miscellaneous correctable usages like 'to' for 'two'. Besides these, there could be higher-level improvements, like better transitions, more sophisticated scene-setting and so on.

Furthermore, research by Marcia Farr Whiteman (Farr Whiteman 1981a) shows that the picture is not as simple as it appears. Farr Whiteman investigated 32 speech and writing samples from white as well as black working-class eighth-grade pupils in a southern Maryland school district. She was able to demonstrate, first of all, that phonological features of the youngsters' speech which differed from the regional standard pronunciation almost never showed up in writing. This result provides general support for Trudgill's (1975a) distinction between matters of *accent*, having to do with pronunciation, and matters of *dialect*, involving morphology and syntax. More interesting were her results for some of the suffix features that are often mentioned in discussions of the educational implications of socially disfavored language. As earlier research had also shown, Farr Whiteman found that the verbal '-s' suffix in the present tense with third-singular subjects was absent with over 80 per cent of such verbs in the speech of the black youngsters, and less than 15 per cent in the speech of whites. Similarly, the plural '-s' suffix was absent from almost 30 per cent of plural nouns in the speech of the black subjects, but less than 4 per cent of the plural nouns used in the spoken samples by the white children. As linguists who study VBE would predict, these suffixes are absent in a substantial number of instances in the writing of the black students, 50 per cent in the case of verbal '-s' and about 27 per cent in the case of plural '-s'. But, surprisingly, these suffixes were also missing in the writing of the white youngsters, a remarkable 31 per cent frequency for verbal '-s' and over 13 per cent for plural '-s'. These results are displayed in figure 9.1, from Farr Whiteman's figure 2 (Farr Whiteman 1981a:158).

Farr Whiteman was further able to replicate her results using data from a national assessment of writing by young people for whom data on ethnicity, region, and education were available. Again, these '-s' suffixes were often absent in the compositions by whites who would not be expected to show the same absence in their speech.

There are three observations here which need an explanation. First, the black youngsters have substantially more suffix absence in their speech than white speakers do.[8] Second, black speakers have less suffix absence in writing than they do in speech. Third, white speakers have *more* suffix absence in writing than they do in speech. The difference in the speech of the black and white children is nothing new; it is just one more instance

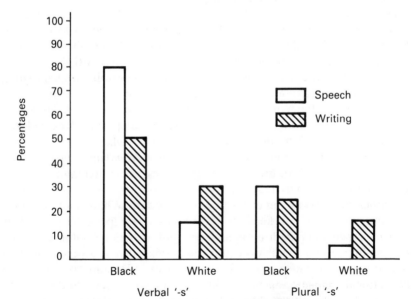

Figure 9.1 Percentage of '-s' suffix absence in speech and writing for southern Maryland black and white eighth-grade pupils
Source: data from Farr Whiteman (1981a:158)

of the differences in linguistic structure between VBE and white vernaculars. This may be due, as we saw in chapter 7, to the putative creole history of VBE, or to the divergence process that some linguists see, or to some other sociolinguistic process. The second fact has often been explained by assuming that VBE-speaking children, growing up in the USA, would be familiar with standard white lects through the broadcast media, and their school and other social contact experiences. It would be clear that standard English is expected in school tasks like writing, and this would lead them to suppress the features of VBE they expect will not be appropriate. Since the standard forms are less familiar, they will not be entirely suppressed; hence the pattern of greater – but not complete – use of the suffixes in writing. It is the third observation that calls this explanation into question. Why should the white children not show the same pattern of less suffix absence in writing? Why should they omit the suffixes so much more in writing?

The explanation that Farr Whiteman gives is that learning to write is to be seen as the acquisition of a new code. As in other stressful language acquisiton situations – pidgin formation, some stages of first language acquisition, 'baby talk', and the kind of speech used to foreigners who do not share the speaker's language – suffixes are vulnerable. While developing facility in writing skills all learners, regardless of their spoken language background, are likely to omit nonsalient features such as these suffixes under the stress of code-acquisition.

If this explanation is valid, can we not dispense with the argument based on spoken language differences? Is it not superfluous to have two accounts for the same result? The answer is that the result is not quite the same in the case of the black youngsters as it is with the whites. Recall that the differences between the two groups are observed in writing as well as in speech. We still need an account for the higher frequency of '-s' absence in the written work by the black children. If the acquisition factor affects both black children and white children, but black children are also influenced to omit written suffixes because suffixes are not required by their spoken language structure, we would expect exactly what we observe. Both groups show suffix absence in writing, but black learners have a higher frequency.

One would expect another result as well, as Farr Whiteman points out. Assuming that the speakers of VBE continue to speak VBE as their primary language system even as instruction in writing continues, they would still have *this* influence towards suffix absence even as writing becomes more familiar. As white youngsters get more practice with writing, the acquisition factor would tend to fade, leaving little reason to continue to leave out the suffixes that are not absent in their speech. The expected result would be that, as time went on, white children would show sharp declines in suffix omission, while the black children would show a much slower decline. This is precisely what Farr Whiteman reports (Farr Whiteman 1981a:162). Using the data from the national assessment of writing, she compared children of nine (the approximate age of the children from southern Maryland in her primary study) with all the older writers in the data. For plural '-s', suffix omission is 35 per cent less in the work of older black writers than in the writing samples of 9-year-old black children. The older white writers showed a striking 78 per cent less omission than did the 9-year-old white children. Tabulating the absence of '-ed' in words where the '-ed' suffix creates a consonant cluster – a well-known site for deletion in spoken VBE – she found about 42 per cent less absence in the writing of the older blacks compared with black 9-year-olds. In the white group, there was 74 per cent less absence in the work of older writers. The comparable differences in the case of verbal '-s' is much less striking, but is still in the predicted direction; older black writers have 60 per cent less omission while the written work of the older white writers contained 66 per cent less.[9] In general, these data support both a spoken language effect and the acquisition effect. It is hard to over-emphasize the importance of recognizing the dual influence on speakers of disfavored varieties of a language. If only the acquisition factor is recognized, it will appear that working-class black children are simply slower at acquiring this kind of writing skill. Coming to this conclusion is likely to invite racist or classist explanations along the lines that black or lower-status children lack the ability that higher-status white children have, since they respond more slowly to the same instruction. If more evidence is needed that a racist explanation is incorrect, we need only consider that Cheshire independently came to the same conclusion as I have just presented, on the basis of her work with white working-class young people in Reading (Cheshire 1984:552):

All children tend to make mistakes of this kind [that is, inappropriate use and omission of suffixes] when they are first learning to write . . . However, the fact that children were still making these mistakes at secondary school suggests that they may be caused by linguistic confusion between SE [Standard English] and the nonstandard variety.

I would still endorse the advice Wolfram and I (Wolfram and Fasold 1974:203–6) offered as a way of dealing with writing for speakers of disfavored lects. We suggested that mechanical 'errors' should be divided into two categories and treated separately. One category would consist of unconventional spellings that are not related to the child's accent, punctuation, capitalization, and other problems neophyte writers have getting used to the new way of using language. The other would consist of infelicities of written style that are related to the structure of the child's spoken language. The first category should be addressed first, since these problems will be common to all learners and can be expected to respond to instruction and practice most readily. At first, the teacher following this advice would not mark as incorrect any of the items in the second category. For example, the composition by the boy from Pennsylvania given earlier as an example would have only the italicized items corrected at this stage, as below:

> I walked inside and seen crates. I opened one and there were them things that guy had pitched. So *i* [I] took *to* [two] crates and went to play. Then *i* [I] started to throw the things. When they got all *i* [I] went home to go [to] bed.

Once progress in first-category mechanics is made, then children can begin to receive instruction on the grammatical differences between their spoken language and the conventions of written language. The teacher should expect that progress in this area will be noticeably slower and should not interpret the slower progress as a sign of any inherent inferiority on the child's part. The same suggestion has been made in Britain by Richmond (1979) and endorsed by Cheshire (1984:555).[10]

Trudgill (1975a:79–83) suggests in addition that there are some forms of writing for which dialect-related 'errors' are really not inappropriate and need *never* be corrected. Personal letters represent one such case and creative writing is another. The criterion he has in mind is that there is no need to adjust language use that comes most naturally to a writer unless there is a penalty for not doing so. If a writer's intended audience is not going to think the less of him or her for using disfavored linguistic forms, there is no reason to avoid using them. Trudgill finds academic essays 'problematical' because he sees no inherent reason why nonstandard forms should not be used in essays. However, a student will no doubt be penalized if the essay is to be evaluated by an examiner within the educational system, because 'some examiners are likely to mark them down for using non-standard grammar.'

Some years ago, I came across an essay written entirely in nonstandard English which none the less won a national essay contest in the USA. The contest was not conducted by any school, but by a liberal political action organization, the American Civil Liberties Union (ACLU). The rules of the contest, conducted in 1970, required contestants to write on the subject: 'The Bill of Rights: Is It for Real?' The national first-prize winner was Goldie Holt of Nashville, Tennessee. Part of her prize-winning essay follows:

Normal is what normal be and they tells a black man he ain't normal. He can't be right cause he's too dark and black is evil. I guess it ain't nobody's fault, it's just the ways we been brought up. But seems like to me they should see that when they says you got the right to talk then shoots you down when you talks too loud, that when they says you got the right to assemble then calls the dogs, firehose, and troops on you, it ain't right! Things have come to that, though, and no one says they the blame! That Bill of Rights means something to me but that ain't no good. It got to mean something to everybody else.

Among the five judges who evaluated the essays at the national level were Julian Bond, then a civil rights activist and since a successful political leader on the state and national level, and Maya Angelou, a noted black writer who herself has used VBE forms in her work. I concur with the judges that the essay is not damaged for having been written as it was; rather it is the more effective because of its dialect forms. On the other hand, Trudgill has a point; most academic essays will not be evaluated by an ACLU committee that includes Maya Angelou and Julian Bond.

Speaking

The issue of whether or not attempts should be made to change the accents or dialects of school children who speak socially disfavored forms of language has been much discussed by applied sociolinguists (for example, Wolfram and Fasold 1974:177–85; Trudgill 1975a:65–87; J. R. Edwards 1979a:118–19). The consensus among them is that teaching spoken standard English is unnecessary, possibly harmful and very probably ineffective. As was pointed out in the last chapter, changing your speech patterns, where sociolinguistic variables are concerned, entails a change in your perception of your social identity. No amount of emphasis on standard English speech forms in a classroom will prepare someone to make a change in her own identity. In any case, evidence from videotaped classroom observations by Lucas (1986) suggests that noticing and overtly correcting disfavored speech forms is too demanding a task to expect teachers to carry out consistently. During whole-group and small-group activities and during interactions between a teacher and an individual pupil, less than half the nonstandard lect forms used by the children were corrected. During 'special events' – a youngster presenting a composition or a group of children acting out a scene – only 10 per cent of the nonstandard forms used were corrected. Children might well draw the implicit conclusion (the right conclusion, in my own view) that using standard spoken forms is not terribly crucial if their nonstandard speech is usually not corrected (cf. V. Edwards 1984:567 on inconsistency in the correction of written material). J. R. Edwards's (1979a:119) advice on the subject of spoken language in schools is eminently reasonable: 'Rather, the teacher should speak in a manner natural to himself, and accept that the children are doing the same. The fact that the children, over their school career, will have a long exposure to SE surely reduces the necessity for any active teaching with regard to oral speech production.'

LANGUAGE TESTING

Lectal bias

One more area where sociolinguists believe educators will be interested in the results of their research is language testing. Screening tests for normal language development and achievement tests evaluating language use are repeatedly given to children in schools (in developed countries at least). So ubiquitous are standardized tests in the USA that Wolfram (forthcoming) suggests that they be added to death and taxes as a third inevitable event. The general procedures for developing and administering standardized tests is reasonable enough on the face of it. A set, or several alternative sets, of test items are constructed and test-administered to samples of the population that they will eventually be used to test. Items which turn out to be unreliable or not adequate in one way or another are modified or thrown out. Eventually, the test is 'normed': that is, the developers of the test determine that the scores they have from large samples of a population of schoolchildren closely approximate the range and distribution of the scores that the whole population would get if it were possible to give it to everyone. Now an individual score can be compared to these 'normal' scores, and an interpretation given concerning the child's language development or achievement level. For instance, if a youngster gets a score that is sufficiently below the normal range for his or her age on a test of language development, that child will probably be diagnosed as having a language disorder and remedial treatment will be recommended.

Anyone who has read up to this point can probably anticipate the problem I am going to raise. We know it is the case that there are youngsters (and older people too, of course) who speak language varieties with grammatical rule systems that are different from the standard school language. Test developers, of course, are themselves well-educated people who are thoroughly familiar with accepted standards of 'correct' language. It follows naturally that test items will tend to check children taking the test against these standards of correctness. Furthermore, to the extent that these standards conform more closely to the normal spoken language of the majority of children than they do to particular minority populations, the norming procedure will work as it is supposed to only for the majority. Children from groups whose spoken language is systematically different from what the test-constructors consider correct will likewise systematically get lower scores on the standardized tests.

Wolfram (forthcoming, chapter 11) illustrates how this works with the following three examples from a real test currently in use, the 'Language Use' section of the California Achievement Test:

(1) Beth $\{ \begin{smallmatrix} \text{come} \\ \text{came} \end{smallmatrix} \}$ home and cried.

(2) Can you {went/go} out now?

(3) When {can/may} I come again?

Imagine a young boy who speaks a somewhat rustic kind of English, like the boy in the example given earlier who wrote about how he went into a cave and 'seen crates'. Quite possibly the linguistic system of his spoken language has 'come' as the form for both the present and simple past of 'to come', similar to certain standard English verbs such as 'to hit'. If this young man is not to get a point counted against his language use achievement by virtue of this item, he must be alert to the fact that his past form 'come' is not good enough on a test like this, and he must know what the 'good enough' form is. He cannot rely on what 'sounds right' (that is, he cannot count on his internalized linguistic system or his 'inner language knowledge' as Wolfram calls it). Another child, a speaker of a more mainstream kind of English which calls for the distinction between 'come' and 'came', can get one point in favor of her language use achievement level simply by relying on inner language knowledge.

In the second example, both children appear to have an equal opportunity to get their answer correct. The reason is that 'go' will sound right and 'went' will sound wrong to both, if they rely on their inner language knowledge. But the first youngster is still at risk, because he may well have developed a 'sounds right so it must be wrong' strategy, like the college student in the example cited earlier who settled on 'my reason are' after considering and rejecting 'my reason is'. If he applies this strategy here, he will select 'Can you went out now?' precisely *because* it sounds wrong. Ironically, this strategy would give the 'correct' answer in the first question since 'Beth came home' would not sound quite right to him.

In the colloquial American English of even high-status speakers, 'can' is common in permission contexts, such as the one evoked in Wolfram's third example. Here, both children face the same challenge. They have to realize that the natural-sounding form 'can' is not going to be accepted on a test like this and that the stiffer, more formal, 'may' should be selected. Even here, though, you can argue that the second youngster is in a better position, since she has fewer of these instances where something sounds right but will be marked wrong to remember.[11]

By Wolfram's calculation, no fewer than 14 of the 25 items in this test are about the distinction between standard and nonstandard vernacular forms. Nor is this an isolated case; elsewhere (Wolfram 1983), he shows that the Grammatical Closure subtest of the Illinois Test of Psycholinguistic Abilities (ITPA) has 24 items (out of 33) that would conform to the grammar of either US VBE or Appalachian English, but would be marked incorrect when the test was scored. This does not mean that children who have these kinds of English will inevitably make the wrong choice in every case. In fact, Wolfram (1983:26–8, forthcoming) gives a number of reasons why they often would *not* choose the option that would be marked wrong. A youngster with a nonstandard lect who made a choice that matched his or her inner language knowledge but would be marked wrong in only 25 per cent of the places in the ITPA where this would be possible, and made no other mistakes, would get a score of 27 on the ITPA subtest. A speaker of standard English who relied on inner knowledge of language in exactly the same way, and made no other mistakes, would get the full 33 points. In percentages, this would mean that the nonstandard English speaking child would get less than 82 per cent of the possible score by doing exactly the same thing that would give the standard English speaking child 100 per cent. Wolfram (forthcoming) cites research which indicates that this 25 per cent estimate is too conservative. In the studies he cites, nonstandard lect alternatives were actually selected more than half the time. Furthermore, the effect of hypercorrection, leading a child to make a choice against the rules of his or her spoken language precisely because it sounds right, adds to the problem.

Nonstandard lectal features and acquisitional features

One complicating fact is that a number of the distinctive features called for by the mature grammars of nonstandard lects are the same as features that turn up during the acquisition of standard lects by children (cf. Wolfram 1979:6–8). For example, standard English grammar contains a prohibition against more than one negative within a clause.[12] The grammars of many nonstandard lects of English allow or require what linguists call negative concord. This means that a negative marker with the main verb may (in some varieties *must*) be repeated with any indefinite noun phrases in the same clause that follows the verb. These varieties, then, have 'He didn't find nothing', with concordant negation in 'nothing', where standard English requires either 'He didn't find anything' or 'He found nothing'. As it happens, negative concord appears at one stage in the speech of children learning standard English, but disappears later. Similarly, children learning standard English commonly use pronunciations like 'toof' for adult standard 'tooth'. In some working-class varieties in Britain, as well as in US VBE, final [f] is the expected pronunciation where the standard lect has final [θ]. These observations make it appear that older children and adults who speak lects which have these features are suffering from arrested language development. To many educators, speech therapists, and other people who are not linguists, this seems to be too much of a coincidence. They remain skeptical when linguists argue that nonstandard lects have as much structural adequacy and integrity as the favored lects. Some take the position that nonstandard lects simply *are* incompletely-learned standard lects, and need to be remedied for that very reason.

We saw something similar in the discussion of writing. Some of the features in the work of people learning to write paralleled aspects of nonstandard lects. Is this an incredible coincidence twice over? Research in linguistic variation shows us that there is nothing coincidental about it. In fact, this apparent coincidence is exactly what variation theory would predict. To see why this is so, we have to recall some of the discussion from the two previous chapters.

In developmental linguistics, there is the recognition of the distinction between connatural and abnatural changes. Remember that connatural changes, in general, are those that make a language or language variety conform to what is most natural for the neurobiological aspects of language. In pronunciation, connatural changes lead to unmarked patterns. Taking the case of 'toof' and 'tooth', for example, we find that [θ], the final sound in the favored pronunciation, has all the hallmarks of a highly-marked consonant, especially in syllable-final position. For example, very few languages have [θ] among their distinctive sounds; it is often replaced by less marked sounds when creoles are lexified by languages like English (we saw in chapter 7 that English-lexified creoles typically have [t] for syllable-initial languages [θ]), and it is acquired relatively late by children learning languages that have it. Furthermore, in syllable-final position, consonants that are pronounced with the lips or at the extreme back of the mouth are less marked than those pronounced in the middle part of the mouth. The consonant [f], pronounced by touching the lower lip to the upper teeth, is less marked in syllable-final position than [θ] would be, since [θ] is pronounced by moving the tongue to the teeth. As a result, developmental linguistics provides us with a natural account for why children should go through an acquisitional stage at which 'both' would be pronounced 'bofe' and 'tooth' as 'toof'.

None of this says anything about why the same features would exist in nonstandard lects, but research on linguistic variation suggests an explanation here, too. According to developmental linguistics, as well as other research in variation, languages will tend to undergo connatural change unless there are particular forces, generally sociocommunicative, leading to abnatural change. In the absence of these forces, we would predict that English would, for example, eventually replace syllable-final [θ] with [f]. This has *not* happened for English in general, but only in some nonstandard varieties. Can we account for this? The answer is yes.

As we have seen, recent research on language variation strongly indicates that linguistic change is to be expected within lower-middle strata of social organization; just the people who typically speak socially disapproved lects. Furthermore, among the forces promoting abnatural change and similarly inhibiting connatural change are literacy (leading to such abnatural spelling pronunciations as 'off-ten' for 'often') and the conscious awareness of social approval in languages. These forces are centered in the higher-status, more literate and standard lect speaking parts of societies (at least in Western ones). Variation theory, then, leads us to *expect* this 'coincidence'. Children will typically introduce connatural forms temporarily during acquisition, precisely because they are natural in the sense of developmental linguistics. If a connatural change takes hold in the mature linguistic system, variation theory predicts it will happen precisely in those communities that use nonstandard lects. An analogous account can be given for negative concord and other common features of nonstandard lects (cf. Wolfram 1979:7 for a sketch of the account for negative concord).

I still have not said anything about the parallel phenomenon in writing. According to Farr Whiteman, the loss of suffixes like '-s' in the writing of speakers of standard lects has to do with the stress of learning a new code. It is entirely plausible that this setting might induce writers to resort to 'natural' forms. Indeed, if some synthesis eventually occurs between Bickerton's bioprogram hypothesis and the notions of marking reduction and natural change in developmental linguistics, we would have a striking parallel. Remember that Bickerton's support for the bioprogram hypothesis is partially based on cases of language acquisition in the absence of adequate models of mature language. Under these conditions, young language learners depend heavily on putative inborn (dare we say unmarked or 'natural'?) linguistic structures. If Bickerton's idea is even partially correct and can be integrated with other discoveries in variation analysis, it would not be surprising to find neophyte writers exploiting the same resources as first-generation learners of Hawaiian Creole did. The result again would be just what we observe. The same features that turn up and later decline in the writing of speakers of standard lects are the ones which are a permanent part of nonstandard lects. The explanation in both cases would be rooted in the developing notion of neurobiological linguistic naturalness.

Solutions to lectal bias

A strong case can be made for the contention that many tests in common use for the assessment of language development and achievement are systematically biased against youngsters who speak nonstandard lects (cf. Vaughn-Cooke 1980 for a survey of several commonly-used tests in the USA). I have to make clear, though, in just what sense a bias is seen. If language development or language achievement is understood as meaning development or achievement in the language system children are acquiring in a natural way within their own community, then there is bias. Since the constructors of the tests implicitly assume that properly developing language means a properly developing *favored* lect, a youngster who is normally developing a disfavored lect will be diagnosed as having language disorders. Furthermore, the nature of language development seems to be such that distinctively nonstandard features will often resemble features observed during a child's acquisition of a standard lect. As a result, children who are normally developing a nonstandard lect are quite likely to test as suffering from slow development.

If, on the other hand, a test like this is used to measure achievement in recognizing *standard* language forms, then it might be an adequate measure of this kind of 'achievement'. Yoder (1970:411–12) says that a standardized test: 'could be used at various stages of instruction as an index of progress in developing the additional language or dialect system. Ironically, the more culturally biased such tests are, the more benefit they will be in this case, so long as they are used as a basis for describing differences instead of deficits.'

There are two major problems with this. In the first place, as Wolfram (forthcoming) points out, the instructions for the administration and interpretation of the common standardized language assessment tests typically do *not* say the test is measuring 'progress in developing [an] additional language or dialect system'. Rather, they state that the test is measuring general language development. In the second place, even if the tests *were* used to measure how well children can recognize the difference between favored and disfavored linguistic forms, it would imply (1) that developing this ability is worthwhile and (2) that schools are efficiently and effectively teaching this skill to youngsters who speak disfavored lects. My own judgement is that these are both dubious propositions.

A number of solutions to the problem of lectal bias in testing has been suggested. Vaughn-Cooke (1983) has reviewed seven of them. She has been able to show that quite a few which seem reasonable at first glance are actually not satisfactory at all. One such solution would be to keep the same test, but norm it separately for minority communities. Applying this solution would mean that on a test such as the ITPA Grammatic Closure subtest, separate normal scores would be computed for, say, speakers of VBE. The lectal bias would still be there but, since any individual child's score would be compared to the normal scores for VBE speakers rather than to those for the general population, the chance for misdiagnoses of language disorder would be sharply reduced. The problem with such a solution stems from the fact that the normal scores for VBE speaking children would be lower than for mainstream children. This would leave open the possibility of misuse of this fact. The lower norms could easily be misinterpreted as indicating that VBE-speaking children and children from other linguistic minorities as a group were slower and less successful at learning language. Such misuse of 'scientific, statistical data' would be intolerable.

Another possibility would be to eliminate items on the test that represent lectal bias. Aside from the fact that this would cause more than half the items in some test sections to be removed, it raises the possibility of the opposite problem from the one we have been discussing. There is no reason to believe that youngsters who speak nonstandard lects have more speech disorders than other children; neither is there any reason to think they have *fewer*. The elimination of certain test items might cause a genuine disorder not to show up. One attempt at this solution described by Vaughn-Cooke led to the elimination of items ending in [θ], since VBE speakers have [f] instead. But suppose a youngster who is acquiring VBE uses [s] in the place of [θ], saying 'toos' where VBE phonology would give 'toof' and standard English 'tooth'. This child might not receive needed therapy because the disorder in the articulatory acquisition would not show up during the test. Frustration with the persistence of the lectal bias problem has led some organizations of black professionals in the USA to call for a complete moratorium on standardized testing until the problem has been corrected. This solution would only be temporary but, while the moratorium remained in effect, there would be the risk that children with genuine treatable disorders would not get the attention they need.

Some solutions with merit have been suggested. For the time being, the brightest hope seems to lie with the enlightened language diagnostician. Wolfram (forthcoming) makes a number of suggestions for the serious language specialist, and has published a booklet for language professionals (Wolfram 1979). Language diagnosticians who want to reduce the effect of lectal bias will have to become familiar with the linguistic features of the disfavored lects they are likely to encounter, either by reading descriptions of these lects or through their own observations. Wolfram (1979:4–5) points out that speech pathologists and other educators in the language field may have confidence in their ability to make the necessary observations and that they may already be acting on the basis of their own informal observations in some cases. Another suggestion he makes is to experiment with nonstandard scoring of the available standardized tests, instead of treating features that are part of the mature lect in the child's community as an instance of a disorder or lack of achievement. Furthermore, diagnosticians should try to supplement formal test results with an observation of a child's language use in more natural settings. Wolfram (forthcoming) adds analogous suggestions for people with the responsibility for interpreting the results of standardized tests.

In the long run, a most promising proposal has been made by Stockman and Vaughn-Cooke (1986). They note that what really matters, at the level of grammatical organization at least, is the ability to code fundamental semantic relations, like *action*, *state*, and *possession*. Far less important is *how* these concepts are coded, and the social evaluation of the linguistic structures that are used. To take one of their examples; a phrase like 'John's hat' codes the possessor–possession relation in standard English. In VBE, and perhaps other kinds of English, the same job is done with 'John hat'. If it is recognized that the relationship is represented by both constructions, the VBE child will be given credit for having acquired the ability to code the relationship, and not erroneously be taken not to know about possession for want of a suffix. Their contention is supported with rather striking evidence. Using data from four studies of language acquisition, including middle-class children as well as both black and white youngsters from working-class families, they compared the acquisition of semantic categories across stages of development. Looking for the development of the ability to code fundamental semantic concepts rather than the more superficial structures that are likely to be involved in sociolinguistic variables, they found that:

the comparative analysis of these four developmental studies supports the expectation that normally developing nonstandard speakers build their surface linguistic forms on the same kind of semantic base that standard speakers do . . . the results of the current analysis can be interpreted as adding to the growing evidence that semantic categories such as *action*, *state*, *location*, and *possession* represent universal regularities in early language.

The development of standardized tests which take advantage of this kind of approach would go a long way towards the elimination of lectal bias.

Apart from the lectal bias issue, Wolfram (forthcoming) raises two other potential problems with assessment where minority group children are involved. The first problem directly involves language, but the language in the *test* instead of the child's language. Test formats quite commonly use highly formal linguistic registers that could easily be baffling to children who have never encountered language use like this before. Wolfram cites this question from an armed forces test: 'To prevent scum from forming in a partly-used can of paint, one should _____'. This item contains several features that are rare in ordinary conversation, such as the fronting of the infinitival clause, the use of impersonal 'one', and the fill-in-the-blank format. Along the same lines, asking for synonyms or antonyms as a way of determining whether a youngster knows the meaning of a word can throw an unfair road-block in front of a child who does not have much experience of metalinguistic analysis such as synonymy or antonymy. If the goal is to see if a child can identify synonyms, a question asking for a synonym is appropriate, but perhaps not as a way of

determining if the youngster is familiar with the meaning of the word.
The other problem has to do with the testing context as a *speech situation* in the sense of Hymes (1962) which we saw in chapter 2. Recall that Hymes proposed a three-tiered structure consisting of speech situations, speech events, and speech acts. As Labov (1976) has pointed out, even the act of asking a boy to tell everything he knows about a toy fire engine in front of him is full of traps based on differences that might exist between what the child and the tester feel to be an appropriate speech situation. First, the youngster is in a two-way conversation with an adult stranger; something that may not be done in his own social group. Second, success on the test depends on the child saying a lot about the fire engine, while children might be expected to say as little as possible to adults in the home community. Finally, the question requires the child to do what his experience would indicate is totally unnecessary: namely, give a detailed description of something that is right before the eyes of the person hearing the description. Even before the child gives an answer, he may have to bring himself to perform in a speech situation that strikes him as bizarre, and respond to a language register that he is unfamiliar with.

ETHNOGRAPHY OF EDUCATION

Some sociolinguistic research has moved beyond the influence of the specific linguistic features of socially disfavored lects and examined potential culture clash between schools and minority social groups. This kind of research is conducted with the outlook and methods of the ethnography of communication, which we considered in chapter 2. This kind of research does not look so much for linguistic patterns expected in school which conflict with children's naturally-learned language; rather, the ethnography of education looks at how youngsters are expected to act in school, compared to behavior that is expected and admired in their own groups.

An excellent example of just this kind of research was conducted by Shirley Brice Heath (1983). As you would expect in this kind of research, Heath collected her data by spending an extended period of time (nearly ten years) living in the community location. The communities she studied are located in the Piedmont area of the Carolinas in the south-eastern USA. Her work is an ethnography of communication of communities called Roadville and Trackton, two textile mill towns within a few miles of each other. Roadville is a white working-class community and Trackton is home to families of black workers. In addition to her study of the use of language in everyday life in the two communities, Heath examines what happens to their children when they enter school, and her own rather successful efforts to get teachers to understand and deal with the cultural differences that had only puzzled them previously.

One example of a culture clash was the notion of a 'story' for teachers, compared to the concept of 'story' in the two communities. The school concept was different from the local idea of a story in each of the communities, but in different ways. For Roadville speakers, the most highly-valued stories are ones told on oneself, that place the teller in a slightly bad light, but are about an incident the central character learned an important lesson from (they end in a kind of moral). Above all, the story must be factual; elaborations on what actually took place are only possible if they are clearly identified as exaggerations. Young children learn to tell stories in this favored format at an early age, with coaching from adults, as in the following exchange between a woman and her 5-year-old niece:

Aunt Sue: Tell yo' mamma where we went today.
Wendy: Mamma took me 'n Sally to the Mall. Bugs Bunny was=
Aunt Sue: =No, who was that, that wasn't Bugs Bunny.
Wendy: Uh, I mean, Peter, no, uh a big Easter bunny was there, 'n we, he, mamma got us some eggs=
Aunt Sue: ='n' then what happened?
Wendy: I don't 'member.
Aunt Sue: Yes, you do, what happened on the climbing=
Wendy: =me 'n' Sally tried to climb on this thing, 'n' we dropped, I dropped, my eggs, some of 'em.
Aunt Sue: Why did you drop your eggs? What did Aunt Sue tell you 'bout climbin' on that thing?
Wendy: We better be careful.
Aunt Sue: No, 'bout eggs 'n' climbing?
Wendy: We better not climb with our eggs, else 'n' we'd drop 'em.

Wendy is not allowed to misidentify the bunny as Bugs Bunny or Peter Rabbit; he must be correctly identified as the Easter bunny. She is coached to include a part of the story crucial for the moral, namely that Aunt Sue had warned the children about climbing, and the little girl is gently brought to state the exact lesson she was supposed to have learned, that she should not climb while carrying eggs. The story has just the right format for a highly-valued adult story; the teller is the central character who has made an error, the facts are related in sequence and accurately, and the lesson the central character learned is the story's culmination.

In school, children are expected to recite – or 'tell stories' – of two different kinds. In social studies or science lessons, the recitations are of a type Heath (1983:294–310) calls *nonfictive*. Here, children are expected to display what they learned in an earlier lesson. School nonfictive stories share many of the features of the kind of stories that are highly valued in Roadville; they are elicited by an adult (the teacher), coaching from the adult occurs to keep the story in line, and the account is expected to be accurate and orderly. The major differences are that the storyteller is not the central character showing how he or she learned from a failure, and there would not have to be a concluding moral to the story. There is a fairly good match between school and community expectations here and Heath (1983:298) reports that 'Roadville children, especially girls, excel in class when they are requested to recall a straightforward account or retell a lesson.'

Children are supposed to tell the other kind of story, the *fictive* story, in language arts lessons, when they are asked to make up stories, or pretend they are a character in a reading lesson story. In fictive stories, children are expected to show creativity and imagination. Fictive stories present a conflict for Roadville children, because telling an imaginary story at home would bring punishment for lying. One particularly perceptive third-grade girl actually showed she recognized the difference between good stories at home and in school (Heath 1983:294–5). On the way home, she had entertained the other children on the school bus with a tale about how she would bring her dog to a party planned for the end of school. After they left the bus, her friend challenged her for telling about something she knew would never happen. The first child's defense was: 'What are you so, uh, excited about. We got one kinda story mamma knows about, and a whole 'nother one we do at school. They're different and you know it.' The other child's response was: 'You better hope mamma knows it, if she catches you making up stuff like that.'

In the Trackton community, a highly-valued feature of oral stories is 'talkin' junk'. The kind of narrative that is considered a real story in Trackton has a basis in fact, but with a good bit of 'junk' in the form of exaggeration and flights of fancy added. A story may well be about the teller but, unlike Roadville stories, they do not involve the teller learning from a failure, but rather how the protagonist overcomes odds through cleverness, toughness, and a willingness to ignore conventional rules of behavior. Someone who wants to tell a story has to compete aggressively for the floor and stories are often created cooperatively by more than one speaker. One Trackton boy tells a story that no doubt has a basis in truth, about how the school principal caught him in the hall at school without a 'pass' (Heath 1983:181–2): 'and he come roun' de corner like he knowed I was dere. I took out runnin' [pause] now don't ever run 'less'n'you know you don't hafta stop. Dat was my mistake. It was good while it lasted. I run all the way down Main.'

At this point the youngster starts 'talkin' junk' in earnest. He leads the principal on a chase out of the school and into the town. Once there, Spider Man (a cartoon super-hero) throws his web over the principal and a big cockroach comes out of an old building and starts to bite the trapped principal, who begs the boy to rescue him. After extracting a promise from the principal not to punish him for the hallway infraction, the narrator rescues the principal, who fails to keep his side of the bargain: 'So I let 'im up, and call off dat roach and dat spider web, and we went back to school. But he didn't do what he say. He git me, 'n' he took dat paddle to me, and to' [tore] me up.' Even after being betrayed and punished, the young boy is undaunted, courageously enduring the principal's worst 'tearing up'.

As you might suppose, Trackton children are in a better position to move from their community concept of a story to fictive stories in school. Heath reports that they are particularly fascinated by stories about animals or fanciful human characters read to them by teachers and often look for these books to read for themselves later. When they were asked to create stories by tape-recording them for later transcription and editing, many were able to record quite imaginative stories. On the other hand, nonfictive stories were more difficult for them to handle to the teachers' satisfaction.[13] The way oral activities are conducted in the community also brought Trackton children into conflict at school. The practice of winning a chance to talk by overcoming competing efforts to get attention does not go down well in school where the teacher expects to assign the chance to talk to children who ask for it by quietly raising their hands. Teachers, when they were asked to comment on children who were identified as having discipline and academic problems, would remark that a child 'talks out of turn and interrupts fellow classmates' or was 'verbally and physically aggressive'.

Labov (1972a, chapter 6; 1982a) contends that a clash between the values assumed in public schools and the values that are indigenous to urban black young people, especially pre-adolescent and adolescent boys, has more to do with low scores on tests of reading ability than linguistic features themselves. His research in New York City showed that test scores on reading for young men who were *not* members of street groups – where membership is a sign of successful participation in the vernacular culture – generally had scores that indicated performance below their grade level. But there were quite a few who were on-grade, and a few who were reading above grade level. Among those in the same neighborhood who *were* members of street groups, only one was marginally on-grade. The rest were well below grade level and some had abysmally low scores (Labov 1972a:247–9). This distinction between youngsters from the same social class in the same neighborhood seems to point to social values as a critical factor. In Labov's view, it is not the case that the poor readers fail for lack of ability. He and his colleagues observed a great deal of evidence of intelligence, resourcefulness, and verbal skill about the group members. Rather, it is because they were so *successful* in their own communities that they had no need to conform to the alien values they encounter in school. The less socially successful youngsters who did not have street group status were apt to compensate, in a way, by becoming more successful in school.[14]

In general, values described by Miller (1958) – toughness, smartness, trouble, excitement, autonomy, and fate – are the ones that guide members of the vernacular culture. These values inevitably lead to conflict in school. Even 'smartness' refers to the ability to outmaneuver others, not the kind of ability that is good for solving abstract problems. Cheshire (1982:154–5) found this same list to be valid for the group of boys in Reading, England, 'who often met at the adventure playgrounds when they should have been at school.' She was able to construct a 'vernacular culture index' by using six characteristics that were consistent with Miller's list: skill at fighting; the carrying of a weapon; participation in minor criminal activities; favoring certain kinds of jobs (such as mechanic or soldier); dress and hairstyle; and swearing. The resulting index correlated strongly with the use of socially stigmatized speech forms. Extensive use of disfavored sociolinguistic variables, in turn, is an indication that school and its associated values have not had much influence on these young men.

Quite a good case can be made for the role of culture–value conflict in the problems children from minority communities have in school. The techniques and outlook of the ethnography of communication have proved effective in identifying some of these points of contrast. How to translate these insights into effective action is far less clear. Heath reports considerable success in getting teachers in the communities she worked in to conduct their own ethnographic inquiries and to adapt their teaching methods on the basis of what they found out. However, in the 'epilogue' at the end of the book, the reader is left with an impression that the success was somewhat transient, and that social and institutional forces the teachers cannot control reversed many of the advances they had made earlier.

In his earlier discussion Labov (1972a:253–4) made a specific recommendation that inner-city schools like those in New York recruit young men with intimate knowledge of the vernacular culture to aid teachers in motivating their students. Apparently, this idea has never been tried, at least not successfully. In his later treatment of the same subject, Labov (1982a) declines to 'set out a blueprint' for an educational plan that incorporates the insights of ethnographic research. His recommendations here are more general; he suggests that 'competitive and individualistic' learning techniques of the school which he sees as major sources of conflict give way to the 'forces of social cooperation and energy' from the vernacular culture. Exactly how this is to be done seems yet to be discovered. Personally, I am not optimistic that it will be found in the foreseeable future.

BILINGUALISM AND BILINGUAL EDUCATION

Another field related to education where sociolinguists have tried to make a contribution is bilingualism and bilingual education. This area no doubt deserves more attention than it is getting here, but several strands of research need to be mentioned, at least. Some sociolinguists have examined the variable rule concept as a way of understanding the process of acquiring second languages (for example, Dickerson 1975; Dickerson and Dickerson 1977; Fasold 1984b; Adamson 1987). It is possible that the variable rule can play a role in developing a model for language learning in spite of its theoretical decline in variation analysis, and the variable rule computer methods may well serve as a statistical tool, as they do in variation studies. Other scholars have examined language contact, taking context and variation into account in more general terms (Wolfram 1974b; Wolfram et al. 1979; Poplack 1980; Sankoff and Poplack 1981; Poplack and Sankoff 1984; Poplack, Sankoff, and Miller 1988). This line of research seems to offer considerable promise for our future understanding of how learning a second language really works.

The spread of English as an inter-language in parts of the world where it is not spoken natively has sparked the interest of another group of sociolinguists. These scholars are interested in the structural properties of English as it is learned by people who may rarely hear English spoken by a native speaker. There is a lively controversy about whether or not these 'world Englishes', as they are sometimes called, should be understood and taught as legitimate entities, or whether the standards in force in English-speaking countries should be taught in other places in the world and, if so, to what extent. There is a journal which focuses on these issues (*World Englishes*) as well as a number of books (for example, Bailey and Görlach 1982; Kachru 1982, 1986; Trudgill and Hannah 1982; Platt, Weber, and Ho 1984) and several anthologies (for example, Pride 1982; L. Smith 1983; Quirk and Widdowson 1985).

SOCIOLINGUISTICS AND THE LEGAL PROFESSION

In recent years, sociolinguistic research has proven useful to legal interests in an amazing variety of ways. At least four of the main thrusts of sociolinguistics that I have discussed in this book have proved directly useful where language and the law is concerned. Work in linguistics and the law has been aptly summarized by Roger Shuy (1984b, 1986).

Discourse analysis

Quite a lot of the studies Shuy has summarized involves what we might call the discourse analysis of language in the courtroom. A study by Charrow and Charrow (1979), for example, showed that instructions to juries could be made somewhat more comprehensible not only by reducing the amount of legal jargon, but by changes in grammar, such as eliminating passive constructions and nominalizations. Studies done by O'Barr and his colleagues (O'Barr 1982) suggests that people respond more positively to witnesses who use direct and assertive speech rather than tentative and indirect speech strategies. Some of these contrasting speech features are similar to those used by Robin Lakoff to illustrate women's speech style. In O'Barr's findings at least, these speech features were more closely related to status than to the speakers' sex.

Another facet of O'Barr's research, and similar work by Walker (1982), has to do with overlapped speech. We have seen that simultaneous talk sometimes represents a momentary trouble point in the turn-taking system, but is a valued aspect of high-involvement conversational styles. O'Barr's results indicate that overlap is likely to be seen as troublesome in his data. Subjects who viewed re-enactments of courtroom trials involving overlapped speech saw it as evidence that attorneys had less control and that they were less fair and less intelligent than when there were no overlaps. Walker found that if the overlap was initiated by a witness, attorneys considered it an encroachment on their authority. Interestingly, O'Barr turned up some differences by sex in this area. Male subjects tended to see lawyers who overlapped the talk of witnesses as skilful and competent. Female subjects regarded the lawyers who were involved in overlap as less skilful. If it is the case that the witnesses, rather than the attorney, generally end the overlap by stopping their talk prematurely, then we have possible support for Leet-Pellegrini's research which we reviewed in chapter 4. Recall that her findings indicated that men have a tendency to see conversation as a contest to be won. A lawyer who 'wins' by shutting down the witness's competing talk would naturally be seen as skilful and competent by men if Leet-Pellegrini is right. Her research indicates that women, on the other hand, are more likely to see conversation as a cooperative activity. If so, then overlap might be seen as a breakdown in the cooperative venture going on between the attorney and the witness. Since the attorney is in charge, the attorney can be seen by women as lacking the skill to maintain a cooperative spirit.

Some of Shuy's own work illustrates some of the more intriguing contributions of linguistics to legal issues. An area in which he has assisted defense attorneys and provided expert testimony has to do with the use of recorded conversations as evidence. Usually such evidence is collected by an informer hired by a law enforcement agency. The informer's job is to do everything possible to provide a context where the individual suspected of doing something illegal will say something to incriminate himself or herself. In the process, the informer typically repeatedly brings the illegal activity into the conversation. When a case in which the prosecution is using this kind of evidence goes before a jury, a phenomenon Shuy (1984a) calls the *contamination principle* is often the result. Imagine that a jury listens to a recorded conversation involving several people, including the defendant and the informant. Imagine further that some of the participants in the conversation use profanity and obscenity, but that the defendant never does. The jury is likely to come away with the impression that they have heard a conversation with a group of people swearing, and that the defendant was one of them. The same thing can happen when illegal activities are discussed and a defendant is part of the conversation. The jury can come to the conclusion that the defendant was contributing to the conversation and is probably guilty.

One of Shuy's ways of applying his expertise to cases like this is to do a topic analysis of the conversation, one of the areas of discourse analysis. In one such case that Shuy describes (Shuy 1982), a man, referred to as 'Arthur Jones', was accused of trying to hire someone to murder his wife and the judge in their divorce case. The man who made the accusation, called 'Roy Foster', was a former employee of a company that Jones owned. Foster reported to the US Federal Bureau of Investigation (FBI) that Jones had asked him to commit the murders. The FBI equipped Foster with hidden recording equipment and asked him to try to get an actual recording of Jones in the act of soliciting the murders. The resulting tape-recording indeed contains some discussion of Jones's wife and a judge and of 'doing' them, because Foster had made considerable effort to bring about a conversation on these topics. In developing the argument that these were Foster's topics, not Jones's, Shuy presented an analysis of the topics, who introduced them, and how they were responded to by the other person in the conversation.

In our discussion of language and gender, we saw evidence to indicate that topic-handling in conversations is not necessarily balanced. In cross-gender conversations, men generally introduce more topics successfully: that is, topics are then developed by the female half of the interaction. Women introduce fewer topics that are later supported by men and have to work harder to get men to attend to their topics. Implicit in these results is the possibility that someone in a conversation can bring up a topic which is never supported by another person in the conversation. In

other words, the other person can drop the topic. Although Foster and Jones are both men, Shuy noticed that the overall pattern was for Foster to introduce topics that were not taken up by Jones.[15] In fact, Shuy observed Jones using at least one of the methods Pamela Fishman (1983) found men used to *resist* supporting topics in cross-gender conversations. One of Jones's patterns was to respond to Foster's topic introductions with minimal responses that included typical back-channel utterances like 'uh' and 'well'. As Fishman pointed out, men would resist topic support by using back-channels not within-turn, but *as* turns, and Jones apparently did the same thing. Interestingly, although Shuy does not have the Fishman study in his bibliography, he uses practically the same term she does, referring to Jones' 'minimal responsiveness' to describe the same phenomenon Fishman calls 'minimal responses'. Besides these back-channel-like responses, Jones would sometimes say nothing at all, or he would change the subject or comment on a marginal aspect of the topic Foster had brought up.

In any case, Shuy was able to show that Foster introduced topics 26 times in two recorded conversations while Jones introduced topics only nine times. The distribution of the 22 topics in the first conversation is illustrated in figure 9.2. This is a clear indication that Foster was doing a lot more work than Jones to control what the conversation was about. It is particularly clear, as figure 9.2 illustrates, that Foster *recycled* his topics – that is, he kept coming back to them – because Jones did not respond in a satisfactory way. Furthermore, although Jones and Foster did bring some of the topics to a close, Shuy tried to show the jury that the proposal to hire someone to commit murder was never concluded. The discourse analysis of these conversations made clear just what they were: an effort by one member of a conversation, the FBI informant, to get another member to discuss an incriminating topic in the face of considerable resistance by the other speaker. This probably would not have been obvious to the jury without a linguist to discover and explain an important part of the discourse structure of the events. The result was that the recorded conversations were a weaker part of the prosecution case than they might otherwise have seemed to be.

Pragmatics and discourse

Pragmatics, of course, involves how meanings beyond the ones precisely expressed in linguistic structures are conveyed and understood. This makes it a potentially useful tool for the analysis of language in legal contexts. A central topic in pragmatics, as we saw in chapter 6, is *presupposition*. An utterance that conveys a presupposition has a powerful potential to *create* the assumption of the truth of the presupposition in the mind of a hearer. In chapter 6, I asked you to imagine that someone had said, 'The principal chief of the Kuikus delivered the petition.' Ordinarily, if you heard something like this you would take it for granted that there was some such group as the Kuikus and that they had a principal chief.

Loftus (1981) conducted an experiment to determine whether asking a question containing a presupposition could make a witness remember something that had actually not occurred. The setting did not actually involve a law case, but used university students (here we go again!) as subjects. By prearranged plan, two men suddenly came into a psychology class while the class was in session. One stood by the door, while the other picked up a book he said he had left on a table in front. The man who came for the book, the taller of the two, got into a brief argument with the instructor, and both men then left. About 40 minutes later, the 147 students in the class were given a questionnaire designed to test how well they remembered the incident. One of the questions was crucial, and was not the same on all the questionnaires. One-third of the students were asked 'Was the moustache worn by the tall intruder light or dark brown?' Another third was asked 'Did the intruder who was tall and had a moustache say anything to the professor?' The other third got a question about the tall man's eyebrows (this was a control question).

A day later, the same students were given another questionnaire of ten questions, all of which began 'did you see?' The ninth question asked if the students saw a moustache on the taller intruder. Of those who got the original questionnaire with the question about eyebrows, only 4 per cent remembered a moustache on the tall man. For those who got the question about the color of the moustache, a much higher proportion, 26 per cent, said yes, the taller man had a moustache.[16] An even greater proportion of the remaining subjects, the ones who had been asked if the intruder with the moustache had said anything, said the tall man had a moustache (39 per cent).[17] Both questions about the moustache *presuppose* that the taller intruder had a moustache, but there is a difference. The question about the color of the moustache questions a proposition about a moustache at the same time it presupposes its existence. The question about whether the tall man had said anything to the professor questions a proposition about the man, not the moustache. In any case, Loftus's experiment demonstrates the power of presuppositions to change what someone reports about what they have seen.

Another area where linguists have been able to apply some of the insights of pragmatics is in communicating to laypeople what the law has said. Roger Shuy (1988), along with psychologist Jana Staton, became involved with an effort along these lines by the US Social Security Administration (SSA), which is responsible for administering the national old-age pension program. The SSA had become aware that the notices they sent to citizens were faulty in some ways and, furthermore, that the flaws might engender lawsuits by citizens' groups who would contend that the law had not been adequately interpreted for them. The SSA faced an immense logistical problem since they send literally millions of letters each year. One solution is to store pre-written paragraphs on a computer and make the computer construct letters by assembling these paragraphs. Sometimes the results are disorganized to the point of being funny, as this excerpt from one such notice illustrates (Shuy 1988:157):

YOU CANNOT QUALIFY FOR MONTHLY BENEFITS BASED ON ANOTHER PERSON'S SOCIAL SECURITY RECORD WHEN YOU ARE ENTITLED TO AN EQUAL OR LARGER INSURANCE BENEFIT BASED ON YOUR OWN EARNINGS RECORD.
BASED ON THE INFORMATION GIVEN TO US, YOU WERE BORN ON 07/25/19.
IF YOU NEED MEDICARE SERVICES BEFORE YOU RECEIVE YOUR HEALTH INSURANCE CARD, YOU MAY USE THIS NOTICE AS PROOF OF COVERAGE. YOU SHOULD RECEIVE YOUR CARD WITHIN 4 WEEKS.

Shuy and Staton participated in a training program in which, among other things, they taught some of the skills of pragmatics and discourse analysis to SSA officials. Agency employees learned to identify the topics that needed to go into the notices, and how to order them in a reasonable way. They learned something about speech acts so that they could identify the speech acts that would be part of the notices and how directly or indirectly to express them. They were introduced to the concept of conversational implicatures, so that desired implicatures would be reliably generated and undesirable ones avoided. The results can be illustrated with the following excerpt from the revision of another notice, after the training program was under way (Shuy 1988:163):

You may be able to get more money because of a recent court decision about Supplemental Security Income (SSI). These questions and answers will help you decide if the court decision applies to you.
What did the Court say?
The court said that we have to change the way we figure how much SSI we pay to some people. The change applies only to married couples living together in Massachusetts at some time since January, 1977.
Does the court decision mean that any couple can get more SSI?
No. The only couples who may get more money are those where only one person got SSI and the other person had income.

It appears that this effort was one of the more successful applications of sociolinguistics, as Shuy (1988:174) reports:

SSA admitted its weakness, coopted the linguist who had been working against them in the lawsuit, asked for help, created a well-protected administrative entity that nourished the project, took the advice and procedures outlined above, instituted training programs for staff, and, finally implemented the new language policy. Today, the clear-writing project at SSA is considered to be one of the strong points of the Agency.

A somewhat similar situation was faced by Labov (1988) and his colleagues, this time directly in the context of a lawsuit. The case involved a suit concerning alleged discrimination by a corporation against black people and women. A complicated state of affairs developed when a national suit on the issue was partially settled in a way that involved a payment of claims to litigants. In order to collect these payments, the litigants would have to give up their claims in a local suit on the same issue. A legal notice was prepared informing the workers involved in the class action suit that they could collect payments, but only by dropping the local suit. Labov, his colleague Anthony Kroch, and two other specialists were called in to examine this notice and an accompanying letter to determine if it was biased towards inducing the workers to accept the national settlement when it might, in the end, be to their disadvantage.

Part of Kroch's testimony involved the conversational implicatures of expressions like 'at least'. In chapter 5, we discussed *scalar* phenomena and the implicatures they generate. Since 'warm', for example, is lower on a scale than 'hot' but higher than 'cool', if I assert that the coffee is warm, what I say entails that it is warmer than 'cool' but *implicates* that it is less than 'hot', although I can cancel the implicature by adding something like 'in fact, it's hot'. The expression of 'at least' is not scalar, but marks the lower boundary of a continuum. The material sent to the workers contained the assertion 'it is likely that it will be *at least* several years even after trial of this case before it is finally known whether plaintiffs . . . will receive any back pay' (emphasis added). Like scalars, a bound marker such as 'at least' has an entailment and an implicature. To say 'at least several years' entails that it will not be less than several years, but implicates that it might well be much more than several years, although the implicature seems not to be quite as strong as scalar implicatures are. The words 'even' and 'any', which also appear in the assertion, likewise carry implicatures that are well known in the study of linguistic pragmatics, and Kroch pointed these out to the court. The cumulative effect of these implicatures favored the conclusion that the workers should accept the terms of the national settlement and give up the local suit.[18]

Linguistic variation

In the same article, Labov (1988) discusses a trial in which a man was charged with making telephone bomb threats against an airline in Los Angeles. It was immediately clear to Labov, as it was to other linguists involved in the man's defense, that the actual bomb threats (which had been recorded) were made by a speaker from eastern New England, while the defendant was from New York City. To people who had spent most of their lives in California, where the case was to be tried, these accents sound similar. Labov saw his task as going beyond convincing the judge that his opinion should be believed because of his own expertise. He wanted to present objective evidence which itself would be compelling to a nonlinguist. Using a standard scholarly reference on north-eastern US accents, and charts displaying instrumental measurements of the vowels of the bomb-threat speaker and of the defendant, Labov was able to bring the judge to the point where he could himself directly interpret the instrumental evidence that showed the different vowel systems of the two speakers. One particularly telling aspect of Labov's testimony came in reference to the caller's utterance of the line 'I hope you're on that.' The caller had pronounced the *a* ([æ]) of 'that' as a high front vowel, so that it sounded almost like 'they-ut'. In fact, the official transcript had transcribed the line as 'I hope you're on there.' Labov played back the telephone threat recording on high-quality equipment, which made it clear that the word was actually 'that'. He pointed out that the phonological environment for [æ]-raising in New York is different from the environment in eastern New England. In New York, a following voiceless stop, like the [t] of 'that', inhibits [æ]-raising completely, so that the pronunciation on the tape is not a real possibility for a New Yorker. In eastern New England, while a following voiceless stop, in Bailey's terms, would be a *marked* environment, application of [æ]-raising has reached this environment, so that a speaker from that part of the country might well raise the vowel of 'that' so that it would sound like the vowel of 'there' to speakers with more conservative accents. In spite of some damaging circumstantial evidence against him, and largely on the basis of the linguistic testimony, the accused man was acquitted.

The defendant in a case tried in Northern Ireland was not so fortunate. The case, described by James Milroy (1984), again involved identifying a telephone caller with a person accused of a crime, this time blackmail. Milroy himself was not involved in the defense of the accused man, but he later analyzed recordings of the telephone calls and of the defendant's speech along similar lines to those Labov had used in the bomb-threat case. In the case of four of the five extortion calls, Milroy found that the caller could not possibly have been the defendant. As he puts it (Milroy 1984:67–8), 'It is not a matter of opinion that these two accents are different: the differences are audible, verifiable and consistently maintained . . . the differences are not merely random variations in pronunciation of occasional words, but . . . they are consistent and systematic. The details analyzed point to structural differences between dialects that are of a high order of generality and abstraction.' For example, after a vowel in the Ulster Scots accent, the consonant spelled 't' is often pronounced together with a glottal stop ([ʔ]), or only a glottal stop is pronounced. In the mid-Ulster accent used by the accused man, this glottalization is rather rare. The caller who made four of the blackmail telephone calls used a glottal pronunciation for post-vocalic 't' 100 per cent of the time, pronouncing 'it', for example, as [Iʔ] and *wait* as [weʔt]. In recordings of the defendant's voice, there are no glottalized pronunciations at all (and neither are there any in the recording of the other extortion call). In other words, the evidence is very similar to the kind Labov presented in the Los Angeles case. In the case of the remaining telephone call, the accent is similar to the accused man's, but still seemed to be someone else.

Although the defense did call a linguistic expert witness (not Milroy), he did not present factual evidence directly as Labov did, but gave testimony that, in his expert opinion, the voices on four of the telephone recordings were similar to each other, but not to that of the defendant. The jury gave this testimony little weight. In the face of the confident testimony of several witnesses – including one of the victims and a police officer – that the voice on the telephone recordings *was* that of the accused, they apparently saw it as an opinion that was probably mistaken. The man was convicted and sentenced to ten years in prison. Although it is doubtful, it is conceivable that the man who went to jail might have been the caller with the different accent from the other four, and might have been a masked intruder who broke into the victims' house and was never recorded. Even granting that, as Milroy (1984:70) points out, 'at least one very unpleasant blackmailer remains at large.'

The ethnography of speaking

The ethnography of speaking uses analysis of language in the context of its related culture to help understand the meaning of utterances in context. This kind of thrust has also been used in the study of language and law. Danet (1980), for example, has examined the questions to, and responses of, a witness in a particular trial from this perspective. This approach is particularly valuable when people from one cultural background are being tried in another cultural context. Gumperz (1983a) was able to provide an ethnographic analysis of discourse conventions in Philippine languages which led to the dismissal of perjury charges against a Filipino physician on trial in the USA. The issue of the need for interpreters when people are being tried in a language they may not know well – including deaf speakers of sign languages – is another area where linguistics can make a contribution. Eugene Brière (1978), for example, had an influence on the Court Interpreter's Act of 1978 in the USA, which addresses this issue.

SOCIOLINGUISTICS AND THE MEDICAL PROFESSION

Although people tend to think of 'going to the doctor' as being mostly about physical examinations and laboratory tests, a crucial part of a physician's work is the medical interview. This is essentially a matter of linguistic interaction in a reasonably well-defined setting and so has been a natural site for research by sociolinguists, and by other social scientists focusing on language. Cicourel (1980) and Shuy (1984b) provide a review of some of these studies, and two fairly recent anthologies of some of the actual research have been assembled by Di Pietro (1982) and by Fisher and Todd (1983). Somewhat as in the application of sociolinguistics to education, some of the early work had to do with the interaction between speakers of disfavored lects and doctors, who generally spoke socially approved language varieties (for example, Shuy 1976). It became immediately obvious that the kinds of language use pattern examined by discourse analysts, ethnographers of communication, and students of linguistic pragmatics were much more important than the use of suffixes or negative concord. Accordingly, most of the recent research on language and medicine has been from these perspectives.

Not too surprisingly, quite a few of these kinds of studies are about questions and responses, often making use of speech act theory and Grice's work in linguistic pragmatics (LaCoste 1976; Simonin 1977; Fisher 1982; West 1983). Others, like Frankel (1983) examine the details of interactional organization more or less in the style of the work on turn-taking I treated in chapter 3. However, probably most of the research on the sociolinguistics of medical interviews takes a broader look at the entire doctor–patient interaction (Cassell and Skopek 1977; Maseide 1982; Cicourel 1983; Fisher 1983; Shuy 1983; A. Todd 1983).

One approach to the interactional analysis of medical interviews can be illustrated from the work of Tannen and Wallat (Tannen and Wallat 1986, 1987). They conducted a detailed analysis of a pediatric examination, conducted in the presence of the mother of the child being examined, and while a videotape was being made. The pediatrician was part of an interdisciplinary team including various medical and social service specialists. The little girl being examined was an 8-year-old child suffering from cerebral palsy.

A concept used in discourse analysis (as well as in other fields) that Tannen and Wallat found useful was the notion they call the *knowledge schema*. A schema is a kind of set of associated information. For example, when talking about dining out, because you can assume a 'restaurant schema' you can say 'the waitress brought the menu', using 'the' even though you have not mentioned the waitress or the menu before. You assume that whoever you are talking with has waiters or waitresses and menus as part of their 'restaurant schema' as you do, so you talk as if they are already part of what is being talked about. A problem in medical interviews, according to Tannen and Wallat's analysis, is that medical professionals and laypeople might have very different schemas about health issues. To make the matter even more problematic, the layperson's schema is likely to be *resilient*, so that if the physician says something in the medical interview that does not fit the patient's schema, it might simply not register at all. This apparently happened during the treatment of the child with cerebral palsy.

Due to the muscle weakness that is a consequence of the disease, the little girl breathed with quite a lot of noise when asleep. This was a matter of much anxiety for her mother, who at one point interrupted the examinations to ask about it (Tannen and Wallat 1986:307):

Mother: She worries me at night.
Because uh . . . when she's asleep
I keep checking on her so she doesn't⌉
Doctor: ⌊As you
know the important ⌉
Mother: ⌊ I keep thinking she's not
breathing properly.
Doctor: As you know the important thing is that she does have
difficulty with the use of her muscles.

The doctor went on to explain that there was no breathing obstruction, but that the noisy breathing was due to the muscle weakness. The girl's mother seemed to accept this reassurance, but, later in the examination, when the pediatrician was listening to the child's heart and asked the girl to breathe deeply, the breathing was very noisy. Her mother interjected, 'That's the particular noise she makes when she sleeps.' The doctor went on with the examination, but the girl's mother persisted, 'That's the kind of noise I hear when she's asleep at night.' At that point the doctor again reassured the mother that there was no interference with the youngster's breathing.

This was not the end of the matter, however. After the examination, the doctor summarized the results for both parents. The summary included some quite important information that might need more discussion, and also a repetition directed to the child's father of the doctor's reassurances about the girl's noisy breathing. When the doctor asked for questions, the following exchange took place (Tannen and Wallat 1986:308):

Mother: No:, except . . . that . . . with this . . . uh . . . about the
heavy . . . wheezing sound,
Doctor: ⌊ mhm ⌉

Mother: would a doctor be able . . . to tell . . . if it's congestion
she's having
Doctor: ⌊ right

or ⌉
Doctor: ⌊ Her lungs are very clear.
. . . Although she sounds . . . very raspy when she breathes. That's more the air going in and out. She has no wheezes.

It seemed that the schema evoked for the mother by the girl's noisy breathing included the idea that her respiratory tract was congested. The doctor's response, since it did not involve treating congestion, did not fit in the mother's schema. As a result, it did not take hold as a reassurance. Tannen and Wallat provided a way of understanding the problem, but they do not provide a direct solution (Tannen and Wallat 1986:309):

> The difficult question, then, is how doctors' and patients' schemas may be made congruent. It is likely that much talk that is generated in medical settings represents schemas that are, from the point of view of medical science, erroneous and unfounded. The most frustrating aspect of this, which has just been demonstrated, is that they are also stubborn.

In addition to the research on medical interviews involving physicians who are primarily treating physical disorders, there is a substantial literature on the interaction in psychotherapy (for example, Labov and Fanshel 1977; R. Lakoff 1977a; Wodak 1981). Much of this research has been influential not only in the study of therapeutic interviewing, but also on discourse analysis in general.[19]

In spite of considerable effort, the impact of linguistics in general and sociolinguistics in particular on the medical profession has been rather less than we might have hoped (Shuy 1986:55). Sociolinguists have not succeeded in accumulating the success stories that they have with the legal profession. There is still the promise, though, that we will yet find a way to combine what we have learned in sociolinguistics with the knowledge and experience of people in the medical profession, with beneficial results.

SUMMARY

Sociolinguists have made considerable effort in applying their findings to the problems of everyday experience. The first and perhaps most extensive efforts have been in language arts education. A controversy about the cognitive deficit that speakers of socially disfavored lects were supposed to have surfaced in the 1960s. The work of sociologist Basil Bernstein served as the focus of this controversy, although much of what Bernstein had said was poorly understood and malinterpreted. It now seems reasonable to believe that what Bernstein was actually describing was a language use style that is a natural outgrowth of dense-network social organization, not a cognitive or language deficit at all.

Applied to reading and writing, the main issue that sociolinguists addressed in early studies was the difference between the spoken language of minority group children and the structure of the language in reading books and expected in written work. The proposal that reading materials be presented to children from these communities in their own (stigmatized) lects met with massive resistance, was never proved to be effective, and no longer has any significant support. In writing, research such as that carried out by Farr Whiteman suggests that disfavored lects can interfere with learning to write standard English, but not in a totally straightforward way. Some sociolinguists, myself included, still advocate tolerating disfavored sociolinguistic variants in early writing efforts, and perhaps permanently for some kinds of writing. Concentrated efforts to teach spoken standard English in classrooms seems doomed to failure, and there are few sociolinguists who see it as possible or desirable.

Language testing is another educational area that has received considerable attention from linguists. It can be demonstrated that children from mainstream social groupings can be expected to score much higher on many tests of language development or achievement simply by relying on what 'sounds right' to them, compared with children who speak disfavored language varieties doing exactly the same thing. Ultimately a suggestion by Stockman and Vaughn-Cooke (that the ability to code semantic relationships should be measured, rather than the surface linguistic elements used to code them) shows considerable promise as a way to eliminate lectal bias in language testing. In the short run, it seems the best way to neutralize bias is to rely on informed and sensitive language educators in schools.

The ethnography of communication has also been applied to educational problems. Exemplary work in this area in a rural context has been conducted by Heath, while Labov has made a similar effort where urban black young people are concerned. In spite of the case that can be made for the role of culture clash in the educational difficulties of minority group children, efforts to reduce culture clash between schools and communities have been discouraging.

The investigation of language contact and bilingualism informed by some of the results of sociolinguistic variation analysis is a major and promising new application. Sociolinguistic knowledge also plays an important role in the relatively new interest in 'world Englishes'.

Considerable effort and some bright successes can be found in the interaction of sociolinguistics and legal issues. There have been many specific applications of discourse analysis, pragmatics, the ethnography of communication, and variation analysis in language and law contexts. Sociolinguists like Roger Shuy, William Labov, and John Gumperz have been directly involved in court cases as sources of linguistic expertise. It is also clear that sociolinguistic knowledge can make a substantial contribution to efforts to interpret clearly what laws say for ordinary citizens who are not lawyers. A striking contrast in the results of two court cases (one described by William Labov which led to the acquittal of an innocent man and the other, described by James Milroy, which undoubtedly ended with a guilty man going free) suggests that evidence on language variation is far more effective when it is directly presented in court, rather than simply having a linguist testify as to his expert opinion only.

Sociolinguistic research has been applied to the medical profession, with perspicacious results. The nature of problems that can arise in medical interviews are now clearer as a result, but this is an area that seems to have more promise than accomplishments.

NOTES

1 A particularly good objective discussion of Bernstein's work on language is J. R. Edwards 1979a, chapter 2.

2 This article by Labov, called 'The logic of nonstandard English', was originally published in *Georgetown University Round Table on Languages and Linguistics 1969* and has been much reprinted. One of these is in Giglioli (1972).

3 At the time, it was necessary to overstate the case. In the early part of the twentieth century it was generally assumed that languages with literary traditions were inherently superior to unwritten languages. Bloomfield, like many American linguists of the time, had worked on (unwritten) native American languages and had come to appreciate their grammatical intricacy. His statement may seem extreme now, but at the time trivializing writing was a necessary and effective rhetorical device to evoke respect for unwritten languages.

4 I base this on many years of experience presenting this line of reasoning to groups of teachers.

5 I will bring up some of what Labov thinks are more important problems shortly.

6 A point emphasized by Arthur Spears (1987:53–4), another member of the panel on the divergence issue.

7 The expression 'got all' means 'were used up'. It is commonly used in this area and is due to Pennsylvania Dutch influence.

8 A similar pattern in the writing of working-class youngsters in the town of Reading, England, is reported by Cheshire (1984:550).

9 A possible reason is that, since the verbal '-s' suffix in English occurs *only* in the present tense, *only* with third-person subjects, and *only* with singular number, it never becomes very salient, and the acquisition factor remains in effect longer.

10 At least one composition guidebook written for college students (Hacker and Renshaw 1979) takes up the issue of nonstandard dialect influence. They advise students to 'keep their words flowing' and not to try to eliminate these features when writing early drafts. Later, at the proof-reading stage, they advise reading their work aloud 'in a

formal voice' (in an effort to tap the writer's receptive competence in formal English) as a way of bringing disfavored linguistic forms to their own attention.

11 If both children apply the 'sounds right so it must be wrong' strategy, the *nonstandard* English speaking child will do better; he will get the first and third items correct, while the child with the mainstream variety will be marked correct only for the third. There is no real advantage to the first youngster, though. First, I have no doubt that the strategy would be very much to the disadvantage of any child who used it consistently on the test as a whole, even if it worked for these three examples. Second, the child with the more standard English would have much less motivation to use the strategy, since her inner language knowledge will give the right answer much more consistently than is true of the other youngster. Third, even if the strategy *did* work, it would not measure the child's language use achievement in any sense, but rather the ability to outwit testmakers.

12 Except when one of them is a prefix, as in 'He's not unhappy'.

13 One teacher said about Trackton children that 'they'll never tell a story straight – if there ever was a grain of truth in what they say, it's lost when they get through with it' (Heath 1983:269).

14 Interestingly, Heath (1983:360) seems to have observed just this phenomenon in the experience of Nellie, one of the Trackton children: 'Her inability to compete with her Trackton peers on the plaza and to build fanciful stories has apparently left her ready for accepting the slow, methodical, step-by-step teaching of reading and arithmetic in the primary-grade classes.'

15 One of the criteria Shuy used, althoug a relatively minor one, to identify the boundaries between topics was pause. Recall that Sacks, Schegloff, and Jefferson's (1974) analysis of turn-taking indicates that topic shift is most likely when gaps become extended enough to become lapses.

16 This difference was statistically significant: $z = 3.05$, $p < 0.001$.

17 The difference between the two presupposing questions was not quite significant by a one-tailed z-test.

18 Although the judge indicated that he was generally favorably impressed by Kroch's testimony and that of the others in the group, he ultimately ruled against the workers.

19 A somewhat similar application of sociolinguistics that is not really psychotherapy might be interactional analysis of misunderstandings in human relationships. The outlines of what this application might be like can be seen in Tannen (1986). The insights of discourse analysis and perhaps the ethnography of communication show promise that they can pinpoint relatively minor interactional problems before they become major.

Bibliography

Abdulaziz Mikilifi, M. H. 1978. Triglossia and Swahili-English bilingualism in Tanzania. In Fishman, Joshua (ed.), *Advances in the Study of Societal Multilingualism*, 129–52. The Hague: Mouton.

Adamson, H. Douglas, 1987. Analyzing prototype linguistic categories with the VARB rule 2 program. In Denning et al. 1988:1–12.

——1988. *Variation Theory and Second Language Acquisition*. Washington, DC: Georgetown University Press.

Adler, Max. 1977. *Pidgins, Creoles and Lingua Francas: A Sociolinguistic Study*. Hamburg: Helmut Buske Verlag.

Algeo, John, 1975. Synchope and the phonotactics of English. *General Linguistics*, 15:71–8.

Allen, Donald and Guy, Rebecca. 1978. *Conversation Analysis: The Sociology of Talk*. The Hague: Mouton.

Anshen, Frank. 1975. Varied objections to various variable rules. In Fasold and Shuy 1975:1–10.

Arkowitz, H., Lichtenstein, E., McGovern, K. and Hines, P. 1975. The behavioral assessment of social competence in males. *Behavior Therapy*, 6:3–13.

Aronovitch, C. D. 1976. The voice of personality: stereotyped judgements and their relation to voice quality and sex of speaker. *Journal of Social Psychology*, 99:207–20.

Ash, Sharon and Myhill, John. 1986. Linguistic correlates of inter-ethnic contact. In D. Sankoff 1986:33–45.

Atlas, J. and Levinson, Stephen. 1981. *It*-clefts, informativeness and logical form: radical pragmatics (revised standard version). In Cole, Peter (ed.), *Radical Pragmatics*, 1–61. New York: Academic Press.

Austin, J. L. 1962. *How to Do Things with Words* (ed. J. O. Urmson). New York: Oxford University Press.

Bach, Kent and Harnish, Robert. 1979. *Linguistic Communication and Speech Acts*. Cambridge, MA: The MIT Press.

Bailey, Beryl. 1965. Toward a new perspective in Negro English dialectology. *American Speech*, 40:171–7.

Bailey, Charles-James. 1973a. *Variation and Linguistic Theory*. Arlington, VA: Center for Applied Linguistics.

——1973b. Variation resulting from different rule ordering in English phonology. In Bailey and Shuy 1973:211–52.

——1974. Some suggestions for greater consensus in creole terminology. In DeCamp and Hancock 1974:88–91.

——1980. Conceptualizing dialects as implicational constellations rather than as entities bounded by isoglossic bundles. In Göschel, J., Ivic, P., and Kehr, K. (eds), *Dialekt und Dialektologie: Ergebnisse des Internationalen Symposions 'Zur Theorie des Dialects'*, Marburg/Lahn, 5–10 September 1977 (Beiheft N. F. 26 der *Zeitschrift für Mundartforschung*), 234–72. Wiesbaden: Franz Steiner.

——1981. Theory, description and differences among linguists (or, what keeps linguistics from becoming a science). *Language and Communication*, 1:39–66.

——1982. *On the Yin and Yang Nature of Language*. Ann Arbor, MI: Karoma.

——1987. Variation theory and so-called 'sociolinguistic grammars'. *Language and Communication*, 7(4):269–91.

——and Maroldt, Karl, 1977. The French lineage of English. In Meisel, J. (ed.), *Pidgins-Creoles-Languages in Contact*, 21–53. Tübingen: Gunther Narr Verlag.

——and Shuy, Roger (eds). 1973. *New Ways of Analyzing Variation in English*. Washington, DC: Georgetown University Press.

Bailey, Guy. 1987. Are black and white vernaculars diverging?, Section IV. *American Speech*, 62(1):32–40.

——and Maynor, Nathalie. 1985a. The present tense of *be* in southern black folk speech. *American Speech*, 60:195–213.

——and Maynor, Nathalie. 1985b. The present tense of *be* in white folk speech of the southern United States. *English World-Wide*, 6:199–216.

——and Maynor, Nathalie. 1987. Decreolization? *Language in Society*, 16(4):449–74.

Bailey, Richard and Manfred Görlach. 1982. *English as a World Language*. Cambridge: Cambridge University Press.

Baratz, Joan and Roger Shuy (eds). 1969. *Teaching Black Children to Read*. Washington, DC:Center for Applied Linguistics.

Barron, N. 1971. Sex-typed language: the production of grammatical cases. *Acta Sociologica*, 14(1–2):24–72.

Basso, Keith. 1971. 'To give up on words': silence in Western Apache culture. In Giglioli 1972:67–86.

——1979. *Portraits of 'The Whiteman': Linguistic Play and Cultural Symbols among the Western Apache*. Cambridge: Cambridge University Press.

Bates, Elizabeth and Benigni, Laura. 1975. Rules for address in Italy: a sociological survey. *Language in Society* 4(3):271–88.

Baugh, John. 1983. *Black Street Speech*. Austin, TX: University of Texas Press.

Bauman, Richard and Sherzer, Joel (eds). 1975. *Explorations in the Ethnography of Speaking*. London: Cambridge University Press.

——1982. *Case Studies in the Ethnography of Speaking*. Austin, TX: Southwest Educational Development Laboratory.

Bautista, Ma. Lourdes. 1980. *Address in Philipino Radio Dramas: Alternation and Co-occurrence Rules*. Philippine Journal of Linguistics, 11(2):44–63.

Bean, Susan. 1978. *Symbolic and Pragmatic Semantics: A Kannada System*. Chicago: University of Chicago Press.

Befu, H. and Norbeck, E. 1958. Japanese usage of terms of relationship. *Southwest Journal of Anthropology*, 14:66–86.

Berdan, Robert. 1975. The necessity of variable rules. In Fasold and Shuy 1975:11–26.

Berko-Gleason, J. 1978. Sex differences in the language of children and parents. In Garnica, O. and King, M. (eds), *Language, Children and Society*. London: Pergamon Press, 149–58.

——and Greif, E. B. 1983. Men's speech to young children. In Thorne, Kramarae, and Henley 1983:140–52.

Berlin, B. and Kay, Paul. 1969. *Basic Color Terms*. Berkeley, CA: University of California Press.

Bernstein, Basil. 1971. *Class, Codes and Control, Volume 1*. London: Routledge and Kegan Paul.

——1972. A sociolinguistic approach to socialization; with some reference to educability. In Gumperz and Hymes 1972:465–97.

Bickerton, Derek. 1971. Inherent variability and variable rules. *Foundations of Language*, 7:457–92.

——1973. The structure of polylectal grammars. In Shuy, Roger (ed.), *Sociolinguistics: Current Trends and Prospects. Georgetown University Round Table on Languages and Linguistics 1972*, 17–42. Washington, DC: Georgetown University Press.

——1975. *Dynamics of a Creole System*. Cambridge: Cambridge University Press.

——1979. Beginnings. In Hill, Kenneth (ed.), *The Genesis of Language*, 1–22. Ann Arbor, MI: Karoma.

——1980. Decreolization and the creole continuum. In Valdman and Highfield 1980:107–28.

——1981. *The Roots of Language*. Ann Arbor, MI: Karoma.

——1984. The language bioprogram hypothesis. *The Behavioral and Brain Sciences*, 7:173–221.

——1986. Beyond *Roots*: the five-year test. *Journal of Pidgin and Creole Languages*, 1(2):225–32.

——1988. Creole languages and the bioprogram. In Newmeyer 1988, Volume II:268–84.

Blocker, Diane. 1976. And how shall I address you? A study of address systems at Indiana University. *Working Papers in Sociolinguistics* 33. Austin, TX: Southwest Educational Development Laboratory.

Bloomfield, Leonard. 1933. *Language*. New York: Henry Holt and Company.

Blount, Ben. 1981. Sociolinguistic theory in anthropology. *International Journal of the Sociology of Language*, 31:91–108.

Bodine, Ann. 1975. Androcentrism in prescriptive grammar: singular 'they', sex-indefinite 'he' and 'he or she'. *Language and Society*, 4:129–46.

Boër, Steven and Lycan, William. 1973. Invited inferences and other unwelcome guests. *Papers in Linguistics*, 6(3–4):483–506.

Brady, Michael. 1980. *Computational Models of Discourse*. Cambridge, MA: The MIT Press.

Brend, R. 1975. Male-female intonation patterns in American English. In Thorne and Henley 1975:84–7.

Brewer, Jeutonne. 1973. Subject concord of *be* in early black English. *American Speech*, 48:5–21.

——1979. Nonagreeing *am* and invariant *be* in early black English. *The SECOL Bulletin*, 3(2):81–100.

Brière, Eugene. 1978. Limited English speakers and the Miranda rights. *TESOL Quarterly*, 12(3):235–45.

Brouwer, D., Gerritsen, M., and De Haan, D. 1979. Speech differences between women and men: on the wrong track? *Language and Society*, 8:33–50.

Brown, Gillian and Yule, George. 1983. *Discourse Analysis*. Cambridge: Cambridge University Press.

Brown, Penelope. 1980. How and why are women more polite: some evidence from a Mayan community. In McConnell-Ginet, Borker, and Furman 1980:111–36.

——and Levinson, Stephen. 1978. Universals in language use: politeness phenomena. In Goody, Esther (ed.), *Questions and Politeness*, 56–311. Cambridge: Cambridge University Press.

Brown, Roger and Gilman, Albert. 1960. The pronouns of power and solidarity. *American Anthrplogist*, 4(6):24–9 (1962). Also in Giglioli 1972:252–82 and J. Fishman 1968:252–75.

——and Ford, Marguerite. 1961. Address in American English. *Journal of Abnormal and Social Psychology*, 62:454–62. Also in Hymes 1964:234–44.

Browne, Allen. 1986. Univocal *or* – again. *Linguistic Inquiry* 17(4):751–3.

Butters, Ronald. 1987. Linguistic convergence in a North Carolina community. In Denning et al. 1987:52–60.

Camaioni, Luigia. 1981. The problem of appropriateness in pragmatic development. In Parret, Sbisà, and Verschueren 1981:79–92.

Cappella, Joseph. 1979. Talk-silence sequences in informal conversations. I. *Human Communication Research*, 6:3–17.

——1980. Talk and silence sequences in informal conversations II. *Human Communication Research*, 6:130–45.

——and Planalp, Sally. 1981. Talk and silence sequences in informal conversations III: interspeaker influence. *Human Communication Research*, 7:117–32.

Carroll, John and Casagrande, Joseph. 1958. The function of language classifications in behavior. In Maccoby, Eleanor, Newcomb, T. H., and Hartley, E. L. (eds), *Readings in Social Psychology* (3rd edn), 18–31. New York: Holt.

Cassell, E. and Lucienne Skopek. 1977. Language as a tool in medicine: methodology and theoretical framework. *Journal of Medical Education*, 52:197–203.

Cedergren, Henrietta. 1986. Metrical structure and vowel deletion in Montreal French. In D. Sankoff 1986:293–300.

——and Sankoff, David. 1974. Variable rules: performance as a statistical reflection of competence. *Language*, 50:333–55.

Chafe, Wallace. 1980. Integration and involvement in speaking, writing and oral literature. In Tannen 1982c:35–50.

Charrow, Robert and Charrow, Veda. 1979. Making legal language understandable: a psycholinguistic study of jury instructions. *Columbia Law Review*, 79(7):1306–74.

Cherry, L. 1975. Teacher-child verbal interaction: an approach to the study of sex differences. In Thorne and Henley 1975:172–83.

Cheshire, Jenny. 1982. Linguistic variation and social function. In Romaine 1982b:153–66.

——1984. Indigenous nonstandard English varieties and education. In Trudgill 1984b:533–45.

Chomskey, Noam. 1957. *Syntactic Structures*. The Hague: Mouton.

——1965. *Aspects of the Theory of Syntax*. Cambridge, MA: The MIT Press.

——1981. *Lectures on Government and Binding*. Dordrecht: Foris.

——1988. *Language and the Problems of Knowledge*. Cambridge, MA: The MIT Press.

——and Halle, Morris. 1968. *The Sound Pattern of English*. New York: Harper and Row.

Cicourel, A. 1980. Language and medicine. In Ferguson, Charles and Heath, Shirley Brice (eds), *Language in the USA*, 407–29. Cambridge: Cambridge University Press.

——1983. Language and the structure of belief in medical communication. In Fisher and Todd 1983:221–39.

Coates, Jennifer. 1986. *Women, Men and Language*. London: Longman.

Cole, Peter and Morgan, Jerry L. 1975. *Syntax and Semantics: Speech Acts*. New York: Academic Press.

Contini-Morava, Ellen. 1983. Relative tense in discourse: the inference of time orientation in Swahili. In Klein-Andreu 1983:3–22.

Corum, Claudia, Smith-Stark, T. Cedric, and Weisler, Ann (eds). 1973. *Papers from the Ninth Regional Meeting of the Chicago Linguistic Society*. Chicago: Chicago Linguistic Society.

Coulmas, Florian. 1979. On the sociolinguistic relevance of routine formulae. *Journal of Pragmatics*, 3(3–4):239–66.

——1981. *Conversational Routine*. The Hague: Mouton.

Coulthard, Malcomb. 1977. *An Introduction to Discourse Analysis*. London: Longman.

Crosby, F. and Nyquist, L. 1977. The female register: an empirical study of Lakoff's hypothesis. *Language in Society*, 6:313–22.

Danet, Brenda. 1980. Language in the legal process. *Law Society Review*, 14(3):445–564.

de Beaugrande, Robert. 1983. Text production: toward a science of composition. *Advances in Discourse Processes, 11*. Norwood, NJ: Ablex.

——and Dressler, Wolfgang Ulrich. 1981. *Introduction to Text Linguistics*. New York: Longman.

DeCamp, David. 1971. Toward a generative analysis of a post-creole speech continuum. In Hymes 1971b:349–70.
——and Hancock, Ian (eds). 1974. *Pidgins and Creoles: Current Trends and Prospects.* Washington, DC: Georgetown University Press.
DeGelder, Beatrice. 1981. Attributing mental states: a second look at mother-child interaction. In Parret, Sbisà, and Verschueren 1981:237–50.
Denning, Keith, Inkelas, Sharon, McNair-Knox, Faye and Rickford, John (eds). 1988. *Variation in Language: NWAVE-XV at Stanford.* Stanford, CA: Stanford University Linguistics Department.
Dennis, Jamie and Scott, Jerrie. 1975. Creole formation and reorganization: evidence for diachronic change in synchronic variation. Paper presented at the International Conference on Pidgins and Creoles, Honolulu.
Dickerson, Lonna. 1975. The learner's interlanguage as a system of variable rules. *TESOL Quarterly,* 9:401–7.
——and Wayne Dickerson. 1977. Interlanguage phonology: current research and future directions. In Corder, S. Pit and E. Ronlet (eds), *Interlanguages, Pidgins and their Relation to Second Language Pedagogy,* 18–29. Librairie Droz, Neufchâtel: Faculté des Lettres and Genève.
Dillard, J. L. 1972. *Black English.* New York: Random House.
Di Pietro, Robert. 1982. *Linguistics and the Professions.* Norwood, NJ: Ablex.
——Frawley, William, and Wedel, Alfred (eds). 1983. *The First Delaware Symposium on Language Studies.* Newark, DE: University of Delaware Press.
Dittmar, Norbert. 1976. *Sociolinguistics: A Critical Survey of Theory and Application.* London: Edward Arnold.
Downes, William. 1984. *Language and Society.* London: Fontana.
Dubois, B. L. and Crouch, I. 1975. The question of tag questions in women's speech: they don't really use more of them, do they? *Language in Society,* 4:289–94.
Edelsky, C. 1976. Subjective reactions to sex-linked language. *Journal of Social Psychology,* 99:97–104.
Edwards, John R. 1979a. *Language and Disadvantage.* New York: Elsevier
——1979b. Social class differences and the identification of sex in children's speech. *Journal of Child Language,* 6:121–7.
——and Giles, Howard. 1984. Applications of the social psychology of language: sociolinguistics and education. In Trudgill 1984a:119–58.
Edwards, V. 1984. British Black English and education. In Trudgill 1984b:546–58.
Ekka, F. 1972. Men's and women's speech in Kurux. *Linguistics,* 81:21–31.
Elyan, O., Smith P., Giles, H., and Bourhis, R. 1978. RP-accented female speech: the voice of perceived androgyny? In Trudgill, P. (ed.), *Sociolinguistic Patterns in British English,* 122–31. London: Edward Arnold.
Erteschik-Shir, Nomi. 1979. Discourse constraints on dative movement. In Givón 1979b:441–68.
Ervin-Tripp, Susan. 1969. Sociolinguistics. In Berkowitz, L. (ed.), *Advances in Experimental Social Psychology,* Volume 4, 93–107.
——1972. Sociolinguistics. In Pride and Holmes 1972: 225–40. Excerpt from Ervin-Tripp 1969.
——1987. Cross-cultural and developmental sources of pragmatic generalizations. In Verschueren and Bertuccelli-Papi 1987:47–60.
Evans-Pritchard, E. 1948. Nuer modes of address. *The Uganda Journal,* 12:166–71. Also in Hymes 1964:221–7.
Fang, H. Q. and Heng, J. H. 1983. Social changes and changing address norms in China. *Language in Society,* 12(4):495–508.
Farr Whiteman, Marcia. 1981a. Dialect influence in writing. In Farr Whiteman 1981b:153–66.
——1981b. *Writing: The Nature, Development, and Teaching of Written Communication.*

Volume 1, Variation in Writing: Functional and Linguistic-Cultural Differences. Hillsdale, NJ: Lawrence Erlbaum Associates.

Fasold, Ralph. 1972a. Decreolization and autonomous language change. *Florida FL Reporter*, 10:9ff.

——1972b. *Tense Marking in Black English.* Washinghton, DC: Center for Applied Linguistics.

——1973. The concept of 'earlier-later': more or less correct. In Bailey and Shuy 1973:183–97.

——1975. The Bailey wave model: a dynamic quantitative paradigm. In Fasold and Shuy 1975:27–58.

——1976. One hundred years from syntax to phonology. In Steever, Sanford, Walker, Carol, and Mufwene, Salikoko (eds), *Papers from the Parasession on Diachronic Syntax*, 79–87. Chicago: Chicago Linguistic Society.

——1981. The relation between black and white speech in the South. *American Speech*, 56(3):163–89.

——1984a. *The Sociolinguistics of Society.* Oxford: Basil Blackwell.

——1984b. Variation theory and language learning. In Trudgill 1984a:245–62.

——and Schiffrin, Deborah (eds). 1989. *Language Change and Variation.* Amsterdam: John Benjamins, B.V.

——and Shuy, Roger (eds). 1975. *Studies in Language Variation.* Washington, DC: Georgetown University Press.

——and Shuy, Roger (eds). 1977. *Analyzing Variation in Language.* Washington, DC: Georgetown University Press.

Feagin, Crawford. 1979. *Variation and Change in Alabama English.* Washington, DC: Georgetown University Press.

——1986. More evidence for major vowel change in the South. In D. Sankoff 1986: 83–96.

Ferguson, Charles and DeBose, Charles. 1977. Simplified registers, broken language and pidginization. In Valdman 1977:99–128.

Figueroa, John. 1971. Creole studies. In Hymes 1971b:503–8.

Fillmore, Charles. 1968. In Bach, Emmon and Harms, Robert (eds). *Universals in Linguistic Theory*, 1–90. New York: Holt, Rinehart and Winston.

Fischer, John. 1958. Social influences on the choice of a linguistic variant. *Word*, 14:47–56. Also in Hymes 1964:483–8.

Fisher, S. 1982. The decision-making context: how doctors and patients communicate. In Di Pietro 1982:51–81.

——1983. Doctor talk/patient talk: how treatment decisions are negotiated in doctor-patient communication. In Fisher and Todd 1983:221–39.

——and Todd, A. (eds). 1983. *The Social Organization of Doctor-Patient Communication.* Washington, DC: Center for Applied Linguistics.

Fishman, Joshua. 1968. *Readings in the Sociology of Language.* The Hague: Mouton.

——1972a. *Advances in the Sociology of Language*, Volume I. The Hague: Mouton.

——1972b. *Advances in the Sociology of Language*, Volume II. The Hague: Mouton.

——1982. Whorfianism of the third kind: ethnolinguistic diversity as a worldwide societal asset. *Language in Society*, 11(1):1–14.

Fishman, Pamela. 1980. Conversational insecurity. In Giles, Robinson, and Smith 1980:127–32.

——1983. Interaction: the work women do. In Thorne, Kramarae, and Henley 1983:89–102.

Ford, Jerome. 1974. The semantics of direct address pronouns in French. *The French Review*, 47(6):1142–57.

Franco, Fabia and D'Odorico, Laura. 1987. Context-discourse matching in baby talk. In Verschueren and Bertuccelli-Papi 1987:213–28.

Frank, Francine and Anshen, Frank. 1983. *Language and the Sexes.* Albany, NY: State

Bibliography 321

University of New York Press.

Fraser, Bruce. 1974. A partial analysis of vernacular performative verbs. In Shuy, Roger and Bailey, C.-J. (eds), *Towards Tomorrow's Linguistics*, 139–58. Washington, DC: Georgetown University Press.

——1987. Pragmatic formatives. In Verschueren and Bertuccelli-Papi 1987:179–94.

Friedrich, Paul. 1966. Structural implications of Russian pronominal usage. In Bright, Williams (ed.), *Sociolinguistics*, 214–59. The Hague: Mouton.

——1972. Social context and semantic feature: the Russian pronominal usage. In Gumperz and Hymes 1972:270–300.

García, Erica. 1979. Discourse without syntax. In Givón 1979b:23–50.

Gazdar, Gerald. 1979. *Pragmatics*. New York: Academic Press.

——1980. Pragmatics and logical form. *Journal of Pragmatics*, 4:1–13.

——1981. Speech act assignment. In Joshi, Aravind, Webber, Bonnie, and Sag, Ivan (eds). *Elements of Discourse Understanding*, 64–83. Cambridge: Cambridge University Press.

Geertz, Clifford. 1960. Linguistic etiquette. In Geertz, Clifford, *The Religion of Java*, 248–60. Glencoe, IL: The Free Press. Also in J. Fishman 1968:282–95.

——1972. Linguistic etiquette. In Pride and Holmes 1972:167–79. Excerpt from Geertz 1960.

Geiger, Richard. 1979. Third-person reference in German. *Papers in Linguistics*, 12(3–4):535–52.

Geis, Michael and Zwicky, Arnold. 1971. On invited inferences. *Linguistic Inquiry*, 2:561–5.

Geoghegan, W. 1971. Information processing systems in culture. In Kay, Paul (ed.), *Explorations in Mathematical Anthropology*. Cambridge, MA: MIT Press.

Giglioli, Pier Paulo (ed.). 1972. *Language and Social Context*. Harmondsworth: Penguin.

Gilbert, Glenn (ed. and trans.). 1980. *Pidgin and Creole Languages: Selected Essays by Hugo Schuchardt*. Cambridge: Cambridge University Press.

——1985. Hugo Schuchardt and the Atlantic creoles: a newly discovered manuscript 'On the Negro English of West Africa'. *American Speech*, 60(1):31–63.

Giles, Howard. 1973. Accent mobility: a model and some data. *Anthropological Linguistics*, 15:87–105.

——and Marsh, P. 1979. Perceived masculinity and accented speech. *Language Sciences*, 1:301–15.

——, Robinson, W. P., and Smith, Philip (eds). 1980. *Language: Social Psychological Perspectives*. Oxford: Pergamon Press.

——and Smith, Philip. 1979. Accommodation theory: optimal levels of convergence, 45–65. In Giles, Howard and St. Clair, Robert (eds). *Language and Social Psychology*. Oxford: Basil Blackwell.

——, Smith, Philip, Browne, C., Whiteman, S., and Williams, J. 1980. Women's speech: the voice of feminism. In McConnell-Ginet, Borker, and Furman 1980: 150–6.

Givón, Talmy (ed.). 1979a. From discourse to syntax: grammar as a processing strategy. In Givón 1979b:81–114.

——1979b. *Syntax and Semantics 12: Discourse and Syntax*. New York: Academic Press.

Goodwin, M. H. 1980. Directive-response speech sequences in girls' and boys' task activities. In McConnell-Ginet, Borker, and Furman 1980:157–73.

Goody, Jack and Ian Watt. 1963. The consequences of literacy. *Comparative Studies in Society and History*, 5:304–45.

Gordon, David and Lakoff, George. 1971. Conversational postulates. In *Papers from the Seventh Regional Meeting of the Chicago Linguistic Society*, 63–94. Chicago: Chicago Linguistic Society. Also in Cole and Morgan 1975:83–106.

Graff, David, Labov, William, and Harris, Wendell. 1986. Testing listeners' reactions to phonological markers of ethnic identity: a new method for sociolinguistic research. In D. Sankoff 1986:45–58.

Greif, Esther Blank and Gleason, Jean Berko. 1980. Hi, thanks, and goodbye: more routine information. *Language in Society*, 9(2):159–66.

Green, Georgia. 1982. Review Givón: 1979. *Language*, 58:672–80.

Grice, H. Paul. 1975. Logic and conversation. In Cole and Morgan 1975:41–58.

Grimshaw, Allen. 1982. A cross-status dispute in ongoing talk: conflicting views of history. *Text*, 2(4):323–58. [Published 1983]

Gumperz, John. 1982. The linguistic bases of communicative competence. In Tannen 1982a:323-34.

——1983a. Fact and inference in courtroom testimony. In Gumperz 1983b:430–45.

——1983b. *Language and Social Identity*. Cambridge: Cambridge University Press.

——and Hymes, Dell (eds.). 1964. The ethnography of speaking. *American Anthropologist*, 66(2) Part II, 26.

——(eds). 1972. *Directions in Sociolinguistics*. Oxford: Basil Blackwell.

Guttman, Louis. 1944. A basis for scaling qualitative data. *American Sociological Review*, 9:139–50.

Guy, Gregory. 1980. Variation in the group and the individual: the case of final stop deletion. In Labov 1980b:1–36.

Haas, Mary. 1944/1964. Men and women's speech in Koasati. *Language*, 20:142–9. Also in Hymes 1964:228–33.

Haberland, Hartmut and Skutnabb-Kangas, Tove. 1981. Political determinants of pragmatic and sociolinguistic choices. In Parret, Sbisà, and Verschueren 1981:285–312.

Hacker, Diana and Betty Renshaw. 1979. *A Practical Guide for Writers*. Cambridge, MA: Winthrop Publishers.

Hahn, Frederick. 1911. *Kurukh Grammar*. Calcutta.

Hakulinen, Auli. 1987. Avoiding personal reference in Finnish. In Verschueren and Bertuccelli-Papi 1987:141–55.

Hall, Robert, 1966. *Pidgin and Creole Languages*. Ithaca, NY: Cornell University Press.

Halliday, M. A. K. 1985. *An Introduction to Functional Grammar*, London: Edward Arnold.

——(ed.) 1987. *New Developments in Systemic Linguistics*. London: Pinter.

Halliday, Michael and Hasan, Ruqaiya. 1976. *Cohesion in English*. London: Longman.

Hancher, Michael. 1979. The classification of cooperative illocutionary acts. *Language in Society*, 8(1):1–14.

Hancock, Ian. 1971. A survey of the pidgins and creoles of the world. In Hymes 1971b:509–25.

——1977. Appendix: Repertory of pidgin and creole languages. In Valdman 1977:277–94.

——1980. Gullah and Barbadian: origins and relation. *American Speech*, 55:17–35.

Haugen, Einar. 1975. Pronominal address in Icelandic: from you-two to you-all. *Language in Society*, 4:323–39.

Heath, Shirley Brice. 1983. *Ways with Words*. Cambridge: Cambridge University Press.

Holmes, Janet. 1986. Functions of *you know* in women's and men's speech. *Language in Society*, 15(1):1–22.

Hopper, Paul. 1979. Aspect and foregrounding in discourse. In Givón 1979b:213–42.

——1983. Ergative, passive, and active in Malay narrative. In Klein-Adreu 1983:67–88.

——and Thompson, Sandra Annear. 1980. Transitivity in grammar and discourse. *Language*, 56(2):251–99.

——1984. The discourse basis for lexical categories in universal grammar. *Language*, 60(4):703–52.

Horn, Laurence. 1972. *On the Semantic Properties of the Logical Operators in English*. Bloomington, IN: Indiana University Linguistics Club.

——1973. Greek Grice. In Corum, Smith-Stark, and Weisler 1973:205–14.

——1984. Toward a new taxonomy for pragmatic inference: Q-based and R-based implicature. In Schiffrin, Deborah (ed.), *Meaning, Form and Use in Context: Linguistic*

Applications. Georgetown University Round Table on Languages and Linguistics 1984, 11–42. Washington, DC: Georgetown University Press.
——1985. Metalinguistic negation and pragmatic ambiguity. *Language*, 61:121–74.
Horvath, Barbara. 1985. *Variation in Australian English: The Sociolects of Sydney*. Cambridge: Cambridge University Press.
Hymes, Dell. 1962. The ethnography of speaking. In Gladwin, T. and Sturtevant, William (eds), *Anthropology and Human Behavior*, 13–53. Washington, DC: Anthropological Society of Washington. Also in J. Fishman 1968:99–138.
——(ed.). 1964. *Language in Culture and Society*. New York: Harper and Row.
——1971a. Introduction to Part III. In Hymes 1971b:65–90.
——1971b. *Pidginization and Creolization of Languages*. Cambridge: Cambridge University Press.
——1972a. Models of the interaction of language and social life. In Gumperz and Hymes 1972:35–71.
——1972b. Toward ethnographies of communication: the analysis of communicative events. In Giglioli 1972:21–44.
——1974. *Foundations in Sociolinguistics: An Ethnographic Approach*. Philadelphia: University of Pennsylvania Press.
Ide, Sachiko. 1979. A sociolinguistics analysis of person references by Japanese and American children. *Language Sciences*, 1(2):273–93.
——1982. Japanese sociolinguistics: politeness and women's language. *Lingua*, 57(2–4):357–86.
Jacobson, Sven. 1982. *Syntactic Variation: Theory and Practice*. Umeå, Sweden: Umeå Papers in English, No. 3.
Jaffe, J. and Feldstein, S. 1970. *Rhythms of Dialogue*. New York: Academic Press.
Jones-Jackson, Patricia. 1986. On the status of Gullah on the Sea Islands. In Montgomery and Bailey, 1986:63–72.
Jonz, John. 1975. Situated address in the United States Marine Corps. *Anthropological Linguistics*, 17(2):68–77.
Jucker, Andreas. 1986. *News Interviews: A Pragmalinguistic Analysis*. Amsterdam: John Benjamins, B.V.
Kachru, Braj. 1982. *The Other Tongue: English Across Cultures*. Oxford: Pergamon Press.
——1986. *The Alchemy of English: The Spread, Functions and Models of Non-Native Englishes*. Oxford: Pergamon Press.
Karttunen, Lauri and Peters, Stanley. 1979. Conventional implicature. In Oh, Choon-Kyu and Dinneen, Daniel (eds), *Syntax and Semantics 11: Presupposition*, 1–56. New York: Academic Press.
Katz, Jerrold. 1977. *Propositional Structure and Illocutionary Force*. New York: T. Y. Crowell.
Kay, Paul. 1978. Variable rules, community grammar and linguistic change. In D. Sankoff 1978:71–84.
——and McDaniel, Chad. 1979. On the logic of variable rules. *Language in Society*, 8(2):151–89.
Keenan, Edward. 1971. Two kinds of presupposition in natural languages. In Langendoen, D. Terence and Fillmore, Charles (eds), *Studies in Linguistic Semantics*, 45–54. New York: Holt, Rinehart and Winston.
——and Ochs, Elinor. 1979. Becoming a competent speaker of Malagasy. In Shopen 1979:113–60.
Keillor, Garrison. 1985. *Lake Wobegon Days*. New York: Viking.
Kemp, William. 1979. L'histoire récente de *ce que, qu'est-ce que* et *qu'osque* à Montréal: trois variantes en interaction. In Thibault, Pierette (ed.), *Le Français parlé: Etudes sociolinguistiques*. Edmonton: Linguistic Research.
Kempf, Renate. 1985. Pronouns and terms of address in *Neues Deutschland. Language in*

Society, 14(2):223–38.

Kempson, Ruth. 1975. *Presupposition and the delimitation of semantics.* Cambridge: Cambridge University Press.

Key, M. R. 1975. *Male/Female Language.* Metuchen, NJ: Scarecrow Press.

Kiparsky, Paul. 1971. Historical linguistics. In Dingwall, William Orr (ed.), *A Survey of Linguistic Science.* College Park, MD: University of Maryland Linguistics Department.

——and Kiparsky, Carol. 1971. Fact. In Steinberg and Jakobovits 1971: 345–69.

Kirsner, Robert. 1983. On the use of quantitative discourse data to determine inferential mechanisms in grammar. In Klein-Andreu 1983:237–58.

Klein, Wolfgang and Dittmar, Norbert. 1979. *Developing Grammars: The Acquisition of German Syntax by Foreign Workers.* Berlin: Springer Verlag.

Klein-Andreu, Flora (ed.). 1983. *Discourse: Perspectives on Syntax.* New York: Academic Press.

Kramer, Cheris. 1975. Sex-related differences in address systems. *Anthropological Linguistics*, 17(5):198–210.

Kroch, Anthony. 1978. Towards a theory of social dialect variation. *Language in Society*, 7(1):17–36.

——1989. Function and grammar in the history of periphrastic *do.* In Fasold and Schiffrin 1989:133–72.

Laberge, Suzanne. 1978. The changing distribution of indefinite pronouns in discourse. In Shuy, Roger and Shnukal, Anna (eds), *Language Use and the Uses of Language*, 76–87. Washington, DC: Georgetown University Press.

Labov, William. 1963. The social motivation of sound change. *Word*, 19:273–307.

——1966. *The Social Stratification of English in New York City.* Washington, DC: Center for Applied Linguistics.

——1969. Contraction, deletion and inherent variability of the English copula. *Language*, 45(4):715–62.

——1970. The logic of nonstandard English. In Alatis, James (ed.), *Linguistics and the Teaching of Standard English to Speakers of Other Languages and Dialects. Georgetown University Round Table on Languages and Linguistics 1969.* Washington, DC: Georgetown University Press.

——1972a. *Language in the Inner City.* Philadelphia: University of Pennsylvania Press.

——1972b. Rules for ritual insults. Chapter 8 of Labov 1972a:297–353.

——1972c. *Sociolinguistic Patterns.* Philadelphia: University of Pennsylvania Press/Oxford: Basil Blackwell.

——1976. Systematically misleading data from test questions. *Urban Review*, 9:146–69.

——1978. Where does the sociolinguistic variable stop? A reply to B. Lavandera. *Texas Working Papers in Sociolinguistics*, 44. Austin, TX: Southwest Educational Development Laboratory.

——1980a. Is there a creole speech community? In Valdman and Highfield 1980:369–89.

——(ed.). 1980b. *Locating Language in Time and Space.* New York: Academic Press.

——1980c. The social origins of sound change. In Labov 1980b:251–66.

——1982a. Competing value systems in the inner-city schools. In Gilmore, Perry and Glatthorn, Allan (eds), *Children In and Out of School*, 148–71. Washington, DC: Center for Applied Linguistics.

——1982b. Objectivity and commitment in linguistic science: the case of the Black English trial in Ann Arbor. *Language in Society*, 11(2):165–202.

——1984. Field methods of the project on linguistic change and variation. In Baugh, John and Sherzer, Joel (eds), *Language in Use*, 28–53. Englewood Cliffs, NJ: Prentice-Hall.

——1987. Are black and white vernaculars diverging?, Section II. *American Speech*, 62(1):5–12.

——1988. The judicial testing of linguistic theory. In Tannen, Deborah (ed.), *Linguistics in Context: Connecting Observation and Understanding. Advances in Discourse Processes*

24. Norwood, NJ: Ablex.

——1989. The exact description of a speech community: short *a* in Philadelphia. In Fasold and Schiffrin 1989:1–57.

——forthcoming. The three dialects of English. In Eckert, Penelope (ed.), *Quantitative Analyses of Sound Change in Progress*. New York: Academic Press.

——and Cohen, Paul, Robins, Clarence, and Lewis, John. 1968. *A Study of the Nonstandard English of Negro and Puerto Rican Speakers in New York City*. United States Office of Education Final Report, Research Project No. 3288.

——and Fanshel, David. 1977. *Therapeutic Discourse*. New York: Academic Press.

——and Harris, Wendell. 1986. De facto segregation of black and white vernaculars. In D. Sankoff 1986:1–24.

LaCoste, M. 1976. *Interrogation-interrogatoire*. Paris: Publications du groupe communication et travail.

Lakoff, George. 1971. On generative semantics. In Steinberg and Jakobovitz 1971:232–96.

——1987. *Women, Fire and Dangerous Things*. Chicago: University of Chicago Press.

Lakoff, Robin. 1972. Language in context. *Language*, 48(4):907–27.

——1973a. Language and women's place. *Language and Society*, 2:45–79.

——1973b. The logic of politeness: or minding your *p*'s and *q*'s. In Corum, Smith-Stark, and Weisler 1973:292–305.

——1975. *Language and women's place*. New York: Harper and Row.

——1977a. Psychoanalytic discourse and ordinary conversation. *Interfaces*, 8:2–13.

——1977b. What you can do with words: politeness, pragmatics and performatives. In Rogers, Andy, Wall, Bob and Murphy, John (eds), *Proceedings of the Texas Conference on Performatives, Presuppositions and Implicatures*, 79–106. Arlington, VA: Center for Applied Linguistics.

——1977c. Women's Language. *Language and Style*, 10(4):222–47.

Lambert, Wallace and Tucker, G. Richard. 1976. *Tu, vous, usted: A Social-Psychological Study of Address Patterns*. Rowley, MA: Newbury House.

Lavendera, Beatriz. 1978. Where does the sociolinguistic variable stop? *Language in Society*, 7(2):171–82.

——1984. Creative variation: shifting between personal and impersonal in Spanish discourse. Sonderforschungsbereich 99, Universität Konstanz.

Leaverton, Lloyd. 1973. Dialect readers: rationale, use and value. In Laffey, James and Shuy, Roger (eds), *Language Differences: Do They Interfere?* Newark, DE: International Reading Association.

Leech, Geoffrey. 1980. *Language and Tact*. Amsterdam: John Benjamins, B. V.

——1983. *Principles of Pragmatics*. London: Longmans.

Leeds-Hurwitz, Wendy. 1980. The use and analysis of uncommon forms of address: a business example. *Working Papers in Sociolinguistics*, 80. Austin, TX: Southwest Educational Development Laboratory.

Leet-Pellegrini, H. 1980. Conversational dominance as a function of gender and expertise. In Giles, Robinson, and Smith 1980:97–104.

Lefebvre, Claire. 1981. The double structure of questions in French: a case of syntactic variation. In Sankoff, David and Cedergren, Henrietta (eds), *Variation Omnibus*, 229–38. Edmonton: Linguistic Research.

——1989. Some problems in defining syntactic variables: the case of WH questions in Montreal French. In Fasold and Schiffrin 1989:351–66.

Lemon, Nigel. 1981. Language and learning: some observations on the linguistic determination of cognitive processes. In Lloyd, Barbara and Gay, John (eds), *Universals of Human Thought: Some African Evidence*, 201–14. Cambridge: Cambridge University Press.

LePage, Robert. 1977. Processes of pidginization and creolization. In Valdman 1977:222–58.

——1980a. Hugo Schuchardt's creole studies and the problem of linguistic continua. In

Lichem, K. and Simon, H. (eds), *Hugo Schuchardt:Schuchardt-Symposium 1977 in Graz, Vorträge und Aufsätze*. Vienna: Austrian Academy of the Sciences.

——1980b. Theoretical aspects of sociolinguistic studies in pidgin and creole languages. In Valdman and Highfield 1980:331–68.

——and Tabouret-Keller, Andrée. 1985. *Acts of Identity*. Cambridge: Cambridge University Press.

Levinson, Stephen. 1983. *Pragmatics*. Cambridge: Cambridge University Press.

——1987. Minimization and conversational inference. In Versheuren and Bertuccelli-Papi 1987:61–130.

Lightfoot, David. 1982. *The Language Lottery*. Cambridge, MA: The MIT Press.

Lilje, Gerald. 1972. Uninvited inferences. *Linguistic Inquiry*, 3(4):540–2.

Linde, Charlotte. 1977. Information structures in discourse. In Fasold and Shuy 1977:226–36.

——1984. *The Creation of Coherence in Life Stories*. Norwood, NJ: Ablex.

——and Labov, William. 1975. Spatial networks as a site for the study of language and thought. *Language*, 51(4):924–39.

Loftus, Elizabeth. 1981. Mentalmorphosis: alterations in memory produced by the mental bonding of new information to old. In Long, John and Baddeley, Alan (eds), *Attention and Performance*, 9:417–36. Hillsdale, NJ: Lawrence Erlbaum Associates.

Longacre, Robert. 1983. *The Grammar of Discourse*. New York: Plenum.

Lucas, Ceil. 1986. 'I ain't got none/You don't have any': Noticing and correcting variation in the classroom. In Montgomery and Bailey 1986:348–58.

Lyons, John. 1980. Pronouns of address in *Anna Karenina*: the stylistics of bilingualism and the impossibility of translation. In Greenbaum, Sidney, Leech, Geoffrey, and Svartik, Jan (eds), *Studies in English Linguistics: For Randolph Quirk*, 253–49. London: Longmans.

Macaulay, R. K. S. 1978. Variation and consistency in Glaswegian English. In Trudgill 1978:132–43.

Martyna, W. 1980. The psychology of the generic masculine. In McConnell-Ginet, Borker, and Furman 1980:69–78.

Maseide, P. 1982. Analytical aspects of clinical reasoning: a discussion of models for medical problem solving. In Di Pietro 1982:241–65.

Mayerthaler, Willi. 1981. *Morphologische Natürlichkeit*. Wiesbaden: Akademische Verlagsgesellschaft Athenaion.

——1988. *Morphological naturalness*. Ann Arbor, MI: Karoma.

Mayo, C. and Henley, Nancy (eds). 1981. *Gender and Non-Verbal Communication*. New York: Springer-Verlag.

McCawley, James. 1968. The role of semantics in a grammar. In Bach, Emmon and Harms, Robert (eds), *Universals in Linguistic Theory*, 171–204. New York: Holt, Rinehart and Winston.

——1981. *Everything that Linguists have Always Wanted to Know about Logic*. Chicago: University of Chicago Press.

McConnell-Ginet, S. 1983. Review of Orasanu et al. (eds): *Language, Sex, and Gender* and Vetterling-Braggin (ed.): *Sexist Language*. *Language* 49(2):373–91.

——Borker, R., and Furman, N. (eds). 1980. *Women and Language in Literature and Society*. New York: Praeger.

McCormack, William. 1977. Introduction. In McCormack, William and Wurm, Stephen (eds), *Language and Thought: Anthropological Issues*, 3–10. The Hague: Mouton.

McDavid, Raven and McDavid, Virginia. 1951. The relationship of the speech of American Negroes to the speech of whites. *American Speech*, 26:3–17.

McKay, D. and Fulkerson, D. 1979. On the comprehension and production of pronouns. *Journal of Verbal Learning and Verbal Behavior*, 18:661–73.

McLaughlin, Margaret and Cody, Michael. 1982. Awkward silences: behavioral antecedents and consequences of the conversational lapse. *Human Communication Research*, 8(4):299–316.

Mehrota, R. R. 1982. Non-kin forms of address in Hindi. *International Journal of the Sociology of Language*, 32:121–37.

Merritt, Marilyn. 1977. The playback: an instance of variation in discourse. In Fasold and Shuy 1977:198–208.

——1982. Repeats and reformulations in primary classrooms as windows of the nature of talk engagement. *Discourse Processes*, 5(2):127–45.

Miller, George and McNeill, David. 1969. Psycholinguistics. In Lindzey, G. and Aronson, E. (eds), *The Handbook of Social Psychology* 3. Reading, MA: Addison-Wesley.

Miller, W. 1958. Lower-class culture as a generating milieu of gang delinquency. *Journal of Social Issues*, 14(3):5–19.

Milroy, James. 1982. Probing under the tip of the iceberg: phonological 'normalization' and the shape of speech communities. In Romaine 1982b:35–48.

——1984. Sociolinguistic methodology and the identification of speakers' voices in legal proceedings. In Trudgill 1984a:51–72.

Milroy, Lesley. 1980. *Language and Social Networks*. Oxford: Basil Blackwell.

——1982. Social network and linguistic focussing. In Romaine 1982b:141–52.

——1987. *Observing and Analyzing Natural Language*. Oxford: Basil Blackwell.

——1988a. New perspectives in the analysis of sex differentiation in language. Paper presented at the First Hong Kong Conference on Language and Society.

——1988b. Review of Horvath 1985. In *Language in Society*, 17(4):577–81.

——and Margraine, Sue. 1980. Vernacular language loyalty and social network. *Language in Society*, 9(1):43–70.

Mitchell, Stephen. 1979. Address and decision-making in modern Swedish. *Anthropological Linguistics*, 21(2):61–9.

Mittwock, Anita. 1983. Backward anaphora and discourse structure. *Journal of Pragmatics*, 7(2):129–40.

Mochizuki, Michiko. 1980. Male and female variants for 'I' in Japanese. *Papers in Linguistics*, 13(3–4):453–74.

Moles, Jerry. 1978. The influence of differential 'power' and 'solidarity' upon predictability of behavior: a Peruvian example. *Anthropological Linguistics*, 20(1):38–51.

Montgomery, Michael and Bailey, Guy (eds). 1986. *Language Variety in the South: Perspectives in Black and White*. University, AL: University of Alabama Press.

Morris, Charles. 1938. Foundations of the theory of signs. In Neurath, O., Carnap, R., and Morris, C. (eds), *International Encyclopedia of Unified Science*, 77–138. Chicago: University of Chicago Press. Reprinted as Morris, Charles. 1971. *Writings in the General Theory of Signs*. The Hague: Mouton.

Moulton, J. 1981. The myth of the neutral 'man'. In Vetterling-Braggin 1981:100–15.

Mufwene, Salikoko and Gilman, Charles. 1987. How African is Gullah and why? *American Speech*, 62(2):120–39.

Mühlhäusler, Peter. 1986. *Pidgin and Creole Linguistics*. Oxford: Basil Blackwell.

Myhill, John. 1984. Pragmatic and categorical correlates of VS word order. *Lingua*, 66:177–200.

——1988. The rise of *be* as an aspect marker in Black English Vernacular. *American Speech*, 63(4):304–25.

——and Harris, Wendell. 1986. The use of the verbal *-s* inflection in BEV. In D. Sankoff 1986:25–32.

Nemoianu, Anca. 1980. *The Boat's Gonna Leave: A Study of Children Learning a Second Language from Conversations with other Children*. Amsterdam: John Benjamins, B. V.

Newmeyer, Frederick. 1980. *Linguistic Theory in America*. New York: Academic Press.

——(ed.). 1988. *Linguistics: The Cambridge Survey*. Cambridge: Cambridge University Press.

O'Barr, William. 1982. *Linguistic Evidence: Language Power and Strategy in the Courtroom*. New York: Academic Press.

Ochs, Elinor. 1973. A sliding sense of obligatoriness: the polystructure of Malagasy oratory.

Language in Society, 2:225–43. Also in Baugh, John and Sherzer, Joel (eds), *Language in Use*, 167–82. Englewood Cliffs, NJ: Prentice-Hall.
——and Schieffelin, Bambi. 1979. *Developmental pragmatics*. New York: Academic Press.
Ochs Keenan, Elinor. 1974. Norm-makers, norm-breakers: use of speech by men and women in a Malagasy community. In Bauman and Sherzer 1974:125–43.
——1975. The universality of conversational implicature. In Fasold and Shuy 1975:255–68. Also in Fasold, Ralph (ed.), *Variation in the Form and Use of Language*, 234–47. Washington, DC: Georgetown University Press, 1983.
Olstain, Elite and Weinbach, Liora. 1987. Complaints: a study of speech act behavior among native and non-native speakers of Hebrew. In Verschueren and Bertuccelli-Papi 1987:195–210.
Ong, Walter, S. J. 1977. *Interfaces of the word*. Ithaca, NY: Cornell University Press.
Palakornkul, Angkab. 1975. A sociolinguistic study of pronominal usage Bangkok Thai. *International Journal of the Sociology of Language*, 5:11–42.
Parret, Herman. 1983. *Semiotics and Pragmatics: An Evaluative Comparison of Conceptual Frameworks*. Amsterdam: John Benjamins, B.V.
——Sbisà, Marina, and Verschueren, Jef (eds). 1981. *Possibilities and Limitations of Pragmatics*. Amsterdam: John Benjamins, B.V.
Paulston, Christina Bratt. 1974. Language universals and sociocultural implications in deviant usage: personal questions in Swedish. *Studia Linguistica*, 29(1,2):1–15.
——1975. Language and social class: pronouns of address in Swedish. *Working Papers in Sociolinguistics*, 29. Austin, TX: Southwest Educational Development Laboratory.
Payne, Arvilla. 1980. Factors controlling the acquisition of the Philadelphia dialect by out-of-state children. In Labov 1980b:143–78.
Pelletier, J. 1977. Or. *Theoretical Linguistics*, 10(4):661–74.
Pitts, Walter. 1986. Contrastive use of verbal -*z* in slave narratives. In D. Sankoff 1986:73–82.
Platt, John, Weber, Heidi and Ho, M. L. 1984. *The New Englishes*. London: Routledge and Kegan Paul.
Polanyi, Livia. 1982. Literary complexity in everyday story telling. In Tannen 1982c:155–70.
Polythress, Vern. 1982. Hierarchy in discourse analysis: a revision of tagmemics. *Semiotica*, 40(1/2):107–37.
Poplack, Shana. 1980. Sometimes I'll start a sentence in Spanish *y termino en español*: toward a typology of code-switching. *Linguistics*, 18(7/8):581–618.
——and Sankoff, David. 1984. Borrowing: the synchrony of integration. *Linguistics*, 22:99–135.
——and Sankoff, David. 1987. The Philadelphia story in the Spanish Caribbean. *American Speech*, 62(4):291–314.
——Sankoff, David, and Miller, Christopher. 1988. The social correlates and linguistic processes of lexical borrowing and assimilation. *Linguistics*, 16(1):47–104.
Pride, John. 1982. *New Englishes*. Rowley, MA: Newbury House.
——and Holmes, Janet. 1972. *Sociolinguistics*. Harmondsworth: Penguin.
Prindle, Tamae. 1981. Polite forms of Japanese speech. *Anthropological Linguistics*, 23(5):209–14.
Quirk, Randolph and H. G. Widdowson. 1985. *English in the World: Teaching and Learning Language and Literatures*. Cambridge: Cambridge University Press.
Reardon, Kathleen. 1982. Conversational deviance: a structural model. *Human Communication Research*, 9(1):59–74.
Reed, Carol. 1981. Teaching teachers about teaching writing to students from varied linguistic social and cultural groups. In Farr Whiteman 1981b:139–52.
Reisman, Karl. 1974. Contrapuntal conversations in an Antiguan village. In Bauman and Sherzer 1974:110–24.
Richmond, J. 1979. Dialect features in mainstream school writing. *New Approaches to Multiracial Education*, 8:10–15.

Rickford, John. 1974. Insights of the mesolect. In DeCamp and Hancock 1974:92–117.
——1975. Carrying the new wave into syntax: the case of Black English BIN. In Fasold and Shuy 1975:162–83.
——1986. *Dimensions of a Creole Continuum*;. Stanford, CA: Stanford University Press.
——1987. Are black and white vernaculars diverging?, Section VII. *American Speech*, 62(1):55–62.
Romaine, Suzanne. 1982a. *Socio-Historical Linguistics*. Cambridge: Cambridge University Press.
——1982b. *Sociolinguistic Variation in Speech Communities*. London: Edward Arnold.
——1988. *Pidgin and Creole Languages*. London: Longman.
Ross, John. 1973. A fake NP squish. In Bailey and Shuy 1973:96–140.
Russell, Joan. 1982. Networks and sociolinguistic variation in an African urban setting. In Romaine 1982b:125–40.
Sachs, Jacqueline. 1975. Cues to the identification of sex in children's speech. In Thorne and Henley 1975:152–71.
Sacks, Harvey. 1972. On the analyzability of stories by children. In Gumperz, John and Hymes, Dell (eds), *Directions in Sociolinguistics*, 325–45. Oxford: Basil Blackwell.
——Schegloff, Emanuel, and Jefferson, Gail. 1974. A simplest systematics for the organization of turn-taking for conversation. *Language*, 50(4):696–735.
Samarin, William. 1967. *A Grammar of Sango*. The Hague: Mouton.
——1984. Socioprogrammed linguistics. *The Behavioral and Brain Sciences*, 7:206–7.
Sanches, Mary and Blount, Ben. 1977. *Sociocultural Dimensions of Language Use*. New York: Academic Press.
Sankoff, David (ed.). 1978. *Linguistic Variation: Models and Methods*. New York: Academic Press.
——(ed.). 1986. *Diversity and Diachrony*. Current Issues in Linguistic Theory 53. Amsterdam: John Benjamins, B.V.
——1988. Sociolinguistics and syntactic variation. In Newmeyer 1988, Volume IV.
——and Cedergren, Henrietta, Kemp, William, Thibault, Pierette, and Vincent, Diane. 1989. Montreal French: language, class, and ideology. In Fasold and Schiffrin 1989:107–18.
——and Laberge, Suzanne. 1978. The linguistic market and the statistical explanation of variability. In D. Sankoff 1978:227–38.
——and Labov, William. 1979. On the uses of variable rules. *Language in Society*, 8(2):189–222.
——and Poplack, Shana. 1981. A formal grammar for codeswitching. *Papers in Linguistics*, 14(1):3–46.
Sankoff, Gillian. 1975. A quantitative paradigm for the study of communicative competence. In Bauman and Sherzer 1975:18–49. Also in G. Sankoff 1980:47–80.
——1980. *The Social Life of Language*. Philadelphia: University of Pennsylvania Press.
——and Brown, Penelope. 1976. The origins of syntax in discourse: a case study of Tok Pisin relatives. *Language*, 52(3):631–66. Also in G. Sankoff 1980:211–55.
Sapir, Edward. 1921. *Language*. New York: Harcourt, Brace.
——1929. The status of linguistics as a science. *Language*, 5:207–14. Also in Mandelbaum, David (ed.), *Selected Writings of Edward Sapir in Language, Culture and Personality*, 160–6. Berkeley, CA: University of California Press, 1958.
Saville-Troike, Muriel (ed.). 1977. *Linguistics and Anthropology. Georgetown University Round Table on Languages and Linguistics 1977*. Washington, DC: Georgetown University Press.
——1982. *The Ethnography of Communication*. Oxford: Basil Blackwell.
Schatz, Henriette. 1986. *Plat Amsterdams in its Social Context*. Amsterdam: P. J. Meertens-Instituut voor Dialectologie, Volkskunde en Naamkunde.
Schatzman, L. and Straus, A. 1955. Social class and modes of communication. *American Journal of Sociology*, 60:329–38.

Schegloff, Emmanuel. 1972. Sequencing in conversational openings. In J. Fishman 1972b:91–125. Also in Gumperz and Hymes 1972:301–24.

Schenkein, Jim. 1978. An introduction to the study of 'socialization' through analyses of conversational interaction. *Semiotica*, 24(3/4):277–304.

Schiffrin, Deborah. 1981. Tense variation in narrative. *Language*, 57(1):45–62.

——1984a. How a story says what it means and does. *Text*, 4(4):313–46.

——1984b. Jewish argument as sociability. *Language in Society*, 13(3):11–36.

——1985. Conversational coherence: the role of well. *Language*, 61(3):640–67.

——1986. Turn-initial variation. In D. Sankoff 1986:367–80.

——1987. *Discourse Markers*. Cambridge: Cambridge University Press.

Schmidt, Rosemarie and Kess, Joseph. 1986. *Television Advertising and Televangelism: Discourse Analysis of Persuasive Language*. Amsterdam: John Benjamins, B. V.

Schneider, Edgar. 1983. The origin of the verbal -*s* in Black English. *American English*, 58(2):99–113.

Schneider, Gilbert. 1966. *West/African Pidgin-English*. Athens, OH: Gilbert Donald Schneider.

Schuchardt, Hugo. 1889. Beiträge zur Kenntnis des englischen Kreolisch: II. Melaneso-Eglishes. *Englishe Studien*, 13:158–62. Edited and translated in Gilbert 1980:14–29.

——1914. *Die Sprache der Saramakkaneger in Surinam*. Amsterdam: Johannes Müller. Edited and translated in Gilbert 1980:89–126.

Schultz, M. 1975. The semantic derogation of woman. In Thorne and Henley 1975:64–75.

Schumann, John. 1978. *The Pidginization Process: A Model for Second Language Acquisition*. Rowley, MA: Newbury House.

Scollon, Ronald and Scollon, Suzanne. 1979. *Linguistic Convergence: An Ethnography of Speaking at Fort Chipewyan, Alberta*. New York: Academic Press.

Scotton, Carol M. and Wanjin, Zhu. 1983. *Tóngzhi' in China: language change and its conversational consequences. Language in Society*, 12(4):477–94.

Searle, John. 1969. *Speech Acts*. Cambridge: Cambridge University Press.

——1975. Indirect speech acts. In Cole and Morgan 1975:59–82.

——1979. *Expression and Meaning*. Cambridge: Cambridge University Press.

——1983. *Intensionality*. Cambridge: Cambridge University Press.

——and Vanderveken, Robert. 1985. *Foundations of Illocutionary Logic*. Cambridge: Cambridge University Press.

Sherzer, Joel. 1977a. The ethnography of speaking: a critical appraisal. In Saville-Troike 1977:43–58.

——1977b. Semantic systems, discourse structures, and the ecology of language. In Fasold and Shuy 1977:283–93.

Shopen, Timothy (ed.). 1979. *Languages and their Speakers*. Cambridge, MA: Winthrop Publishers.

Shuy, Roger. 1976. The medical interview: problems in communication. *Primary Care*, 3:365–86.

——1982. Topic as the unit of analysis in a criminal law case. In Tannen 1982a:113–26.

——1983. Three types of interference to an effective exchange of information in the medical interview. In Fisher and Todd 1983:189–202.

——1984a. Entrapment and the linguistic analysis of tapes. *Studies in Language*, 8(2):215–34.

——1984b. Linguistics in other professions. *Annual Review of Anthropology*, 13:419–45.

1986. Language and the law. *Annual Review of Applied Linguistics* 7:50–63.

——1988. Changing language policy in a bureacracy. In Lowenberg, Peter (ed.), *Language Spread Language Policy: Issues, Implications, and Case Studies. Georgetown University Round Table on Languages and Linguistics 1987*, 152–74. Washington, DC: Georgetown University Press.

Silva-Corvalán, Carmen. 1983. Tense and aspect in oral Spanish narrative: context and meaning. *Language*, 59(4):760–80.

Simonin, J. 1977. *Analyse interactionnelle de systèmes question–réponse dans la pratique d'interview.* Neuchâtel: Travaux du Centre de Recherchee Sémiologiques.

Slobin, Dan. 1963. Some aspects of the use of pronouns of address in Yiddish. *Word,* 19:193–202.

——Miller, Stephen, and Porter, Lyman. 1968. Forms of address and social relations in a business organization. *Journal of Personality and Social Psychology,* 8(3):289–93.

Smith, L. (ed.). 1983. *Readings in English as an International Language.* Oxford: Pergamon Press.

Smith, Philip. 1980. Judging masculine and feminine social identities from content-controlled speech. In Giles, Robinson, and Smith 1980:121–6.

Smith-Hefner, Nancy. 1981. To level or not to level: codes of politeness and prestige in rural Java. *Papers from the Parasession on Language and Behavior,* 211–17. Chicago: Chicago Linguistic Society.

Spears, Arthur. 1982. The Black English semi-auxiliary *come. Language,* 58:850–72.

——1987. Are black and white vernaculars diverging?, Section VI. *American Speech,* 62(1):48–55.

Sperber, Dan and Wilson, Dierdre. 1986. *Relevance.* Cambridge, MA: Harvard University Press.

Sreedhar, M. V. 1977. Standardization of Naga Pidgin. *Journal of Creole Studies,* 1:157–70.

——1979. The functions of bilingualism in Nagaland. *International Journal of the Sociology of Language,* 22:103–14.

Steinberg, Danny and Jakobovits, Leon (eds). 1971. *Semantics: An Interdisciplinary Reader in Philosophy Linguistics and Psychology.* Cambridge: Cambridge University Press.

Steinsholt, Anders. 1962. *Målbryting i Hedrum.* Oslo: Universitetsforlaget.

Stewart, William. 1966. Nonstandard speech patterns. *Baltimore Bulletin of Education* 43(2–4):52–65.

——1967. Sociolinguistic factors in the history of American Negro dialects. *Florida FL Reporter* 5(2):1ff.

——1968. Continuity and change in American Negro dialects. *Florida FL Reporter* 6(1):3ff.

Stockman, Ida and Vaughn-Cooke, Fay. 1986. Implications of semantic category research for the language assessment of non-standard speakers. *Topics in Language Disorders* 6(4):15–250.

Streeck, Jurgen. 1983. *Social Order in Child Communication: A Study in Microethnography.* Amsterdam: John Benjamins, B. V.

Stubbs, Michael. 1980. *Language and Literacy.* London: Routledge and Kegan Paul.

——1983. *Discourse Analysis: The Sociolinguistic Analysis of Natural Language.* Chicago: University of Chicago Press.

——1986. *Educational Linguistics.* Oxford: Basil Blackwell.

Tagliamonte, Sali and Poplack, Shana. 1988. How Black English *Past* got to the present: evidence from Samaná. *Language in Society* 17(4):513–34.

Tannen, Deborah (ed.). 1982a. *Analyzing Discourse: Text and Talk. Georgetown University Round Table on Languages and Linguistics 1981.* Washington, DC: Georgetown University Press.

——1982b. Oral and literate strategies in spoken and written narratives. *Language,* 58:1–21.

——1982c. *Spoken and Written Language: Exploring Orality and Literary Advances in Discourse Processes 9.* Norwood, NJ: Ablex.

——1983a. Ethnic style in male–female conversation. In Gumperz 1983b:217–30.

——1983b. When is an overlap not an interruption. In Di Pietro, Frawley, and Wedel, 1983:19–29.

——1984a. *Coherence in Spoken and Written Discourse. Advances in Discourse Processes, 13.* Norwood, NJ: Ablex.

——1984b. *Conversational Style: Analyzing Talk among Friends.* Norwood, NJ: Ablex.

——1986. *That's Not what I Meant!* New York: William Morrow.

——forthcoming. Interactional Sociolinguistics. In Bright, William (editor-in-chief). *Oxford International Encyclopedia of Linguistics*. Oxford: Oxford University Press.

——and Wallat, Cynthia. 1986. Medical professionals and parents: a linguistic analysis of communication across contexts. *Language in Society*, 15:295–312.

——1987. Interactive frames and knowledge schemas in interaction: examples from a medical examination/interview. *Social Psychological Quarterly*, 50(2):205–16.

Taylor, D. 1951. Sex gender in Central American Carib. *International Journal of American Linguistics*, 17(2):102–4.

Thompson, Sandra Annear. 1983. Grammar and discourse: the English detached participial clause. In Klein-Andreu 1983:43–66.

Thorne, Barrie and Henley, Nancy (eds). 1975. *Language and Sex: Difference and Dominance*. Rowley, MA: Newbury House.

Thorne, Barrie, Kramarae, Cheris, and Henley, Nancy (eds). 1983. *Language, Gender and Society*. Rowley, MA: Newbury House.

Todd, A. 1983. A diagnosis of doctor–patient discourse in the prescription of contraception. In Fisher and Todd 1983:135–57.

Todd, Loreto. 1974. *Pidgins and Creoles*. London: Routledge and Kegan Paul.

——1984. *Modern Englishes: Pidgins and Creoles*. Oxford: Basil Blackwell.

Trudgill, Peter. 1972. Sex, covert prestige and linguistic change in the urban British English of Norwich. *Language in Society*, 1:179–95.

——1974a. Linguistic change and diffusion: description and explanation in sociolinguistic dialect geography. *Language in Society*, 2(2):215–46.

——1974b. *The Social Differentiation of English in Norwich*. London: Cambridge University Press.

——1975a. *Accent, Dialect and the School*. London: Edward Arnold.

——1975b. Linguistic geography and geographical linguistics. In Board, Christopher, Chorley, Richard, Haggett, Peter, and Stoddart, David (eds), *Progress in Geography*, 229–52. London: Edward Arnold.

——1983a. *On Dialect*. Oxford: Basil Blackwell.

——1983b. *Sociolinguistics: An Introduction to Language and Society*, revised edition. Harmondsworth: Pelican.

——(ed.). 1984a. *Applied Sociolinguistics*. London: Academic Press.

——(ed.). 1984b. *Language in the British Isles*. Cambridge: Cambridge University Press.

——1986. *Dialects in Contact*. Oxford: Basil Blackwell.

——and Hannah, Jean. 1982. *International English*. London: Edward Arnold.

Turner, Lorenzo Dow. 1949. *Africanisms in the Gullah Dialect*. Chicago: The University of Chicago Press.

Valdman, Albert (ed.). 1977. *Pidgin and Creole Linguistics*. Bloomington, IN: Indiana University Press.

——and Highfield, Arnold. 1980. *Theoretical Orientations in Creole Studies*. New York: Academic Press.

Valian, Virginia. 1981. Linguistics and feminism. In Vetterling-Braggin 1981:68–81.

van Dijk, Teun. 1980. *Macrostructures: An Interdisciplinary Study of Global Structures in Discourse, Interaction and Cognition*. Hillsdale, NJ: Erlbaum.

Vanek, Anthony and Darnell, Regna. 1977. Direct discourse as interactional reality. *International Review of Slavic Linguistics*, 2(2–3):189–214.

Vaughn-Cooke, A. Fay. 1980. Evaluating the language of Black English speakers: implications of the Ann Arbor decision. In Farr Whiteman, Marcia (ed.), *Reactions to Ann Arbor: Vernacular Black English and Education*, 24–54. Washington, DC: Center for Applied Linguistics.

——1983. Improving language assessment in minority children. *Asha* 25:29–34.

——1986. Theoretical frameworks and language assessment. *Concerns for Minority Groups* in *Communication Disorders*. *ASHA Reports 16*. Rockville, MD: American Speech, Language and Hearing Association.

——1987. Are black and white vernaculars diverging?, Section III. *American Speech*, 62(1):12–32.

Verschueren, Jef. 1987. The pragmatic perspective. In Verschueren and Bertuccelli-Papi 1987:3–6.

——1985. *International News Reporting: Metapragmatic Metaphors and the U-2*. Amsterdam: John Benjamins, B. V.

——and Bertuccelli-Papi, Marcella. 1987. *The Pragmatic Perspective: Selected Papers from the 1985 International Pragmatics Conference*. Amsterdam: John Benjamins, B. V.

Vetterling-Braggin, M. 1981. *Sexist Language*. Totowa, NJ: Rowman and Littlefield.

Walker, Ann G. 1982. Patterns and implications of cospeech in a legal setting. In Di Pietro 1982:101–12.

Warner, W. Lloyd, Meeker, Marchia, and Eells, Kenneth. 1960. *Social Class in America*. New York: Harper Torchbooks.

Washabaugh, William. 1980. Brainstorming creole languages. In Valdman and Highfield 1980: 129–38.

Weiner, E. Judith and Labov, William. 1983. Constraints on the agentless passive. *Journal of Linguistics*, 19(1):29–58.

Weinreich, Uriel, Labov, William and Herzog, Marvin. 1968. Empirical foundations for a theory of language change. In Lehmann, W. P. and Malkiel, Yakov (eds), *Directions for Historical Linguistics*, 95–188. Austin, TX: University of Texas Press.

West, Candace. 1983. 'Ask me no questions . . .' An analysis of queries and replies in physician–patient dialogues. In Fisher and Todd 1983:75–106.

——and Zimmerman, Don. 1977. Women's place in everyday talk: reflections on parent–child interaction. *Social Problems* 24(5):521–9.

——1983. Small insults: a study of interruptions in cross-sex conversations between unacquainted persons. In Thorne, Kramarae, and Henley 1983:103–18.

Whorf, Benjamin Lee. 1940. Science and linguistics. *Technology Review*, 42(6):229–31,247–8. Also in Carroll, John (ed.), *Language, Thought, and Reality: Selected Writings of Benjamin Lee Whorf*, 207–19. Cambridge, MA: MIT Press, 1957.

Wierzbicka, Ana. 1985. Different cultures, different languages, different speech acts. *Journal of Pragmatics*, 9:145–78.

Williamson, Juanita. 1971. Selected features of speech: black and white. In Williamson, Juanita and Burke, Virginia (eds), *A Various Language: Perspectives on American Dialects*, 496–507. New York: Holt, Rinehart and Winston.

Wilson, Dierdre. 1975. *Presuppositions and Non-Truth Conditional Semantics*. New York: Academic Press.

Wittermans, Elizabeth. 1967. Indonesian terms of address in a situation of rapid social change. *Social Forces*, 46:48–51.

Wodak, Ruth. 1981. How do I put my problem? Problem presentation in therapy and interview. *Text*, 1/2:181–213.

Wolfram, Walt. 1969. *A Sociolinguistic Description of Detroit Negro Speech*. Washington, DC: Center for Applied Linguistics.

——1974a. The relationship of white Southern speech to Vernacular Black English. *Language*, 50:498–527.

——1974b. *Sociolinguistic Aspects of Assimilation*. Arlington, VA: Center for Applied Linguistic.

——1975. Variable constraints and rule relations. In Fasold and Shuy 1975:70–88.

——1979. *Speech Pathology and Dialect Differences*. Arlington, VA: Center for Applied Linguistics.

——1980. *A*-prefixing in Appalachian English. In Labov 1980b:107–42.

——1983. Test interpretation and sociolinguistic differences. *Topics in Language Disorders* 3(3):21–34.

——1985. Variability in tense marking: a case for the obvious. *Language Learning* 35(2):229–53.

——1987. Are black and white vernaculars diverging?, Section V. *American Speech*, 62(1):40–8.

——1989. Structural variability in phonological development: final nasals in Vernacular Black English. In Fasold and Schiffrin 1989:301–32.

——forthcoming. *Dialects and American English*.

——and Christian, Donna. 1976. *Appalachian Speech*. Arlington, VA: Center for Applied Linguistics.

——and Christian, Donna, Leap, William and Potter, Lance. 1979. *Variability in the English of Two Indian Communities and Its Effect on Reading and Writing*. Final report, US National Institute of Education, Grant No. NIE-G-77-0006.

——and Fasold, Ralph. 1974. *The Study of Social Dialects in American English*. Englewood Cliffs, NJ: Prentice-Hall.

Wolfson, Nessa. 1979. The conversational historical present alternation. *Language*, 55:168–82.

——1982. *CHP: The Conversational Historical Present in American English Narrative*. Dordrecht: Foris.

——and Manes, Joan. 1979. Don't dear me. *Working Papers in Sociolinguistics*, 53. Austin, TX: Southwest Educational Development Laboratory.

Yaeger-Dror, Malcah. 1986. Changements en chaîne dans le français montréalais. In D. Sankoff 1986:223–38.

——1989. Patterned symmetry of shifting and lengthened vowels in the Montreal French Vernacular (MFV). In Fasold and Schiffrin 1989:59–84.

Index